*The World of Athens*

A Athens from the north-east. Early 19th century A.D.

B Athens from the north-east. Early 20th century A.D.

JOINT ASSOCIATION OF
CLASSICAL TEACHERS' GREEK COURSE
BACKGROUND BOOK

# The World of Athens
## AN INTRODUCTION TO
## CLASSICAL ATHENIAN CULTURE

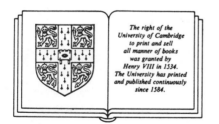

*The right of the
University of Cambridge
to print and sell
all manner of books
was granted by
Henry VIII in 1534.
The University has printed
and published continuously
since 1584.*

CAMBRIDGE UNIVERSITY PRESS
CAMBRIDGE
NEW YORK   PORT CHESTER
MELBOURNE   SYDNEY

Published by the Press Syndicate of the University of Cambridge
The Pitt Building, Trumpington Street, Cambridge CB2 1RP
40 West 20th Street, New York, NY 10011, USA
10 Stamford Road, Oakleigh, Melbourne 3166, Australia

First published 1984
Reprinted 1985 (twice), 1986, 1987 (twice), 1988, 1989, 1990

Printed in Great Britain at the University Press, Cambridge

Library of Congress catalogue card number: 83–23989

*British Library Cataloguing in Publication Data*

The world of Athens. – (Joint Association of
Classical Teachers' Greek course)
1. Athens – History
I. Series
938'.5   DF285

ISBN 0 521 26789 7 hard covers
ISBN 0 521 27389 7 paperback

WD

# CONTENTS

# PREFACE

*The World of Athens* introduces the mature reader to the history, culture, values and achievements of Classical Athens. It requires no knowledge of ancient Greek. It begins with a Historical Introduction which sketches the history of Athens from earliest times till the destruction of Athenian democracy in 322 B.C. This is followed by extracts from Pericles' famous Funeral Speech, one of the classic contemporary statements about what made Athens 'great'. There are then seven chapters on different aspects of the Athenian world, and the book closes with a Postscript on other worlds which impinged on the Athenian and drew a reaction from it. Finally, there are a Greek alphabet with a simplified English transliteration and pronunciation guide, a Glossary of terms used, maps, a list of cross-references with *Reading Greek* (see below) and an index. Greekless readers should note that some of the terms in the Glossary have been given in their Greek *as well as* their English form. Those who care to, can use the guide to the Greek alphabet to see how Greek works and how close to the Greek our traditional spellings and pronunciations of the words are.

Many hands have worked on this book. In its original form it was a series of notes produced for *Reading Greek* (*Text* and *Grammar*, C.U.P. 1978), an introduction to ancient Greek for maturer beginners produced between 1974 and 1979 in Cambridge by a Project team (Dr P.V. Jones, Dr K.C. Sidwell and Miss F.E. Corrie) under the auspices of the Joint Association of Classical Teachers (J.A.C.T.). When the Project ended, Mr J.M. Wilkins, in conjunction with Dr Jones and the Project's distinguished Advisory Panel of scholars, brought the scattered notes together and produced proposals for, and working drafts of, a complete book. Individually and collectively the Advisory Panel set to work, and *The World of Athens* is the result.

Since the whole book has been the work of so many hands, and all of it subject to Advisory Panel discussion and editorial review, we agreed not to assign sole responsibility for any chapter to any individual. But as editor I should like here to acknowledge the help of the Panel with deeper thanks than any of them can know: Mr J.J. Paterson (University of Newcastle upon Tyne) for work on the Historical Introduction; Dr B.A. Sparkes (University of Southampton) for work on Chapter 1 and for all the illustrations except those for 7.64–82; Professor J.P. Gould (University of Bristol) for work on Chapters 2, 3 and 7; Dr P.A. Cartledge (Clare College, Cambridge) for work on Chapters 4 and 5; Mr G.L. Cawkwell (University College, Oxford) for work on Chapter 6; Dr V.E.S. Webb (University of Newcastle upon Tyne) for work on Greek art in Chapter 7; and Sir Desmond Lee for the translations other than from Homer. To John Wilkins, our best thanks for establishing the firm foundations on which the book could be built. One final act of thanks to Elizabeth Thurlow for indexing so thoroughly and meticulously. It is important to stress that all responsibility for balance, coverage, presentation, use of sources, glossing and transliteration rests entirely with the Project.

<table>
<tr><td>Department of Classics,</td><td>Peter V. Jones</td></tr>
<tr><td>University of Newcastle upon Tyne</td><td>Director, J.A.C.T. Greek Project</td></tr>
<tr><td>January 1984</td><td></td></tr>
</table>

Passages from the *Iliad* and the *Odyssey* are taken from the translations by Richmond Lattimore, copyright 1951 and 1965 University of Chicago. Acknowledgement is due to the late Richmond Lattimore and the University of Chicago Press for the use of this material.

# NOTES

1 We have made the usual compromise in turning Greek words into English, opting sometimes for the traditional form, sometimes for the strict transliteration. On p. 359 we have given a simple version of the Greek alphabet, with pronunciation and our rules of transliteration, and in the subsequent Glossary we have given the original Greek of all proper names and some of the technical terms defined (with exact transliterations into English). Those interested can therefore discover for themselves how the original Greek forms were spelt and how they sounded.

2 Greek proper names ending in '-e' or '-es' are normally pronounced 'ee' and 'eez' in English. In *some* cases we have marked a vowel long (ē or ō), e.g. 'Athēnē' ('Atheenee'), where it seemed to us important.

3 All dates are B.C. unless stated otherwise.

4 All writers quoted are given a brief pen-sketch in the Glossary. Where inscriptions are quoted, the references are as follows:

> Austin/Vidal Naquet = *Economic and Social History of Ancient Greece*, Batsford 1977
>
> Fornara = C.W. Fornara, *Translated Documents of Greece and Rome* (vol. 1) *Archaic Times to the End of the Peloponnesian War* (2nd edn), Cambridge 1983
>
> $IG^2$ = *Inscriptiones Graecae* (2nd edn)
>
> M and L = Meiggs and Lewis, *A Selection of Greek Historical Inscriptions to the End of the Fifth Century*, Oxford 1969
>
> LACTOR = London Association of Classical Teachers' source books
>
> Rhodes = LACTOR 9
>
> *SEG* = *Supplementum Epigraphicum Graecum*
>
> Tod = M.N. Tod, *Greek Historical Inscriptions* (vol. 2), Oxford 1948

5 The Glossary (pp. 359–73) contains the most important names, institutions and terms used in this book which we think may not be familiar. Any not found there will be found in the Index (pp. 389–405). For place-names, consult the Index and maps at the front of the book (p. xiii).

6 Numbers in brackets in the text indicate chapters and paragraphs of this book (e.g. (4.23)); H.I. = Historical Introduction (pp. 1–61), and P. = Postscript (pp. 353–8).

7 Square brackets [ ] round an author's name indicate that, though the work in question has been assigned to him in the past, it is probably not by him.

# FURTHER READING

By far the best thing to do by way of further reading is either to learn ancient Greek and start reading texts in the original, or to buy translations (Penguin Classics carry an excellent range). You should start with Homer. The following books are recommended:

**General**
S. Hornblower *The Greek World 479–323 BC* Methuen 1983
J.K. Davies *Democracy and Classical Greece* Fontana 1978
K.J. Dover (ed.) and others *Ancient Greek Literature* Oxford University Press 1980
K.J. Dover *The Greeks* BBC Publications 1980
A.M. Snodgrass *Archaic Greece* Dent 1980

**Values and society**
K.J. Dover *Greek Popular Morality in the time of Plato and Aristotle* Blackwell 1974
M.I. Finley *Economy and Society in Ancient Greece* Penguin Books 1983
N.R.E. Fisher *Social Values in Classical Athens* Dent 1976
Jean-Pierre Vernant *Myth and Society in Ancient Greece* Harvester 1980

**Literature**
M.I. Finley *The World of Odysseus* Penguin Books 1979
J. Griffin *Homer* Oxford University Press (Past Masters) 1980
O.P. Taplin *Greek Tragedy in Action* Methuen 1978
B. Vickers *Towards Greek Tragedy* Longman 1973
K.J. Dover *Aristophanic Comedy* University of California Press 1972

## Thought

W.K.C. Guthrie *Socrates*   Cambridge University Press 1971
W.K.C. Guthrie *The Sophists*   Cambridge University Press 1971
G.E.R. Lloyd *Magic, Reason and Experience*   Cambridge University Press 1979

## Art and society

J. Boardman *Athenian Red Figure Vases*   Thames and Hudson 1975
J. Boardman *Athenian Black Figure Vases*   Thames and Hudson 1974
R.E. Wycherley *The Stones of Athens*   Princeton University Press 1978
J.J. Pollitt *Art and Experience in Classical Greece*   Cambridge University Press 1972

## Religion

W. Burkert *Homo Necans* (tr. Peter Bing)   University of California Press 1983

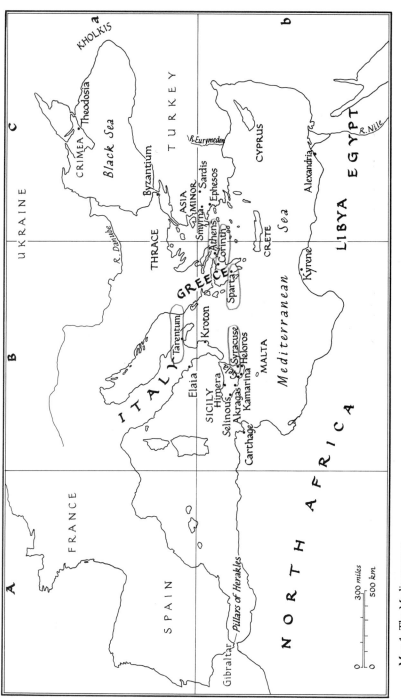

Map 1 The Mediterranean.

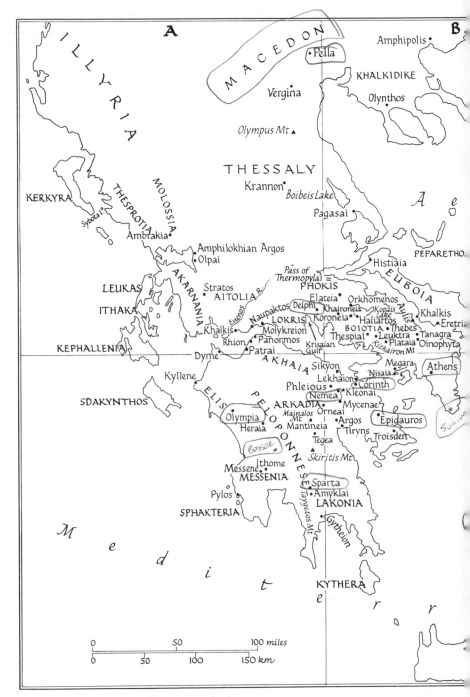

Map 2 Greece and the Aegean islands.

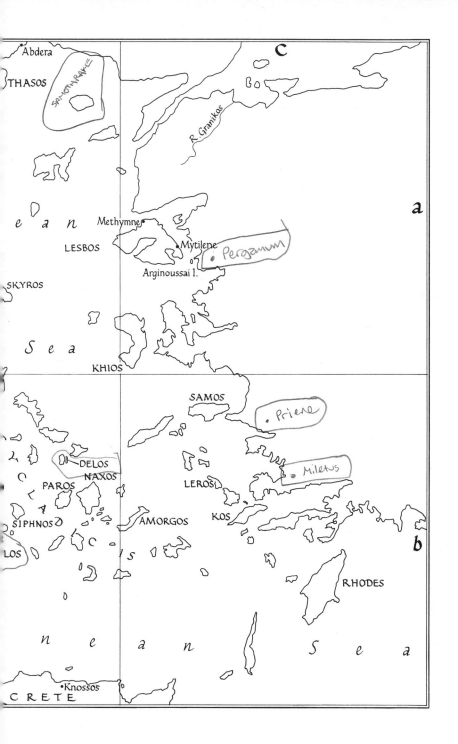

Abdera

THASOS

SAMOTHRAKE

C

Bo

R. Granikos

a

e a n

Methymne

LESBOS

Mytilene

Pergamum

Arginoussai I.

SKYROS

S e a

KHIOS

SAMOS

Priene

DELOS

NAXOS

PAROS

LEROS

Miletus

SIPHNOS

AMORGOS

KOS

LOS

b

RHODES

n e a n

S e a

Knossos

C R E T E

Map 3 Attica.

**A**

Epidamnos

Apollonia

KERKYRA

**B**

Amphipolis

Eion

Methone

Poteidaia

Mende

Skione

Torone

THESSALY

PHOKIS

EUBOIA

LOKRIS

Khalkis

Eretria

Tanagra

Oinophyta

AKHAIA

Athens

AIGINE

KEKRYPHALEIA

Dipaia

Argos

Tegea

Ithome

Halieis

Sparta

| 0 | 50 | 100 miles |
|---|----|-----------|
| 0 | 50 | 100 | 150 km |

Map 4  The Athenian empire.

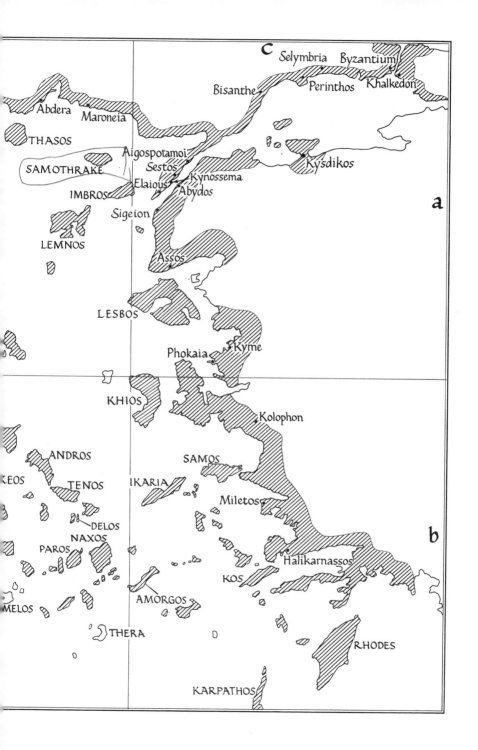

c

Selymbria    Byzantium
                    Khalkedon
Bisanthe    Perinthos

Abdera    Maroneia

THASOS

Aigospotamoi    Kysdikos
SAMOTHRAKE    Sestos
        Elaious    Kynossema
IMBROS    Abydos

    Sigeion
                        a
LEMNOS

    Assos

LESBOS

    Phokaia    Kyme

KHIOS

        Kolophon

ANDROS    SAMOS

XEOS    TENOS    IKARIA
        Miletos
    DELOS
    NAXOS                b
PAROS            Halikarnassos
    KOS
    AMORGOS
MELOS
        THERA            RHODES

    KARPATHOS

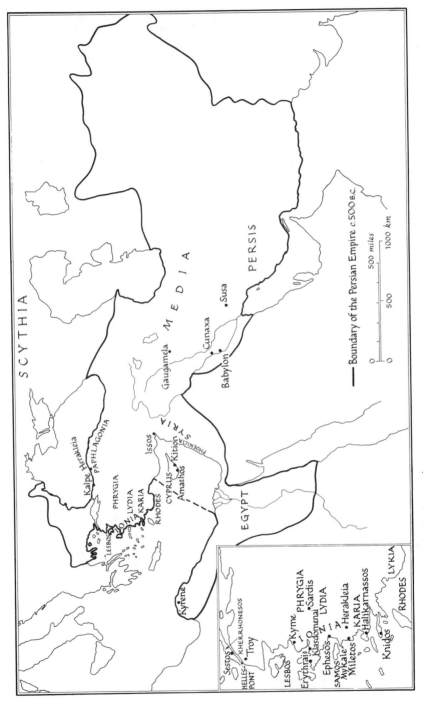

Map 5 The Near East and the Persian empire.

# Introduction: an outline history of Athens to the death of Alexander the Great

## Early Greek history: Minoans, Mycenaeans, Homer and the Dark Age 2200–900

H.I.1 Some time after 640 at Athens, a one-time Olympic victor called Kylon attempted a coup, while the attention of the citizens was turned to a religious festival (always a favourite moment for subversion). The plan failed and, although Kylon escaped, his followers were killed, despite the promise of safe conduct. This incident is the first in the history of Athens of which we have more than the barest information. The reliable historical memory of some of the other Greek cities might extend back a generation or two earlier, but not much further. Yet the Greeks were well aware that they had been around for a long time before the seventh century. They filled in the gaps with highly detailed but largely imaginary stories. The long and complex processes of development in the cities were often ascribed to the work of one mythical lawgiver or statesman (Theseus at Athens, Lykourgos at Sparta). The epic poems of Homer, the *Iliad* and *Odyssey*, which took on the form in which we have them at some time in the eighth century, had at their base a much earlier world of local kings and their rich palaces. The historian Herodotus, in the fifth century, thought that the Trojan War, which formed the subject of the poems, took place about 800 years before his own day. Eventually the scholar Eratosthenes (*c.* 274–194) calculated the dates of the war as 1193–1183. It was pure chance, rather than insight, if he got it roughly right.

H.I.2 Archaeology enables us to know rather more than the Greeks themselves about their origins. The excavations of Sir Arthur Evans at Knossos in Crete and other more recent explorations of sites have revealed a society of rich, labyrinthine palaces, which flourished from *c.* 2200 to 1450 (the Minoan civilisation, so called after Minos, the legendary Cretan king). The inhabitants of these sites were not Greek; but their culture had

1

HI:1   The throne room of the Mycenaean palace, Pylos. 1300–1200.

a significant influence on the people on the mainland. About 2000 there were major cultural changes in Greece. Possibly new people settled in many areas. They eventually developed their own palace culture which lasted from *c.* 1600 to 1200 at sites like Mycenae, Tiryns and Pylos (the Mycenaean civilisation). We now know that at least some of these people spoke Greek, because hundreds of clay tablets written in a script known as Linear B were found at Pylos, and in 1952 Michael Ventris demonstrated that the script was a form of Greek.

H.I.3 The Mycenaean palaces were destroyed about 1200. Many sites were abandoned entirely. There followed an unsettled period, the Dark Ages (1100–900), which the Greeks remembered as a time of wanderings and movements of people.

**Colonisation, early aristocratic government, Theseus and the unification of Attica; Sparta (900–640)**

H.I.4 There is a sense in which this Greek restlessness survived for centuries. Already in perhaps the ninth century Greeks, among whom Athens, according to the legends, played a significant part, were settling in Ionia on the coast of Asia Minor. Then later from about 750, traders, discontented aristocrats, and farmers searching for a better life, founded colonies in Sicily and south Italy, in southern France, Spain, North Africa and by the Black Sea.

H.I.5 The Greek communities, as they emerged from the Dark Ages, in

HI:2  Clay tablet with text in Linear B script, from Pylos. C. 1200.

the eighth century had only the most simple forms of political organisation. Local aristocratic lords (*basileis*) fiercely guarded their independence, acknowledging only reluctantly any form of central control.
Loyalty to family, clan and followers came first. Hēsiod, a farmer from
Askra in Boiotia, who lived in the second half of the eighth century, vividly
described in his poem *Works and Days* the activities of the 'gift-devouring'
nobles of his own community who sat in judgement over the petty
squabbles of the local people.

Gradually, and doubtless with difficulty, local loyalties began to focus
upon one city community and the nobles came to acknowledge the central
authority of one family who held the kingship. In Athens, for example, it
was the hero Theseus who was supposed by tradition to have unified
Attica and to have provided in the city a central council in which the local
lords could meet. The story points to one of the most remarkable features
about Athens: the territory of Attica around the city was exceptionally
large for a Greek state. However, the unification of this area was not the
act of one man, but a long process extending down into the fifth century.
The rivalry between local families continued to dominate the politics of
Athens until at least 500.

By tradition the successors to Theseus ruled in Athens as kings. However, by the seventh century the king (*basileus*) no longer exercised great
powers. He was only one of a board of annually appointed officers of state,
the nine *arkhontes* (s. *arkhōn*). These *arkhontes* went on to become life
members of the Council which sometimes met on the Hill of Arēs in Athens
(the Areopagus). These official posts were not open to all citizens. A group
of aristocratic families maintained their exclusive right to hold them.
Wealthy and well-born, they described themselves as Eupatridai ('sons of
good fathers').

**H.I.6** In the classical period, when the opponents of the democratic system of Athens sought a model for an alternative society, they turned their eyes to Sparta which had evolved in an idiosyncratic manner. Sparta was the amalgamation of four villages, perhaps in the tenth century, on the bank of the river Eurotas in the southern Peloponnese. The unification of these communities was probably responsible for the unique institution of the dual kingship. There were two royal families in Sparta, the Agiadai and the Eurypontidai, which both provided a king. The two kings were advised by a council of elders, chosen from men over sixty years of age (the *gerousia*). Rather later there were also five annually elected officials called *ephoroi*. Those with full citizen rights (the Spartiatai) assembled regularly to approve or reject proposals which were put to them. However, citizenship was narrowly defined. The Spartiatai were only those who from an early age had undergone a rigorous state upbringing (*agōgē*) and after the age of twenty had been elected to one of the *sussitia*, dining clubs or messes. This training was designed to foster loyalty and obedience and it undoubtedly ensured that the Spartan army was a more disciplined and efficient military force than most of the citizen militias of the other Greek states.

From the early eighth century Sparta began to expand, and overcame first the neighbouring communities of the Eurotas valley. Some of these towns were given the status of *perioikoi* ('dwellers around'), who had local autonomy to some extent but were liable to military service. Then at the end of the eighth century the Spartans crossed Mount Taygetos to the west

HI:3  Bronze armour found in a warrior's grave at Argos. Late 8th century.

and annexed Messenia. Two generations later, in the middle of the seventh century, the Messenians rose in revolt. It seems to have been a hard war, during which the Spartan poet, Tyrtaios, wrote his poems, as a rallying cry for good order and bravery in battle. After it was over, Messenia was annexed and ceased to exist as a separate state for nearly three hundred years. The Messenians were reduced to the servile status of 'helots'. Their land was divided up and an allotment (*klēros*) was given to each Spartiate. The Messenian helot was forced to work the land and to pay half the produce to his absent Spartiate master.

The annexation of Messenia was Sparta's answer to the needs which led other Greeks to send out colonies. It is significant that Sparta only ever established one colony at Taras (Tarentum) in South Italy. Further, the grant of a *klēros* to each Spartiate enabled him to devote himself to his life in the Spartan community and gave each a basic economic independence. Spartiates were able to describe themselves as *homoioi* ('equals'). This enabled Sparta to escape many of the economic and social tensions which afflicted other Greek communities in the seventh century.

**From aristocracy to tyranny: Kylon, Drakon, Solon and Peisistratos (640–530)**

H.I.7 The government of most Greek states lay in the hands of aristocracies of one sort or another. Indeed, concentration on the later democracy at Athens or on Sparta's unique system of government can obscure the fact that for most Greek communities, throughout the classical period and after, their characteristic form of government was oligarchy based on wealth and birth. There were dangers, however, in defining the ruling class too narrowly. The increasing wealth of the communities in the seventh century was, in part, distributed among men who were outside the ruling aristocracies and came to resent their lack of influence. The adoption of weapons and tactics of the heavy-armed hoplites brought men together to train and march. A spirit of comradeship was inspired and, with it, a growing awareness of the armed citizens' potential power. In many communities over the next century or more, there emerged a man, resentful at exclusion from power, who exploited the discontents and the military might of the citizens to seize personal power (Aristotle much later noted that tyrants combined the roles of general and leader of the people, *dēmagōgos*). Such a usurper was known as a *turannos* ('tyrant') – the word, non-Greek in origin, did not necessarily carry with it implications of cruelty or oppression.

HI:4   A hoplite phalanx. C. 640.

The abortive coup by Kylon in Athens, with which this chapter began, was just such an attempt to seize power as a tyrant. Kylon was supported by his father-in-law, Theagenes, the tyrant of neighbouring Megara. The tyrants tended to form a club for mutual aid and protection. Kylon failed; but the sources for discontent remained.

It is a vital moment in the development of any society when the laws by which it is to be governed are defined and published for all to read. By tradition in 621/0* the Athenian law-giver, Drakon, published a law-code which later became proverbial for its harshness (hence, 'draconian'). It may represent a response by the Eupatridai to the discontent on which Kylon was hoping to play. His law on homicide survives in detail. It regularises the procedures for dealing with the killing of others and to some extent limits the powers of the family of the dead man in the revenge which they might exact. Indeed, this may be the real significance of the law-code. It is early evidence for the assertion of central control over local family loyalties.

H.I.8 In addition to all the other troubles which afflicted the Athenians at the end of the seventh century, the system of land tenure increasingly came to be seen as an unacceptable burden. Peasants found themselves crippled by debts. Enslavement could follow. Other landowners resented the traditional payment of one-sixth of their produce to their lords. The times looked ripe for tyranny. As some tyrants had been prepared to enforce land redistribution and cancellation of debts, the solution could seem attractive. At this moment, in 594/3, Solon was appointed *arkhōn* at

*The Athenian year ran from June to June (cf. 2.42), so '621/0' means 'in the year beginning June 621 and ending May 620'.

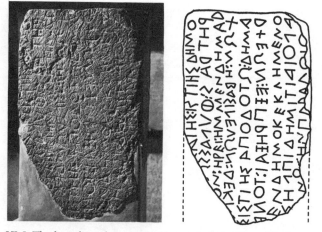

HI:5 The front face of an inscribed law-code from Khios with the writing set vertically and *boustrophēdon* (see p. 277). Early 6th century.

Athens and tried to provide solutions to the problems of the age. Solon is the first real personality of Athenian history. He was a superb propagandist. In poems designed to be recited and remembered, he set out in somewhat enigmatic terms his aims and achievements. Solon sought an alternative to tyranny: 'It did not please me to do anything with the violence of a tyrant.' He alleviated the oppression of crippling debt. His solution was sometimes called the *seisakhtheia*, 'the shaking-off of burdens'. On the political level, Solon broke the exclusiveness of the Eupatridai. He defined four classes on the basis of agricultural wealth. From now on, the wealthiest in society, whether or not they were Eupatridai, could hold the chief offices of state. Alongside the traditional council of the Areopagus, Solon established a people's Council (*boulē*) of 400 representatives. Solon was the archetypal man of compromise and mediation:

> To the people (*dēmos*) I have given such privilege as is enough,
> Neither taking away nor adding to their honour;
> While those who had power and were famed for their wealth,
> For them I took care they should suffer no injury.
> I stood, holding out my strong shield over both,
> And I did not allow either to triumph unjustly.          (Solon, fr. 5)

Like so many men of moderation after him, by offering something to everyone, Solon succeeded in satisfying no one. He lived just long enough to see that he had failed.

HI:6  The foundations of the archaic temple of Athēnē on the Acropolis of Athens. C. 525.

H.I.9 Despite, or even because of, Solon's political reforms, the local nobles of Attica continued to squabble over their right to leadership in the Athenian community. In 561/0 one such noble, Peisistratos, a military hero, whipped up popular support and took over Athens as tyrant. His control was far from absolute. Twice he was thrown out by his political enemies. Twice he made a comeback. In 546 he consolidated the tyranny at Athens and from then on managed to remain in power until his death in 528/7. He made no radical changes to the political system, simply ensuring that his own supporters were among the *arkhontes* every year.

Under Peisistratos Athens flourished. Grandiose building projects, the beautiful black-figure pottery from Athenian workshops, the poets, attracted by patronage and the remodelled Great Panathenaic festival, all testified to the increasing self-confidence of the Athenians of this period.

### From tyranny to democracy: Hippias and Kleisthenes (530–500)

H.I.10 Peisistratos was able to hand on his rule to his son Hippias. It is a notable feature of Greek tyranny that it rarely lasted in a city for more than a couple of generations, before its early supporters turned against it and discontented aristocrats made a comeback. So it was in Athens. Hippias was faced with increasing aristocratic opposition, even from men who had once co-operated with the regime (Kleisthenes of the family of Alkmaion, for example, then in exile, had previously been *arkhōn* at Athens in 525/4). In 514 two aristocratic lovers, Harmodios and Aristogeiton, plotted to murder Hipparkhos, Hippias' brother. At the procession of the Panathenaia, the conspirators panicked. Hipparkhos was slain. But Harmodios was killed in the attempt and Aristogeiton died later under torture. Hippias survived and his tyranny became harsher. Exiled aristocrats attempted to seize a frontier post in Attica,but got no further. If they were to succeed, they needed more help. So they turned to Sparta, which had a reputation for being sympathetic to the appeals of the opponents of tyrannies. At Delphi, the Alkmaionid family won the favour of the priesthood of the Oracle, by offering to rebuild the sanctuary of Apollo. Whenever the Spartans consulted the oracle, they received the reply: 'First free Athens.' Eventually, in 510 the Spartan king, Kleomenes, responded by driving Hippias and his family out of Athens.

H.I.11 Kleomenes probably expected that Athens would retaliate by returning to an aristocratic form of government which would naturally continue to show good will to Sparta for her actions against the tyrant. For a couple of years this was what happened, until the Alkmaionid Kleisthenes failed in his political struggle with his leading opponent Isagoras and in 508/7 'joined the people [*dēmos*] to the company of his followers', in a striking phrase of the historian Herodotus (*Histories* 5.66). The details of the package of proposals which were designed to attract general support can be found later (see 5.24). Kleisthenes created ten new artificial geographical *phulai* (tribes) which cut across the natural boundaries of the four old kinship-based ones and probably enabled men who had previously been refused citizenship to be enrolled. Each tribe was composed of groups of village units, *dēmoi* (demes) (s. *dēmos*), scattered over Attica. These *dēmoi* had their own local political set-up and became the focus of the citizen's loyalties and attention. They gave the ordinary Athenian a new sense of participation, and a new feeling of self-confidence; he no longer had to live in the shadow of duty to the local lord. It is assumed that Kleisthenes must have got his measures through the assembly of the Athenian citizens (*ekklēsia*) which had existed in a formal manner since at least the time of Solon. Here may be the clue to the real significance of his programme of reform. He gave the *ekklēsia* a new sense of power with which it could come to expect and eventually to demand that all matters of significance should be submitted to it for discussion and then decision. This opened the way for the radical democracy of the later fifth century. However, Kleisthenes presumably expected that aristocrats like himself would continue to exercise a predominant influence on the assembly. Indeed, for the next eighty years, nearly all the leaders of the people were of aristocratic birth.

In Herodotus' opinion, the effects of the new democracy were heady, invigorating and immediate. When, in 506, Kleomenes of Sparta tried to reassert control of Athens, his expedition collapsed ignominiously and the Athenians were also able to defeat the Boiotians and Khalkidians who sought at the time to take advantage of the threat to Athens to seize territory in Attica. 'This proved', claimed Herodotus, 'if proof were needed, how noble a thing freedom is' (*Histories* 5.78).

### The Persian Empire and the 'Ionian revolt' (560–490)

H.I.12 No Greek of the mainland at the end of the sixth century who raised his eyes from the day-to-day activities of his own community could have failed to see the clouds rolling in from the East. Under the vigorous leadership of Cyrus from 558, the Persians had taken over the kingdom of the Medes and gradually moved west. The Greeks of Ionia on the coast of Asia Minor would have become aware of the new power in 546 when, to their astonishment, Cyrus defeated Croesus, king of Lydia, their powerful suzerain. Indeed, Cyrus followed up his victory by annexing the Greek cities of the coast. When Sparta chose to respond to this by sending an embassy to Cyrus to tell him to keep off the Greek communities, Cyrus replied in puzzlement, 'Who are the Spartans?'

Cyrus' successors continued the conquests of the Eastern Mediterranean and in 512 Dareios crossed into Thrace and Macedonia, the region south of the Danube. But in 499 the Ionian cities decided to rise in revolt. Aristagoras from Milētos arrived in Greece to secure support for the cities. He even tried to persuade the Spartans to consider the conquest of the Persian Empire itself. The canny king Kleomenes, so the story goes, asked him how far away Susa, the Persian administrative capital, was. When Aristagoras replied that it was three months' journey away, Kleomenes dismissed him contemptuously. However, Aristagoras had greater success at Athens and Eretria, who promised ships. The Athenians could not forget that the ex-tyrant Hippias was in contact with the Persian court, perhaps hoping for support for an eventual restoration. The campaigns of the next five years were a curious mixture of success and failure for the Greeks. However, when in 494 Milētos fell to the Persians and was razed, the

HI:7 Xerxes standing behind Dareios seated on his throne, Persepolis. Early 5th century.

revolt collapsed. The interference of Athens and Eretria must have caused Dareios to become even more determined to bring about a scheme which he had probably been contemplating for many years, the subjugation of the European Greeks. He demanded from the Greek cities the signs of submission, gifts of earth and water. Some felt their interests lay in giving in. Others, including Athens, were defiant. Dareios, it is said, had a servant who constantly reminded him 'Do not forget the Athenians.'

**The Persian Wars: Marathon (490)**

H.I.13 In 490 the Persian forces crossed the Aegean. Eretria, on the island of Euboia, was betrayed to them and was burned. From there the Persians crossed to the nearest convenient landing place in north-east Attica, the bay of Marathon. The Athenians had to make the decision whether to await the enemy at Athens or to march out to meet them. The generals, under the nominal leadership of Kallimakhos, decided to march. At the same time they sent a message to Sparta to beg for help through the first 'Marathon' runner, Pheidippides. The Spartans, forced to delay by religious scruple, eventually arrived just too late for the battle.

When the Athenians reached Marathon, they waited for a few days. The main inspiration of the Athenians at this time was an exotic swashbuckler, Miltiades. Born into the heart of the Athenian aristocracy he had spent much of his life as the ruler of the Thracian Kherronēsos (the Gallipoli peninsula), the vital strategic area commanding the entrance to the Hellespont. From there he had fled back to Athens in 493, as the Persians advanced, and was now one of the Athenian generals. It was he who urged

HI:8   The Athenian burial mound at Marathon (cf. 6:2).

the Athenians to attack at Marathon. The Athenians, their line extended to avoid being enveloped by the superior numbers of the Persian forces, advanced at the double to close as swiftly as possible with the enemy. Although worsted in the centre, the Athenians on the right wing and their Plataian allies on the left were able to break down the Persian resistance. The Persians fled in confusion to their ships. It was a famous victory. The 192 Athenian dead were buried on the field under a vast mound. The remarkable achievement of the Athenians was extolled in song and painting. For those who were there it was the high point of their lives. Aeschylus, the tragic poet, whose brother died in an act of heroism during the battle, was proud of nothing in his life so much as his membership of the Old Comrades who had fought at Marathon on that day, the Marathōnomakhai.

### Themistokles, the silver from Laureion, the Athenian navy (490–480)

H.I.14 The Persians were bound to be back. The Athenians could not forget that if they had lost Marathon, then the Persians would probably have reimposed the ageing tyrant, Hippias, upon them again. So it is no surprise to find that the democracy, buoyed up by the victory over Persia, but aware that it was still a prime target for the enemy, was deeply suspicious of those of its aristocratic leaders who had connections with the exiled Peisistratids and the Persians. In 487 the *ekklēsia* used for the first time the device of ostracism (see Glossary) to rid the city of a man whose loyalty was suspect. The first victim, Hipparkhos, a relative of the Peisistratids, confirmed people's fears by fleeing to Persia. In the following years ostracism was resorted to regularly.

H.I.15 In 483 there was a lucky strike of a rich vein of silver in the state-owned mining district of Laureion in Attica. The first reaction of the Athenians was to distribute the profits from this windfall among themselves; but they were persuaded to devote the money to the creation of the greatest fleet in Greece. By 480 this fleet was to number 200 ships. The author of this fateful proposal was Themistokles, son of Neokles. Almost alone of the leaders of the people in Athens about this time, he was not from a politically distinguished, aristocratic family. However, tales of his rise from poverty-stricken obscurity should not be believed. As *arkhōn* in 493/2, he had already displayed his interest in Athens' naval potential by beginning the transformation of the area of Peiraieus into a fortified dockyard and port for Athens. Ten years later, he committed the Athenians to the development of her fleet. This decision was not only important for the renewed war with Persia, but it had a decisive effect on Athenian development for the next century or so. 'Lay hold of the sea' was Themistokles' advice.

### The Persian Wars: Thermopylai and Artemision, Salamis, Plataia and Mykale (480–479)

H.I.16 Dareios was never to get his revenge. Delayed by revolts within the Persian empire, he died in 486 and was succeeded by his son Xerxes. Preparations were made for an overwhelming land force which was to be accompanied closely by a large navy. No one Greek state on its own could expect to face up to such numbers. In the autumn of 481 and again in the spring of 480 many Greek states met at the Isthmus of Corinth to set aside their quarrels and create a league to defeat Persia. Although many communities, particularly those in the north who were most vulnerable to Xerxes' attacks, held aloof or submitted without a fight to Persia, thirty-one Greek states were to add their names to the victory monument which was to be dedicated at Delphi: only thirty-one of the many Greek states, but never before and certainly never again did the Greeks display such unity. In the next century, when the cities were exhausting themselves with their inter-state quarrels, some men longed for a new ideal of Panhellenic unity and looked back to the days of the Persian Wars to provide themselves with a model of what could happen. At the meetings of the new alliance it was agreed that Sparta should assume overall command both on land and sea, although Athens' contribution of the largest navy might have entitled them to command of the fleet. The decision was unsurprising in view of the large number of Peloponnesian states which were present.

### Thermopylai and Artemision

**H.I.17** The Greeks first of all dispatched a force to attempt to hold the pass of Tempe in the north near Mount Olympus. However once they got there, they realised that there were other routes into the Thessalian plain and that it would have been easy for Xerxes to turn the Greek position at Tempe. So the question arose: where could they make a stand? Doubtless many Peloponnesian states would have advocated defence at the Isthmus of Corinth; but this would have meant abandoning Boiotia and even Athens without a fight. Somewhere to the north had to be found. The Greeks decided on the pass in central Greece between the sea and mountain, where there were hot sulphur springs, Thermopylai ('Hot Gates'). At sea the Greek fleet took up position at Artemision at the north end of the island of Euboia. They hoped that they could prevent the Persian fleet making contact with the army as it moved south.

The Spartan king Leonidas commanded the Greeks at Thermopylai, although the presence of a Spartan contingent of only 300 as part of the Greek army raises doubts about how wholehearted was Spartan support for the expedition. Xerxes originally tried to take the Greek position by frontal assault. This was a disastrous failure. For two days the Persians could not make any headway. Then they were informed of a mountain

HI:9  A Greek hoplite. *C. 500.*

track which led round to the rear of the Greek forces. The crack Persian forces, the Immortals, were sent round by this path and defeated the Phokian contingent who were guarding the way. Warned of the impending arrival of the Persians in his rear, Leonidas, for reasons which remain obscure, dismissed most of the Greek forces, but remained in the pass with the Spartans and contingents from Thespiai and Thebes. Leonidas was killed and his force overwhelmed after a heroic defence. Acts of gallantry so often serve no long-term purpose except to inspire others by the remembrance of them. For Leonidas and the Spartans, the lyric poet Simonides produced a famous epitaph:

> Stranger, go tell the Spartans that we lie here
> Obedient to their laws.        (Quoted in Herodotus, *Histories* 7.228)

On sea the Greeks were aided by the weather. The Persian naval forces lost large numbers in a series of storms. They were then surprised by the Greek ships, which captured a number of ships off Artemision. There were several further, indecisive engagements, until news arrived of the defeat at Thermopylai. At that the Greek fleet set off south.

### *Salamis* (cf. 6.37)

H.I.18 Faced with the imminent arrival of the Persians, Themistokles managed to persuade the Athenians to abandon their city and cross over to Troisden, Aiginē and Salamis. According to an oracle, they were to put their trust in a 'wooden wall', which Themistokles interpreted as the new Athenian fleet. Despite opposition from some of the allies, Themistokles bullied the Greeks into halting their fleet by the island of Salamis.

The Persians could not ignore or by-pass the Greek fleet at Salamis. So an engagement was inevitable. Xerxes was lured, perhaps in part by a trick of Themistokles, into the narrow channel between Salamis and the mainland. Here the Persian fleet was crushed after a fierce battle.

### *Plataia*

H.I.19 It was now late September 480; so Xerxes decided to retire the largest part of his army to the north of Greece to find supplies for the winter. He himself returned to Asia Minor, perhaps fearing that the news of Salamis would inspire revolts among the Ionian Greeks. The army was left in the control of his son-in-law, Mardonios.

In the spring of 479 Mardonios tried through diplomacy to detach

HI:10   Air view of Salamis from the north-west.

Athens from the Greek alliance. The offer was tempting, particularly because the Athenians were far from certain that the Spartans would be willing to fight north of the Isthmus again. But, as tradition had it, the Athenians made a resolute reply: 'So long as the sun keeps his present course in the sky, we Athenians will never make peace with Xerxes.' To the Spartans they explained their determination to resist with words which showed just what it meant to be a Hellēn (a Greek) (see 1.1). This meant that for a second time Athens was evacuated and reoccupied by the Persians in the summer. After sacking the city once again, Mardonios retired into Boiotia.

The desperate appeals of the Athenians to Sparta eventually had their effect. Despite initial wavering, the Spartans put together the largest force ever to be sent out of the Peloponnese. It included 5,000 Spartiates and was commanded by Pausanias, who was acting as regent for Leonidas' young son Pleistarkhos. This Peloponnesian force marched north to link up with the Athenians and eventually to face the Persians in the territory of the Boiotian town of Plataia, where Mount Kithairon slopes down to the river Asopos.

For nearly two weeks the Greeks manoeuvred and endured the constant attacks of Persian cavalry. Finally Pausanias attempted a complex night march to a better position closer to the town of Plataia. Dawn found the Greek units in confusion and Mardonios was tempted to attack. The Spartans and the troops from Tegea bore the brunt and with impressive discipline drove the Persians back. In the fight Mardonios was killed and the Persians turned and fled. The Persian threat to the Greek mainland was over.

## Mykale

**H.I.20** At sea the Greek fleet in 479, much smaller than the one assembled in the previous year, was commanded by the Spartan king Leotykhidas. Tempted by the prospect that the Asiatic Greek cities would be inspired to revolt from Persia, the Greeks sailed to Samos. The Persians were unwilling to face the Greek ships at sea again; the memory of Salamis was too fresh. So they beached their ships at Mykale, a promontory on the mainland opposite Samos, and joined the Persian forces already stationed there. Leotykhidas landed his own forces and stormed the Persian position. Persian resistance collapsed. At a vital moment in the battle, many of the Ionian contingents in the Persian forces deserted and helped the Greeks. Their action was significant, although Herodotus was exaggerating when he described it as a second Ionian revolt.

HI:11 Remains of the serpent column from Delphi, erected in 479 to commemorate those who fought against the Persians.

### The Greeks versus the Carthaginians in Sicily: Himera 480

**H.I.21** By the sort of coincidence which delights historians, both ancient and modern, at the very moment when the Greeks of the mainland were fighting 'to ensure that no part of Greece should see the day of slavery', as one of their victory monuments put it (M and L, 26), their fellow Greeks in the western colonies faced their own great threat to their independence. The dominant power in the west was the North African state of Carthage. The Greek colonies, particularly those which had been settled on Sicily since the late eighth century, had long been an irritating barrier to Carthage's power in the island. At this time, the cities were controlled by a group of quarrelsome tyrants, of whom the most prominent was Gelon of Syracuse. As a result of a quarrel between two of the tyrants, Carthage received an invitation to intervene, which she eagerly accepted. The Carthaginians in 480 besieged the Sicilian city of Himera. Gelon led a large Syracusan force to the rescue, which destroyed the Carthaginian forces in a fierce battle outside the city. The Carthaginians were forced to sue for peace immediately. The parallel with what was happening in Greece was so striking that the story arose that the battles of Himera and Salamis had taken place on the same day.

### The aftermath of the Persian Wars: Pausanias, the Delian League (478) and the walls of Athens

**H.I.22** It would be wrong to suppose that the war with Persia ended with the victories of 480/79. The war was to continue for decades. After Mykale, the Greeks held a debate at Samos over what was to be done. The Spartans, anxious not to be committed to the long-term defence of the Greeks of Asia, even suggested that the Ionians should be transported back to mainland Greece and resettled. However, the Athenians opposed such radical action. That winter of 479 the Greek fleet moved north to the Hellespont. Here the Athenians stayed to lay siege to Sestos, even though most of the rest of the Greek forces returned home.

In 478 Pausanias, the victor of Plataia, took control of the Greek fleet and sailed to Cyprus. After winning over most of the island, he directed the fleet to the Hellespont, where he succeeded in driving the Persian garrison from Byzantium. It was here that his extravagant and arrogant behaviour outraged his fellow Greeks. He was eventually recalled by Sparta to face charges. He managed to escape conviction and returned as a private individual to the scenes of his recent escapades. He re-established himself at

Byzantium and eventually had to be driven out of there by the Athenians under Kimon. Returning to Sparta some years later, he allegedly involved himself in subversive activities. The Spartan authorities lost patience and starved him to death, after he had taken refuge in a temple. A puzzling end to an enigmatic career.

**H.I.23** It may well be that the activities of Pausanias in Byzantium were only the last straw for the Greek allies, who came to see that Athens with her fleet and interest in the corn supply route from the Black Sea was more likely than Sparta to be a vigorous champion of their interests. In 478 the Greek allies rejected the successor to Pausanias, when he arrived from Sparta, and turned to the Athenians. In the winter of 478/7 at a meeting on the island of Delos, Athens and the other allies from the Aegean founded a voluntary league, one of whose avowed objects was 'to compensate themselves for their losses by ravaging the territory of the king of Persia' (Thucydides, *Peloponnesian War* 1.96). To this end each member was expected to contribute each year either ships or a cash payment (tribute – *phoros*) which was to be supervised by Athenian officials called Hellēnotamiai ('treasurers of the Greeks'). The deviser of this scheme was the Athenian leader Aristeides. To him fell the task of drawing up an assessment of the contributions to be made by each state and deciding which states should contribute ships, and which tribute in money (5.78ff.).

**H.I.24** Themistokles seems to have had little to do with the Delian League either at its creation or later. But he was responsible at this time for a development of the greatest consequence for Athens. He got the Athenians to devote their energies to the rebuilding of the walls round Athens and the defence of the Peiraieus. Sparta protested and even proposed that all city fortifications in Greece should be dismantled as a gesture of goodwill between the Greek states. Sparta herself had always been unfortified. Themistokles used various delaying tactics to divert the Spartans until the work of rebuilding was well under way. He then presented them with a *fait accompli* and stated defiantly that the Spartans should recognise that the Athenians were capable of making up their own minds about their own interests and those of people in general. In such a way Themistokles served notice that Athens no longer accepted the leadership of Sparta. Twenty years later the work was completed and extended by the Long Walls which were built to join the city of Athens and the Peiraieus. The rebuilding of Athens' defences was Themistokles' last great achievement for Athens. At some time in the 470s he was ostracised and went to live in Argos in the Peloponnese, where he may have been a centre of intrigue. He was accused by the Spartans of being involved with

Pausanias. When the Athenians sent men to arrest him, Themistokles fled and, by odd irony, finished his days at the Persian court. He died at Magnesia on the river Meander (Maiandros). Contemporaries were struck by the curious fates of both Themistokles and Pausanias, the leaders of the Greek defence against Persia.

### Kimon and the Delian League against Persia (476–449)

**H.I.25** The forces of the Delian League were soon in action. The leader and inspiration of the League's war against Persia was Kimon, son of Miltiades, the Athenian hero of Marathon. 'No one humbled the Great King more than Kimon. He gave him no rest when he had been driven from Greece, but followed hard on his heels before the barbarian could recover his breath and make a stand' (Plutarch, *Life of Kimon* 12). About 476 he captured Eion near the mouth of the river Strymon, the last major Persian stronghold west of the Hellespont. About 475 Kimon captured the island of Skyros in the north Aegean. While the allies may have been pleased at the suppression of a pirate base, some cannot have failed to notice that this action was not directed against Persians directly and that Athens was the main beneficiary. On the island a huge skeleton was discovered, which was claimed as the bones of the Athenian hero Theseus. A settlement of Athenians on the island soon followed. Similar doubts could have been raised by the action in the late 470s to force the city of Karystos, on the island of Euboia, to join the League.

At some time after 469 Kimon carried the fight against the Persians to

HI:12 Theseus welcomed home to Athens by Athēnē. C. 475.

HI:13 Athēnē reading a list of
Athenian dead. C. 460.

Asia Minor. He drove them from the coastal regions of Karia and Lykia
and then at the river Eurymedon, which flows through Pamphylia to the
south coast of Asia Minor, he decisively defeated the Persian forces on land
and sea. 200 Phoenician ships which constituted the main part of the
Persian Mediterranean fleet were destroyed (6.37). They represented
Xerxes' last real attempt to restore his fortunes.

In 459 Egypt revolted from Persian control. A force of 200 ships of the
Delian League sailed to the Nile Delta, where to start with they had significant success. For six seasons they maintained a hold in the Delta; but
in 454 the Persians destroyed the whole force, a major disaster for the
Athenians.

Since 462/1 Kimon had been ostracised. In 451/0 he took up the command again, but died fighting in Cyprus in 449. After this hostilities
ceased. Some sources claim that there was a formal agreement between
Athens and Persia, the so-called 'Peace of Kallias'.

**From Delian League to Athenian Empire: the rise of Pericles (470–440)**
(cf. 5.78ff.)

**H.I.26** About 470 the island of Naxos, no longer having any taste for

HI:14  A fragment from the Athenian Tribute Lists for the year 440/39. The inscription lists the proportion offered to Athēnē from the annual tribute paid by Athens' allies.

the continuing burden of providing forces for the League, broke her oath of allegiance and tried to withdraw at a time when the threat from Persia was still alive. It was forced back into the League. The island lost its fleet and walls and was told to contribute money which went to the building of more ships for the Athenian navy. Athens could argue that Naxos had no right to opt out while the war against Persia was being prosecuted. The island state of Thasos in the north Aegean might have felt a more justified sense of grievance when in 465–463 Athens and the League reacted violently to the island's attempt to withdraw. After all, the defeat of the Persians at Eurymedon had effectively removed the threat to the Aegean. Nevertheless, after a long siege Thasos capitulated. It lost its defensive walls; its navy was handed over to the Athenians; it had to pay an indemnity and tribute. In all this Athens was the main beneficiary.

Probably in 454 the Delian League treasury was moved to the Acropolis in Athens. From that date a quota of one-sixtieth of the cities' money tribute was dedicated to the goddess Athēnē. The lists of the amounts were inscribed on stone and fragments of many of these have survived. They testify to the extent of the League, which now included most of the islands of the Aegean and the cities of the northern coast of the Aegean and down the coast of Asia Minor.

H.I.27 It is impossible to set a date on the moment when the Delian League was transformed into the empire (*arkhē*) of Athens. It was a long and gradual process. Perhaps the most significant feature was the creation of a belief in the minds of ordinary citizens of Athens that not only were they entitled to enjoy the prosperity which came with the fruits of empire but also that the success of the self-confident, radical democratic system which emerged at Athens in the middle of the century was intimately bound up with the possession of the empire. This belief, justified or unjustified as it might be, dominated Athenian thinking for over a century. The man who played a key role in the creation of this confident imperialism was Pericles, son of Xanthippos, a member on his mother's side of the aristocratic Alkmaionids (see H.I.11).

Early in his career, in 462/1, Pericles co-operated with the political leader, Ephialtes, in his attack on the privileges and powers of the ancient Council of the Areopagus. What exactly was done is far from clear; but the attack on the powers of this ancient institution is a sign of the trend towards a radical democracy which had no wish to see its decisions influenced or impeded by any unrepresentative and non-responsible body, however venerable. Ephialtes was successful, but stirred up violent animosity. In 461 he died in mysterious circumstances. At much the same time Pericles introduced a nominal payment for those who sat on the juries. Payment for office, for jury-service and even for attendance at the *ekklēsia* was to become one of the most characteristic features of the radical democracy. In 458/7 the *arkhōn*ship was opened up to men from the third of Solon's wealth classes (see 5.26). It was Pericles who was probably the inspiration of the lavish building programme which from 450 onwards was to provide Athens with the Parthenon and other shrines and buildings on the Acropolis, and theatres and gymnasia elsewhere in the city. Artists and architects, such as Pheidias, Iktinos and Mnesikles, worked on the schemes. These buildings represented the culmination of Athens' revival after its destruction in the Persian Wars. Pericles' aim was clearly to make Athens a city fit to be leader of an empire and he was happy to use the tribute which came from that empire to finance the project.

H.I.28 Athens inspired and attracted poets and artists in the second half of the fifth century on a scale unexampled in the rest of Greece. The tragic poet, Sophocles (*c*. 496–406), an Athenian citizen, played his full role in the public life of his city as general and financial expert in addition to his achievements as a poet. His younger Athenian contemporary Euripides (485–406) produced work which reflected the teachings of the intellectuals (sophists) who were attracted to Athens. Pericles had as his mentor one of the first philosophers to settle in Athens, Anaxagoras from Klasdomenai.

From 443 Pericles was the dominant leader of the people in Athens. His popularity, his patronage of the arts, the building schemes, all aroused

HI:15  The Acropolis of Athens from the west.

memories of Peisistratos. But there is no reason to suppose that his power rested on any exceptional office. His influence depended ultimately on his ability to carry a majority in the Athenian *ekklēsia* with him (cf. 5.33).

## The break with Sparta and the First Peloponnesian War 464–445

**H.I.29** The aggressive and self-assertive growth of Athenian power since the Persian Wars was bound to be a matter of concern to the other Greek states, not least to Sparta. The sudden reversals in attitude and policy in both Sparta and Athens in the fifty years after the Persian Wars are best explained by the likelihood of arguments within each state over the proper reaction to the actions of the other. In Athens Kimon was openly a sponsor of Sparta's interests, even to the extent of provocatively naming one of his sons Lakedaimonios. Kimon's view was that the real enemy remained Persia and that it was essential to preserve the co-operation between Sparta and Athens which had contributed so much to the defeat of the Persians. He believed that there was no reason why

Greece could not have joint leaders whose spheres of influence did not conflict. Others were much more ready to try to exploit any weakness of Sparta in these years. Many Spartans would not have regretted abandoning the sea war against Persia after 478. On the other hand, Athens' successes with the Delian League could be seen as a challenge to Sparta's own network of alliances with neighbouring states (called the 'Peloponnesian League'), built up over many years. The point was that the Peloponnesian League was a much less centralised alliance than the Delian and was not well adapted to making a co-ordinated response to the rise of Athens.

H.I.30 Not that Sparta could do much about Athens in any case, because in the fifteen years after the Persian Wars they were faced with challenges to their dominance of the Peloponnese. Their misfortunes culminated in 464 with a huge earthquake which devastated the town and caused great loss of life. The helots, the servile Greek population of Lakonia and of Messenia, chose this moment to revolt. Although the Spartans were able to bottle up the helots on Mount Ithome in Messenia, they appealed to their allies including Athens to send help to bring an end to the revolt (cf. 6.29). Despite opposition, Kimon was able to persuade the Athenians to send him with a contingent to help with the siege of the helots on Ithome. Unfortunately the behaviour of the democratic Athenian soldiers, who may have come to sympathise with the Messenians, worried the Spartans, who summarily dismissed them with the statement that they were no longer needed. Athenian irritation was considerable and Kimon's humiliation at the hands of the Spartans was one of the charges which helped to get him ostracised in 461. His policy of co-operation with Sparta was abandoned and the Athenians became much more ready to make life difficult for the Spartans in the Peloponnese. This change was signalled by an alliance between Athens and Argos about 460. Argos was certainly an enemy of Sparta and at that time may even have been at war with Sparta. This event can be taken as the opening of the First Peloponnesian War, which was carried on in a rather desultory fashion down to 446. At about the same time, 460/59, Megara, after a border dispute with Corinth, withdrew from the Peloponnesian League, to which they had both belonged, and made an alliance with Athens. This secured Athenian control of the northern end of the Isthmus and made it very difficult for Sparta to operate in central Greece.

In the first years of the war, 459–457, Sparta's allies in the north of the Peloponnese, particularly Corinth, bore the brunt of the fighting. The most significant gain in these years was Athens' capture of the island of Aiginē in 457.

H.I.31 Sparta's first major contribution to the conflict also came in 457, when a sizeable force crossed the Corinthian Gulf to intervene in the dispute in central Greece between Doris and Phokis. While there, they linked up with the Thebans and moved towards the border with Attica. The Athenians came out to meet them at Tanagra. The Spartan victory in a hard-fought battle confirmed the myth of the invincibility of the Spartan phalanx; but it did not herald a long-term success for them. Sixty days later the Athenians, under their general Myronides, defeated the Boiotian forces at Oinophyta. Athens now was the dominant power in Greece, controlling both Boiotia and Phokis. These were great days for the Athenians. Their confidence was well illustrated by an expedition of the Athenian general Tolmides with a fleet which sailed round the Peloponnese. The fleet burned the Spartan port of Gytheion and made raids on numerous other spots. This was followed up by Pericles in 454 with attacks in and around the Corinthian Gulf.

H.I.32 The war became a stalemate. After ten years Athens' land empire crumbled. In 447 the Boiotians defeated the Athenians at the battle of Koroneia. The island of Euboia revolted in 446 and, when Pericles crossed with a force, Megara seized the opportunity to massacre the Athenian garrisons. At the same time the Spartan king Pleistoanax led a Spartan army into Attica. In response Pericles rushed back from Euboia. It is likely that Pleistoanax's expedition was primarily intended to prevent Athens intervening in Megara's revolt. Once this had been achieved, Pleistoanax retired without coming near to Athens itself. This withdrawal enabled Pericles to return to Euboia and put down the rebellion there. There were those in Sparta who felt that Pleistoanax had missed his chance in failing to press home his attack. Perhaps the Spartan king had already begun the negotiations with Pericles which in the winter of 446 were to lead to the signing of a thirty years' peace between Sparta and Athens. The basis of the peace was that both sides accepted the status quo. Athens gave up her claims to a land empire in central Greece and ceased to interfere directly in the Peloponnese. Nevertheless, she did hold on to Aiginē and a base in the Corinthian Gulf at Naupaktos.

### The Second Peloponnesian War 431: preliminaries

H.I.33 It is clear that there were those on both sides who were keen to make the peace work, since the terms included a clause which provided for arbitration of the disputes which were bound to arise. In reality the peace settled nothing and at Sparta, in particular, many could not help resenting the way in which Athens had muscled them out of the limelight since the Persian Wars. The reaction soon set in. In 445 King Pleistoanax was prosecuted and went into exile for his actions in the previous year's invasion of Attica; the rumour went round that the only explanation of his failure to follow up his advantage was bribery by Pericles.

An incidental remark in Thucydides (1.40) reveals just how belligerent the mood still was at Sparta. In 440 Samos revolted from the Athenian empire and Athens was forced to send a major expedition under all ten *stratēgoi* (generals), including Pericles. At that moment it is clear that the Spartans themselves voted for war against Athens, but were unable to carry a majority of the members of the Peloponnesian League with them. In this sort of atmosphere it was only a matter of time before hostilities were renewed.

**H.I.34** The flashpoint came in the late 430s when Athens again came to be seen to be dabbling in affairs which did not concern her, to the particular irritation, this time, of Corinth. The island of Kerkyra in north-west Greece, although a colony of Corinth, was involved in a dispute with her mother city, which flared up into open warfare in 435. Two years later Kerkyra sought a defensive alliance with Athens which, to the fury of Corinth, the Athenians accepted. Over the winter of 433/2, Athens and Corinth clashed on a question of jurisdiction concerning Poteidaia, a city in Khalkidike in northern Greece, which was both a colony of Corinth and a tribute-paying member of the Delian League. Corinth now urged her fellow members of the Peloponnesian League to join her in making protests against Athens to the Spartans. Aiginē and Megara added their own complaints to those of Corinth. What was the use of the Peloponnesian League, if Sparta was not willing to uphold the interests of its members? Corinth added: 'Do not force us in despair to join a different alliance.' The threat to the continued existence of the Peloponnesian League was probably unnecessary. The Spartan 'hawks', led by the ephor Sthenelaidas, had such a clear majority in favour of war that they were able to ignore the counsel of caution presented by the Spartan king Arkhidamos. Once Sparta was ready for war, her allies were eager to join in. The winter of 432/1 was spent on fruitless negotiation as Sparta desperately and unsuccessfully tried to find both legal and moral justification for breaking the peace. Thucydides, the Athenian historian of this, the Second Peloponnesian War, recognised clearly that, even more than the incidents and quarrels which led up to the outbreak, what inspired Sparta to action was the unsettled business of the fifty years since the Persian Wars, the Spartans' fear and envy of Athens' growth and power.

It is a curious irony that the king who recognised that this would be a difficult war to win gave his name to the first ten years of fighting, which are often known as the Arkhidamian War.

## The Second Peloponnesian War: Plataia, the plague at Athens, the death of Pericles 431–429

**H.I.35** It was Thebes who took the initiative. The town of Plataia, an old ally of Athens, had stalwartly refused to be incorporated into the Boiotian confederacy. One night in the early spring of 431 a force of Thebans was let into Plataia by sympathisers. However, the surprise attack failed and the Plataians captured and subsequently killed the Thebans. In response to urgent appeals, the Athenians sent a force to help Plataia. Over the next four years the Thebans continued action against the city and from 429 had the help of the Spartans in besieging it (6.29). Despite the ingenious counter-measures which the Plataians took to defend their city, they were forced to capitulate in 427. Curiously, Athens had done little to aid them. At Theban insistence, revenge was exacted upon the defenders. Each prisoner was asked 'Have you done anything to aid the Spartans and allies in the present war?' When, inevitably, he could offer no answer he was taken off to execution. The city was razed. The fate of Plataia illustrates one of the most unpleasant aspects of this war. Plataia stands at the head of a lengthy roll call of small communities, like Skione and Mēlos, which were caught up in the fighting and suffered grievously at the hands of the protagonists.

**H.I.36** One of the main reasons for the Spartan king Arkhidamos' initial opposition to the war could have been that the experience of the First Peloponnesian War raised doubts about how any such war could be won. As there could be no question of besieging Athens, the Spartans decided upon regular invasions of Athenian territory in early summer to cut down the ripening grain and devastate the countryside. The longest of these invasions, in 430, lasted probably no more than 40 days; yet 'at the beginning of the war some thought that the Athenians might survive a year; others reckoned two; no one reckoned they would last more than that' (Thucydides, *Peloponnesian War* 7.28). In a way the attempt almost worked. The Athenian farmers were demoralised by having to crowd into the protection of the city at the time of invasion and then to watch from the walls their farmlands ablaze. At the time of the second invasion in 430, a virulent plague, apparently brought by ship from the east, broke out in

Athens, and spread rapidly through the population. The historian Thucydides caught the plague, but survived to give a vivid account of the suffering. The disaster almost broke the Athenian spirit. There was a reaction against Pericles who was tried and fined. There was even an attempt to open peace negotiations with Sparta; but nothing came of it.

H.I.37 In 429 Pericles died, a victim of the plague. The passing of the man who had dominated democratic politics for several decades was bound to have a profound effect on Athens. After Pericles things could never be the same, only worse, if the contemporary sources are to be believed. For the historian Thucydides, the leaders who emerged from the shadow of Pericles were petty, self-seeking rabble-rousers. This view was confirmed by the comic playwright Aristophanes, who from 427 produced plays which satirised and ridiculed the leaders of the people during the Peloponnesian War. It is Aristophanes, also, who provides a clue to the source of this prejudice – snobbishness. The demagogue, Kleon, is nicknamed the 'Tanner', while Hyperbolos, another leader, is the 'Lamp-maker'. The point of these sneers is that, whereas down to Pericles the majority of leaders of the people were of aristocratic birth, after the death of Pericles the new breed of politicians could not trace their ancestry back through many generations of nobility. In reality the new men were wealthy; but they derived their income not just from farming, the characteristic pursuit of a gentleman in Athens, but also from exploiting slaves in small factories. These men were also well educated (particularly in the new, sophisticated skills of rhetoric) and experts in particular fields, such as finance and the navy. As for their conduct of the war, in the immediate aftermath of Pericles' death no radically new strategies emerged.

### Mytilenean revolt; Phormion at Naupaktos; movements in north-west Greece 428–426

H.I.38 For Pericles the key to Athens' survival was to avoid a direct confrontation on land with Sparta and to maintain the fleet which was to be used to keep the sea lanes open, to harass the enemy, and to maintain Athens' grip on her empire. In 428 Mytilēnē led the island of Lesbos (except the town of Methymne, which had a democratic government) in revolt from the Athenian empire. The Athenians blockaded the island and, despite the promise from Sparta of a fleet to help, Mytilēnē was forced to surrender in 427. The initial reaction of the Athenian *ekklēsia* was severe: a vote to execute all adult males and sell the women and children into slavery. However, overnight opinion changed and on the next day the debate was reopened. Kleon was intransigent; terror, he argued, was a necessary weapon for an imperial power. On the other hand, the politician Diodotos was convinced that a more moderate policy would be most beneficial. The *ekklēsia*, by a small majority, changed its mind and decided to confine its most severe punishment to the minority in Mytilēnē who could be proved to have fomented revolt. News of this change of heart, carried across the Aegean by trireme, reached Mytilēnē just in time to stop the general massacre being carried out. The whole incident has been used to illustrate the fickleness of the Athenian democratic assembly. On the other hand there have been few enough governments in later history who have had the magnanimity and courage to admit a mistake.

H.I.39 It would be wrong to think of Pericles' policy for Athens as a purely defensive one. The Athenians were quite prepared to use their forces, particularly their fleet, wherever it looked as though something might be gained without seriously endangering Athenian power. One area where this seemed to hold out good prospects was the Corinthian Gulf and Ambrakia and Akarnania in the west. In 429 the Athenian admiral, Phormion, operating from the Athenian base at Naupaktos on the northern shore of the entrance to the gulf, was able to inflict two surprise defeats on larger Peloponnesian fleets (cf. 6.38–9). Although Phormion disappeared from the scene in the next year (it is not known what happened to him), the Athenians kept up their probing in the region.

The presence of the forces of both sides in the west was probably indirectly responsible for another of the ugly features of the age, civil war (*stasis*) in a community between the wealthy oligarchs who looked to Sparta for support and the democrats who expected Athens to back them. On the island of Kerkyra fighting broke out between groups in 427. Athenian forces intervened and cynically stood by while the democrats massacred their opponents. These events inspired Thucydides to his most impassioned piece of political analysis (3.14ff.).

In 426 the Athenian general Demosthenes tried to offer greater protection to Naupaktos by invading Aitolia. He was defeated and it was only with difficulty that the Athenian survivors struggled back to Naupaktos. Later in the year Demosthenes was able to redeem himself, when a Peloponnesian force first attempted to attack Naupaktos and then attacked Amphilokhian Argos. At Olpai Demosthenes, commanding both Athenian and local troops, outwitted the Peloponnesians and inflicted the first major defeat of the war. A significant role in the success was played by light-armed troops.

## Sicily, Pylos and Sphakteria 427–5

**H.I.40** It is a surprising and noteworthy fact that the war with Sparta and her allies did not absorb all the energy and attention of the Athenians. In 427 when her old ally in Sicily, the city of Leontinoi, appealed to Athens for help against Syracuse, Athens responded by sending a small fleet. It may be that she was motivated in part by the hope of cutting grain supplies to the Peloponnese from Sicily. However, given Athens' long-standing interest in the area since the middle of the century, it is likely that the Athenians were primarily inspired by the possibility of making further accessions to her empire and winning new sources of wheat. This would explain the disappointed reaction, when in 424 the Sicilian states temporarily settled their disputes and sent the Athenian forces home. All three Athenian generals were punished on their return.

**H.I.41** It was an incident in 425, when the Athenians sent a new fleet to reinforce their men in Sicily, which for the first time in this war promised to tip the balance significantly. The Athenian fleet under the generals Sophocles and Eurymedon rounded the southern Peloponnese and were forced by bad weather into the great natural harbour of Pylos in Messenia. The long island of Sphakteria protected the bay. Demosthenes, who had been so active in the north-west in the previous two years, was accompanying the fleet, even though he held no official post. He realised the potential of Pylos as a base from which the Messenian helots might be inspired to revolt from Sparta. He was left behind with a small contingent to build a fort at the northern end of the bay. The Spartans were so disturbed by the news, that they called off their normal invasion of Attica early and rushed troops to the area. The Spartan forces tried to blockade the Athenians. Four hundred and twenty hoplites and their helots were landed on the island of Sphakteria to deny it to the Athenians. They then tried an unsuccessful direct assault on Pylos, during which the Spartan Brasidas distinguished himself.

The Athenian fleet turned back to help Demosthenes. They entered the bay and defeated the Peloponnesian fleet. To their horror the Spartans now realised that their troops were cut off on the island of Sphakteria. Their first reaction was to make an offer of peace, which was turned down at Athens. Much later some Athenians came to regret this rejection; but at the time the Spartans offered very little.

Unfortunately the Athenian blockade of the Spartan forces on Sphakteria was not completely effective and the whole operation dragged on indecisively. In Athens Kleon attacked the incompetence of the generals, incautiously claiming that he could have done better himself. To Kleon's undoubted amazement, Nikias, one of the board of *stratēgoi*, in an act of complete irresponsibility said that he could have the job, if he wanted it. Forced to make good his boast, Kleon had the common sense to take the experienced Demosthenes with him. To the astonishment of many, Kleon and Demosthenes were successful. They led an assault on the island. Two hundred and ninety-two hoplites from the Spartan forces were taken as prisoners, of whom some 120 were Spartiates. This was a most serious loss to Sparta. For the rest of the war, their every action was governed by fears about the fate of the Spartan prisoners at Athens. Sparta stopped the invasions of Attica and tried to renew offers of peace (cf. 6.22).

H.I.42 The success of Pylos was a boost to Athenian morale. They became even more adventurous. In 424 they entered into secret negotiations with democratic elements in Boiotia who had been excluded from power since 447, as a prelude to risings in the cities of Boiotia and the overthrow of the Boiotian confederacy. The plan went wrong and in a large-scale battle at Dēlion the Boiotians defeated the Athenians, a desperate blow to the renewed confidence of Athens (cf. 6.13).

## War in north-east Greece and the Peace of Nikias 424–421

H.I.43 There was one area of the Athenian empire which was vulnerable to Spartan intervention – the cities in north-east Greece, on Khalkidike, which could be reached overland from the Peloponnese. In 424 an appeal came to Sparta from cities in this area which were ready to revolt. At Sparta the leading advocate for intervention was the enterprising Brasidas, who had already distinguished himself in action at Pylos and elsewhere. He was given a force of 700 helots, who were armed as hoplites; to them he added another thousand mercenaries. Significantly, no Spartiates were to be sent so far from home. Brasidas marched north and began to win over cities of the Athenian empire by a mixture of personal charm, persuasion and threat. His most notable success was the capture of Amphipolis. The Athenian *stratēgos*, Thucydides, failed to prevent this and was blamed by the Athenian people for the loss. During the enforced leisure of exile, he was able to tour Greece to gather material from both sides for the history of the war, which he had begun at its outbreak.

H.I.44 Under the shock of Brasidas' continuing success, the Athenians agreed to a truce for one year in 423. The Spartans obviously hoped that this would lead to a more permanent peace. This truce unfortunately was not observed in Khalkidike. At the end of the truce, in 422, Kleon, as one

HI:16   Air view of Sphakteria and the bay of Pylos from the north.

of the generals, took a force to the north to counter Brasidas. The main goal was Amphipolis. Outside the city Kleon was drawn into battle. The Athenians were routed and Kleon killed. Brasidas, who had shown himself to be one of the most vigorous and charismatic of Spartan generals, also died from his wounds.

**H.I.45** These events served to illustrate something which had been evident since the outbreak of hostilities: this war could not be won. Neither side was likely to lose except by some act of gross stupidity. In the winter of 422/1 both sides began to think seriously of peace. The Spartans wanted back their men who had been captured at Pylos; on the other side Athens wanted Amphipolis back. In 421 a fifty years' peace was agreed on the basis of the return by both sides of most places which had been captured by fighting. The main Athenian negotiator was Nikias who gave his name to the settlement. The Peace of Nikias brought an end to the Arkhidamian war.

Unfortunately, if the war had been unwinnable, the peace was unworkable. The negotiations had been carried on between Athens and Sparta. It was left to Sparta to persuade her allies to accept the agreement. Although she got a majority vote in favour of the peace in the Peloponnesian League, the major states, like Corinth and Boiotia, simply refused to carry out their part. They saw no advantages in the peace for them. In an attempt to emphasise the new position in inter-city relations, Sparta and Athens followed up their peace with an alliance, after which to Sparta's immense relief Athens returned the men captured at Pylos.

## The rise of Alkibiades, the battle of Mantineia, the destruction of Mēlos 420–416

**H.I.46** There was a new factor in the complex diplomacy of the next few years. After thirty years of peace with Sparta, Argos, an independent state which had not suffered in the war, became the natural leader for those groups which were dissatisfied with the actions of the two great powers. For a time it looked as though a new grouping of powers, including Corinth and Argos, might emerge to challenge Sparta. In addition at Athens there was increasing irritation with Sparta's failure to fulfil her side of the Peace of Nikias. The mood was brilliantly exploited by the most flamboyant personality in Athens in this period, Alkibiades, son of Kleinias. Noble by birth and brought up in the household of Pericles, Alkibiades was a throw-back to an earlier breed of aristocratic politicians who were primarily motivated by the pursuit of personal *timē*. For Alkibiades, the democracy of Athens was the stage on which he was play- ing the star role; no one was to be allowed to elbow him from the limelight. In 420 Alkibiades persuaded the Athenians that there was advantage to be got from exploiting the dissatisfaction in the Peloponnese.

As a consequence Athens made an alliance with Argos, Elis and Mantineia, although she did not repudiate her agreements with Sparta. In 418 King Agis of Sparta led an expedition against Argos. This developed into a confrontation with the allies of Argos, including Mantineia and Athens. On the plain of Mantineia in a battle of confused movement, the Spartans overwhelmed the forces opposed to them (cf. 6.9–10). The battle of [First] Mantineia helped to confirm the myth of Spartan invincibility and enabled her to reassert her control of the Peloponnese.

**H.I.47** There followed a period of 'phoney' war in which Sparta did little to follow up her success or to harass Athens. The Athenians were able to continue their aggressive imperialism. In 416 they captured the island of Mēlos, one of only two islands in the Cyclades which were not part of the Athenian Empire. Mēlos claimed to be a Spartan colony and its sympathies lay with the Spartans. After a siege, the island capitulated and received harsh punishment. All men of military age were put to death and the

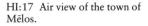
HI:17  Air view of the town of Mēlos.

women and children sold into slavery. Thucydides used the incident to explore the nature and justification of imperialism.

### The Sicilian Expedition 415–413

**H.I.48** In the winter of 416/15 envoys came from one of Athens' allies in Sicily, the city of Egesta, to beg for help in a war against Selinous, which had called in Syracuse on her side. This appeal revived Athens' long-standing ambitions in the area. Alkibiades was strongly in favour of intervention, while Nikias counselled caution. The Athenians, not seriously distracted by warfare in Greece, enthusiastically voted for a large fleet to be sent with Alkibiades, Nikias and Lamakhos in charge. They had no clear brief, apart from doing what they could to help their allies; but most Athenians would have been anticipating new conquests and additions to their empire.

**H.I.49** Just before the fleet sailed in early summer 415 (cf. 6.40), Athenians awoke to find that some of the Hermai, busts of Hermes, which stood outside both public and private houses as a symbol of good fortune, had been defaced during the night. This act of sacrilege was taken as a sign of ill omen for the coming expedition. Calls were made for an investigation. In addition, at a meeting of the *ekklēsia*, just before the fleet sailed, Alkibiades was accused of taking part in sacrilegious, mock celebrations of the sacred Mysteries of Eleusis (see 2.53). Alkibiades tried without success to get the matter cleared up before he sailed. What lay behind these acts is far from clear. An aristocrat, Andokides, was arrested along with others

HI:18  Marble head of a Herm
(cf. 2:14) mutilated in 415.
Early 5th century.

and turned state's evidence; in a later speech *On the Mysteries* he did little
to clarify the events. The profanation of the Mysteries was probably no
more than a blasphemous, private entertainment. Alkibiades' alleged
involvement was a gift to his political enemies. The mutilation of the
Hermai was discussed at a dinner party several days before it occurred.
While it could have been no more than an aristocratic 'dare' (this sort of
vandalism had happened before, according to Thucydides), it may have
been a deliberate political act to try to prevent the fleet sailing. If so, it
could be significant that it originated in the dining-clubs of young aristocrats which in a few years were to play a sinister role in the attempt to overthrow the democracy (cf. 5.33).

Despite everything, the fleet sailed. However, before it saw action, the
Athenians decided to recall Alkibiades to face his accusers. In response
Alkibiades fled to Sparta, where he proceeded to give his best advice on
how to overcome his mother city.

H.I.50 Nikias and Lamakhos were left in charge of the Athenian fleet.
The war did not go particularly well for them. The response from potential
allies in Sicily was disappointing. However, by the winter of 415/14, the
Athenian fleet was anchored in the Great Bay of Syracuse and the
Athenians had begun siege works around the city. In 414 Lamakhos was
killed and Nikias, who had originally had great doubts about the whole
enterprise, was left in sole command. Nevertheless, the Athenians came
close to success until the Spartans, acting on the advice of Alkibiades, sent
a commander, Gylippos, to rally the Syracusan resistance. In 413,
although Nikias was reinforced with troops and ships under the command
of Demosthenes and Eurymedon, no progress was made. The Syracusans
blockaded the Athenian fleet in the harbour after fighting in which

HI:19 The stone quarries at Syracuse.

Eurymedon was killed. In a desperate attempt to break out, the Athenian fleet was defeated. Nikias and Demosthenes began a retreat by land, constantly harried by the Syracusans. The two commanders lost contact with each other and were defeated separately. Despite assurances which were given when they surrendered, both were executed. The surviving Athenian prisoners were herded into a makeshift prisoner-of-war camp in the stone quarries of Syracuse.

This was the greatest action of this war, and, in my opinion, the greatest action that we know of in Greek history – to the victors the most brilliant of successes, to the vanquished the most disastrous of defeats. (Thucydides, *Peloponnesian War* 7.87)

### Sparta, Persia, the oligarchic coup at Athens 413–411

H.I.51 The expedition to Sicily was not a sudden, irrational whim, nor was it misconceived from the start. Indeed, it came close to success. Nevertheless, the loss of the fleet and of many thousands of men presented Athens' enemies with a remarkable opportunity. Sparta had already been spurred into action. In 413 she placed a permanent fort at Dekeleia in

Attica. Athenian freedom of movement was restricted all the year round
and the fort also became a sanctuary for runaway slaves. In the Athenian
Empire a number of states revolted in 412. Sparta began the building of a
new fleet to try to exploit discontent in the Aegean.

Perhaps the most decisive mistake in the war was made by Athens when
they chose to support the revolt of Amorges in Karia from the Persian
empire in 414/13. The Persians now showed renewed interest in the
Aegean and, in the hope of winning back control of the Greek cities of Asia
Minor, made friendly contact with Sparta. The main Persian negotiator,
Tissaphernes, the satrap (Persian governor) of the south-west of Asia
Minor, was pleased to find that the Spartans were quite ready to bargain
away the rights of the Greeks of Asia in return for Persian monetary
support for their fleet.

H.I.52 These were tough years for Athens. The citizens had to struggle
to raise the funds to continue the war and to keep hold on their empire.
They were forced to melt down gold statues and to draw on the 1,000
talents' reserve which had been set aside for emergencies at the beginning
of the war. In 411 the Athenian fleet was based at Samos and it was there
that their officers were contacted by Alkibiades. Life had become rather
awkward for him in Sparta. For both personal and political reasons he had
left Sparta and gone to the court of Tissaphernes. Alkibiades' offer was
that he would persuade the Persians to stop supporting Sparta, if, in return,
the Athenian officers would bring about the overthrow of the radical
democracy at Athens, so that Alkibiades could return home. Peisandros,
an oligarchic leader, went with this proposal to Athens. There he proposed

HI:20  A silver tetradrachm with the head of the Persian governor (satrap)
Tissaphernes. Late 5th century.

only that 'they should not continue democracy in the same way'. The tempting bait was an alliance with Persia. Even though Alkibiades proved totally unable to fulfil his promise, the oligarchic coup went ahead. This was the moment that many of those critics of the radical democracy had been waiting for. The population of Athens was terrorised into the creation of a body of 400 who were to take immediate control of the government. The reaction in Samos was immediate. If the democracy had been banished from Athens, it was still alive among the Athenian forces at Samos. Indeed, the absence of so many citizens from the city may have been the key to the oligarchs' initial success. The democrats at Samos now recalled Alkibiades, who was perfectly willing to offer his services to anyone for personal advantage.

H.I.53 The news of the reaction at Samos caused a split in the oligarchs at Athens. One of the promises at the beginning of the revolution had been that a body of some 5,000 of the better-off Athenians who could provide hoplite armour at their own expense was to have full citizen rights and be eligible for election to state office. This was justified on the principle that those who contributed most to the Athenian war effort should be the ones to direct how their money and energies were to be used. However, the idea of the 5,000 was being used by the extreme oligarchs as a cover. It soon became clear that they had no intention of ever creating such a group. There were some within the oligarchic ruling group, men like Theramenes, who realised that the oligarchs would have to come to terms with the Athenians at Samos. They pressed for the creation of the 5,000. After only four months the 400 found themselves unable to bring about peace with Sparta or to fulfil any of their promises. About September 411 they were overthrown and replaced with the rule of the 5,000. The rule of the 5,000 was a significant move away from extreme oligarchy. So in 410 it was not difficult for the traditional democracy to be restored in Athens. The failure of the oligarchic revolution of 411 taught a powerful lesson. The Athenian radical democracy enjoyed wide support among Athenians who would not easily surrender the powers and privileges which they had gained. In future any more restrictive system of government could only be imposed on them by the force of arms of a foreign power.

### Persia, Lysandros, Arginoussai, Aigospotamoi: the end of the war 411–404

H.I.54 Even before the restoration of the democracy at Athens, the democratic fleet in the Aegean was winning victories, at Kynossema in the

Kherronēsos in 411 and at Kysdikos in 410. In the years following, under the leadership of Alkibiades among others, the Athenians had a series of successes in the Hellespont region. In 407 Alkibiades was able to return to Athens and be rehabilitated.

In the same year, 407, the Persian king Dareios sent his younger son, Cyrus, to supervise the west of Asia Minor with orders to help the Spartan war effort. At much the same time Sparta put Lysandros in charge of their navy. These two struck up a good relationship, which ensured that Persia with reasonable efficiency financed the Spartan fleet for the rest of the war. In the spring of 406 the new combination had its first success when it defeated an Athenian fleet near Notion on the coast of Asia Minor. Although Alkibiades had not been present at the battle, he was held responsible for the failure. So, instead of returning to Athens to face prosecution, he retired to a castle in the Kherronēsos, from where he made a last dramatic appearance to advise the Athenian fleet just before the battle of Aigospotamoi.

H.I.55 Later in 406 the Spartan admiral Kallikratidas succeeded in blockading the Athenian fleet, now commanded by Konon, in Mytilēnē. In response to this danger, the Athenians managed to put together a new fleet which sailed and met Kallikratidas in battle off the Arginoussai islands near Lesbos. The Peloponnesian fleet was crushed and Kallikratidas was lost overboard. On the Athenian side 13 ships were sunk and 12 disabled and a squadron under two Athenian trierarchs, Theramenes and Thrasyboulos, was ordered to pick up survivors. A storm blew up and prevented the rescue mission. Several thousand Athenians drowned.

Eight of the board of ten *stratēgoi* had been present at Arginoussai. Of them, six decided to return to Athens, where they were immediately brought before the *ekklēsia*. Their victory had been overshadowed by the great loss of Athenian lives. The people's grief was whipped up into a fury by the evidence of a survivor. The proposal was put that the *ekklēsia* should take a single vote on the collective guilt of the generals. When it was objected that this was unconstitutional, the howl went up that it was intolerable if anyone prevented the people from doing what it wanted to do. The generals were condemned and the unfortunate six who had come home were executed. There could be no more vivid verification of where power ultimately lay in the radical democracy.

H.I.56 The next year, 405, saw the centre of action return to the Hellespont. While Lysandros and a Peloponnesian fleet were besieging Lampsakos late in the year, an Athenian fleet beached on the opposite side of the Hellespont at Aigospotamoi. For five days Lysandros refused to give battle. But on the final evening, when the Athenians disembarked, Lysandros caught them unawares. At a stroke and without resistance he captured almost the entire Athenian fleet. The Athenian *stratēgos*, Konon, escaped to Cyprus with nine ships. The state trireme, *Paralos*, was sent to bring the news to Athens that she no longer had the means to continue the war.

It was night when the *Paralos* arrived in Athens. As news of the disaster spread, a howl of grief rose up first from the Peiraieus, then among the Long Walls and into the city, as one man passed the news to another. That night no one slept. (Xenophon, *Hellenika* 2.2.3)

The first reaction of the Athenians was renewed defiance. After all, the likely prospect was the total destruction of the city and the killing and enslavement of its population, the sort of treatment which Athens herself had meted out on more than one occasion. After long negotiations, in which the Athenian Theramenes played a prominent part, by spring 404 the Athenians were ready to accept the Spartan conditions. Athens was not to be destroyed. Instead she lost her empire; her fleet was limited to 12 ships, the defences of the Peiraieus and the Long Walls were to be demolished, all exiles were to be recalled, and Athens was to become a Spartan satellite, obliged to recognise Spartan leadership.

## Theramenes and the rule of the Thirty: democracy restored 404–400

H.I.57 Lysandros arrived in the spring of 404 to preside over the demolition of the Long Walls. Later in the summer he returned to add his support to another oligarchic coup in Athens. This time the Athenians were cowed into establishing a board of thirty men to look after affairs until a new constitution could be drawn up. The thirty included men like Kritias and the ubiquitous Theramenes. Many such men had been in exile since the revolution of 411 or, like Kritias, had fallen foul of the democracy in the intervening years. By the terms of the peace all such exiles were permitted to return to Athens. To back up their take-over, the Thirty got Sparta to send a garrison of 700 men. Under the eyes of these troops the Thirty instituted a reign of terror against their political and personal enemies. This grim period is vividly described in a speech *Against Eratosthenes* (he was one of the Thirty) by one of the victims, the wealthy *metoikos* and speech-writer Lysias, whose brother was put to death.

H.I.58 As in 411 the oligarchs soon fell out. Theramenes tried to resist the purges, but was denounced by Kritias and condemned to death. This was a violent end to an extraordinary career. Theramenes, the son of the distinguished Athenian general Hagnon, had played a full part in the oligarchic revolution of 411, yet had turned against the extreme oligarchs in sufficient time to enable him to remain and participate in the restored democracy. However, after the defeat of Athens, he was still able to become one of the ruling Thirty, probably with greater enthusiasm than his supporters were prepared later to admit. The twists and turns of the career of this Athenian opportunist, which need no deeper explanation than personal ambition, earned him the nickname of '*kothornos*' (the actor's boot which fitted either foot).

Democratic exiles from Athens found refuge in a number of Greek cities, including Thebes, where politicians were unhappy with the peace settlement and were prepared to support anyone who might disrupt it despite a Spartan prohibition on harbouring exiles. From Thebes, the democrats, led by Thrasyboulos, occupied the Athenian fort of Phyle in the winter of 404/3. From there they captured the Peiraieus and in a fight succeeded in killing some of the Thirty, including Kritias. When the Spartan king, Pausanias, arrived, he realised that it would be impossible to suppress the democratic revival; so he turned to a policy of reconciliation. The supporters of the Thirty were to receive an amnesty and were to be permitted to go to live in Eleusis, which became virtually a separate state. This haven for oligarchs survived until 401/400, when it was once again incorporated in the Athenian state. The restoration of all the features of the radical democracy was a gradual process over the years following 403, including a revision of the law codes and the reintroduction of state pay which had been abolished by the oligarchs in 411.

## Death of Socrates 399

H.I.59 In 399 the philosopher, Socrates, was brought to court on a charge of 'refusing to recognise the gods of the state and introducing other new gods. He is also guilty of corrupting the youth' (Xenophon, *Memorabilia* 1.1.1).

The specific charges were not just a cover for a political charge. It is true that Socrates had among his pupils men like Kritias, who had played a significant role in the oligarchic rule of Athens; but no one could deny that Socrates had fulfilled loyally the duties of a citizen of the democracy and on one notable occasion had refused to co-operate with the Thirty. The charges were serious in themselves. Socrates was found guilty and, taking a high moral stance, refused the opportunity to have his sentence commuted to a heavy fine. He was forced to drink hemlock and died in the dignified manner which was to be an example to generations of martyrs. The killing of their master and guide inspired in his followers, such as the philosopher Plato, a hatred for the democratic system. However, it is difficult to see Socrates as the victim of Athenian democracy. What the case did show was how profoundly conservative the Athenian democracy was, how suspicious of innovation and of change.

## Sparta in victory 404–396

H.I.60 Victory in the Peloponnesian War restored Sparta to the leadership of Greece. The history of the thirty years after 404 is the story of how Sparta threw away that opportunity in part through bad luck, but mainly through insensitivity, selfishness and arrogance towards the other Greek states.

Sparta inherited the Athenian Empire. However, Lysandros created immense ill will in the empire by establishing in many of the cities a narrow oligarchy of ten men, backed up by a Spartan *harmostēs* ('controller') and garrisons. Although the Spartans overthrew this policy when Lysandros' power waned, the damage had been done and the resentment at Spartan interference remained.

Secondly Sparta ignored the interests of her allies in the war. She took all the booty for herself and Athens was bound to Sparta. Thebes and Corinth got no reward for their labours. In the decade after the end of the war they consistently refused to play their part in the Spartan alliance.

H.I.61 Finally the Spartans were drawn into conflict with Persia, which had done so much to aid their success in the Peloponnesian War. When King Dareios died in 405/4, his eldest son, Artaxerxes, took over. However, Cyrus, his young son, resented this and planned an expedition from his base in the west of Asia Minor. In 401 Cyrus took the field and appealed to Sparta for help. This put Sparta in a difficult position, for although she owed a great deal to Cyrus' good will in the last years of the Peloponnesian War, if Cyrus lost, she might be drawn into a direct confrontation with Persia. The Spartans hedged their bets by unofficially sending a force to join the Greek mercenaries in Cyrus' army. Cyrus was killed and his army defeated in battle at Cunaxa, not far from Babylon. The march home of the 10,000 Greeks from the very heart of the Persian Empire is vividly described by a leading participant, the Athenian Xenophon, in his *Anabasis* ('March Up Country').

The Greek cities of Asia Minor which had also supported Cyrus now expected Persian retribution and appealed to Sparta for protection.

Despite the fact that, a decade earlier, the Spartans had been quite ready to sign away the freedom of the Greeks of Asia in return for Persian aid (H.I.51), they now rose to the occasion in a manner befitting the leaders of the Greeks. A series of Spartan commanders and troops were sent out, culminating in the great expedition of the new Spartan king Agesilaos in 396. Agesilaos tried to turn the venture into a crusade, modelled on the Greek expeditions against Troy, even to the extent of trying to offer sacrifice at Aulis, like Agamemnon.

### Discontent with Sparta, the Corinthian War, Athens' revival 396–390

**H.I.62** For those in Greece who were discontented with Sparta, the absence of Agesilaos in Asia Minor provided a golden opportunity. The Athenians, even after the restoration of the democracy, had abided by the letter of their agreement with Sparta. They were hardly in a position to do otherwise. Nevertheless, their loss of power and influence must have irked them. So when, in 395, the Thebans approached Athens for help against Sparta, the Athenians readily made a treaty. Then, after the new alliance had been successful in a battle at Haliartos against the Spartans, in which Lysandros was killed, Corinth and Argos joined in. Xenophon, in his history of this period, claims that the war against Sparta was inspired by Persian bribes offered to the Greek states. Such an account entirely ignores the deep-rooted antagonism which Sparta had stirred up throughout Greece. This new conflict centred on the Isthmus and so gained the name of the 'Corinthian War'.

In 394 the Spartans won a great victory at the battle of the Nemea river against the allied forces. It was inevitable that Agesilaos would be recalled from Asia Minor to help. He reappeared in Greece in the high summer of 394 and inflicted another defeat on the enemy at Koroneia in Boiotia. These successes meant that the allies refused to face the Spartan army in pitched battle again in this war.

**H.I.63** In the same year, 394, Sparta suffered a major defeat at sea. A large Persian fleet, commanded by the Persian satrap Pharnabasdos and the Athenian mercenary Konon, destroyed the Spartan navy at the battle of Knidos. The Persians followed this up by sailing round the Aegean and driving out Spartan garrisons, thus bringing to an end Spartan short-lived control of the sea empire which she had inherited from Athens. After consulting with the allies at the Isthmus of Corinth, Konon persuaded Pharnabasdos to take the fleet to Athens to help in the task of rebuilding the Long Walls. Here Konon received a rapturous welcome. His position as a mercenary general in the pay of the Persians was forgotten; instead he was hailed as an Athenian who restored the fortunes of Athens. All the old confidence flooded back. In 389 the Athenian *stratēgos*, Thrasyboulos, took an Athenian fleet through the eastern Aegean to revive Athens' control over her empire after a brief, enforced interruption. The Persians had cleared the Spartans from the seas, and Athens slipped into the power vacuum left in the Aegean with an ease based on long experience. Nothing could better illustrate how deeply ingrained in the minds of the Athenians were the ways of imperialism.

The war on land, which soon got bogged down in the usual stalemate, was most notable in 390 for the ominous defeat at Lekhaion near Corinth of a force of Spartans by a troop of mercenaries. These were led by the Athenian Iphikrates and, significantly, were armed as peltasts with a light shield and javelin (cf. 6.21).

### The King's Peace 386

**H.I.64** As in the Second Peloponnesian War, Persia was the only power likely to be able to break the deadlock. In 392 the Spartan Antalkidas had been unsuccessful in trying to get a peace which involved Persia. Five years later in 387/6, he was able to win the backing of the Persian king, Artaxerxes, who sent down the terms of a peace in which Persian control of the Greek cities of Asia Minor was acknowledged by the rest of the Greeks and all the other Greek cities, both small and large, were to be left autonomous. These terms were backed up by a threat that the Persian king would make war on anyone who refused to accept them. This, the King's Peace, was the first 'common peace' (*koinē eirēnē*), in that it did not apply only to one group of states, but was designed to impose a general peace on all the Greek cities. In theory a noble idea, this peace was in practice made to solve a particular problem in the interests of Persia and Sparta. It did not provide any real basis for continued peace in Greece. There was no accepted idea of how the principle of autonomy was to be defined, no procedure for arbitration. Athens made the best of a bad job. At least she now had her fortifications and a fleet and the possibility was open to her to build up alliances in the Aegean.

### Sparta's misuse of power at Mantineia, Phleious, Thebes and against Athens

**H.I.65** The King's Peace gave Sparta another chance to reassert her role as the leading state in Greece, a chance which once again, and for the last time, she squandered by a remarkable display of callous self-interest.

Sparta was determined to impose her control on the Peloponnese and ensure that in future no combination of states such as those which had started the Corinthian War should appear again in Greece.

In 385 the city of Mantineia was overcome. Her fortifications were demolished and the population divided among the four villages of which Mantineia had originally been composed. In 383 Sparta had responded to a group of exiles from the city of Phleious in the northern Peloponnese, by ordering their restoration. When, in 381, the exiles complained of ill-treatment in Phleious, the Spartans marched against the city. Phleious endured a siege of over one-and-a-half years. When she gave in, a new oligarchic constitution was imposed on the city, which had been democratically ruled, and for a time a Spartan garrison was left to ensure the people's compliance. Doubts were raised even in Sparta about this intervention.

**H.I.66** In 382 Sparta was given the chance of intervening in the north, when some cities in the Khalkidike area appealed to her for help against the growing power of a league of northern cities, centred on the city of Olynthos. The Spartan campaign was successful in eventually reducing Olynthos itself. It was while he was leading reinforcements to the north that the Spartan commander, Phoibidas, encamped near Thebes, received a request from a group favourable to Sparta within the city of Thebes itself. With their help Phoibidas was able to take over the Kadmeia, the acropolis of Thebes, on the day of a religious festival and then impose a pro-Spartan government on the city. This outrageous interference in the internal affairs of another state in time of peace and in blatant contravention of the King's Peace upset even some of the Spartans. Phoibidas, who had probably acted without orders from home, was fined, but not before the Spartan king Agesilaos had neatly expressed the prevailing philosophy of Sparta in these years:

If the action of Phoibidas is harmful to Sparta, then he deserves to be punished. If, on the other hand, it will benefit Sparta, we should remember our established rule that in such cases a man may use his own initiative. The point to be examined is simply this: has this action been good or bad for Sparta? (Xenophon, *Hellenika* 5.2.32)

**H.I.67** For the historian Xenophon, who in general was pro-Spartan, the capture of the Kadmeia was an irreligious act that was bound to be punished. Punished it was. Late in 379 Theban exiles, based on Athens, entered Thebes and massacred the pro-Spartan Thebans and forced the Spartan garrison to surrender. Sparta responded by sending out King Kleombrotos with an expedition. As it was late in the year, there was little that could be done and Kleombrotos soon returned home, although he did leave a contingent under a *harmostēs* (controller), called Sphodrias, at Thespiai in order to keep an eye on the situation.

In 378 Sphodrias conceived his own plan to win glory, a night attack on the Peiraieus of Athens. The whole attempt was a fiasco. Dawn rose to reveal Sphodrias and his force still miles from their target. At that very moment there were envoys from Sparta in Athens. They protested that the Spartan government had not sanctioned any such action and that Sphodrias would be punished. Indeed, Sphodrias himself expected condemnation and failed to return home. Nevertheless his trial went ahead and, to the shocked outrage of the Greek world, Sphodrias was acquitted, thanks to the surprise intervention of King Agesilaos. It was the king's view that, despite Sphodrias' manifest guilt, Sparta needed soldiers like him. An expression of such cynicism was unsurprising in the mouth of the defender of Phoibidas.

### The Second Athenian League 378–377 (cf. 5.98–9)

**H.I.68** Concern at Sparta's actions during these years was widespread and was exploited effectively by Athens. Athens and Thebes were drawn together and probably agreed to an alliance in 378. Athens then reorganised her existing allies, including Thebes, into a new league of states, the Second Athenian League. Its purpose was 'to make the Spartans leave the Greeks to enjoy peace in freedom and autonomy'. Athens was making a bid to take over Sparta's role as champion of the principles of the King's Peace. Such laudable aims would meet with general acceptance; but some states might pause and remember how a similar confederacy, the Delian League, in the fifth century, had been created to counter Persian aggression but had developed into the Athenian Empire. To allay such fears the Athenians issued a decree, proposed by Aristoteles, in 377 which was in effect a front-page advertisement for the League, in which Athens renounced many of the features of her fifth-century empire which had proved so objectionable. There was to be no interference in the internal constitutions of member states, no tribute and no Athenian settlements on allied territory. Over the next three years some 70 states joined the new League.

### The war against Sparta: the battle of Leuktra 376–371

**H.I.69** The war against Sparta was prosecuted in a most desultory fashion. Athens was worried at the way Thebes was exploiting the war to build up her control of the cities of Boiotia. The war cost money. There can be no doubt that Athens found it increasingly difficult to meet the financial burdens of these years. In 378/7 the tax on property, the *eisphora*, which was levied to pay for the war, was reorganised. Citizens were placed in groups, *summoriai*, each of which became responsible for a share of the burdens. As financial difficulties continued to dominate public policy in Athens for the rest of the fourth century, it is no surprise to find that some of the most prominent and influential politicians of the age were experts in finance and that the financial posts which they held became steadily more important.

**H.I.70** By 371 Athens was more worried by the aims of Thebes than by those of Sparta. In that year Athens persuaded the main belligerents to agree to peace at a conference at Sparta. Unfortunately a serious dispute arose, when the Thebans tried to insist on signing the peace on behalf of the cities of Boiotia. The Spartan king Agesilaos refused, because he was unwilling to acknowledge Thebes' control of the Boiotian League. After an angry exchange, the Thebans were excluded from the terms of the peace. Within three weeks, King Kleombrotos had invaded Boiotia. The Thebans, led by Epameinondas, came out to face him at Leuktra (cf. 6.26). The Spartan army was decisively defeated. Out of 1,000 dead some 400 Spartiates were killed, along with Kleombrotos himself.

The battle of Leuktra was a surprise to the whole of Greece. Thebes had developed the arms and tactics to defeat the Spartan phalanx. Spartan power was broken not just because of the loss of men at Leuktra. The resentment and ill will which her actions had inspired in the other Greek states now burst forth in undisguised delight as Spartan control of the Peloponnese was dismantled in the years after Leuktra. The states of the Peloponnese seized their opportunity to assert their independence and were backed up by repeated expeditions into the Peloponnese by Epameinondas and the Thebans during the 360s. In 370/69 Messene, with Theban help, became an independent state for the first time for 300 years. Sparta never recovered this territory. In the early 360s the cities of the central Peloponnese formed a new Arkadian League. Yet in all this the most significant fact was that Sparta was not attacked directly, although on two occasions Epameinondas did come close to the city. The Spartan myth was not entirely destroyed.

**H.I.71** The 360s were the heyday of Theban power. Early on, Athens turned against Thebes and by 368 she was allied to Sparta. For much of the decade Athens intervened in the Peloponnese to try to counterbalance Theban influence. In addition the Athenians continued a vigorous policy by sea to recover influence, particularly in the north Aegean. The Thebans even responded to this by building their own fleet in 364.

In the Arkadian League a split developed between those who favoured Thebes and those who turned to Sparta and Athens to protect them from increasing Theban interference. In 362 Epameinondas led a force into the Peloponnese to help those states which adhered to Thebes. At Mantineia he met an army of those Arkadian states which opposed him, Sparta and Athens (6.27). Adapting the tactics which had won at Leuktra, Epameinondas and the Thebans were again successful. But when Epameinondas was killed in the moment of victory, the Thebans failed to press home their victory. After the battle a new 'common peace' was made on the basis that each state should keep what it had. It mattered little that the Spartans refused to sign, still vainly demanding their right to Messene.

**H.I.72** In the last sentences of his history, Xenophon summed up the situation after the battle of [Second] Mantineia: 'There was even more uncertainty and confusion in Greece after the battle than there had been before' (*Hellenika* 7.5.27). This was too gloomy an assessment. What had been created was an equilibrium in which no one state could claim to be predominant. Thebes was a significant power in central Greece, but undertook no further expeditions into the Peloponnese. Athens was the dominant power at sea. Sparta could no longer control the states of the Peloponnese. This was the logical outcome of centuries of development of the city-states of Greece. Competitive, self-assertive, and deeply suspicious of neighbours, the cities were never able to join in some larger, cooperative, united organisation of Greeks. Panhellenism remained the pipe-dream of philosophers; it could never form a part of practical politics. In such a world any state which appeared to be aiming to be pre-eminent inevitably caused the other Greek cities to combine to resist its influence. A balance was bound to emerge.

### The collapse of the Second Athenian League 357–355

**H.I.73** Athenians could feel satisfied with the revival of the city as the major naval power and the steady growth of Athenian gains in the Aegean. Despite Athenian promises at the time of the formation of the Second League, Athens tended to behave increasingly like an imperial power again. The League continued even after its original objective (to oppose Sparta's predominance) was no longer relevant. States found that they could not secede from the League. Demands for payments to League funds became more regular. The League fleet was used for Athens' purpose.

Eventually in 357 the major members of the League revolted. The so called Social War lasted until 355, when Athens allowed those states which wanted to leave the League to do so. In the years after peace was made other allies slowly drifted away from Athens.

**H.I.74** It was bound to take the Athenians time to adapt to their new situation. They had to be persuaded that democracy could survive without an empire. In a brave pamphlet *On the Peace* in 355, the speech-writer Isokrates argues that Athens should give up her imperial aspirations. Xenophon in a work produced at the same time, the *Poroi* ('Revenues'), sought to demonstrate that with peace Athens was bound to thrive as a trading centre and had no need of income from an Empire. It was left to the politician Euboulos to put these principles into action. In the period after 355 Euboulos, a financial expert, enabled Athens to make a financial recovery by a careful husbanding of resources and an avoidance of major military commitments.

### The rise of Philip II of Macedon: Demosthenes at Athens 359–348

**H.I.75** From the ranks of the Athenian political advocates of the new realism there emerged Demosthenes, a speech-writer and advocate in his thirties. By the late 350s, however, he was to turn against Euboulos, to try to awaken his fellow Athenians to the new threat which he saw in the north, King Philip II of Macedon. His speeches, in which he tried to bully the Athenians into action, can with point be described as 'Churchillian', for generations of patriotic politicians were to copy their elaborate phrasing and impassioned invective.

**H.I.76** The object of Demosthenes' hatred, King Philip II of Macedon, came to power in 360/59 at the age of twenty-four. The Macedonians were

HI:21  A gold stater of Philip II of Macedon (d. 336) with a laureate head of Apollo and a charioteer. 348–336.

Greek in origin, though other Greeks tended to sneer at their backwardness and distinctness. The amalgamation of local and Greek culture has been vividly demonstrated in recent years by the discovery of the tombs of the Macedonian royal family at Vergina. Philip inherited a kingdom threatened by neighbouring tribes and disturbed by the claims of pretenders. Philip soon dealt with the pretenders and, after beginning the reformation of the Macedonian army, first defeated the invading tribes and then went on to deal with his major task of securing the border territories of Macedon. It was inevitable that these actions should concern Athens in particular, as she had long-standing interests in north Greece. In 357 Philip took Amphipolis. The Athenians were particularly enraged because they always claimed that Amphipolis was theirs, although they had not controlled it since 424. Some Athenians were under the impression that Philip had promised to return Amphipolis to them. Whatever the truth of the matter, Philip held on to the city and the Athenians were sufficiently roused to declare war on him, a war which they were hardly able to prosecute effectively.

H.I.77 By 352 Philip had taken control of Thessaly and then turned against the Kingdom of Thrace and the League of the cities of Khalkidike, which was dominated by the state of Olynthos. Against this background, Demosthenes desperately tried to get the Athenians to intervene, first by his 'Philippic' speech of 352/1 and then in a series of speeches in 349/8 in which he urged Athens to back Olynthos. Despite his bluster, Demosthenes was unable to produce an answer to the two basic problems: how could Athens fight effectively in an area where she had no bases and how could a major campaign be financed? In fact, Athens did manage to send considerable numbers of troops to Olynthos, but to no avail. In 348 Philip razed the city and sold the population into slavery. He also kept those Athenians who were captured there. Their fate was to influence Athenian policy for the next two years.

## The Peace of Philokrates 346

H.I.78 Philip saw no future in antagonising Athens unnecessarily and right from the time of the capture of Olynthos he sent messages offering the prospect of peace. Towards the end of 347 Athens responded by sending an embassy of ten men including Philokrates, who had proposed the mission, and Demosthenes and his later political rival Aiskhines. Philip produced a proposal not just of peace, but also of alliance, backed up by vague, but tempting, promises of help for Athens.

These negotiations took place against the background of the so-called 'Sacred War' in central Greece. In 356 Phokis had seized the Oracular Shrine of Delphi and for ten years Phokis had fought off the attacks of her enemies, including Philip. Everyone realised that this war provided Philip with an excuse to intervene in central Greece at a time which suited him.

**H.I.79** The Athenians were caught between the desire to keep Philip out of Greece and the need for a peace with Philip. When the Athenian embassy returned from Philip, it was only with difficulty that its leader, Philokrates, was able to get the Athenians to agree to a peace and an alliance between Philip and Athens and her allies. Phokis was abandoned to her fate.

Immediately Philip entered central Greece and put an end to the Sacred War. He presided over the Pythian Games and then returned to Macedon. Of course, since he now controlled Thermopylai and was champion of the rights of the shrine at Delphi, he had both the opportunity and the excuse to intervene in Greece again if he so chose.

Philip's return home should have been taken as an indication that he was not interested in direct control of the Greek cities. He certainly wished to have good relations with the cities and to get respect in return; but the centre of his attention was probably elsewhere. It may be that he had already conceived of the plan to attack Persian control of Asia Minor. Unfortunately the Greek cities could not let things be.

### Demosthenes and Aiskhines at Athens: the final defeat of the Greeks by Philip (346–338)

**H.I.80** In Athens the peace of Philokrates very soon became unpopular, as Athenians felt some guilt at the way Phokis had been left in the lurch and no great benefits came to them from Philip as promised. Demosthenes managed to climb on this bandwagon of resentment, to dissociate himself from the process of peace-making. He led the attack on the politicians involved in peace negotiations. In particular, in 343, his case against Aiskhines, his one-time colleague, came to court. The speeches by both sides illustrate the formidable difficulties faced by a jury in a highly charged political case in Athens. Demosthenes and Aiskhines presented totally incompatible accounts of events which had taken place, often in public, only three or four years earlier. Aiskhines was acquitted by a small margin. Nevertheless the mood of antagonism against Philip, stoked up by Demosthenes and others, prevailed in Athens.

**H.I.81** By 340 the Athenians came to see Philip's steady gains in the

HI:22 The Lion Monument set up at Khaironeia, Boiotia, to commemorate the Sacred Band of Thebans who fell there in the battle of 338.

north as a threat to their grain route. Philip was besieging Byzantium and, indeed, later in the year, actually did seize the grain fleet in response to Athens' continuing provocations. In 340 Demosthenes got his way. Athens and her allies declared war on Philip.

In 339 the squabbles in the Amphiktyonic Council, the group of states who presided over the affairs of Delphi, gave Philip the excuse he needed to intervene. Athens was terrified that she would be left isolated. She succeeded in making an alliance with Thebes and Boiotia. But in the summer of 338 Philip decisively defeated the Greek allies at Khaironeia in Boiotia.

Philip dealt harshly with Thebes. The Boiotian confederacy was again broken up and Thebes was garrisoned. Athens got more lenient treatment, probably because Philip wanted her as an ally and did not want the task of reducing Athens. Philip promised to send no troops into Attica. Although Athens was forced to break up what was left of her alliance, she was left in control of a number of islands and, as a present from Philip, was given Oropos, a city which had been the source of constant dispute between Thebes and Athens.

In 337 Philip invited the Greek cities to send delegates to a conference at Corinth. A general peace was agreed. All the mainland states south of Olympos, except Sparta and some island states, became members of a federal union, 'the Greeks'. The so-called League of Corinth promptly allied with Philip and joined him in a declaration of war on Persia, for which Philip was elected *hēgemōn* ('leader').

Philip, however, was not destined to lead the crusade against Persia. At the wedding celebrations for his daughter on the eve of his departure on the expedition in 336, Philip was stabbed to death by one of his bodyguard.

### Alexander the Great 336–323

**H.I.82** Philip was succeeded by his twenty-year-old son, Alexander. It is impossible to write a biography of this man. His true character has disappeared entirely under a mass of myth and hero-worship. The historian can only concentrate on his campaigns.

Many Greek states could not repress their glee at the death of Philip. In Athens Demosthenes was overjoyed. However, Alexander swiftly marched into Greece and, without bloodshed, asserted his authority and later put down a Theban revolt. This sharp, effective action put an end to subversion.

With Greece restored to loyalty, Alexander embarked on the great adventure, the attack on Persia, in 334. At the battle of the river Granikos in 334, he defeated the Persians and went on to liberate most of Asia Minor from Persian control. In the next year he defeated Dareios, the Persian king, at the battle of Issos. Dareios fled and offered a peace which

HI:23  Portrait of Alexander.
C. 340–330.

Alexander turned down, a sign that he was now intent on the conquest of the whole of the Persian Empire. In 332 and 331 Alexander occupied the countries of the eastern end of the Mediterranean and conquered Egypt, where he laid down plans for a great new city, Alexandria.

In 331 Alexander marched into the heart of the Persian Empire. At Gaugamela in Mesopotamia Dareios was once again defeated by Alexander and fled into the remoter parts of the Persian Empire. There he fell victim to one of his own satraps.

H.I.83 The years following saw the great marches to the east through Persia, past the Caspian Sea, to Kandahar (another 'Alexandria'), then north through the Hindu Kush to Samarkand and Tashkent, where Alexander found a wife, Roxane. Between 327 and 325 Alexander marched into north-west India and the Punjab. At the river Hyphasis his troops cried 'enough' and Alexander could not persuade them to travel further. There followed a long and agonising march back to Babylon. There he made plans for an Arabian expedition. In the middle of 323 he fell ill of a fever and died after thirteen years of hectic conquest and endeavour. His senior officers were to carve out kingdoms for themselves from the empire which he had won.

H.I.84 While Alexander was away, the Spartan king, Agis, led an abortive revolt in the Peloponnese, which Alexander's representative, Antipater, put down. Athens remained quiet. For much of the period an Athenian financial expert, Lykourgos, carefully supervised the revenues of the city and presided over a period of prosperity and public building (in particular the rebuilding in stone of the theatre of Dionysos at the foot of the Acropolis).

In 330 Demosthenes and Aiskhines had a re-run of their old rivalry. The occasion was the prosecution by Aiskhines of an Athenian, Ktesiphon, who had proposed to reward Demosthenes for his services to Athens with the grant of a crown. The speeches of Aiskhines and Demosthenes turned into a review of Athenian policy towards Macedon. Aiskhines failed and his public career ended.

### The end of democracy in Athens 324–2

H.I.85 When the news arrived of Alexander's death, Athens joined other northern Greek states in revolt against Macedon. When the Macedonian commander, Antipater, marched south, he was besieged in Lamia near Thermopylai during the winter of 323/2. However, in the summer of 322 Antipater defeated the Greeks at the battle of Krannon.

Although the defeat was not severe, the Greek cities' contingents melted. 'Thus was the cause of freedom most shamefully abandoned' (Plutarch, *Life of Phokion* 26).

Antipater imposed hard terms on Athens. A Macedonian garrison was established at Mounykhia. The democratic system of government was to be abolished and a new constitution with the franchise restricted to the well-off was introduced. In 322 Athens' experiment in democracy had been destroyed.

This outline survey of Greek history is bound to reveal how endemic war was. War, albeit usually confined to the few months of summer, with brief intervals of peace, was the natural order of things. The Greek city-states were fiercely independent and their competitiveness made it impossible to unify them or to devise the proper means for regulating relations between states. Comparative peace could only be imposed upon the cities by the intervention of an external power (6.5).

## Pericles' Funeral Speech of 430

The Funeral Speech put into the mouth of Pericles, Athens' most famous statesman, by the historian Thucydides is the most famous statement of what made Athens great. It was given to commemorate those slain in battle. You should read these selections in close conjunction with Chapter 3, and 4.77ff.

We have chosen Crawley's (1876) translation (slightly adapted). It is not the easiest to read, but it does represent more faithfully than others the style of the original:

. . . But what was the road by which we reached our position, what the form of government under which our greatness grew, what the national habits out of which it sprang; these are questions which I may try to solve before I proceed to my panegyric upon these men; since I think this to be a subject upon which on the present occasion a speaker may properly dwell, and to which the whole assemblage, whether citizens or *xenoi*, may listen with advantage.

37. Our constitution does not copy the laws of neighbouring states; we are rather a pattern to others than imitators ourselves. Its administration favours the many instead of the few; this is why it is called a *dēmokratia*. If we look to the laws, they afford equal justice to all in their private differences; if to social standing, advancement in public life falls to reputation for capacity, class considerations not being allowed to interfere with *aretē*; nor again does poverty bar the way. If a man is able to serve the state, he is not hindered by the obscurity of his condition. The freedom which we enjoy in our government extends also to our ordinary life. There, far from spying jealously on each other, we do not feel called upon to be

HI:24  A public commemoration for those Athenians who died in the first year's fighting of the Peloponnesian War. C. 430.

angry with our neighbour for doing what he likes, or even to indulge in those hard looks which cannot fail to be offensive, although they inflict no positive penalty. But all this ease in our private relations does not make us lawless as citizens. Against this, fear is our chief safeguard, teaching us to obey those in office and the laws, particularly such as regard the protection of the injured, whether they are actually on public display, or belong to that code which, although unwritten, yet cannot be broken without acknowledged disgrace.

38. Further, we provide plenty of means for the mind to refresh itself from business. We celebrate games and sacrifices all the year round, and the elegance of our private establishments forms a daily source of pleasure and helps rid us of irritations; while the size of our city draws the produce of the world into our harbour, so that to the Athenian the fruits of other countries are as familiar a luxury as those of his own.

39. If we turn to our military policy, there also we differ from our enemies. We throw open our city to the world, and never by alien acts exclude *xenoi* from any opportunity of learning or observing, although the eyes of an enemy may occasionally profit by our openness, trusting less in system and policy than to the native spirit of our citizens; while in education, where our rivals from their very cradles

by a painful discipline pursue courage, at Athens we live exactly as we please, and yet are just as ready to encounter every legitimate danger. In proof of this it may be noticed that the Spartans do not invade our country alone, but bring with them all their allies; while we Athenians advance unsupported into the territory of a neighbour, and fighting upon a foreign soil usually defeat with ease men who are defending their homes. Our united force was never yet encountered by any enemy, because we have at once to attend to our navy and to dispatch our citizens by land upon a hundred different services; so that, wherever they engage with some such fraction of our strength, a success against a detachment is magnified into a victory over the nation, and a defeat into a reverse suffered at the hands of our entire people. And yet if, given as we are to ease, not toil, and to natural, not enforced, courage, we are still willing to encounter danger, we have the double advantage of escaping the experience of hardships in anticipation and of facing them in the hour of need as fearlessly as those who are never free from them.

40. Nor are these the only points in which our city is worthy of admiration. We cultivate refinement without extravagance and knowledge without effeminacy; wealth we employ more for use than for show, and place the real disgrace of poverty not in owning up to the fact but in declining to fight it. Our public men have, besides politics, their private affairs to attend to, and our ordinary citizens, though occupied with their own business, are still fair judges of public matters; for, unlike any other nation, regarding him who takes no part in these duties not as unambitious but as useless, we Athenians are at least able to judge, even if we cannot originate, and instead of looking on discussion as a stumbling-block in the way of action, we think it an indispensable preliminary to any wise action at all. Again, in our enterprises we present the singular spectacle of courage combined with careful calculation, each carried to its highest point, and both united in the same persons; although among others decision is usually the fruit of ignorance, while reflection leads to hesitation . . .

41. In short, I say that as a city we are the school of Hellas; while I doubt if the world can produce a man, who where he has only himself to depend upon, is equal to so many emergencies, and graced by so happy a versatility, as the Athenian. And that this is no mere boast thrown out for the occasion, but plain matter of fact, the power of the state acquired by these habits proves. For Athens alone of her contemporaries is found when tested to be greater than her reputation, and alone gives no occasion to her enemies to blush at the antagonist by whom they have been defeated, or to her subjects to question her title by merit to rule. Rather, the admiration of the present and succeeding ages will be ours, since we have not left our power without witness, but have shown it by mighty proofs; and far from needing a Homer for our panegyrist, or other of his craft whose verses might charm for the moment only for the impression which they gave to melt at the touch of fact, we have forced every sea and land to be the highway of our daring, and everywhere, whether for evil or good, have left imperishable monuments behind us. Such is the Athens for which these men, in the assertion of their resolve not to lose her,

nobly fought and died; and well may every one of their survivors be ready to suffer in her cause.

42. Indeed if I have dwelt at some length upon the character of our country, it has been to show that our stake in the struggle is not the same as theirs who have no such blessings to lose, and also that the panegyric of the men over whom I am now speaking might be by definite proofs established. That panegyric is now in a great measure complete; for the Athens that I have celebrated is only what the heroism of these and their like have made her, men whose fame, unlike that of most Hellenes, will be found to be only commensurate with their deserts. And if a test of worth be wanted, it is to be found in their closing scene, and this not only in the cases in which it set the final seal upon their merit, but also in those in which it gave the first intimation of their having any. For there is justice in the claim that steadfastness in his country's battles should be as a cloak to cover a man's other imperfections; since the good action has blotted out the bad, and his merit as a citizen more than outweighed his demerits as an individual. But none of these allowed either wealth with its prospect of future enjoyment to unnerve his spirit, or poverty with its hope of a day of freedom and riches to tempt him to shrink from danger. No, holding that vengeance upon their enemies was more to be desired than any personal blessings, and reckoning this to be the most glorious of hazards, they joyfully determined to accept the risk, to make sure of their vengeance and to let their wishes wait; and while committing to hope the uncertainty of final success, in the business before them they thought fit to act boldly and trust in themselves. Thus choosing to die resisting, rather than to live submitting, they fled only from dishonour, but met danger face to face, and after one brief moment, while at the summit of their fortune, escaped, not from their fear, but from their glory.

43. So died these men as became Athenians. You, their survivors, must determine to have as unfaltering a resolution in the field, though you may pray that it may have a happier issue. And not contented with ideas derived only from words of the advantages which are bound up with the defence of your country, though these would furnish a valuable text to a speaker even before an audience so alive to them as the present, you must yourselves realise the power of Athens, and feed your eyes upon her from day to day, till you become an *erastēs* of her; and then when all her greatness shall break upon you, you must reflect that it was by courage, sense of duty, and a keen feeling of honour in action that men were enabled to win all this, and that no personal failure in an enterprise could make them consent to deprive their country of their *aretē*, but they laid it at her feet as the most glorious contribution that they could offer. For this offering of their lives made in common by them all they each of them individually received that renown which never grows old, and for a sepulchre, not so much that in which their bones have been deposited, but that noblest of shrines wherein their glory is laid up to be eternally remembered upon every occasion on which deed or story shall call for its commemoration. For heroes have the whole earth for their tomb; and in lands far from their own, where the column with its epitaph declares it, there is enshrined in

every breast a record unwritten with no tablet to preserve it, except that of the heart. These take as your model, and judging happiness to be the fruit of freedom and freedom of courage, never decline the dangers of war. For it is not the worthless that would most justly be unsparing of their lives; these have nothing to hope for; it is rather they to whom continued life may bring reverses as yet unknown, and to whom a fall, if it came, would be most tremendous in its consequences. And surely, to a man of spirit, the degradation of cowardice must be immeasurably more painful than the unfelt death which strikes him in the midst of his strength and patriotism!

44. Comfort, therefore, not condolence, is what I have to offer to the parents of the dead who may be here. Numberless are the chances to which, as they know, the life of man is subject; but fortunate indeed are they who draw for their lot a death so glorious as that which has caused your mourning, and to whom life has been so exactly measured as to terminate in the happiness in which it has been passed. Still I know that this is a hard saying, especially since we talk of those of whom you will constantly be reminded by seeing in the homes of others blessings of which once you also boasted: for grief is felt not so much for the want of what we have never known, as for the loss of that to which we have been long accustomed. Yet you who are still of an age to beget children must bear up in the hope of having others in their stead; not only will they help you to forget those whom you have lost, but will be to the state at once a reinforcement and a security; for never can a fair or just policy be expected of the citizen who does not, like his fellows, bring to the decision the interests and apprehensions of a father. While those of you who have passed your prime must congratulate yourselves with the thought that the best part of your life was fortunate, and that the brief span that remains will be cheered by the fame of the departed. For it is only the love of honour that never grows old; and honour it is, not gain, as some would have it, that rejoices the heart of age and helplessness.

45. Turning to the sons or brothers of the dead, I see an arduous struggle before you. When a man is gone, all are accustomed to praise him, and however outstanding your *aretē* should become, you will still find it difficult not merely to overtake, but even to approach their renown. The living have envy to contend with, while those who are no longer in our path are honoured with a goodwill into which rivalry does not enter. On the other hand, if I must say anything on the subject of female *aretē* to those of you who will now be in widowhood, it will be all comprised in this brief exhortation. Great will be your glory in not falling short of your natural character; and greatest will be hers who is least talked of among the men whether for good or for bad.

46. My task is now finished. I have performed it to the best of my ability, and in word, at least, the requirements of the law are now satisfied. If deeds be in question, those who are here interred have received part of their honours already, and for the rest, their children will be brought up till manhood at the People's expense: the state thus offers a valuable prize, as the garland of victory in this race of valour,

for the reward both of those who have fallen and their survivors. And where the rewards for *aretē* are greatest, there are found the best citizens.

And now that you have brought to a close your lamentations for your relatives, you may depart. (Thucydides, *Peloponnesian War* 2.36–46)

# 1
# The physical environment

## The Greek world

1.1 In 480 the Persians destroyed the city of Athens but later in the same year found themselves unexpectedly defeated in a naval battle off the island of Salamis. The following spring they offered the Athenians an alliance, and the Athenians found their own Greek allies fearful that they might accept. The historian Herodotus has the Athenians allay these unfounded suspicions in the following words:

> If we were offered all the gold in the world, or the most beautiful and fertile land imaginable, we would never be willing to join our common enemy and be party to the enslavement of Greece . . . first, there is the burning and destruction of our temples and the images of our gods which compels us to exact from the perpetrators the greatest vengeance we can rather than come to terms with them. Then there is our Greek heritage – the bond of blood and language, our holy altars and sacrifices, and our common way of life, which it would ill become Athens to betray . . . as long as a single Athenian survives there will be no terms with Xerxes. (Herodotus, *Histories* 8.144; see H.I.18–19).

To be Greek was to share a common outlook more than a common country, and to a large extent the same attitude prevails today. One need only recall that in modern times the Greek monarch has been officially styled not 'King of Hellas' but 'King of the Hellenes'.

1.2 The Greek world in antiquity never covered the same territory as modern Greece but was both more extensive and more fragmented. Greece was to be found wherever Greek was spoken, and many Greeks settled far away from their original homeland. Small independent communities of Greeks were established to the west, in South Italy and Sicily, in southern France and Spain, to the east along the coast of modern Turkey, as far south as Libya and Egypt, and as far to the north-east as the Black Sea

(5.75). By the eighth century Greeks were used to hearing stories about faraway places, such as those found in the early epic poem, Homer's *Odyssey*, and after a period of intensive foreign settlement which scattered Greek families over the Mediterranean and beyond (*c.* 750–550), travellers' tales and more authentic information widened their horizons both factually and imaginatively. But the experience of the vast majority of Greeks was very limited. Comparatively few were traders, travellers or émigrés, and for most, life was constrained by their immediate needs, the demands of the family farm and the working year, and by the physical barriers of the landscape around them.

## Landscape

1.3 There are two major features in the landscape of Greece and its surrounding areas: the mountains and the sea. The dominant colours are the grey of the limestone, the green and brown of the vegetation and the blues of the sea and sky. The mountains shut off one small area of plain from another and run in complex chains, constantly dominating the horizon. Although the majority do not rise high, there are a few of noted prominence, e.g. Mt Olympos in the north, 2,917 m and the Taygetos mountains, which overlook Sparta, 2,407 m (cf. Ben Nevis 1,342 m, Mt Whitney in California (the highest mountain in the United States, excluding Alaska) 4,418 m). The presence of the mountains and the difficulty of communication over the ridges must have hampered political unity and have helped to entrench the Greeks in the small, independent settlements which became the hallmark of classical Greek life. A settlement and its surrounding territory was called a *polis* (pl. *poleis*). The low, wooded hills which formed the boundaries of these *poleis* made effective borders to them and allowed communities to develop separately, even though physically close; for a traveller, the *polis* of Megara lay only 50 km from Athens, that of Thebes 70 km, and that of Corinth 100 km. With their limited resources, it was rare for *poleis* to grow to any great size; Athens was unique in being the urban centre of an unusually large *polis* which embraced the whole of Attica (2,500 sq. km) (cf. 4.8). Some islands individually comprised one *polis*, but it was not unknown for a large island to consist of more than one (e.g. Lesbos: 1,630 sq. km consisted of five *poleis*).

1.4 Most settlements were in the plains where reasonably fertile soil supported various crops. The rivers which made their way through the plains were liable to dry up in high summer and to flood in winter, so the Greeks could not use them to any extent for navigation. However, as the coastline is deeply indented with gulfs and promontories, no point on the Greek mainland is much more than 60 km from the sea, so it was the sea, not the rivers, which provided their waterways. Sailors in these waters were unlikely to lose sight of land for long, and the landmarks and islands offered some security from treacherous conditions. However, it was the very existence of these islands, the steep cliffs and the rugged coastlines that created dangerous currents and down-draughts and made navigation the hazardous business that it was.

### Climate

1.5 Apart from some mountainous areas of the central Peloponnese and Crete, southern Greece enjoys the type of climate called 'Mediterranean': winter rains and summer droughts. In the winter rainfall is heavy but intermittent, and there are many days when the sky is clear, the sun warm and the breeze only cool, though the north wind occasionally has the bite that characterises it in more northerly countries. In summer there is virtually no rain for two to four months, apart from an occasional thunderstorm or brief mist, and the intense heat of noontime can bring activity to a halt. However, for about forty days in the latter half of summer the hot air rising over the Sahara draws the cold air from Europe down over the Aegean, so that the sea is boisterous, sailing is hampered, and navigation northwards well-nigh impossible; these winds are the strong, steady 'Etesians', what the Greeks today call the *meltemi*.

1.6 Until modern heavy industrialisation the atmosphere everywhere had a piercing clarity which sharpened the outline of landscape and buildings, and which enabled distant landmarks to be seen: Corinth's citadel from the Athenian Acropolis (over 80 km), the island of Mēlos from Cape Sounion (over 100 km). Unlike the cold of northern Europe which invites a private, indoor existence, the Mediterranean climate encourages men to live their lives out of doors, constantly observed by one another and made to feel the need to succeed in front of other men and to fear the open shame of failure (cf. 3.9). The effect of climate on the whole character of the Greek people was referred to by many writers. Here is Aristotle in chauvinistic vein:

The peoples who live in cold climates and in European areas are full of energy, but rather lacking in intelligence and skill; they therefore in general retain their freedom but lack political organisation and the ability to control their neighbours. The peoples of Asia on the other hand are better endowed with intellect and skill but lack energy and so remain in political subjection. But the people of Greece occupy a middle geographical position and correspondingly have a share of both characteristics, both energy and intelligence. They therefore retain their freedom and have the best of political institutions; indeed if they could achieve political unity they could control the rest of the world. (Aristotle, *Politics* 7.7, 1327b) (cf. P.1; H.I.72).

## Raw materials

1.7 The three major natural resources of the Greeks were building stone, clay and timber. The building stone was mainly limestone, but in some areas (e.g. the island of Paros and the hills of Attica) high-grade marble was present. The clay was used in the production of baked pottery, roof-tiles, architectural decoration and small-scale figurines, and in particular for unbaked sun-dried bricks, an almost universal building material for houses, and even used in fortification walls. Timber, plentiful even up to the last century, was used in great quantities in the construction of houses, as a component of larger buildings, public as well as private, and for fuel. However, for ship-building timber, Athens was heavily dependent on outside sources, mainly the kings of Macedon, where the high mountains produced the necessary pine and fir trees (4.57).

1:1  A potter's yard in the modern suburb of Maroussi, Athens.

1:2  Workmen splitting marble in a quarry on Penteli, Attica.

◦  **1.8** Metals, however, were rare. Copper was mainly imported from Cyprus; it was the first metal to be smelted, and *khalkeus* – a 'coppersmith' (from *khalkos* meaning 'copper') – was the word later used for all smiths. Silver (together with lead) was mined in southern Attica (see 1.19) and also on the island of Siphnos; gold in Thrace to the north of the Aegean and again on Siphnos; both metals were used in the manufacture of coinage and luxury objects. Iron, though it exists sporadically in mainland Greece, was mined in only a few places (e.g. Lakōnia) and may have been imported from the islands, Thrace or from the west. Tin, used with copper in the manufacture of bronze for armour, statues, containers, etc., is not a natural resource in Greece and was most likely supplied initially by the Phoenicians.

## Vegetation

◦  **1.9** Whilst the plains provided some small areas of high fertility which
◦ bore succulent fruits, the shallow soils amidst the bare rocks of the hillsides
◦ supported trees and wild flowers, gorse and scrub, but were generally
◦ unsuitable for cultivation. To increase the area of cultivable land, terracing
◦ was adopted, probably as commonly then as now in Greece, though even

1:3 The grape harvest. Late 6th century.

so only 20% of the total land area was capable of growing the most important crops: cereals, olives and vines.

Greeks were aware of how unproductive their land was. This can be illustrated by a passage from Xenophon, returning from a year away in Persia as a mercenary (H.I.61). Here he keenly praises the site of Kalpē (modern Kerpe) on the southern shore of the Black Sea, furnished with natural features and resources that Greeks prized highly:

Kalpē harbour lies midway on the voyage between Herakleia and Byzantium, and is a bit of land jutting out into the sea, the seaward side being a precipitous cliff, whose minimum height is 35 m while the neck joining it to the mainland is about 120 m across. The area to the seaward side of this neck is large enough to hold a population of ten thousand. The harbour is right at the foot of the cliff and the beach faces west. There is an abundant spring of fresh water just by the sea and commanded by the headland. There is a lot of timber of various sorts and in particular a lot of fine ship-timber right down by the sea. The high land extends about 3 km inland and the soil is good and free from stones; the land bordering the sea is thickly wooded with large trees of all kinds for a distance of more than 3 km. There is a lot more good country with many inhabited villages. The land bears barley and wheat, all kinds of vegetables, apples, sesame, beans, plenty of figs, a lot of vines which produce a good sweet wine, and indeed everything else except olives. (Xenophon, *Anabasis* 6.4.36)

Xenophon might almost be advertising Kalpē as the ideal site for a new Greek settlement, as it afforded nearly all the conditions for peaceful and productive existence, and for trade; olives, the missing item, could be acquired by trading with Athens which exported them on a large scale (see 1.20)

1:4  A satyr treads grapes in a vat. Early 5th century.

1:5  Work at an olive press. Early 5th century.

## Farming

1.10 Ownership of land, which was restricted to full members of a community, was fundamental to Greek society. Wealth was generally based on land, and care for the land of one's ancestors, together with the religious associations of their shrines there, was of prime concern (cf. 4.13). For the peasant farmer with his smallholding and for the aristocrat with his wider estates, security of livelihood and status in the eyes of others were rooted in the maintenance of their inherited property (cf. 4.49ff.).

1:6  A ploughman and his team. Late 6th century.

**1.11** For the majority of Greeks farming was their livelihood, and the year must have fallen into a regular pattern, one not marked by months of the year but by the seasons which demanded different tasks and by the phenomena that marked the onset of changes in the weather, e.g. the appearance and position of the important stars and constellations. Major events in the year were the vintage in September, the ploughing and sowing in October and November, the gathering of olives in November and the grain harvest in May (cf. 4.52). Despite occasional periods of relaxation there would be little prolonged time for rest if the farm were to survive, and the various festivals of thanksgiving that punctuated the year were expressions of real gratitude to the gods, as the food for the coming year was assured, and if the human participants made merry, this reflected an understandable feeling of relief (cf. 2.6). It was on festive occasions that worshippers might offer a precious animal for sacrifice – as food for themselves: the gods had to be satisfied with the savour of the cooking (cf. 2.28ff.). Everyday food consisted mainly of bread and vegetables, and at times even such meagre fare might not suffice. Apollodoros underlines how serious a bad year could be: 'my land not only produced no crops, but that year, as you all know, even the water dried up in the wells, so not a vegetable grew in the garden' ([Demosthenes] (*Against Polykles*) 50.61). Also, the absence of a citizen farmer on a military campaign, normally fought in the summer, might threaten the very survival of his family at home.

1.12 The divisions of the Greek countryside into wooded mountain-sides, hillsides covered with brush and scrub, and the cultivable plains in the valleys dictated the range of farming for the Greeks. The arable lands were sown mainly with barley, which is more resistant to drought than wheat and will grow in relatively poor soils. The other two products of the 'Mediterranean triad' were vines and olives, the latter in particular being able to survive in poor soil. If one is to picture a farmstead, there will be the farmhouse with its adjacent garden of vegetables and fruits, its pigs and chickens, and then an irregular pattern of fields fanning outwards, dividing the land by ridges and furrows into patches of vineyards and olive groves, with perhaps grain growing between the trees. On open spaces exposed to the wind, the farmer lays out his threshing floors. The whole farm is dotted with inconvenient rocks that protrude through the thin covering of soil. In a comedy by the Athenian Menander the definition rings true:

> Poor wretch; what a life! He's a typical Attic farmer,
> Struggling with rocks that yield nothing but savory and sage
> And getting nothing out of it but aches and pains.
>
> (Menander, *Dyskolos* 604–6)

Rocks were sometimes piled into cairns that came to be treated as sacred markers.

1.13 Much of the farm would be open grain land; pasture land was poor, more distant and in short supply. Hence cattle were few, and of these the ox was the most useful for the heavy work on the farm and for the slow and expensive business of haulage. Horses were a sign of a rich man, who would use them for hunting and racing. They were expensive to keep, as they needed grain as feed to maintain them in good condition, and grain was usually required for human consumption. Their harness was rudimentary and, if the horse put his head down to pull, soon choked him. The horse was therefore unsuitable for heavy draught work either on farm or road, while the absence of stirrups limited its usefulness in war (stirrup-less riders being easily unseated) (cf. 6.16). It was only in the lusher parts of northern Greece (Thessaly and beyond) that horses were raised in any numbers. Mules and donkeys would have been a commoner sight in the farms and on the pathways. The pastures were given over to sheep and goats; both were driven up to the mountains in summer where the shepherds would live a remote and isolated life, and in winter the animals were brought back to the protection of the valleys. Sheep and goats, *not* the cow, provided cheese and milk. Hippocrates advised against drinking cows' milk. Modern biological evidence suggests that northern Europeans adapted specially in order to digest it. The short-haired sheep provided valuable soft wool which made very fine cloth. More common were coarser, long-haired sheep. Of the wild animals that roamed the hills, the most common were hares and deer, though wild boars and bears were to be found in the more wooded parts and even lions were not unknown.

**Travel and communications**

**1.14** Owing to the lack of properly surfaced roads and the difficult nature of the Greek terrain, overland travel was arduous and was not lightly undertaken. The majority of people stayed near to home, walking into town or local village for the market, or to the farmlands for their daily tasks. The 7-km walk from Athens to the Peiraieus and the journey back might have been counted by many as an everyday excursion (cf. 1.24). Individuals also travelled by cart, and the range of draught animals used can be seen from Nausikaa taking her companions and the royal washing in a mule-drawn cart to the shore (Homer, *Odyssey* 6.36–92), King Laios on a pilgrimage in a horse-drawn cart being met and killed by his son Oedipus (Sophocles, *Oedipus Tyrannus* 800–13), and Kleobis and Biton substituting themselves for the oxen that had not arrived in time to take their mother to the festival at the sanctuary of Hera near Argos where she was a priestess (Herodotus, *Histories* 1.31). Lighter, more manoeuvrable chariots drawn by horses were the preserve of the wealthy and used for racing and processions. For heavy haulage, e.g. to transport goods such as farm produce, ox carts were needed, but as they had no rotating axle for negotiating corners, they were not used outside the regions of the plains. Pack animals transported goods over longer distances and more rugged terrain.

**1.15** For transport of all kinds, the sea was therefore the usual choice. Although many areas were self-sufficient and had no need of the sea, Athens was the exception, as the amount of cereals grown within Attica was insufficient for the urban population and thus she was particularly dependent on overseas grain (cf. 5.74ff.). Few voyages would have been taken for pleasure, as pirates were a constant source of danger. Nor was a sea voyage possible at all times of the year (1.5, 2.25). The islands lying within the Aegean basin enable sailors to chart their courses by reference to fixed points, but traders did not avoid the open sea. The slow, broad cargo-ships depended on sail and wind, and travelled at an average speed of five knots. Nelson's *Victory*, a much larger and heavier warship with

1:7  A heavy merchantman and a two-level warship. Late 6th century.

sails, averaged seven knots. Ships powered by oars were swifter than sailing ships, but their lighter bulk and the presence of the rowers fitted them for use mainly in time of war. The trireme, with 170 rowers, was the fastest and the finest man-of-war in the classical period, and could reach a speed of seven to eight knots with a continuous power output, or even up to thirteen knots for a short burst of ten to twenty minutes. Greek cargo-ships, with their small number of crew and their heavy loads, had no reason for rationing the supply of food and water, and so could sail for many days and nights without putting in to land; warships, with their complement of about two hundred and their need to be as light as possible, carried few provisions and had to put in frequently to enable the rowers to rest and eat (cf. 6.31ff.).

**1.16** When information needed to be conveyed quickly, a runner could be used, or a beacon fire or fast ship. The most famous runner was Pheidippides, who in two days ran the 250 km from Athens to Sparta to ask for help against the Persians who had landed at Marathon (H.I.13). Beacon fires were used for signalling messages in time of war, e.g. to alert a town to an attack (cf. 1.24), and Thucydides gives an example of the use of a swift ship when the decision to kill the people of Mytilēnē on the island of Lesbos was rescinded in the Athenian assembly (see H.I.38):

Another trireme was at once despatched in haste, for fear that the first might arrive before it and the city be found destroyed . . . the crew made such efforts on the voyage that they took their meals (a mixture of barley, oil and wine) while they rowed, and took it in turns to row and sleep. They were lucky to meet no contrary

1:8 The countryside of Attica with olive trees.

wind, and as the first ship made no haste on its monstrous mission, while the second pressed on as described, the first arrived so little ahead that Pakhes had only just time to read the decree and prepare to carry out its sentence when the second put into harbour and prevented the massacre. (Thucydides, *Peloponnesian War* 3.49, H.I.38).

## Attica

1.17 The roughly triangular promontory of Attica lies in the south-east corner of central Greece and extends over an area of 2,500 sq. km (the size of present-day Luxembourg and slightly larger than the American state of Rhode Island). Two sides of the triangle are bordered by sea, the third to the north-west is marked by the mountains of Kithairon and Parnes which effectively shut off Attica from Boiotia and the rest of central Greece. Although mainly a hilly region, four more mountainous areas (Aigaleos, Pentelikon, Hymettos and Laureion) help to define three major plains: the Thriasian plain on the west, the plain of Athens and Mesogeia (see Map 3).

1.18 Attica was comparatively rich in raw materials; she had clay in abundance and a great variety of building stone. The high-quality marbles from beneath Mt Pentelikon and Mt Hymettos were used for building to a unique extent, the former white and crisp, giving precision to the lines of the buildings on which it was used, the latter of a bluish colour. Of the coarser limestones, there were the hard blue-grey 'Acropolis' limestone, the blue-black Eleusinian, the yellowish-grey Kara from Hymettos and the softer limestone from the Peiraieus area, more workable and so more popular. Hymettos also provided a reddish conglomerate that was a natural concrete, later much used in foundations. A brownish, less weighty limestone was imported from the nearby island of Aiginē. Although the Parthenon temple on the Acropolis of Athens stands out as a supreme example of what Pentelic marble could do, being used for structure, architectural sculpture and even roof-tiles, its uniqueness is emphasised by contrast with the ruined buildings of the market-place which give a more varied and truer picture of the variety of textures and colours that Attic building stones possess (5.87).

**1.19** Silver was the most valuable metal mined in Attica, at Laureion. First extensively exploited just before the sea-battle of Salamis against the Persians in 480, these rich veins provided money for the building of Athens' fleet and were the basis of her power. Lead was mined with the silver at Laureion, but despite the existence of iron in the same area the Athenians knew nothing of these deposits and imported their iron from elsewhere (5.70).

**1.20** Attica is situated in the driest part of Greece with particularly shallow soils on the hills and mountains and was largely under olives, which resist drought; so dependent were the people of Attica on the olive

1:9  Drawn reconstruction of ore washeries near the silver mines at Laureion in south-east Attica.

that it was claimed that it had been a gift of Athēnē to the land and that it had first grown in Attica. Indeed, the farmers in the area concentrated on the production of olives and vines and, to support the populous urban centres such as Athens and Peiraieus, chose to import the necessary grain from the lands round the Black Sea, from North Africa and from Sicily (5.74). Plato likened Attica to 'the skeleton of a body wasted by disease; the rich soft soil has all run away leaving the land nothing but skin and bone' (*Kritias* 111b–c). Despite Plato's gloomy picture, Attica still had a variety of trees: planes, cypresses and elms, and in Athens itself these trees were planted in the market-place. Sacred groves and springs were also greener than the rest of the countryside.

**1.21** In the period from *c.* 600 to 300 Attica was an independent state with Athens as its urban centre, and the people of Attica were all Athenians. This was an unusually large *polis*, even though it was only 60 km from Mt Parnes to Sounion, and 40 km from Marathon to the coast opposite the island of Salamis, which itself belonged to Athens. Before this unification under Athens, there had been a number of independent communities dotted about the countryside and even after Athens had become the centre, country towns and small villages were still in a real sense the rural foci for the farmsteads and hamlets that lay around. The country parishes or local districts (*dēmoi*) were flourishing local centres, and some of the more outlying had little contact with Athens, forming their lives round the older nuclei and directed more by the aristocratic families who had their estates nearby and who earlier had been the local leaders (H.I.5). Rich finds of sixth-century sculpture and pottery show that the townships of Attica had the estates of aristocratic families nearby. Distance as well as the hold which local loyalties had over the country folk may well have disinclined them to attend the political meetings in Athens. Their natural reluctance to uproot themselves from ancestral lands and move into town at the beginning of the Peloponnesian War is noted by Thucydides (cf. 1.1):

They were heavy-hearted and reluctant to leave their homes and the temples with their traditional and time-honoured institutions, to change their way of life, and to leave behind what was to them their native city. (*Peloponnesian War* 2.16)

Perhaps the major festivals would tempt them into town, but most country centres had their own cults, markets and fairs which the local people would more readily attend. Athens was not necessarily where their traditional allegiance lay (cf. 2.52).

**1.22** The towns and villages of Attica had their own character and identity. The small fortified town of Eleusis, 16 km west of Athens, with its Mysteries in honour of Demeter, the agricultural goddess, and her daughter Persephone attracted thousands of worshippers (cf. 2.53); Akharnai, a few kilometres north of Athens, was noted for its charcoal-burners who derived their wood from the slopes of nearby Mt Parnes; Thorikos on the east coast lay near the mining installations of Laureion and presented a more industrialised aspect than the country villages. But the fact that there are few remains of large country houses hinders modern understanding of rural settlement.

1.23 The harbour town of Peiraieus, 7–8 km south-west of Athens, is however an exception. It was not until the early fifth century that the Athenians abandoned their old roadstead of Phaleron Bay where they had beached their ships, but in a few short years they established the port of Peiraieus on and around the neighbouring promontory of Akte. There were three harbours: Kantharos on the west which was the main harbour and commercial emporium with a market on the east side and the *deigma*, a place for displaying goods, and the smaller harbours of Sdea and Mounykhia on the east for warships; all three were noted for their splendid ship-sheds. Later in the century the area was laid out on a grid pattern of streets by Hippodamos, a native of the Greek city of Milētos on the west coast of Asia Minor where a similar street plan was also used. In contrast to Athens, about 7 km away, the harbour town must have looked rigidly organised, with straight streets, well placed houses and open public areas. Besides the naval installations, the town boasted many of the amenities that Athens had, including a set of fortifications that were necessary to protect Athens' trade. By the middle of the fifth century the harbour was linked to Athens by Long Walls, no mean feat of construction given the distance covered and the swampy character of the terrain at the Peiraieus end. The population of Peiraieus was mixed, for not only did foreign traders lodge there but many of Athens' resident aliens (*metoikoi*), some of whom were responsible for Athens' trade and ran businesses such as armouries and banking, lived at the port; the *metoikoi* might also be grain-dealers or carry on such trades as fulling and baking (cf. 4.3, 55, 67ff.).

1.24 This mixture of population meant that the shrines and sanctuaries that dotted the harbour town boasted a greater variety of worship than places less accessible to foreign influence, and such non-Greek deities as Bendis and Kybēlē had shrines there. It was a festival of the Thracian goddess Bendis that occasioned the visit of Socrates and Glaukon to the Peiraieus at the beginning of Plato's *Republic* (2.46):

I went down yesterday to the Peiraieus with Glaukon, son of Ariston. I wanted to say a prayer to the Goddess and also to see what they would make of the festival, as this was the first time they were holding it. I must say that I thought that the local contribution to the procession was splendid, though the Thracian contingent seemed to show up just as well. We had said our prayers and seen the show and were on our way back to town when Polemarkhos, son of Kephalos, caught sight of us in the distance making our way home and sent his slave running on ahead to tell us to wait for him. The slave caught hold of my coat from behind and said 'Polemarkhos says you are to wait.' I turned and asked where his master was. 'He's coming along behind you', he said, 'Do wait.' 'We will', said Glaukon, and soon afterwards Polemarkhos came up; with him were Adeimantos, Glaukon's brother, Nikeratos, son of Nikias, and others who had all apparently been to the procession. (Plato, *Republic* 1.327)

Although the conversation in the *Republic* is imaginary, the setting is real enough and the characters involved belong to the highest society of late fifth-century Athens. Adeimantos and Glaukon were Plato's elder brothers, and the family can be traced back to the mid-seventh century. Nikeratos was the son of the Athenian politician Nikias who was one of the military commanders of the disastrous Athenian expedition to Sicily in 415; the family was extremely rich, with slaves as a main source of income. Kephalos' family also owned slaves and had a lucrative arms factory in the Peiraieus; Polemarkhos' brother was the speech-writer Lysias. However, as Kephalos himself had been invited from Syracuse to Athens by Pericles, the family were not citizens, but *metoikoi*; their wealth and social standing are worth noting. Socrates, the narrator, was by contrast a deliberately poor man.

Since Peiraieus was so vital for Athens' prosperity and safety, there was a system for early warning in the case of attack. Here Thucydides describes a surprise attack by sea on Peiraieus early on during the Peloponnesian War in 429, which, had it been successful, might have brought the war to an end at once:

Knemos and Brasidas and the others in command of the Peloponnesian fleet decided on the advice of the Megarians to make an attempt on Peiraieus, the port of Athens, which the Athenians, reasonably enough because of their superiority at sea, had left open and unguarded. The plan was that each sailor should take his oar, cushion and oar-loop, and that they should then proceed on foot to the sea on the Athenian side, make for Megara as quickly as they could and launch from the docks at Nisaia forty ships which happened to be there and then sail straight to Peiraieus ... They arrived by night, launched the ships from Nisaia and sailed, not for Peiraieus as they had originally intended, thinking it too risky (and because the wind was unfavourable, it was said later) but to the promontory of Salamis that fronts Megara ... Meanwhile beacons were lit to warn Athens of the attack, and the biggest panic of the war ensued. Those in the city thought the enemy had already sailed into Peiraieus, those in Peiraieus thought Salamis had fallen and that an attack on themselves was imminent. Indeed if the enemy had resolved to be a little bolder this might well have happened, and no wind could have prevented it. But at daybreak the Athenians assembled in force at Peiraieus, launched their ships, embarked in haste, and sailed in some confusion to Salamis leaving a garrison to guard Peiraieus. When the Peloponnesians saw that relief was on the way, they made off in haste to Nisaia ... After this the Athenians took stricter precautions for Peiraieus in the future by closing the harbour and by other suitable measures. (Thucydides, *Peloponnesian War* 2.93)

## The city of Athens

### Topography

1.25 The plain of Athens is the largest of those in Attica and is enclosed to the west, north and east by hills (Aigaleos, Parnes, Pentelikon and Hymettos) but is open to the sea on the south. About 6 km inland from the Saronic gulf a precipitous limestone rock rises 120 m from the surrounding plain, the Acropolis (lit. 'citadel'), a natural refuge in time of trouble and the original site of the settlement that developed into the city of Athens. Rocky outcrops – the Areopagus ('the Crag of Arēs') and the Pnyx (which the Athenians assumed to signify 'the Crowded Place'), and the hills of the Nymphs and the Muses – lie in close proximity to it. The plain is sparsely watered, but two seasonal rivers, destructive in winter, much reduced in summer, flow close to the Acropolis: the Kephisos on the west rising in Mt Parnes and flowing into the bay of Phaleron, and the Ilisos on the east rising in Mt Hymettos and flowing into the Kephisos; the brook of the Eridanos is smaller and flows into the Ilisos from Mt Lykabettos to the north. The Acropolis itself holds water all year round, which issues as natural springs lower down the slope, but the many man-made wells show that at no time was the natural water supply sufficient for the needs of the local inhabitants, and by the late sixth century fountain-houses were being built to be fed by underground pipelines, bringing in water from outside the city. A traveller ('Dikaiarkhos') who first saw Athens in the early third century sets the scene:

He then comes to the city of the Athenians; the road is pleasant; the ground is cultivated all the way, and has a kindly look. The city is all dry, not well-watered; the streets are badly laid out because of their antiquity. The houses are mostly mean; few are commodious. Strangers visiting the city might be struck by sudden doubt,

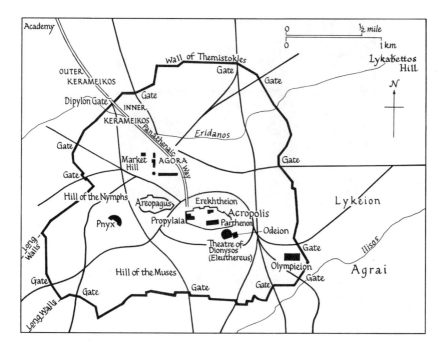

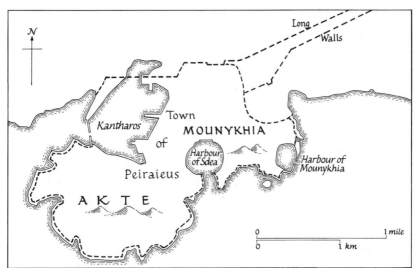

1:10  Plan of Athens showing the line of the Themistoklean Wall, with close-up plan of the Peiraieus showing fourth-century walls.

1:11  Athenian women fetch water from a public fountain (cf. 4:19). Late 6th century.

whether this is really the renowned city of the Athenians; but after a little while one might well believe it.

### Development to the early fifth century

**1.26** There was a small flourishing community established round the Acropolis as early as the Late Neolithic period (3500–3000). Two thousand years later a palace with a defensive wall proclaims the importance the site had slowly acquired, and Athens was one of the major settlements both in Attica itself and in the rest of Greece by 1200. Members of the community lived in houses and caves round the base of the rock, able to repair to the summit in time of danger and having secret access from above to water held within the rock itself.

**1.27** With the collapse of the Mycenaean civilisation by 1100, Athens suffered a decline too, and our evidence for the site between 1100 and 600 is meagre. The chief evidence during these five hundred years is provided by the tombs found to the north-west of the Acropolis; and, as tombs were usually dug beyond the inhabited centres along the tracks that led out of a town, their position – they are placed increasingly further and further out along the Eridanos valley – gives an indication of the gradually increasing size of the living area of Athens. By 600 the concentration of public life around the Acropolis and Areopagus has been dispersed. The Acropolis still remains a focal point, but now mainly of the religious life of the town, and the clefts and rocks in the cliff face which had in the earliest times sheltered the population have become shrines for local cults. Some of the flat ground immediately to the north of the Areopagus, which until *c.* 600 had been an area of fields, private dwellings and family tombs, is now expropriated and develops into the *agora* or gathering ground for the community on formal and informal occasions; and as local cults develop round the Acropolis, so hero cults (see 2.32) become associated with the earlier graves in this *agora* area. This open ground came to be the arena for many communal activities that made up the life of the town: religious, commercial, political, legal, administrative. It was the heart of the community, and the meanings which other forms of the word *agora* carry, such as 'address a public meeting' and 'buy', neatly embrace the variety of activities pursued there, and the comic poet Euboulos later provides a witty list of saleable goods:

You will find everything sold together in the same place at Athens: figs, witnesses to summonses, bunches of grapes, turnips, pears, apples, givers of evidence, roses, medlars, porridge, honeycombs, chick-peas, lawsuits, beestings-puddings, myrtle, allotment-machines [for random jury-selection], irises, lambs, water-clocks [for timing lawcourt speeches], laws, indictments. (Euboulos, fr. 74)

The three major figures of sixth-century Athenian history, Solon, Peisistratos and Kleisthenes, consciously altered the appearance of the city itself in ways which reflect social and political development. Solon (see H.I.7–8) was in a real sense the creator of the early *agora*, and was instrumental in clearing the ground for public use and in establishing the ground below the east slope of the Kolonos Agoraios ('Market Hill') as the administrative centre of the Athenian *polis*.

1.28 The strong, centralised rule which the dictator Peisistratos and his sons exercised in the second half of the sixth century came to be given visible expression in monumental buildings and in public works. Peisistratos' name has been connected (rightly or wrongly) with the foundation in 566 of the four-yearly Great Panathenaic festival, Athēnē's principal festival in classical Athens, and the erection of a large, limestone temple to Athēnē on the Acropolis a few years later emphasises the growing importance of this 'state' cult and Peisistratos' interest in fostering centralised worship. His presence is to be seen in the *agora* which was enlarged in the middle of the century by the expropriation of more properties. Below the Market Hill are slight traces of sixth-century buildings (see 1.33). Peisistratos' sons also saw the virtue of attending to the fundamental needs of the citizens, and improved the amenities of the town by the provision of fountain-houses and aqueducts. However, they displayed a more flamboyant and extravagant attitude than their father. They added marble pedimental figures to the temple on the Acropolis in which Athēnē's venerated wooden image was lodged, and began an even grander temple to Zeus in the south-east sector of the town, the Olympieion (completed 700 years later). In 522 Peisistratos' grandson had an altar to the Twelve Gods erected in the northern part of the *agora* by the side of the Panathenaic Way, a place of refuge and asylum.

**1.29** The radical reordering of the political life of the whole Athenian state which was put in train by Kleisthenes (see H.I.10–11) meant further attention being paid to the *agora*, but once again the identity of the buildings is no easy matter to settle (see 1.33). The *agora* is at this time marked by boundary stones (*horoi*) that staked out the public area as a religious precinct and made it closed to certain types of criminal, a useful reminder of the way in which secular and religious life were closely linked. A group of statues commemorating the tyrant-slayers, Harmodios and Aristogeiton, was set near the Panathenaic Way, a symbol for the newly emerging democracy. The increased amount of political and social life eventually forced a number of the public events to be held away from the *agora*; the meetings of the *ekklēsia* were transferred to the Pnyx west of the Acropolis, and the dramatic competitions, which had been instituted by Peisistratos, took place in the sanctuary of Dionysos Eleuthereus on the south slope of the Acropolis.

**1.30** As no trace of a fortification wall has been found, it is uncertain where it ran, but there is sufficient written evidence to assure its existence, and it may have been built in the 560s when the Acropolis ceased to be a

1:12  A marble boundary stone (*horos*) of the *agora* of Athens, found *in situ*; the inscription says 'I am a boundary stone of the *agora*'. C. 500.

fortress and became a religious sanctuary. The Delphic oracle's advice to the Athenians before the Persian sack of 480, quoted by Herodotus

> Unhappy people, why stay you here? Leave your homes
> And the heights encircled by your city like a wheel
> And flee to the ends of the earth. (Herodotus, *Histories* 7.140.2)

has been connected with the shape of the sixth-century city, with the Acropolis at the centre of a circle of fortification wall. It is also difficult to say by what date Athens had absorbed the other areas of Attica and carried out its unification (see H.I.5), but by 500 Peisistratos' establishment of city cults and Kleisthenes' political reforms had made Athens the centre and indispensable guiding force of all Attica.

### Development in the fifth and fourth century (plan, p. 79)

1.31 The victory the Athenians gained over the Persians at Marathon in 490 inspired them to raise a new temple to Athēnē on the southern part of the Acropolis (the 'Older Parthenon') and to improve the entrance to the sanctuary on its west side by erecting the first new gateway and forecourt since the Mycenaean period. Neither of these ventures was completed, for the Persians sacked the city in 480. When the Persians had been repulsed in 479 and the Athenians returned to their devastated city, they first turned their attention to defence. The fortification walls of the city had been demolished, and the Spartans were urging that they should not be rebuilt, as it was claimed that new walls could provide a defence for the Persians if they once again captured the town. Themistokles had other plans, and a new circuit, more extensive in all directions than the old, was hastily erected. Thucydides records that Themistokles gave instructions to the Athenians:

The whole population of the city was to work on the wall, no building private or public which could provide material was to be spared, all were to be demolished. (Thucydides, *Peloponnesian War* 1.90; H.I.24)

Signs of the hasty construction have been made visible by excavations which have shown that architectural members, tombstones, statues and statue bases were used alongside the more usual materials. The circuit was roughly 6.5 km in length and made use of such neighbouring low hills as those of the Muses and Nymphs; it was furnished with 13 gates and an unknown number of towers and posterns. The main gate was located in the north-west where the wall now ran through the old Kerameikos or

Potters' Quarter. The classical cemeteries are now firmly fixed outside the wall at the sides of the roads that led to different parts of Attica, and the most important was still that in the north-west, now the Outer Kerameikos, the site of the earlier main cemetery. By the side of the roads that fan out from there public grave monuments were set up by the state and family plots were cared for by well-to-do Athenians; it was here too that Pericles gave the traditional Funeral Speech in 431/430 (see pp. 56–61).

1.32 The development and fortification of the Peiraieus as the port of Athens had been begun in the 490s (cf. H.I.24) and was now needed as the vital link with Athens' overseas allies; this led in the 460–450s to the erection of the Long Walls that connected Athens across country to the Peiraieus (Northern Wall) and the coast at the bay of Phaleron (Phaleric Wall; course uncertain); another (Middle Wall), parallel to the original Peiraieus wall and c. 180 m apart from it, was erected in the 440s at the instigation of Pericles. The main Athens–Peiraieus road lay outside the walls on the north side; the space between the Northern and Middle Walls (nicknamed 'the Legs') was used for military purposes, but at the beginning of the Peloponnesian War was a camping-ground for refugees from the country districts of Attica (cf. 4.56ff.; H.I.36).

1.33 Within the new circuit wall so hastily erected, the Athenians turned their attention to the task of building the city anew. The private houses and workshops, with walls of unbaked brick on a foundation of small stones and clay and roofed with tiles of baked clay, were rebuilt piecemeal, some still unfinished fifty years later at the outbreak of the Peloponnesian War (431). As a community, the Athenians first concentrated on rebuilding the *agora*. There was much to do, and old materials were readily used in the reconstruction. Although civic buildings may have existed in the sixth century (see 1.28) it is only in the years leading to the mid-fifth century that substantial civic structures can be recognised. Mention may be made of a Council Chamber (*bouleutērion*) for the Council or steering committee (*boulē*) of the assembly (*ekklēsia*), a Court House (the Ēliaia) to which appeals were taken, a colonnaded building (the Royal Stoa) for the officer of state (the king *arkhōn*) whose prime function was justice; it was here that the officers of state stood on a block of stone (*lithos*) to take their oath to abide by the state's laws, and here also that the 'Laws of Solon', carved on stone, were made accessible to the citizens. Before the middle of the century work had begun on a rotunda (*tholos* and nicknamed *skias* or 'parasol' from the shape of its roof) as a residence for the standing committee (*prutaneis*) of the *boulē*, and on colonnaded buildings, including the Stoa Poikilē (the 'Colonnade with the Paintings'), its walls decorated with murals, including one of the now legendary battle of Marathon (this Stoa has just recently been identified in the *agora*). Kimon, an influential Athenian of the 460s, who may have been instrumental in having some of these buildings erected, is said to have embellished the *agora* with plane trees. A prison (*desmōtērion*) for state debtors and those awaiting trial was erected in the middle of the fifth century alongside the road that led south-west from the *agora* to the Pnyx. Soon after the middle of the century a temple of Hephaistos and Athēnē began to be built on Kolonos Agoraios above the west side of the *agora*, amidst the workshops of the potters and bronzesmiths whose district this was, but work on it was interrupted by the Acropolis building programme.

**1.34** No attempt had been made to rebuild the Acropolis temples in the thirty years following the Persian sack. The ruins of the archaic temple had been patched up to provide a safe home for the old wooden image which they had taken with them when they fled; the foundations of the 'Older Parthenon' had been left bare, to act as a reminder of Persian aggression. But after the middle of the century peace with Persia was a fact, and a new building project, which had the political backing of Pericles and the artistic supervision of Pheidias, was inaugurated after a generation of studied neglect. Work now started on a new temple, the Parthenon, for Athēnē Parthenos ('the Maiden'), which rose on the highest part of the rock over the foundations of its predecessor, a monument to Athens' imperial position. Like all Greek temples, details were picked out in paint; the

1:13 Drawn reconstruction of the north-west corner of the Agora showing (from left to right) the Stoa of Zeus, the small Stoa of the king *arkhōn* in which the laws of Athens were on display, a later arch and the Stoa Poikilē.

temple was not left to stand as the gleaming honeyed marble we know today. It was begun in 447 and completed in 432, a particularly rapid construction for this uniquely intricate and costly building; its massive gold and ivory statue of Athēnē was already in place by 438. In 437 when the major construction work on the Parthenon was completed, work on new entrance gates, the Propylaia, was begun, furnishing a radically new approach to the whole sanctuary. The temple called the Erekhtheion after Erekhtheus, a legendary king of Athens, was built later in the fifth century. It stood in the area which had witnessed the primeval battle of Athēnē and Poseidon for the land of Attica, and which had been the site of the Mycenaean palace and later of the archaic temple housing the venerated wooden image of the goddess. Consequently the new temple took over many of these holy associations from Athens' sacred past, and it was to this temple, not to the Parthenon, that every four years the people of Athens escorted a new robe for Athēnē's wooden statue on the occasion of her most prestigious festival, the Panathenaia. The isolation in which the existing buildings of the Acropolis stand belies their original effect. There were many more structures covering the rock in the fifth and fourth centuries as well as altars, statues, officially inscribed stones and countless personal offerings. As the divine protectors of the Athenian state, especially Athēnē herself, had their local habitation on the rock, it was natural that the treasury of the Athenian empire should be there also under the protection of Athēnē for whom the Parthenon had been built from a tithe of the tribute money (cf. 7.75; H.I. 26; 5.87).

1.35 Little building work was done in the *agora* at the time the Parthenon and Propylaia were being constructed; only a headquarters for the annually chosen military leaders (*stratēgoi*, 'generals') is known to have been erected at this time. In the last thirty years of the fifth century, however, attention was refocused on the town centre. New colonnaded buildings on the west and south, a replacement for the old *bouleutērion* (this was converted into a public records office), the mint and a lawcourt were all erected by the end of the century, and in the middle of the fourth century a new fountain-house was provided, and a square building with an interior colonnade replaced the lawcourt of only two generations earlier. Temples to civic cults and a large altar to Zeus Agoraios were also put up at this time; and a fenced pedestal on which stood statues of the ten tribal heroes of Attica was used as a public notice-board in the *agora* for new proposed legislation, impending lawsuits and lists of men called up for military service. All this building work emphasises the increasingly democratic bias of Athens and the more extensive involvement of the citizens

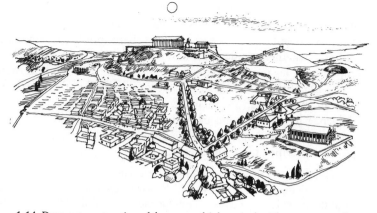

1:14 Drawn reconstruction of the *agora* of Athens in the 4th century, seen from the north-west.

that it brought in its wake. However, despite the growing formalisation of the *agora*, the craftsmen of Athens – potters, sculptors, bronzesmiths – continued to live and work on and around the borders of the public area, and excavated remains of their workshops illustrate the variety of life in the city centre. It will be sufficient to mention the cobbler's shop belonging to Simon, known from Plato's memoirs of Socrates and unearthed near the south-west corner of the *agora*.

**1.36** Areas of Athens other than the Acropolis, *agora* and north-west cemetery have been less thoroughly investigated and give less information. Directly north of the Acropolis may have lain the more strictly commercial area of town, on the east side of the excavated *agora* and in the adjacent area further east still. On the south slope of the rock the theatre was rebuilt under Pericles and again more radically in the middle of the fourth century; a concert hall (*ōdeion*) was built next to the theatre in the 440s, alleged by Plutarch to be in shape an imitation of the tent of the Persian king and claimed by Vitruvius, the Roman architectural writer, to be roofed with timbers of Persian ships (cf. 7.78). The Academy, early established in a grove to the north-west near a sanctuary of the Attic hero, Hekademos, was used by Plato in the fourth century as a base for his philosophical school, and the Lykeion on the east side, on an old foundation, was from the later fourth century onwards linked with the name of Aristotle.

**1.37** Even at the end of the fourth century the size of the city was extremely small by modern standards, one area being within easy walking distance of another. Although large and expensively equipped private houses were not unknown in Athens, most were still basically simple, consisting of a series of small rooms arranged round an inner court. By contrast, private and public money had for generations been spent on public buildings, whether for heated political discussion, athletic or theatrical competitions, legal wrangling or religious celebrations. It was there that the real life of the *polis* had always been lived, and in the fourth century Athenian politicians, in their efforts to castigate their opponents' indulgence in private comfort and display, nostalgically simplified the more public-spirited attitudes of the fifth-century leaders, as in the following speech ascribed to Demosthenes:

The buildings which they left to adorn our city – the temples and harbours and all that goes with them – are on a scale which their successors cannot hope to surpass; look at the Propylaia, the docks, the colonnades and all the other adornments of the city which they have bequeathed to us. And the private houses of those in power were so modest and in keeping with the title of our constitution that, as those of you who have seen them know, the houses of Themistokles, Kimon and Aristeides, the famous men of those days, were no grander than those of their neighbours. But today, my friends, the city is content to provide roads and springs and stucco and other trivialities by way of public works. I am far from wishing to blame those who pioneered such useful works, but I do blame you for supposing they are all that is required of you. For some of the private individuals who hold any public office have built private houses which are grander not only than those of the ordinary run of citizens but even than our public buildings, and others have bought and cultivate estates on a scale undreamed of before. ([Demosthenes] (*On Organisation*) 13.28–9)

# 2
# *The metaphysical environment*

## Introduction: Greek religion and Christianity

**2.1** Christians and Jews believe that there is one god, who made the world and is external to it. He becomes part of it in men's hearts. This god, whose characteristic is love, works for good in the world. He demands not only worship but love and faith from his adherents. Worship takes place in church or synagogue and is normally conducted by a cleric. Faith is expressed through adherence to a creed, which has been established with reference to the god's revealed word, the Bible. The function of the cleric – who often makes his ministry a paid, life-long profession – is to mediate between the god and his adherents and to interpret the Bible to them, to discover the god's will. A prominent feature of the god's will is that his adherents obey a strict moral code of personal behaviour. Faith and obedience in this life are usually related to the life to come. Christianity and Judaism had, and to some extent still do have, a political and social as well as a religious function.

**2.2** For Greeks there were many gods (the pantheon), of which Zeus as leader of the Olympian gods became the head, and they did not make the world. Night (Nux), Void (Chaos), Earth (Gaia) and other deities all existed before them, and still existed after Zeus had forced his way to power. Greek gods are part and parcel of the universe, in some sense its product. A god is frequently endowed with a sphere of interest (several have more than one), and they struggle amongst themselves and with humans to ensure that their interests predominate. The gods are all too human in their personalities and characteristics.

**2.3** The gods demand worship in the sense of human acknowledgement (*nomisdein tous theous* does not mean 'believe in the gods', but to 'recognise' or 'acknowledge' them), but they do not love humans, nor do they

2:1  The Olympian deities *en famille* with Ganymede in the centre and Zeus and Hera on either side. Late 6th century.

impose codes of belief or morality. They require to be recognised for the power they wield and to be respected for it. That done, they will reciprocate and help their favourites. The basis of the relationship between man and the gods is tit for tat, as between man and man. As there is no revealed word, the function of priests – in the main chosen by lot to do the job for one year – was to ensure that the rituals which acknowledged the gods' power were properly carried out. Since there were female and male gods, there were male and female priests.

**2.4** The temple was a palace built for the god to live in. Worship was carried on outside, at the altar where the offering to the god (be it a hundred oxen or a few drops of wine or a cake) was made. There was no such organisation as an official religious body which had political power, nor did individual priests act as counsellors, confessors, (amateur) therapists and social workers. (Medical cures at Epidauros are an exception, as are the activities of the body which advised on religious matters, the *exēgētai*.) When men required to know the will of the god, they went to a seer (*mantis*: not necessarily a priest) or to an oracle to seek advice. Failure to acknowledge the gods might well have some effect on one's life: it had little or no effect on one's afterlife. Ideas of 'guilt' or 'sin' or such problems as that of 'suffering' are generally absent from Greek religion, though such ideas were not unknown in Orphism and appear in the Eleusinian Mysteries (see 2.53).

**2.5** Though the Greek gods could be made fun of, they were very definitely not figures of fun. They might be random and fickle; they were certainly awe-inspiring and terrifying. This did not prevent intellectuals criticising them. The complete absence of a ruling priest-caste in Greek (as in Roman) society, linked with the fierce Greek sense of independence, helped Greek thinkers break with traditional pictures of divine activity in

2:2 The duel between Ajax and Hektor at Troy; Athēnē supports Ajax, Apollo Hektor. Early 5th century.

the world. One of the most important contributions of Greek intellectual thought was to minimise such activity when they speculated about the physical world and human life (cf. 7.6, 11, 14, 76).

### Experience and myth

**2.6** As we have seen, most Greeks were entirely dependent upon the benevolence of nature if life was to continue. In such an environment, Greeks were aware of their powerlessness before natural forces that might overturn the stable order of things without warning. As with many other agriculturally based tribal peoples, it is reasonable to assume that the Greeks both came to terms with, and remained in awe of, the world around them by positing divine powers to account for things beyond their control. Such powers could explain, for example, the unpredictability of the weather or of fertility (in both crops and humans). More generally, they might be used to explain any strange or incomprehensible event – a meteorite, for example, or an instance of odd behaviour, an unexpected illness, or the arrival of a total stranger. For him, anything abnormal might be a literal indication of divine intervention, and need acknowledgement and conciliation.

**2.7** For example, in Book 1 of Homer's *Iliad* a plague strikes the Greek army camped outside Troy. Achilles' human response is to consider how the god responsible (which must be Apollo, who is god of healing and ill-

2:3 In the battle between the Gods and the Giants, Hephaistos flings burning coals, Poseidon the Earthshaker heaves a rock. Early 5th century.

ness) can be appeased, so he appeals for a 'seer or priest or reader of dreams'. Any human being can hope to recognise a god at work, but only those especially receptive to the divine will can interpret the reason and indicate the right way of reconciliation. An incident from Herodotus illustrates an immediate reversal of policy because something odd happened and the oracle was consulted for the meaning. When Cyrus, King of Persia, was conquering Asia Minor, a Greek community on a peninsula of the west coast tried to halt the invasion of his general Harpagos:

While Harpagos was reducing Ionia the Knidians accordingly began to dig through this neck of land, which was about half a mile across, with the object of making their territory into an island. For the isthmus which they were intending to cut through was the link which connected them to the mainland, and bounded their territory. All hands were engaged on this work when the Knidians noticed that the number of injuries, particularly to the eyes, suffered by the workers when the rock was splintered, was unexpectedly and unnaturally large. They therefore sent envoys to Delphi to enquire about this hindrance to the work. The priestess answered them (so their story runs) in iambic verse.

    Do not fortify the isthmus or dig it through:
    Had Zeus wished he would have made an island.

The Knidians on receiving this reply gave up their digging and when Harpagos arrived gave themselves up without striking a blow. (Herodotus, *Histories* 1.174)

Events like these show how the gods could be held responsible for strange or abnormal events which might be directly harmful or simply inexplicable in normal human terms.

**2.8** The Greeks gave names, and in time human personalities, to the divine powers to define the areas in which the power moved, so that appropriate measures of appeasement could be taken. One god often had many functions. Thus Zeus was god of weather, fertility, gold, kings, warfare, counsel, supplication, strangers, beggars, safety, marriage, home and property, and as such he might often seem to work for people in some of his capacities, but not in others. Xenophon records how he had been helped by Zeus in his capacity as god of kings and of safety but then fell foul of him in his capacity as god of propitiation. There were also lesser gods associated with particular places that inspired awe and were considered to have an indwelling divine power – springs, groves and woods, for example, and especially lonely places like hills and mountains, far from human habitation. New divinities too could be added (and old ones die out). Other 'powers' could include dead 'heroes', men whose spirit was thought to protect a place (e.g. Theseus (H.I.5; 2.32)).

**2.9** Besides this understanding drawn from direct experience of supposed intervention from the supra-human world, there was another, probably of equal antiquity – the understanding enshrined in myth. In no sense were myths seen as revealed scriptures, or as the 'truth' about the gods (cf. 7.40). What they helped to do was to define the human condition in relation to that of the gods. Take for example two versions of the myth of Prometheus, the thief of fire from heaven, preserved by the poet Hēsiod (*c.* 700–670):

And Iapetos married Klymene, the Ocean nymph with beautiful ankles, and they went to bed together. And she bore him a son, stout-hearted Atlas, and then far-famed Menoitios and Prometheus,\* subtle and wily, and Epimetheus† prone to error, who was always a disaster to busy men and who first accepted from Zeus the virgin woman he had made. Presumptuous Menoitios far-seeing Zeus cast into

\*Prometheus means 'Forethought'.    †Epimetheus means 'Afterthought'.

2:4  The shade of a hero rises from his tomb mound. Early 5th century.

Erebos, striking him with his smoking thunderbolt because of his presumption and insolent boldness. Atlas stands before the clear-voiced Hesperides at the ends of the earth and must hold up the broad heavens, for this harsh fate was assigned to him by Zeus the all-wise. But he bound the wily Prometheus in strong chains from which there was no escape, and which he fastened to a pillar, and set on him a wide-winged eagle which came to feed on his immortal liver; and all that the wide-winged bird had eaten during the day grew again each night. The eagle was killed by the brave son of fair-ankled Alkmēnē, Herakles, who drove off his tormentor and freed him from his misery. Olympian Zeus who rules on high did not object, wishing the fame of Theban-born Herakles to be still greater on the fruitful earth, and showing this respect and honour to his famous son. And he ceased from the rage he had felt against Prometheus for his defiance of the will of almighty Zeus. For when gods and mortal men came to judgement at Mekone, Prometheus forethoughtfully set out the cut portions of a great ox, intending to deceive Zeus. He put the flesh and the entrails full of fat into the skin on one side and hid them in the ox's stomach; on the other side he put the white bones of the ox, and arranged them with great cunning carefully covering them with shining fat. And the father of gods and men said to him 'Son of Iapetos, most famous leader, I fear the division you have made is most unfair.' So Zeus, whose counsels are eternal, taunted him. The wily Prometheus answered deceitfully with a gentle smile 'Zeus, greatest and most glorious of the immortal gods, choose whichever of the two your heart bids you.' He spoke, of course, to deceive. But Zeus whose counsels are eternal perceived the trick and was not deceived; but he had in mind ills for mortal men which he intended to bring on them in the future. So he took the white fat in both hands, and his blood boiled and rage filled his heart when he saw the white bones and the trick he had been played. And from that day the races of men when they sacrifice at their altars to the immortals burn the white bones.

But Zeus the cloud-gatherer was enraged and said 'Son of Iapetos, always cunning, so you are still up to your tricks, my friend.' Zeus whose counsels are eternal spoke thus in anger. He did not forget the trick which had been played on him and from then on denied wretched mortals the use of tireless fire. But the brave son of Iapetos deceived him and stole the far-seen beam of tireless fire, hiding it in a hollow reed. And high-thundering Zeus was cut to the heart and raged within when he saw the far-seen beam of fire again among men, and at once devised a price for men to pay for it. For the famous lame god, at the will of Zeus, moulded of earth the image of a modest girl; grey-eyed Athēnē gave her a girdle and silver robe, and over her face drew an embroidered veil, marvellous to look at, and round her head set lovely garlands of spring flowers; and the famous lame god set on her head a golden tiara, which he made with his own hands, to please father Zeus. On the tiara he modelled many wonderful figures of the creatures which sea and land produce, marvellously life-like, and all breathing with beauty. And when he had made this lovely evil thing as the price of fire he led her to a place where gods and men were gathered, and she showed her delight at the finery which the grey-eyed daughter of the almighty had given her. And immortal gods and mortal men were amazed when they saw how deep was the trap from which there was no escape for men. For from her the whole female sex is descended, a great curse to mortal men with whom they live, no help in accursed poverty and ready enough to share wealth. They are like drones which are fed by the bees in their roofed hives and are their partners in crime. For the bees are busy all day till the sun goes down and build white honey-combs, while the drones stay at home in the shelter of the hive and fill their bellies with the toil of others. High-thundering Zeus made woman to be a similar curse to mortal men, and partner in vexation.

But Zeus produced another price to be paid. If a man avoids marriage and all the mischief women cause, and never takes a wife, he comes to his declining years with no one to look after him in the miseries of old age. He has enough to live on while he lives, and when he dies his distant relatives divide up his property. A man who does marry and has a good wife after his own heart can balance evil with good while he lives, but he who gets one of the hurtful sort lives with an open wound in his heart and spirit, and an ill that has no cure. (Hēsiod, *Theogony* 507ff.)

The gods keep men's livelihood hidden from them. For you could easily produce in a day enough to keep you in idleness for a year, and hang your rudder up above the smoke and do away with the labour of oxen and hardworking mules. But Zeus hid the way to do so because his heart was angry at the deception practised on him by the wily Prometheus. He contrived grievous cares for men, first hiding fire from them. But the noble son of Iapetos stole it back again for men from Zeus the wise, hiding it in a fennel-stalk, unseen by the Thunderer. And Zeus the cloud-gatherer was angry and said to him, 'Son of Iapetos, there is none cleverer than you, and you are pleased to have stolen fire and tricked me. But you have brought trouble on yourself and on future generations of men, to whom I will give in exchange for fire an evil thing which will delight their hearts and which they will embrace to their ruin.'

Thus spoke the father of gods and men and laughed. And he told famous Hephaistos to make a mixture of earth and water, as quickly as he could, and to put in it human voice and strength, to give it features like an immortal god and the lovely shape of a virgin girl. He told Athēnē to teach her the craft of weaving patterned cloth and Aphrodite to pour golden charm about her head and fierce desire and heavy sorrows; and Hermes, killer of Argos, his servant, he ordered to give her the mind of a bitch and sly ways.

So he spoke, and they obeyed Zeus, Lord and son of Kronos. The lame Hephaistos moulded earth as Zeus commanded into the form of a modest virgin, grey-eyed Athēnē gave her clothes and girdle, and the divine Graces and holy Peithō set golden necklaces about her neck and the fair Seasons crowned her with spring flowers. And the slayer of Argos put into her heart at the will of Zeus the Thunderer lies and specious words and sly ways; and the messenger of the gods gave her a voice and called her Pandora,* because all the gods who live in Olympos had given her gifts, to be the ruin of man and their business.

*Pandora means 'all-endowed'.

2:5  Athēnē decks out Pandora for the temptation of Epimetheus. C. 460–450.

And when the deadly and inescapable snare was complete the father sent the famous slayer of Argos, the swift messenger of the gods, to Epimetheus bearing it as a gift. And Epimetheus forgot that Prometheus had told him never to accept a gift from Olympian Zeus, but to send it back, in case it brought trouble to mortals. But he accepted it and did not perceive the trouble it brought till it was upon him. (Hēsiod, *Works and Days* 42ff.)

**2.10** Together, these stories of Prometheus contain much of the Greek understanding of man's lot. Hēsiod presents in mythological terms the reasons why man was a farmer and a sailor. Fire, the basis both of technology and of cooked food and sacrifice is essential to the story. Sacrifice is presented as a shared act with the gods, and at the same time a symbol of trickery on both sides (reflecting perhaps the cunning of the Greek mind on the human side, and on the other the deceptiveness of the words of the gods in oracles, omens and dreams (see 2.12)). All the responsibilities and problems of life are introduced – women (cf. 3.19), marriage, property and succession, old age, and sickness. These elements collected together in the form of a story define the Greek understanding of the 'human condition'. Again, man's lot is clarified by the contrast first with the life of the gods, then with beasts and finally with the idea of a 'Golden Age' when once upon a time life was easy and man had no need to work.

**2.11** The Prometheus myths constitute Hēsiod's attempt to articulate his understanding of human experience by means of a story which draws extensively on deep-rooted associations of ideas. Such was the inheritance of fifth- and fourth-century Greeks from centuries of religious experience. The inheritance was rich and varied, reflecting the presence of the gods in

2:6 Prometheus gives fire in a stalk of fennel. Late 5th century.

every part of life and almost every place in Greece. Consequently, it is impossible to define 'the Greek idea' of the gods. As a corollary to this, there could be no such thing as heresy or orthodoxy (4.71).

### Contacts with humans

**2.12** Polytheism and cult variation from city to city, together with the multiplicity of human experience and a rich mythological tradition, created an extremely diffuse religion in which much was universally accepted but in which no single element *had* to be accepted if one was to be classed as conventionally pious. But without the hard basis of a creed, or any revealed word, it was extremely difficult to know whether one was keeping the gods happy. Unless the god actually appeared in person or spoke, it would need an expert to interpret the god's will. The more important the enterprise, e.g. the founding of a colony, joining battle or dispatching an expedition, the more important it was to get the best possible advice from the best qualified expert.

### (i) Dreams

**2.13** A common way in which the god might be attempting to contact a person was through a dream. These could be true, or deceitful, as Agamemnon found to his cost in Homer, *Iliad* 2.1ff. when Zeus sent a deceitful dream to trick him into rash action.

If the dream was telling the truth, it was impossible to avoid the consequences, as Croesus found when he dreamt that his son was to be killed by an iron spear (Herodotus, *Histories* 1.34–45). In the following passage, Hippias, the deposed tyrant of Athens, acts on the strength of a dream – and wrongly interprets it:

Hippias, the son of Peisistratos, guided the Persians to Marathon. The previous night he had had a dream in which he seemed to be in bed with his mother, and he interpreted the dream to mean that he would return to Athens, recover the power he had lost, and die in old age in his own country. That was his interpretation at the time, and he continued to act as guide to the Persians, first landing the prisoners from Eretria on an island called Aigilia belonging to the Styrians, and then leading the fleet to anchorage at Marathon and disembarking and drawing up the troops. In the course of all this he was seized by an unusually violent fit of sneezing and coughing. He was an elderly man and a good many of his teeth were loose, as is not uncommon at that age, and the violence of his coughing dislodged one of them and it fell into the sand. He tried very hard to find this tooth and when it was nowhere to be seen, turned to the bystanders with a deep groan and said, 'This land is not ours and we shall never be able to subdue it. My tooth has the only share I ever had in it.' This was how Hippias finally interpreted the meaning of his dream. (Herodotus, *Histories* 6.107ff.)

2.14 Against such a background of confusion, it is not surprising to learn that, when the Athenian state sent a man to sleep in a shrine in order to receive divine guidance in the face of a threat from the Macedonians in the fourth century, the resulting dream was subject to charges of fabrication for political ends:

The people ordered Euxenippos and two others to spend the night in the temple, and he tells us that he went to sleep and had a dream which he duly reported to them. Now, Polyeuktos, if you assumed that he was telling the truth, and that he reported to the people what he actually saw in his dream, what wrong has he done by reporting to the Athenians what the god's instructions had been? But if, as you now allege, you think he misrepresented the god and made a biased report to the people, your right course was not to put forward a decree disputing the dream, but, as the speaker before me said, to send to Delphi and find out the truth from the god. (Hyperides, *Euxenippos* 14)

### (ii) Oracles

2.15 Gods might also contact humans through oracles, and it was to oracular shrines that states as well as individuals tended to turn for advice and help, not just in times of national emergency, but to cope with everyday occurrences too. The most influential oracle was at Delphi, but there were many others throughout the Greek world, using all sorts of different methods of divination – clanging pots, rustling leaves, warbling doves, rushing waters, reflecting mirrors. It is very important to stress here that the function of an oracle is not to foretell the future, but to give advice. It is inevitable that, if the advice is good, the oracle will get the reputation for being *able* to foretell the future, but that is not its function. Equally, it may seem to us pure superstition, but if the Greeks actually did believe that the gods acted through everyday occurrences as a matter of course (and the Greeks *did*), it was logical for them to turn to the experts for interpretation. We turn to experts in politics, economics and social policy with as little or as much chance of success as Greeks turned to their oracle. Again, it is important to understand that, generally speaking (and discounting for the moment myth and legend), the oracle at, for example, Delphi, spoke directly to questioners in perfectly plain and simple terms. There is no good evidence that in the fifth century the Delphic prophetess (Pythia) was in a state of babbling ecstasy and her words had to be interpreted by a priest. Of course the prophetess was inspired, but as any poet knows inspiration does not result in incoherence, but rather in heightened lucidity of perception and utterance. The following practical, down-to-earth questions, answered in equally practical, down-to-earth terms, are typical:

2:7 Delphi.

1   Isyllos the poet asked, in relation to the composition of a paean in honour of Apollo, whether it was better to inscribe the paean. The response was that it was better for both present and future if he inscribe the paean.
2   The cities of Klasdomenai and Kymē were disputing possession of Leukē. They asked which city the god wanted to possess Leukē. The response was: 'Let the city which is first to make sacrifice in Leukē have it. On the day agreed, each party should start at sunrise from its own city.'
3   Poseidonios of Halikarnassos, concerned for welfare of his family, asked 'What is it better for him and his sons and daughters to do?' The response came: 'It will be better for them to worship Zeus Patrōos, Apollo lord of Telmessos, the Moirai, the Mother of Gods, the Agathos Daimon ('Lucky Spirit') of Poseidonios and Gorgis, as their ancestors did; it will be better for them if they continue to perform these rites'.

(Fontenrose, *The Delphic Oracle*)

**2.16** That said, there is a strong *literary* tradition, in both myth and the early history of Greece, of the opacity of oracles and their tendency to deceive. The famous oracle given to the Athenians as the Persians advanced on the city, that Zeus would grant them a wooden wall as a stronghold for themselves and their children, was the subject of much dispute, and had to be given to special readers of oracles to interpret. Even so, the experts were ignored when Themistokles gave his famous interpretation that wooden walls meant the fleet, and Athens should be abandoned to its fate (H.I.18).

**2.17** That the oracle was taken seriously, and expected to answer cogently, is clear from this passage of Xenophon. Xenophon had been advised by Socrates to consult the oracle about whether he should go on an expedition or not:

Xenophon went to Delphi, but he asked Apollo to which of the gods he should offer sacrifice and prayer with a view to the successful completion of a journey he had in mind, and to a safe return. In reply Apollo told him to which gods he should sacrifice. On his return Xenophon told Socrates what the oracle had said. On hearing it Socrates blamed Xenophon because he had not first asked whether he should make the journey or not, but had taken his own decision and then asked how best he could make the journey successfully. But, he added, as he had put the question in the way he had, he must do whatever the god directed. (Xenophon, *Anabasis* 3.1.4ff.)

### (iii) Magic

**2.18** That magic was seen as a medium for divine intervention is strikingly clear from this famous passage on epilepsy, 'the sacred disease'

2:8 The witch Medeia demonstrates her ability at rejuvenation by boiling an old ram; King Pelias is brought forward to be made young again. C. 470.

(written *c.* 400), in which the writer sets out to pour scorn on magicians in favour of a more 'scientific' approach.

> The facts about the so-called sacred disease are as follows. I don't think it is really any more divine or sacred than any other disease; it has its own symptoms and cause, but because of their inexperience and its extraordinary and unique character men supposed it had some divine origin. I think that the kind of men who first attributed a sacred quality to this disease were similar to today's magicians, salvationists, quacks and charlatans who all claim to be very religious and to have superior knowledge. Because they felt helpless and had no effective treatment to suggest, they took refuge in the pretence of divinity and treated the disease as sacred to conceal their own ignorance. ([Hippocrates], *On the Sacred Disease* 1ff.)

We can recognise witchcraft in Kirkē, who turned men to beasts with potions (Homer, *Odyssey* 10.230ff.), and in Medeia, a sorceress related to Kirkē who used magic powers to help Jason get the Golden Fleece. Both these women lived at the edges of the Greek world. Belief in the power of magic seems to have become more common in the fourth century and later, when magical instruments and incantations were increasingly used, particularly tablets cursing an enemy. As we shall see with divination, such beliefs tended to become more elaborate and systematised as time went on.

### (iv) Divination: the seer (mantis)

**2.19** It is important to draw a distinction between the priest (*hiereus*) who was responsible for correct procedure at rituals, and the seer (*mantis*).

2:9  Before setting out for war, a soldier inspects a liver to read the omens for the future. Late 6th century.

They *might* be capable of both functions, but not necessarily. While priests were male or female, could be appointed on an annual basis (elected or drawn by lot), and anyone could stand for the position (though some priesthoods were restricted to certain families), a seer was simply a person with insight into the interpretation of signs. Herodotus tells us that the first seer was Melampos, and that he brought the art to Greece. Since the family of Melampos maintained the tradition, it looks as if the practice of the seer went back to time immemorial and was handed down to future generations of the seer's family. There were other famous families, e.g. the Iamides (sons of Iamos) and Telliades (sons of Tellias), renowned as seers. Some seers would form religious associations which served as oracles; others would exist independently serving the needs of the local population. Two of the most common methods for seers to give advice were by observing the flight of birds and by examining the entrails, especially the livers, of slaughtered beasts (hieromancy) (cf. Euripides' *Ēlektra* 774ff., where the king acts as his own *mantis*). A *mantis* was a paid professional but fifth-century Athenians regarded the oracle at Delphi as the most authoritative source of information. Again, the sort of advice that was sought could be of the most prosaic kind, or it might refer to the mightiest events, e.g. the expedition to Syracuse (see 7.60 for a comic view).

2.20 In time, and certainly by the fourth century, the skill of the *mantis* had become the subject of books, a science which could be understood and practised by anyone. It indicates again how seriously the subject was taken, yet how open to abuse by those who would exploit it (one is reminded of the legal system in the modern world). The passage from Xenophon gives both sides of the picture:

After this Xenophon stood up and said, 'Fellow soldiers, it looks as if we shall have to complete our journey on foot. There are no ships, and it is time we set out. There are no supplies if we stay here. We then,' he went on 'will sacrifice; and you must be ready to fight if ever you did. For the enemy has taken heart again.' The generals then proceeded to sacrifice, the presiding seer being Arexion the Arkadian; Silanos from Ambrakia had by this time deserted on a ship he hired at Herakleia. But when they sacrificed for their departure the omens were not favourable, and they therefore gave up sacrificing for the day. There were some impudent enough to say that Xenophon wanted to found a city at the place and had persuaded the seer to say the omens were not favourable for departure. Xenophon in consequence made an announcement that anyone who wished could be present at the sacrifice next day and ordered anyone who was a seer to participate in the sacrifice; and so there were a good many present when he made the sacrifice. But though he performed the sacrifice three times for their departure the omens were not favourable . . . He sacrificed again on the next day and pretty well the whole army attended the ceremony, as it was of such consequence to them. But there was a shortage of sacrificial victims. Thereupon the generals, though they would not lead them on, assembled them, and Xenophon said 'Perhaps the enemy have joined up and we shall have to fight them. If we were to deposit our equipment in the stronghold and set out in battle order the omens might favour us'. When they heard this the soldiers shouted that there was no need to take things to the stronghold, but that the sacrifice should be made at once. There were no sheep left, but they bought an ox which was yoked to a wagon and sacrificed it. Xenophon asked Kleanor the Arkadian to take special note of any favourable sign, but none was forthcoming . . .

[*There follows an unsuccessful plundering raid for supplies, in which they lose 500 men. They spend the night under arms.* Eventually . . . ]

A vessel arrived from Herakleia bringing barley, sacrificial victims and wine.

Xenophon rose early and sacrificed for departure, and the omens were favourable at the first sacrifice. Just as the ceremonies were completed Arexion the Parrhasian saw an eagle in a favourable quarter, and told Xenophon to lead on. (Xenophon, *Anabasis* 6.4.12ff.)

### Divine grip on humanity

**2.21** Despite attempts by a small minority of fifth-century Greeks to explain the world in human terms, few Greeks doubted that the gods did play a central part in the way the world worked and, as we have seen, their ways could be inscrutable. While men could, for example, grapple with what *dikē* (justice) was in human terms, it was difficult to see how human

2:10  Aktaion is attacked by his own dogs as he is transformed into a deer. Madness is among the hounds, whilst Zeus and Artemis watch. Mid 5th century.

understanding could be squared with the apparently arbitrary, meaningless intervention of divine powers.

**2.22** Consequently, Greeks generally viewed the workings of the gods with a considerable degree of what looks like to us pessimism but was for them hard-nosed realism. Men could be led astray by oracles and dreams; the same god could be responsible for good and bad in the same area (Apollo is god of healing and disease, Dēmētēr could send a good or bad harvest); man was at the mercy of random natural forces. And given Greek values, whereby men scorned weakness and competed for superiority (cf. 3.9, 15), they could not but feel that the gods must feel scorn for them. Here, Solon warns Croesus about the insecurity of the human condition:

You have asked me about the human condition, Croesus. I know well that the gods are all envious and disruptive. In the space of a long life you can see and experience much that you would not wish. I reckon the span of human life to be about seventy years. That number of years gives a total of 25,200 days, omitting the intercalary months. If you allow for the addition of an intercalary month every other year, to keep the seasons in step, you get thirty-five additional months and 1,050 additional days. This gives you a total of 26,250 days in your seventy years, and no day is just like another in what it brings. So you see, Croesus, that human life is a chancy affair. You seem to me to be a very rich man and to rule over a large population, but I still can't call you what you asked until I know that your life has ended well. For the very wealthy man is no happier than the man who has just enough for his daily needs unless he has the good fortune to end his life in prosperity. Many of the richest men are unhappy, many who have moderate means have good luck. The man who is wealthy but unhappy is better off than the man who has good luck in two respects only, whereas the lucky man is better off than the rich and unhappy in many ways. The rich man can satisfy his desires and is better able to bear great calamities, but the other is better off in the following respects. He may be less well placed to gratify his desires or withstand calamity, but his luck keeps him clear of them, and he has sound physique, good health, freedom from trouble, fine children and good looks. If in addition to all this he prospers till the end of his life, he is the man you are looking for and deserves to be called happy. But till he dies do not call him happy but lucky. It is humanly impossible for one man to combine in himself all good things, just as no country can be entirely self-sufficient but if it has one thing will be short of another; and the country which has most is best. So no single human individual is self-sufficient; if he has one thing he lacks another. But the man who continues to have the most advantages and dies peacefully deserves in my opinion, Croesus, this title of happiness. In all things look to the end and final result. For god often gives men a glimpse of happiness only to ruin them root and branch. (Herodotus, *Histories* 1.32ff.)

2.23 Note especially the phrase 'envious and disruptive'. Gods are disruptive (*tarakhōdēs*) because it is impossible to forecast what they will do next, but at least there is one characteristic one can hold on to, and that is that they are envious (*phthoneros*) of good fortune amongst humans (a theme which is much developed by tragedians, cf. 3.17; 7.40ff.).

2.24 The problem became even more acute when men tried to make sense of divine justice (*dikē*). *Dikē* implied justice according to the established rules. Rules could be made to govern human societies, but the Greeks had no divine law-books (such as the Jews had with Leviticus and Deuteronomy). Greeks believed that there were rules and order in the world ('the ordered world' is '*ho kosmos*'), but that the order was in the gods' interests, not men's. Consequently it was extraordinarily difficult to determine exactly what divine justice at any time required. Matters were complicated by the *timē* (honour, respect) that gods demanded from men. Since the gods fought for *timē* amongst themselves, to honour one god might be to offend another. In Euripides' *Hippolytos*, Artemis promises to take revenge on Aphrodite, who has caused the death of Hippolytos because he honoured Artemis too much, Aphrodite not at all:

*Hippolytos*: I wish the gods were subject to men's curse.
*Artemis*: Be easy. Because of your piety and goodness towards me, though your body lies in earth's darkness, the strokes with which Aphrodite in her anger struck you down shall not be unavenged. For I will slay in retribution with my unerring arrows her dearest love among mortals.
(Euripides, *Hippolytos* 1417ff.)

But there were at least some fixed points.

**2.25** (1) If a man transgressed his obligation to the gods, if he became *asebēs* (lacking in piety), then the wrath (*nemesis*) of the gods would be expected to be visited upon him. Thus the orators use safety in a hazardous journey as a proof of innocence:

I have also been attacked for being a ship-owner and a merchant, and we are asked to believe that the gods have preserved me from the perils of the sea merely in order that I should be ruined by Kephisios on my return to Athens. I simply cannot believe, gentlemen, that if the gods thought I had done them wrong they would have been minded to spare me when I was in the utmost danger – for what greater danger is there than a sea-voyage in winter? They had my life in their hands, my person and my property in their power; why should they have preserved me when they could well even have denied my body decent burial? (Andokides (*On the Mysteries*) 1.137)

Obligation to the gods included not only reverence and worship, but also observation of certain special laws given to men – respect for suppliants, heralds, strangers, beggars; in other words, those outside the protection of their own city.

**2.26** (2) Even more important was the gods' concern with homicide and blood-guilt. The death of a man aroused the ancient pre-Olympian powers associated with bloodshed, the Erinyes (Furies). These fearsome goddesses hounded the blood-guilty with madness and terror until the dead man's kin avenged his death. Blood-guilt was considred to pollute the whole city until the murderer had made atonement (cf. 7.11). Sophocles considers

2:11  Neoptolemos cuts the throat of Polyxenē, the Trojan princess, over the tomb of his father, Achilles. C. 570–560.

such pollution (*miasma*) in Thebes at the beginning of *Oedipus Tyrannus*:

I pronounce that no one in this land, where I hold the power and the throne, shall receive or speak to the murderer, nor share prayer or sacrifice with him, nor dispense to him his portion of holy water. All must ban him from their homes, for he has brought pollution on us, as the oracle of the Pythian god has just revealed to me. And in this pronouncement I support the god and the murdered man. (Sophocles, *Oedipus Tyrannus* 236ff.)

2.27 (3) Finally, in a society where the spoken word was the main means of communication, a man made an agreement *under oath* where we would use a contract and signature. The guarantors of these oaths – both private and public (e.g. treaties) – were the gods.


**Human responses**

*(i) Sacrifice*

2.28 One of the most widespread responses in primitive agricultural societies was to sacrifice to the powers of the earth and sky a valuable part of the produce – the first fruits of the harvest, or a fertile young animal. By offering the potentially hostile divine powers the best, an obligation to reciprocate might be created and fertility and survival assured in return. There is evidence that the Minoan and Mycenaean world (1800–1100) used human sacrifice in times of great stress, but for fifth-century Athenians human sacrifice was met only as a feature of the world of myth.

*(a) Fruits of the earth*

2.29 The simplest form of offering was the gift of the products of the earth: placing fruits or cakes made from grain on altars, or pouring out wine or milk or olive oil upon the ground (a practice known as 'libation'). The food was left to decompose or to be taken by animals, the liquid drained into the earth, but both were gifts, withdrawn from the use of men and made over to the divine powers and seen as one act in a process of exchange. By the act of giving, whether a simple gift of wine or the slaughter of a hundred oxen, anxiety was turned into expectation. The idea of a partnership with a powerful source of good was created.

*(b) Animals*

2.30 An animal may also be offered by simply throwing it into a chasm in the earth (this practice survived in the Athenian festival of

2:12  A woman pours an offering from a jug over a flaming altar. At the right stands an incense burner. Early 5th century.

Skirophorion). But in general Greeks had two ways of sacrificing animals: after the ritual slaughter, burning the whole beast (a holocaust), or (more commonly) burning certain parts, with the rest of the beast consumed by the sacrificers in a meal. Those parts were the thigh-bones wrapped in fat. Homer describes here a hecatomb (sacrifice of 100 oxen):

> They washed their hands and took up the barley . . .
> And when all had made prayer and flung down the scattering barley
> First they drew back the victims' heads and slaughtered them and skinned them,
> And cut away the meat from the thighs and wrapped them in fat,
> Making a double fold, and laid shreds of flesh upon them.
> The old man burned these on a cleft stick and poured the gleaming
> Wine over, while the young men with forks in their hands stood about him.
> But when they had burned the thigh pieces and tasted the vitals,
> They cut all the remainder into pieces and spitted them and roasted all carefully and took off the pieces.
> Then after they had finished the work and got the feast ready
> They feasted, nor was any man's hunger denied a fair portion.
>
> (Homer, *Iliad* 1.449ff.)

Note the ceremonial washing, the symbolic 'slaying' with barley grain before life is actually taken, the burning of the thigh-bones, the roasting of the entrails, the tasting of the burnt entrails, the cooking of the meat and finally human consumption of it (1.11).

**2.31** The reason which Hēsiod gives for this pattern of sacrifice is contained in the story of the way in which Prometheus (a pre-Olympian divinity) tricked Zeus, head of the Olympians, into being prepared to accept the bones from a sacrifice (see 2.9). It is suggested that Hēsiod's story, which comes immediately after the gods and men part company, may recall the bonds and divisions between men and gods. The thigh-bones also

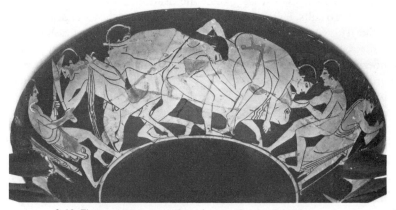

2:13  Five young men struggle with a sacrificial bull, whilst another sharpens the knives. Late 6th century.

2:14  A young man cooks the sacrificial meat on a spit before a Herm (cf. HI:18), whilst a man pours wine over the flames. C. 460.

contained the marrow, the stuff of life, and would be for this reason the most valuable to the gods. As for the human feasting, there is perhaps some sense of sharing with the god, but none of communion in the mystical Christian sense.

2.32 Blood is of greater importance in the other type of sacrifice, the holocaust, the burning of the whole beast. The holocaust was used principally on two occasions. First, in the case of homicide, the removal of a whole beast from the secular to the sacred sphere represented a life for a life and might appease the avenging powers of the underworld (*alastores*, 'Avengers' or Erinyes, 'Furies'), once the dead man's kin were satisfied. Secondly, hero cults. Heroes were local powers, either the great dead of the past, like Theseus (H.I.5), or minor deities who had not been assimilated into the Olympian system, or men within living memory, especially founders of new cities. Brasidas, the fifth-century Spartan general, was accorded hero-status as the founder of Amphipolis, though in fact it had been founded by the Athenian Hagnon. Heroes were felt to be weaker gods, literally in need of physical sustenance lest they haunt the community as ghosts. The blood of the holocaust might provide such nourishment (cf. Homer, *Odyssey* 11.23ff.).

2.33 Private sacrifices either to retain a god's protection over the family and family property, or to secure protection during a journey or for many other reasons were an important part of religious life. The following two

2:15  In the presence of Hermes, Odysseus has slaughtered sheep to raise the shade of Elpenor. C. 450–425.

sacrifices show how integral private ritual was in daily life. It might equally properly be a solemn family event, or part of a feast or party:

> Later on it so happened that Philoneos had a sacrifice to perform in Peiraieus to Zeus Ktēsios, and my father was going to sail to Naxos. So Philoneos decided that the best plan would be to make a single journey of it and see my father (who was a friend of his) as far as Peiraieus, make the sacrifice, and then entertain him. Philoneos' mistress accompanied him to attend the sacrifice. When they reached Peiraieus Philoneos carried out the sacrifice, as you would expect. When he had performed it the woman deliberated whether to give them the drug before or after dinner. After some thought she decided to give it after dinner, thereby serving the plans of this wretched Klutaimēstra . . . When they had dined, as you would expect after sacrifice to Zeus Ktēsios and the entertainment of a friend who was about to set out on a voyage, they set about making libations and sprinkling frankincense. And it was as she was mixing the libation, and as they were offering prayers – prayers, alas, never to be fulfilled – that his mistress poured in the poison. (Antiphon (*Against the Stepmother*) 1.16ff.)

> Moreover there is other evidence we can cite to show that we are the children of Kiron's daughter. For as is natural with a daughter's children, he never performed any sacrifice except in our presence; we were present at and took part in all sacrifices, whether the ceremony was great or small. And we were invited not only to such domestic rites but also taken to the Rural Dionysia, and we sat with him at public entertainments and went to his house for all festivals. He attached particular importance to sacrifices to Zeus Ktēsios, which he performed himself and to which he admitted neither slaves nor free men who were not members of the family; but we shared in the ceremony, laying our hands on the victims, making our offerings with his and playing a full part in all the rites, while he prayed for our health and prosperity in the way you would expect of a grandfather. (Isaios (*On Kiron's Estate*) 8.15)

## (ii) Prayers

2.34 Prayers, however, were more or less fixed in their general shape. This prayer from the *Iliad* is typical. The old man is Khryses, priest of Apollo, who prays that the Greeks (Danaans) may suffer for taking his daughter:

> Over and over the old man prayed as he walked in solitude
> To King Apollo, whom Lēto of the lovely hair bore: 'Hear me,
> Lord of the silver bow who set your power about Khrysē
> And Killa the sacrosanct, who are lord in strength over Tenedos,
> Smintheus, if ever it pleased your heart that I built your temple,
> If ever it pleased you that I burned all the rich thigh pieces

2:16 Ajax prays before
committing suicide over his
upturned sword (cf. 3:8).
C. 475–450.

Of bulls, of goats, then bring to pass this wish I pray for:
Let your arrows make the Danaans pay for my tears shed.'
So he spoke in prayer, and Phoibos Apollo heard him . . .

(Homer, *Iliad* 1.35ff.)

The god is invoked by name or titles which are often numerous; he is reminded of past kindnesses, then the request is made. Without some reference to the ties binding a god to his worshippers there was no ground for expecting divine aid, for the basic assumption was one of reciprocity (cf. 3.13). A prayer was made to the Olympians standing, with hands raised, to the underworld with hands lowered towards the earth. If a priest made the prayer, it would probably be at the altar in the temple precinct (*temenos*, 'a sacred area'); if it was a private ceremony any male – usually the head of the family – would conduct it.

### (iii) Purification

2.35 Purification was part of all rites. Usually a ceremonial washing of hands was all that was needed before a sacrifice, together with purification of the place of sacrifice, thenceforth called the *katharma*, 'the purified place'. More elaborate purification was needed in certain cases, particularly for murderers who were excluded from sacred ground, and after sexual intercourse and childbirth (cf. 4.77ff.). Purification might even be needed if one came into contact with murder. In these matters, as in others, there were official bodies of people in Athens to whom one could apply for advice. One such body were the *exēgētai* in Athens, who were official ministers of Apollo. Some of them were named by the oracle at Delphi for this task, others were elected by the Athenian people from one or two noble families with hereditary authority in such matters (one such family was the Eumolpidai). They advised on such matters as temples, cult procedure, sacrifices, and particularly purification following homicide. When this body could not advise, the matter was referred to Delphi. It is a matter for speculation how far such a body of citizens, controlled from Delphi and seen as ministers of Apollo, could help to initiate a specifically Delphian policy in a place like Athens.

### (iv) Supplication

**2.36** The safety and position of a man in ancient Greece depended primarily upon himself, his family, friends and possessions. These were all the material means available to him for helping or defending himself. Beyond this, a citizen enjoyed the protection of certain rights by virtue of his membership of a city-state. But a stranger or foreigner had no rights. He would naturally be far from friends, family and possessions (cf. 4.17). Already in Homer and Hēsiod the gods are shown to extend their protection to those outside human legal protection. One method of self-preservation in emergency was the act of supplication.

**2.37** To become a suppliant to either a man or a god was to proclaim the abjectness of one's position, and to acknowledge and honour fulsomely the power and position of the other. This was a complete inversion of normal patterns of behaviour and encounters between equals (cf. 3.2). It would then be a slight on the honour and power of the god or man to fail to protect his suppliant.

In a simple supplication of a god, the suppliant merely had to *touch* the altar. More formally, a suppliant donned garlands and carried branches,

2:17 An impious centaur attempts to drag a Lapith woman from a statue of Athēnē where she has taken sanctuary. Late 5th century.

decorated with wool, before approaching the altar to grasp it. While contact with the altar was maintained, any violence offered to the suppliant was an offence against the god and a violation of the sanctity of his power and that of Zeus himself, under his title of Zeus Hikesios (protector of suppliants). Consequently, direct force in removing a suppliant from the altar was rarely resorted to and was all the more shocking when it was used. Less direct methods were sometimes tried; even so the wrath of the gods was not always avoided. Here the politician Theramenes takes refuge at the altar, but little good it does him. He has just been struck off the roll of citizens, and the Thirty Oligarchs in power at the time take this opportunity to get rid of him. Kritias (once a friend of Socrates) was the leader of the Thirty (cf. H.I.57–8).

'I therefore,' concluded Kritias, 'strike the name of Theramenes from the roll, with your unanimous agreement, and we condemn him to death.'

When Theramenes heard this he jumped onto the altar and cried, 'All I ask is basic justice. You must not allow Kritias to strike either me or any of you off the roll just as he pleases; they have passed a law about those on the roll, and you and I must be judged in accordance with it. I know very well, I assure you, that this altar will give me no protection, but I wish to demonstrate that this junta has no respect either for justice or religion. But I am surprised that you, good men and true that you are, are reluctant to defend your rights, knowing very well as you do that your names are as easy to strike out as is mine.'

At this the herald of the Thirty ordered the Eleven to seize Theramenes; they entered with their attendants, led by Satyros, the most brazen and shameless of the gang. Kritias said to the Eleven, 'We hand this fellow Theramenes over to you. He has been condemned according to the law; do you take him to the proper place and carry out the sentence.'

At these words Satyros and his attendants dragged Theramenes from the altar. He as was natural called on gods and men to witness what was being done. But the *boulē* kept quiet. They saw the rail was packed with men of the same sort as Satyros, and that the front of the *bouleutērion* was full of security guards who, they knew, had come armed with daggers. So Theramenes was led away through the *agora* loudly proclaiming his wrongs. (Xenophon, *Hellenika* 2.3.51)

To supplicate *a person*, the suppliant would clasp his or her knee and chin. The person could not refuse the request made of him while contact lasted. It *was* possible to supplicate a human without physical contact, but success was not assured since physical contact between the two parties could not be made. Consider Odysseus' dilemma here: naked, filthy, stranded, he desperately needs help, so he emerges from the bush where he has been sleeping. The girls run in terror from him – all except Nausikaa, daughter of Alkinoos:

Only the daughter of Alkinoos stood fast, for Athēnē
Put courage into her heart, and took the fear from her body,
And she stood her ground and faced him, and now Odysseus debated
Whether to supplicate the well-favoured girl by clasping
Her knees, or stand off where he was and in words of blandishment
Ask if she would show him the city, and lend him clothing.
Then in the division of his heart this way seemed best to him,
To stand well off and supplicate in words of blandishment,
For fear that, if he clasped her knees, the girl might be angry.
So blandishingly and full of craft he began to address her:
'I am at your knees, O queen. But are you mortal or goddess?'

(Homer, *Odyssey* 6.127ff)

Ironically, the words he starts his appeal with mean literally 'I seize your knees'!

### (v) Sanctuaries and temples

2.38 A sanctuary (*temenos*) is a sacred area, 'cut off' from profane human use, because it was a traditionally holy reservation. Many sanctuaries were furnished with a temple or temples, but the size and importance of *temenos* and temple were not related. The magnificence of a temple could reflect political as much as religious pressures. Consequently, temples varied greatly in size and importance. At one extreme a private group called *orgeōnes* might honour a little-known hero, at the other, many thousands of worshippers would come to the great festivals – of Athēnē at Athens or of Zeus at the games of Olympia.

2.39 The temple itself might contain the huge cult statue of the god (Athēnē Parthenos in the Parthenon was 40 feet high) or it might hold only an antique sacred object, often a small wooden effigy of the god. The contrast between cult image and sacred object shows two aspects of divinity: the first imagines the god in human terms, in terms of physical appearance, while the sacred object has religious power in non-human terms of mystery and awe. Thus on the Acropolis the most sacred object was not the statue of Athēnē in the Parthenon but a wooden image of Athēnē Polias in the Erekhtheion (cf. 1.34). The Panathenaic procession culminated before the latter, not in the Parthenon. We might compare this with a supposed 'mask' of Dionysos, a sacred wooden object of immemorial age that was said to have fallen out of the sky at Methymne on Lesbos. Pausanias tells the story:

My next story comes from Lesbos. Some fishermen at Methymne drew up from the sea in their nets a face made of olive wood. In appearance it bore some resemblance to a divinity, but a foreign one not in the normal style of the Greek gods. The Methymnians accordingly asked the Pythian priestess of what god or hero it was an image, and she told them to worship Phallic Dionysos. Accordingly the Methymnians kept the wooden image from the sea for themselves and honour it with sacrifices and prayers; but they sent a bronze replica to Delphi. (Pausanias, *Guide to Greece* 10.19.2)

Worship of the god was usually conducted at an altar – the focus of the *temenos* – outside the temple, to the east. This was one reason why the outside of the temple was the place for elaborate architectural decoration.

### State religion in Athens

**2.40** By the fifth century, shrines and cults proliferated in Attica both to heroes and minor deities, and to Athēnē and the other Olympians. Most civic as well as sacred functions were felt to be under the patronage of the gods: Zeus, Artemis, Athēnē and Hermes in particular oversaw the activities of most officials in the *agora* – so Zeus Boulaios and Artemis Boulaia in the *boulē*, Zeus and Hermes Agoraios in the *agora*, and so on. The presence of the gods gave these institutions authority and permanence. So too for the citizen body, a temple in the *agora* to Apollo Patrōos ('of our ancestors' – Apollo was the mythical ancestor of the Athenian race) and

2:18  The altar of Zeus Phratrios and Athēnē Phratria in the *agora* of Athens; under these titles the deities were concerned with ancestral religious brotherhoods (*phratriai*). Mid 4th century.

one to Zeus Phratrios and Athēnē Phratria ('of the *phratriai*') were nuclei of civic life uniting small groups of citizens. Nearly all citizens belonged to one of the *phratriai*, and many had shrines to Apollo Patrōos in their homes (cf. 4.20). Indeed prospective magistrates were asked specifically about this (see 4.13).

Family tombs of the wealthy, mentioned by Aristotle, show more than anything the conservative influence of religion. These honoured graves were built on country estates, showing that the family had lived there many years and implying that it would continue to do so.

**2.41** Festivals were major public rituals, often lasting several days, and occupying a large part of the civic and sacred year. Traditional honours were paid to the gods, ancient ceremonies for grain and grape harvest lived on, and at the same time the celebrants enjoyed every kind of intellectual, religious and physical excitement. The occasion might be compared to the saint's day celebrations which are held in some countries, though as we shall see the Athenians included tragedies and comedies, athletics and many different forms of religious activity.

**2.42** First, the Athenian calendar.

| *Months of the Athenian civil calendar, with modern equivalents* | |
|---|---|
| Hekatombaiōn | June–July |
| Metageitniōn | July–August |
| Boēdromiōn | August–September |
| Pyanepsiōn | September–October |
| Maimaktēriōn | October–November |
| Poseideiōn | November–December |
| Gamēliōn | December–January |
| Anthestēriōn | January–February |
| Elaphēboliōn | February–March |
| Mounikhiōn | March–April |
| Thargēliōn | April–May |
| Skirophoriōn | May–June |

Each month was a lunar month, so Greeks had the associated problems of keeping the lunar and solar calendar in phase (cf. on Solon, 2.22). Hekatombaiōn for example, began with the new moon in June and extended till the new moon in July.

### (i) The religious year

**2.43** In addition to monthly festivals and sacrifices, two types of annual festival may be distinguished: *dēmos-* or *phratria*-centred festivals, and state festivals. The monthly festivals consisted in sacrifices to the appropriate gods (e.g. the seventh of each month to Apollo), and did not impede, for example, normal work. The *dēmos-* or *phratria*-centred festivals (2.50–2) only involved members of a particular *dēmos* or *phratria*, and as these seem generally to have occurred at different times for different *dēmoi*, a general holiday would not have been in question. During state festivals, everyone took a holiday and the *ekklēsia* only met in grave emergency, while the *boulē*, too, was probably dismissed for these days, with the same proviso. The Athenians in the fifth century prided themselves on the number and magnificence of their festivals. In fact, the number of firmly dated festival days is 130; when the undated festivals are added, about one-half of the days of the year can be shown to have boasted one festival or another. From a number of sources we can show that, for instance, the jury-courts could expect to work 300 days in the year (but the number of days is disputed: it *may* be as low as 150). That leaves some 54 'holidays' in an ordinary year. But we also have a contract given to some workmen to work at Eleusis for a period of 40 days which included the festivals of Kronia, Synoikia and the major state festival of Panathenaia. The conclusion must be that while most people would expect to have a real holiday during state festivals, it was not obligatory.

### (ii) Festivals and religious feeling

**2.44** The festivals were religious events and some of the major state festivals involved all members of the population, both slave and free, citizen and *metoikos* (metic), male and female, adults and children. The gods too were felt to be watching. Pheidias pictured a group of immortals, all set to watch the spectacle, on the Parthenon frieze, which is based on the procession at the Great Panathenaia. No doubt their sympathies and interests were felt to be particularly caught by celebrations on a massive and august scale, or by the involvement of the very best athletes or poets and actors (7.76).

### (iii) The constituents of public ritual

**2.45** Sacrifice we have already discussed (2.28ff.). It formed the climax of many festivals, often on a vast scale, e.g. at the Panathenaia, Athenian communities overseas were required to send a cow as a sacrificial victim, and the rents of public lands were used to buy more animals (the sum involved was the equivalent of two to three thousand skilled men's wages for a day). All but one of the victims was slaughtered at the great altar of Athēnē on the Acropolis. After some of the meat had been set aside for the religious and secular officials of the community, the rest was probably distributed among the people of Attica by *dēmoi* in proportion to the number of demesmen that each contributed to the procession. We should not underestimate the expense and complexities of public ritual.

**2.46** Processions too were centre-pieces of many festivals and again on a very considerable scale of solemnity and grandeur. They would include the bearers of ritual objects and offerings, such as *kanēphoroi* (bearers of gold baskets of grain for throwing at the sacrifice), *skaphēphoroi* (resident aliens who carried trays of such gifts as cakes and honeycombs), carriers of silver bowls, jugs and incense burners, of stools for the officiating priests to sit on and of great awnings under which the priests walked. Many in the procession would carry branches of olive or of oak as sacred emblems. In processions to honour Dionysos, *phalloi* were carried, as well as wine-skins and special loaves of bread called *obeliai*. Such processions would wind their way across Athens (from the Kerameikos across the *agora* to the Acropolis at the Panathenaia) or on longer routes across Attica. At the Dionysia, the wooden image of the god was brought in procession from the Academy to the god's temple by the theatre, to commemorate his first coming to Athens from Eleutherai on the border between Attica and Boiotia. Participants in the great procession of the Eleusinian mysteries walked from Athens to Eleusis (22 km) carrying the 'holy things' of

2:19  A procession moves to an altar for the sacrifice of a bull, a boar and a sheep (*trittus*). C. 500.

Dēmētēr or escorting the initiates, and the wooden image of Athēnē was taken in procession from the Acropolis to the sea at Phaleron (7 km) to be washed by its traditional custodians, members of a family called Praxiergidai.

**2.47** Perhaps less familiar to us as examples of religious worship are contests and competitions in honour of the god. These, no less than sacrifices and processions, were a recurring part of Greek religious rituals. They might take many forms: athletic contests (in chariot racing, running, wrestling, and throwing the discus and javelin); competitions between choirs and professional reciters of heroic poetry, or between teams of playwrights, actors and managers (*khorēgoi*); torch-races (in one case on horseback) ending at an altar. Some festivals combined more than one type of contest, as the Panathenaia combined athletics and torch-races with competitions between Homeric 'rhapsodes'; some might offer only one, as the festivals of Dionysos at Athens featured contests between playwrights and their teams (cf. 7.35–6). We can look at these in two ways, either as shows for the gods to watch and enjoy (as we see them watch and enjoy heroic warfare in the *Iliad*), or as arenas for the conspicuous display of human competitive aggression, giving divine sanction and recognition to an aspect of human behaviour which had in it the seeds of social disruption and conflict (cf. 3.2, 16). Just as Greeks imagined their gods as often in conflict with one another, so they imagined them as understanding and enjoying human conflict. As Patroklos (*Iliad* 23.257ff.) was honoured in death by men competing with each other, so the gods were honoured by

2:20  Some festivals included a torch-race among the events. Later 5th century.

2:21 A choir, taking part in a musical competition at a festival, moves forward to the accompaniment of pipes. C. 480.

the competitive display of human excellence in all its forms – even balancing on a greasy wine-skin!

**2.48** The greatest of these religious competitions were the venue for great gatherings of Greeks from many parts of the Mediterranean. Like the great mediaeval fairs in honour of a saint, they provided the opportunity for the interchange of both goods and ideas. At Olympia, for example, at the games in honour of Zeus which had been celebrated, the Greeks believed, every four years from 776, thousands assembled in a temporary encampment to be witnesses of the greatest athletes in the Greek-speaking world, but also to hold a market and to hear displays of rhetorical and intellectual virtuosity from men such as Gorgias and Lysias (7.19).

### (iv) Festivals and public rituals

**2.49** Processions, sacrifices and contests are constituents of many public rituals. But the major rituals, often lasting several days, have individual characters of their own. We discuss a sample of them in what follows.

### (a) The festival of Panathenaia

This took place every year at the waning of the first moon after the new year in Hekatombaiōn. Every fourth year it was celebrated with extra splendour and called the Great Panathenaia. We have already discussed the contests which took place during the festival and said something of the great procession and sacrifices which were the climax. The procession was to escort up to the Acropolis the new robe (*peplos*), woven every four years with much attendant ritual by girls chosen from Athenian aristocratic

2:22  Olympia.

families, to be presented to Athēnē Polias, the protecting goddess of Athens, not to Athēnē in the Parthenon. As its name implies, the Panathenaia like other such festivals elsewhere (the Paniōnia and Pamboiōtia, for example) was a celebration of the solidarity of the Athenian community under the protection of the great goddess, whose birthday it was imagined as being; a reinforcement of a sense of 'being Athenian' wherever in Attica or overseas one lived, different from and superior to other, non-Athenian Greeks.

### (b) The festival of Apatouria

2.50 The Panathenaia had its counterpart in terms of local religion in the Apatouria, celebrated in the autumn of each year. This festival too was a state festival, but it was not celebrated *en masse* by all Athenians or organised by Athenian state officials. It was organised and celebrated by the individual *phratriai* (hereditary groups of families) and its chief purpose, apart from renewing the religious and secular solidarity of the *phratria*, was as a 'rite of passage' (i.e. a transition from one status to another) to register and attest the status of citizen children. Each *phratria* had a local cult centre. There the members (all of whom were men) celebrated various rituals. For example, on the third day, *koureōtis* (the

2:23 At the Great Panathenaic Festival the new robe (*peplos*) is handed over and will clothe the goddess' image for the next four years. C. 440.

name might mean either 'Day of Youths' or 'hair-cutting') was the occasion for the presentation of the children of *phratria-* members for public 'legitimisation'. New brides would also be presented to *phratriai* on the third day. There were as well drink-offerings (*khoai*) for deceased *phratria*-members.

2.51 The role of the Apatouria was thus to focus religious feeling upon the traditional *phratria*-grouping and the acceptance of children as eligible for citizenship. This emphasises the constant relationship in Athens between the organisation of the institutions of the *polis* and the local loyalties of the people. *Phratria*-membership was not just a practical matter of keeping outsiders out; it combined a positive sense of belonging with a deep feeling of traditional religious values, which could be played on to good effect in the courts (4.20). The Apatouria was a very old festival which existed also in all the Ionian cities of the Aegean and the coast of Asia Minor.

*(c)* Dēmos-*centred rituals*

2.52 But the *dēmoi*, the local village communities of Attica, also had their own public rituals, as the *phratriai* did. From one of them, Erkhia, we have an inscription which lists more than fifty sacrifices in the year, offered to almost forty different divine powers. The gods most frequently honoured at Erkhia are Zeus, Apollo, Kourotrophos ('she who raises the young') and Athēnē. On a few days in the year, men went from Erkhia to Athens (on the other side of Mt Hymettos, or more than 20 km away) to make offerings to the gods of Athens, to Zeus and Athēnē 'of the city', to Apollo Lykeios and to Dēmētēr of Eleusis. In the village itself they had an Acropolis on which were worshipped the same divinities, great or small, as were worshipped in Athens, but also at Erkhia men offered sacrifices to obscure gods such as Zeus Epopiōtēs, the nymphs, the Heroides, the Arrhes, the Tritopalates, and the Herakleidai, and to local heroes such as Leukaspis ('he of the white shield'); even, apparently, to Epops, the hoopoe. The picture has parallels in Christian practice in many Mediterranean and Latin American countries, where loyalty to the local saints may figure as much in religious feeling as acknowledgements of the great gods in the Greek world. In this, Erkhia seems to be typical of the village communities of the Attic countryside (cf. 1.21).

## (d) The Eleusinian Mysteries

**2.53** The public rituals we have so far considered embrace all members of the community, local or national, and have as their object the security and well-being of the whole community. That is in general typical of ancient Greek religion in its public rites, but there are a few exceptions.

The Eleusinian Mysteries, celebrated towards the end of summer, was a festival with some points in common with the Panathenaia – processions, sacrifices, Panhellenic involvement – but was more unusually an exclusive cult with the emphasis firmly upon personal revelation and salvation. A character in Sophocles says 'Thrice blessed are those among men who, after beholding these rites, go down to Hades. Only for them is there life' (Plutarch, *Moralia* p. 21f.; Dindorf fr. 719). The cult, which centred around the myth of Dēmētēr's recovery of her daughter Persephone from the underworld, was administered by Athens as a state festival and overseen by the king *arkhōn*, though its chief priesthood, that of the Hierophantes – 'revealer of holy things' – was in the hands of the Eumolpidai family and that of the Daidoukhos – 'the Torch-holder' – in the hands of the Kerykes family. In contrast to practice in other state cults, these priests wore elaborate clothes. Though the mysteries stressed the difference between the initiated and the uninitiated, entry to initiation was not restricted; anyone, slave or free, citizen or non-citizen, men or women, provided they were Greek speakers, could become initiates, though they had to be introduced by a *mustagōgos* ('leader of the initiates').

**2.54** Initiation was in two stages. The Lesser Mysteries, which were held in Anthestērion (cf. 2.42) at Agrai near the Ilisos outside Athens, were dedicated to Persephone. The *mustai* wore wreaths and carried in procession branches of myrtle. A woman bore on her head the sacred *kernos*

2:24 The torch-bearer (*daidoukhos*) was an important figure in the rituals for the Eleusinian deities. Mid 5th century.

which held a variety of seeds and grains to symbolise Dēmētēr's gifts, as Dēmētēr was goddess of the crops. For the Greater Mysteries in Boēdromiōn (cf. 2.42) a truce of 55 days was declared so that people could travel safely from all over Greece to the festival. The *ephēboi*, youths of eighteen or nineteen, escorted the sacred things (*hiera*) in boxes (*kistai*) to Athens. These objects were a central part of the ritual, but because of the universal awe and respect for the secrecy of the Mysteries in Greece, we have no evidence at all for suggesting what they might have been. On the 15th was held the *agurmos* (gathering); and on the 16th, the day probably known as *halade mustai* ('seaward initiates'), purification rites were held. The initiates bathed in the sea, each with a sucking pig which they later sacrificed. The 18th was spent indoors by the initiates, while the rest of Athens celebrated the festival of Asklepios. On the 19th the initiates went in procession to Eleusis led by Iakkhos, the personified cry ('Iakkhē!') of the celebrants approaching Demeter. They wore garlands of myrtle and carried *bakkhoi* (branches of myrtle tied with wool), as well as provisions on a stick, probably bedding and new clothes. On the evening of the 20th the procession reached Eleusis, lit by torches. The *kernos* was presented to Dēmētēr. On the 21st, sacrifices were made to the two goddesses; a vast offering of ground wheat, enough for 1,000 men, was set aside for this. The revelations which lasted through this night were not made in the open air. For these, uniquely in Greek ritual, took place inside the Telesterion, which at the period of its greatest extent could have held as many as 10,000 *mustai*. Little is known of the central ritual, except that it was divided into

2:25  An ecstatic Dionysos, with
panther-skin cloak and hair wreathed in ivy,
brandishes a fawn he has torn in two.
C. 480–470.

'things said', 'things done' and 'things revealed'. Initiates who were allowed to see the last stage were known as *epoptai* ('viewers'). We can be fairly sure that two things seen by the initiates were light appearing from darkness, and an ear of (Dēmētēr's) wheat being carried round. For the religious effect, we can compare similar simple revelations in the Orthodox Easter services.

**2.55** That the Mysteries provided an intense personal involvement and an emotional experience of the highest order cannot be doubted. Initiation, as the quotation from Sophocles shows, was regarded with reverence. The rites were said to 'inspire those who take part in them with sweeter hopes regarding both the end of life and all eternity'. No wonder that the young aristocrats Alkibiades and his friends aroused such intense hostility in 415 when implicated in a travesty of these very rites. The passion of the investigation into these allegations is one more indication of the immense respect in which the Mysteries were held by all Athenians (cf. H.I. 49).

### (e) The festival of Anthestēria

**2.56** This festival in honour of Dionysos gave its name to the month in which it took place (Anthestērion). Its name derives from the Greek for 'flowers', and the festival took place at a time when the first signs of life in nature, blossom, began to show. The main concern of the festival was with the new wine (i.e. the reappearance of Dionysos) and the spirits of ill omen (cf. 4.82). The festival lasted three days. On day 1 (*pithoigia*, 'jar opening'), the new wine was opened and tested; on day 2 (*khoes*, 'wine-jugs'), there was a procession in which Dionysos rode in a ship-chariot and the wife of the king *arkhōn* was 'married' to him in a 'holy marriage' (perhaps the king *arkhōn* was dressed as Dionysos throughout the ceremony). In the evening, drinking-parties were the order of the day, but each guest brought his own wine and drank it in silence, the very antithesis of community fellowship. The Greek explanation lay in myth. Orestes, infected with blood-pollution for killing his mother, arrived in Athens on *khoes* and in order that he should not be excluded from the celebrations and that the people should not be polluted, the king ordered that all drink their own wine from their own cups. We may prefer to explain the ritual rather as an attempt to put a boundary around the potentially destructive effects of too much alcohol. The third day was *khutrai* 'pots', and of a completely different character. Vegetables were boiled in these pots not for the living but for the spirits of the dead. It was a day of ill omen, when these spirits were said to roam abroad. When the day was over, the householders shouted 'Get out, *kēres* ['evil demons'], the *Anthestēria* is over!'

**2.57** This seems an extraordinary hotchpotch of events, but perhaps makes sense in the light of the ambiguous character of Dionysos. Not only is he god of life, wine and festivities, but he is also god of destruction. Wine itself has ambiguous qualities: it creates good feeling, but it can also release violent, destructive passions. The destructive side of Dionysos is brought out most powerfully by Euripides who, in his tragedy *Bacchae*, shows how Dionysos had the power to drive his followers wild with ecstasy in their search for him. They lost all control over themselves and ripped wild animals apart to get the raw, bleeding flesh inside them and with it, the god of life, Dionysos himself. Euripides has Dionysos in that play say of himself that he is a god most awesome and most gentle to men.

**2.58** This is the other face of Greek religion. On the one hand, we have a civic and political religion whose function was to integrate individuals into society, defining them as 'citizen' or 'member of the family' or 'guest' (cf. 2.51). On the other, we have mystery religions (cf. 2.53) and elements in the worship of Dionysos which seem to have torn people away from their lives as citizens of the civilised world of the *polis* towards something very different. It should be no surprise that women, disqualified from equal participation with men in social life, should appear to have been drawn to these alternative religions (but cf. 3.18; 4.30–1). Anthestēria was a festival whose deeper purpose may have been to defuse and contain some of these wilder aspects of Dionysiac worship.

## Homer

**2.59** In one sense, Homer's gods are very like human beings. In another, they are true gods, of terrifying and awe-inspiring power, grandeur and nobility, who can successfully demand full human respect. As a result the human heroes can at times seem quite at home with the divine presence, treating gods as if they were (almost) fellow human beings, whilst at other times human response is one of dread and awe. One particular result of this ambivalent attitude is that the gods' desire to be present and intervene in human life rather enhances and elevates humanity, for men are seen to be worthy of divine interest.

The following passages illustrate a number of aspects of the gods' behaviour.

**2.60** The gods' random, complete power: here Zeus reaches an agreement with his wife Hera that if she insists on the destruction of Troy, he should be allowed in return to sack any city dear to her that he wishes. Zeus is speaking:

> 'And put away in your thoughts this other thing that I tell you:
> Whenever I in turn am eager to lay waste some city,
> As I please, one in which are dwelling men who are dear to you,
> You shall not stand in the way of my anger, but let me do it,
> Since I was willing to grant you this with my heart unwilling.
> For of all the cities beneath the sun and the starry heaven
> Dwelt in by men who live upon earth, there has never been one
> Honoured nearer to my heart than sacred Troy
> And Priam, and the people of Priam of the strong ash spear.
> Never yet has my altar gone without fair sacrifice,
> The libation and the savour, since this is our portion of honour.'
> Then the goddess the ox-eyed lady Hera answered:
> 'Of all cities there are three that are dearest to my own heart:
> Argos and Sparta and Mycenae of the wide ways. All these,
> Whenever they become hateful to your heart, sack utterly.
> I will not stand up for these against you, nor yet begrudge you.'
>
> (Homer, *Iliad* 4.39ff.)

**2.61** The gods' grandeur: here Poseidon sets off over the sea in his chariot:

> So presently he came down from the craggy mountain, striding
> On rapid feet, and the tall mountains trembled and the timber
> Under the immortal feet of Poseidon's progress.
> He took three long strides forward, and in the fourth came to his goal,
> Aigai, where his glorious house was built in the waters'

Depth, glittering with gold, imperishable for ever.
Going there he harnessed under his chariot his bronze-shod horses,
Flying-footed, with long manes streaming of gold; and he put on
Clothing of gold about his own body, and took up the golden
Lash, carefully compacted, and climbed up into his chariot
And drove it across the waves. And about him the sea beasts came up
From their deep places and played in his path, and acknowledged their
    master,
And the sea stood apart before him, rejoicing. The horses winged on
Delicately, and the bronze axle beneath was not wetted.
The fast-running horses carried him to the ships of the Greeks.
                                                    (Homer, *Iliad* 13.17ff.)

**2.62** The possibility of a close relationship between man and divinity is demonstrated in the next passage.

Odysseus has landed on his homeland of Ithaka, but does not recognise it. Athēnē, his divine protectress, appears in disguise, and Odysseus proceeds to regale her with a long false tale. She replies:

The goddess, gray-eyed Athēnē, smiled on him,
And stroked him with her hand, and took on the shape of a woman
Both beautiful and tall, and well versed in glorious handiworks,
And spoke aloud to him and addressed him in winged words, saying:
'It would be a sharp one, and a stealthy one, who would ever get past you
In any contriving; even if it were a god against you.
You wretch, so devious, never weary of tricks, then you would not
Even in your own country give over your ways of deceiving
And your thievish tales. They are near to you in your very nature.
But come, let us talk no more of this, for you and I both know
Sharp practice, since you are far the best of all mortal
Men for counsel and stories, and I among all the divinities
Am famous for wit and sharpness . . .     (Homer, *Odyssey* 13.287ff.)

**2.63** Human acceptance of divine will: Hektor has been deceived by Athēnē (disguised as Hektor's close relation Deiphobos) into standing and fighting Achilles. Too late, he realises what has happened:

And Hektor knew the truth inside his heart, and spoke aloud:
'No use. Here at last the gods have summoned me deathward.
I thought Deiphobos the hero was here close beside me.
But he is behind the wall and it was Athēnē cheating me,
And now evil death is close to me, and no longer far away,
And there is no way out. So it must long since have been pleasing
To Zeus, and Zeus' son who strikes from afar, this way; though before
    this

> They defended me gladly. But now my death is upon me.
> Let me at least not die without a struggle, inglorious,
> But do some big thing first, that men to come shall know of it.'
>
> (Homer, *Iliad* 22.296ff.)

**2.64** If a Homeric hero had been suddenly placed in fifth-century Athens, he would probably have felt largely at home with men's general attitude to the gods (cf. 4.13), but would have noticed certain important differences: (i) men did not expect a god to be as personally close or to materialise as frequently as a Homeric hero did; (ii) the gods of fifth-century Athens were not seen so consistently as a family; (iii) there was a considerable growth in community worship of the gods (the Homeric heroes simply sacrificed, though there are one or two signs of cult worship in Homer, e.g. the offering of the robe to Athēnē in *Iliad* 6); (iv) there was also considerable state intervention in worship of the gods (state sacrifices and cults, *dēmos* rituals and so on). The forms of worship changed, but men's feelings of the ways in which a god might intervene and of the god's reasons for so doing probably did not.

## Conclusion

**2.65** When the divinities Greeks worshipped seemed to act irrationally, and there were few if any rules of behaviour which could be adduced to mollify them, one may wonder why the religion continued to be so successful in retaining people's loyalty. After all, Zeus was worshipped for longer than (so far) Jesus Christ has been. A Greek may well have replied that it was a matter of observing the world as it actually *was*, rather than as one would like it to be, and if it was irrational and intractable, one did one's best to live with it. Still, there were fixed points, as we have seen. The orator Lysias certainly thought so in the following extract, where the politician Andokides was indicted on charges of impiety:

But think again, envisage in your mind's eye what he did, and you will be able to form a better judgement. This man put on a sacred robe, he acted a parody of the sacred rites before the uninitiated and spoke the forbidden words; he mutilated the gods whom we worship, and to whom our devotions and sacrifices and prayers are offered. For this the priests and priestesses stood and cursed him, facing the west and shaking out their crimson robes as is their ancient and time-honoured custom. And he has confessed. What is more he has broken the law you made debarring transgressors from our holy ceremonies, in defiance of it he has made his way into the city, he has sacrificed at the altars forbidden to him, he has been present at the very rites which he violated, he has entered the Eleusinion and bathed his hands in the holy water. Who can tolerate all this? Can friend or relation or fellow townsmen dare to incur the manifest anger of heaven by showing him indulgence in private? You should indeed today reckon that in pubishing Andokides and getting rid of him you are cleansing the city and freeing it from pollution, expelling a scapegoat and ridding yourselves of a transgressor. For that is what he is. (Lysias, (*Against Andokides*) 6.50ff.)

2.66 At the same time, criticism of the gods had been a feature of intellectual thought of the sixth century (cf. 7.11), and in the fifth century Athens had seen a general broadening of the spectrum of attitudes to the gods, so that the picture is, in fact, less coherent than may appear from the above account. At the end of the day, a Greek might have said that the very existence of himself and his community was some sort of proof that the gods had heeded their prayers and so, to that extent, the longer the tradition of worship in *this* way or *that* way rather than in any other way, the more acceptable it must, by definition, be. Isokrates sums it up precisely:

In religious matters (for it is right to begin with them) our forefathers were neither inconsistent nor irregular in their worship or celebrations. They did not make a sacrifice of three hundred oxen, nor neglect traditional rites at will. They did not celebrate the festivals of foreign cults on a grand scale if there was a feast attached to them, while performing the rites of their own religion at cut price. Their only concern was not to weaken the religion of their fathers or to introduce unwanted innovations; for in their eyes piety consisted not in lavish expenditure but in leaving untouched what their forefathers had bequeathed to them. So the blessings of heaven were visited on them with unbroken regularity and in due season for ploughing and for harvest. (Isokrates (*Areopagiticus*) 7.29ff.)

# 3
# *Human obligations, values and concerns*

## Introduction

**3.1** Greek cultural values – those rules of behaviour transmitted from generation to generation – can be usefully seen in terms of team games. (1) Games are competitive, but there is a permanent tension in a team game between the self-display of the individual and the needs of the team. (2) There is no doubt about the identity of the opposition. (3) You treat the opposition as people to be defeated, and you expect them to do the same to you. (4) Where games are played under the public eye, the game is an arena for conspicuous displays of success (cf. 1.6); excuses count for nothing and results for everything. (5) Finally, it is generally the case that the nearer the top a team reaches, the more difficult it is to stay there and the more dedicated the opposition is to defeating it.

**3.2** Aggressive, self-assertive competition, for which the Greek word is *agōn* (cf. 'agony'), with a clear distinction between friends and enemies, and the sure knowledge that you will be treated as an enemy by the opposition, in the same way as you will be treated as a friend by your own side, and constant awareness that the final arbiter is other people, the public eye – these are three important features of the Greek value-system. Consider how these values make more comprehensible a number of common features of Greek life. The regular assertion that it was a man's duty to help his friends (*philoi*) and harm his enemies (*ekhthroi*) arises from the principle of reciprocal action. In the tragic theatre, poets competed aggressively against each other under the public gaze to secure a prize. A lawcourt trial aimed to ensure that one side won and the other lost, not necessarily to see that justice was done. So in many court cases the issue before the jurors often seems to be 'Who started it?' or 'How shall we deal with these litigants?' rather than 'Where do right and wrong lie?' Conversely, the institution of hospitality shows men helping their *philoi*. Friendship was made tangible by the exchange of gifts, which were visible signs of a relationship. The greater the man, the greater the gift; the greater the gift, the more important to display it.

**3.3** Clearly, a society which embraced only these values and no others would soon tear itself apart. So there were means of saving face or diverting aggression into other channels without the public confrontation implied above. Solon (H.I.8) cut down on one area of extravagant and potentially inflammatory display by regulating against conspicuous displays of wealth at funerals (cf. modern Sicily and South Italy, where in many places the lavishness of a funeral is an index of a family's status). The common use of the lot in selecting candidates for office was one way of selecting a candidate without ranking or judging the others (cf. 5.34). Ostracism was one way of averting open aggression between rival political factions.

**3.4** Competition, public displays of status and power, and pride in helping friends and harming enemies are not the terms in which we explain our behaviour either to ourselves or others. A Greek would find bewildering our value-system, which seems (on the model of the game) to be designed so that the most likely result is a draw (which may explain why cricket is the English game *par excellence*). To us, with our predominantly Christian values, Greek values may seem strange. But for the Greek this system worked. Consequently, when C.S. Lewis described Achilles in the *Iliad* as

3:1 Achilles I: Achilles mourns in his tent as Briseis, his captive girl, is led away by heralds to Agamemnon. C. 480–470.

3:2 Achilles II: Diomedes, Odysseus and Phoinix try unsuccessfully to persuade Achilles to take up arms again for the Greeks. C. 480.

'little more than a passionate boy', he was judging not the poetry, but the culture, through the eyes of one who did not understand how that culture made adult sense to those who lived in it.

### The Homeric background: *timē* and *aidōs*

3.5 In *Iliad* Book 12, Sarpedon, a great Lykian warrior fighting on the Trojan side, asks his companion Glaukos:

> Glaukos, why is it you and I are honoured before others
> With pride of place, the choice meats and the filled wine cups
> In Lykia, and all men look on us as if we were immortals,
> And we are appointed a great piece of land by the banks of Xanthos,
> Good land, orchard and vineyard, and ploughland for the planting of wheat?
> Therefore it is our duty in the forefront of the Lykians
> To take our stand, and bear our part of the blazing of battle,
> So that a man of the close-armoured Lykians may say of us:
> 'Indeed, these are no ignoble men who are lords of Lykia,
> These kings of ours, who feed upon the fat sheep appointed
> And drink the exquisite sweet wine, since indeed there is strength
> Of valour in them, since they fight in the forefront of the Lykians.'
>
> (Homer, *Iliad* 12.310–321)

The passage neatly illustrates three of the main cornerstones of the Greek value-system: society needs the skill of the warrior, and rewards it with *material gifts*, and *public acclaim*. *Timē* is the Greek for 'acclaim'. It is

3:3 Achilles III: whilst Priam and Hekabē mourn, Achilles drags Hektor's body round the walls of Troy and Patroklos' tomb. Late 6th century.

3:4 Achilles IV: Priam brings gifts to ransom his son's body from Achilles. C. 480.

often translated 'honour', but is derived from a word meaning 'value', 'true assessment'. These rewards are *reciprocated* by the warriors' duty of fighting in the front line. When Achilles, the greatest Greek warrior, refuses to fight for the Greeks because of the slight done to him by the king Agamemnon, his old mentor Phoinix tries to persuade him to return to the fighting and to accept Agamemnon's compensatory gift as well:

> No, with gifts promised
> Go forth. The Greeks will honour you as they would an immortal.
> But if without gifts you go into the fighting where men perish,
> Your honour will no longer be as great, though you drive back the battle.
> (Homer, *Iliad* 9.602–5)

Without the physical evidence of compensation in gifts, any Greek might have assumed that Achilles had simply given in.

**3.6** Since public approval was the greatest spur to success, public *disapproval* acted powerfully in the Homeric hero's mind to dissuade him from failing to meet his obligations. The technical term for this sense of feeling men's eyes upon you was *aidōs*, often translated as 'shame'. In the following passage Hektor justifies his decision to fight on against hopeless odds:

> Now, since by my own recklessness I have ruined my people,
> I feel shame before the Trojans and the Trojan women with trailing
> Robes, that someone who is less of a man than I will say of me:
> 'Hektor believed in his own strength and ruined his people.'
> Thus they will speak; and as for me, it would be much better
> At that time, to go against Achilles, and slay him, and come back,
> Or else be killed by him in glory in front of the city.
>
> (Homer, *Iliad* 22.104–110)

**3.7** Described in the above terms, the system seems neat and workable. But we have not mentioned the strong element of competitiveness between heroes to show that they are better than other heroes.

The *Iliad* starts with the public quarrel between Agamemnon and Achilles. The heart of their argument is 'Who deserves public rewards? Those who are the best fighters, or those who are leaders (whether they are right or not)?' In the heat of the moment, Agamemnon (son of Atreus) promises to take the girl of Achilles (son of Peleus) from him, to make up for the girl whom he (Agamemnon) had earlier been forced to give up. The wise old Nestor attempts to find a middle way:

> You, great man that you are, yet do not take the girl away
> But let her be, a prize as the sons of the Greeks gave her
> First. Nor, son of Peleus, think to match your strength with
> The king, since never equal with the rest is the portion of honour

3:5  Ajax I: Ajax raises the dead body of Achilles from the battle field. C. 570.

3:6 Ajax II: Ajax and Odysseus quarrel over the dead Achilles' arms and armour. C. 490.

3:7 Ajax III: The Greek chieftains vote to decide the award of the arms. On the left Odysseus raises his hands in joy; on the right Ajax turns away in sorrow and shame. C. 490.

Of the sceptred king to whom Zeus gives magnificence. Even
Though you are the stronger man, and the mother who bore you was
    immortal,
Yet is this man greater who is lord over more than you rule.
Son of Atreus, give up your anger; even I entreat you
To give over your bitterness against Achilles, he who
Stands as a great bulwark of battle over all the Greeks.

                    (Homer, *Iliad* 1.275–284)

3:8  Ajax IV: Ajax has committed suicide (cf. 2:16) and
now Tekmessa, his captive girl,
compassionately covers his
corpse. C. 480.

In other words, in Homer's world excellence in fighting was only one of a
number of qualities which demanded *timē*. Wealth, the number of a man's
subjects or the quality of advice one gave were all rival claims to status.
Clearly, if such a society was to stand without incessant competition
between its members rendering it incapable of acting in concert, there had
to be some restraints, some sanctions.

### Classical Athens

3.8 Fifth-century Athenians valued competition, conspicuous public
acclaim and reciprocal obligations as strongly as any Homeric hero did.
They also admitted sanctions which helped to ensure that the community
was not permanently torn apart by open personal rivalries (cf. H.I.72).

The most important difference between the world of fifth-century
Athens and that of the Homeric hero was that the nature of combat had
changed radically. Men now fought, not primarily as individuals, but as
part of a hoplite phalanx (cf. 6.17; H.I.7), which depended for its effective-
ness on co-ordination between all its members. The arena for interpersonal
rivalries shifted from the battlefield to other areas – to political, social and
intellectual competitiveness. The Greek festivals (e.g. Panathenaia) and
athletic competitions (especially at Olympia, Delphi, Nemea and the
Isthmus at Corinth) were now important arenas for displays of intellectual
and social as well as athletic rivalry. It is significant that the Greeks knew
no such thing as athletics records. All that was important was to beat your
opponents. There were no prizes for coming second or third. The Theban

3:9 A prize amphora awarded at the Great Panathenaic games, showing Athēnē and a foot-race. C. 520.

poet Pindar, commissioned to write poems to celebrate victories at games, saw athletics, not warfare, as a paradigm for the individual in society:

> Zeus, honour the successful boxer,
> And give him the respect and gratitude
> Of citizen and stranger alike.
> For he has walked the straight road which hates violence
> And has learned well the lessons taught
> By the wisdom of his fathers.
>
> (Pindar, *Olympians* 7.88–93)

Compare with this Pericles' metaphor from athletics quoted on p. 60, section 46.

### (i) Public life and envy

**3.9** In classical Athens the public life of the citizen, especially in the assembly, offered as much scope for visible success as did the battlefield for

3:10 A young man is crowned victor after success in the games. Early 5th century.

Achilles. Here the youthful, but extraordinarily talented and wealthy, Alkibiades explains to the assembly why he should command the expedition to Sicily although Nikias, a respected Athenian elder statesman, had just advised the assembly against him (cf. H.I.46ff.):

Athenians, since Nikias has attacked me on this point let me begin by saying that I have a better claim to command than others and believe that I am qualified for it. Indeed the very things for which I am criticised in fact bring honour to my ancestors and myself and benefit our country. For, after thinking the war had ruined our city, the Greeks came to overestimate its power because of the magnificent showing I made at the Olympic games; I entered seven chariots for the chariot race (a larger number than any private individual before), took first, second and fourth place, and did everything in suitably grand style. Custom honours such successes, and at the same time they give an impression of power. Again, any display I have made at home by providing choruses and the like, though it may have provoked a natural envy in my fellow citizens, gives an impression of power abroad. It is not mere useless folly when a man benefits not only himself but his city at his own expense, nor is it unfair for the ambitious to expect special treatment; the unsuccessful does not find others to take their share in his misfortunes. If we ignore failure we should correspondingly be ready to be looked down upon by success unless we are prepared for everyone to be treated as equal. What I do know is that men of this kind, and all who have attained to any distinction, are unpopular in their lifetime both with their immediate circle and with their contemporaries more generally, but that later generations are eager to claim relationship with them even if there is none, while their own country boasts about them, with no suggestion that they were foreigners or wrongdoers but as fellow countrymen and heroes. That is my own ambition, and that is why my private life is criticised; but what you must ask yourselves is whether you have anyone who manages your public affairs better than I do. (Thucydides, *Peloponnesian War* 6.16ff.)

The importance of this passage is obvious. It underlines perfectly how such an ambitious, politically motivated Athenian valued public display, public success and public recognition (cf. 1.6). But it also sounds a warning note. In a competitive society, the pain of defeated opponents and the envy of those outstripped were the surest signs of success. While to be envied was desirable, those seen to be inferior had a very powerful spur to action.

3.10 Envy carried its own dangers with it. The most serious was the risk of alienating those who envied you. It is a remarkable fact that many of the most well-known figures in fifth- and fourth-century Athens faced some sort of trial which usually resulted in heavy fines, or exile or even death (e.g. Aristeides, Alkibiades, Anaxagoras, Kimon, Pheidias, Demosthenes, Pericles, Themistokles, Xenophon). *Philotimia*, 'love of *timē*', 'ambition' was a double-edged sword. It is not surprising that Greek tragedians saw a pattern in the lives of the great figures of myth who were brought low.

3.11 Nevertheless, for all its dangers, a Greek liked to be envied, and had a strong sense of the public eye upon him. Croesus' son Atys used an irresistible argument to his father when he asked what people would think of him for staying away from the battlefield and the hunt:

> When Croesus persisted in his refusal to let his son join the hunting party, the young man said to him, 'My dear father, in the past I have looked for honour and fame in war and hunting. Now you have barred me from both, though you have no evidence against me of cowardice or lack of spirit. What figure do you think I shall cut on my way to and from the assembly? What will people think of me? And what sort of man will my young wife think she is living with? Either let me go on this hunt, or give me good reason why I should obey your wishes.' (Herodotus, *Histories* 1.38)

## (ii) Dishonour and revenge

3.12 The word for dishonour was *atimia* (cf. *atimos*, 'dishonoured'). It meant that one had not received the *timē* which was normally due. *Atimia* had a range of meanings extending from personal slight to exile from the community with loss of all rights (cf. 5.64). The consequences of *atimia* in any form were grave. Consider here how the threat of political *atimia*, which in fact never materialised, resulted in the most powerful social pressures to take revenge:

> I ask you, gentlemen of the jury, to reckon up what would have been the likely consequences for me, for my wife and my sister if Stephanos had been able to inflict the damage he intended either in his earlier or later action, and how great my shame and misfortune would have been. I was urged, privately, by everyone to avenge

myself for the wrongs he had inflicted on us and was told that I should be extremely cowardly if I did not see that justice was done for my sister, my father-in-law, my sister's children and my own wife – all of them my close relatives. ([Demosthenes] (*Against Neaira*) 59.11–12; cf. 5.51).

The institution of ostracism indicates how sensitive Athenians were to men's feelings of disgrace. The purpose of ostracism was to remove from the city the leader of a political faction which was hindering decision-making (a fault to which a radical democracy was especially prone). As a result, ostracism allowed citizens to express their fear and envy of one more powerful than them. But while an ostracised Athenian was sent into enforced exile for up to ten years, neither he nor his family suffered any loss of rights. This protected the feelings of the exile and precluded revenge. Again, as we have already noted in the introduction (3.3) the use of the lot for the purpose of selecting officers of state was a means of choosing a person without in any way degrading or openly judging the others. The selected candidate won, but this was not at the expense of anyone else's standing in society.

Nevertheless revenge was still seen as a highly commendable reason for action.

Let us acknowledge that we are entirely within our rights in dealing with any enemy if in exacting vengeance for his aggression we give free rein to the anger in our hearts, and that there is proverbially nothing sweeter than retaliation upon enemies, which will now be ours. (Thucydides, *Peloponnesian War* 7.68)

A slighted Athenian was quick to seek redress, and a common way of so doing was through the lawcourts. The following extract is typical:

I regarded the man who had put me in this predicament as an enemy with whom no personal reconciliation was possible. But when I discovered that he had defrauded the city as a whole, I proceeded against him with Euktemon's help, thinking it a suitable opportunity to do the city a service and to avenge my own wrongs. (Desmothenes (*Against Timokrates*) 24.8)

### (iii) Friends and enemies

**3.13** The Greek's world could be divided into three groups – those to whom one owed obligations and from whom they were expected (*philoi*, 'friends'); those to whom one was hostile (*ekhthroi*, 'enemies'); and 'outsiders', those to whom one owed nothing and could completely ignore. The basic assumption underlying these categories can be summarised in one word – reciprocity (cf. 2.34). As you prayed to a god and expected him to be favourable because you had yourself done the god favours (and for no other reason), so you expected your *philoi* to help, your *ekhthroi* to injure. Amongst *philoi* were counted your family, first of all; then friends and others with whom obligations had at one time or other established ties. An *ekhthros* had done some harm in the past, or intended to, or was related to one who had. Here Medeia considers how she will treat Jason, her husband who has deserted her for a new bride:

I will kill my children. No one shall save them. And when I have wiped out all Jason's family I will flee from the land, leaving behind the murder of my own dear children and the awful crime I have dared to do. For I will not tolerate the mockery of my enemies. So be it. What is there for me to live for? I have no country, no home, no refuge from trouble. I was wrong to leave my father's house, yielding to the words of a Greek, on whom with god's help I will be avenged. He will not see the children I bore him alive again nor will he beget more children by his newly-wedded wife, who must die by my poison, unhappy wretch. Let no one think I am a meek weak woman, of no account. I am another sort, kind to my friends indeed but bitter to my enemies – that is how fame is won. (Euripides, *Medeia* 792ff.)

Her desire for revenge was all the sharper because Jason had been the man to whom she was, in theory, most closely bound (cf. *Against Neaira* at 3.12).

3.14 Knowing who friends and enemies were is basic to an understanding of Greek political motivation. Pericles could imagine himself being taunted with an accusation that he had been closely connected with Arkhidamos of Sparta, so that when Arkhidamos invaded Attica he did not ravage Pericles' lands:

Pericles son of Xanthippos, one of the generals, knowing that invasion was imminent, suspected that because Arkhidamos was a friend* of his he might spare his estate from the general devastation. This he might do either as a personal favour or on the instructions of the Spartans who wished to stir up prejudice against him as they had in their demand for his expulsion for the curse. Pericles therefore gave it out in the *ekklēsia* that Arkhidamos was indeed a friend* of his but this friendship would certainly not be detrimental to the city, and in case the enemy refrained from devastating his land and property like those of other people, he gave them up to be public property so that no suspicion should fall on him on their account. (Thucydides, *Peloponnesian War* 2.13)

More broadly, *stasis* (internal civil strife) was endemic in the Greek world (Athens only suffered from it on two occasions, in 411 and 404) and this

*The word is *xenos*, 'guest-friend', often used of an alien with whom one had struck up a close alliance.

can best be understood in terms of discontented groups of individuals who saw their own status under threat from others. Thucydides' brilliant description of *stasis* in Kerkyra highlights the personal nature of the rivalries:

So savage was the course of the party-conflict at Kerkyra, and it seemed even more savage than it was because it was one of the first to occur. Later on, one may say, the whole Greek world was torn by domestic conflict in which the democratic leaders tried to bring in the Athenians, the oligarchs the Spartans. In peacetime there would have been neither justification nor desire for foreign intervention; but in war a revolutionary faction always had excuses to hand for bringing in the foreigner, assistance from whom would bring advantage to the one faction and destruction to its opponents ... Further, the ties of blood became less binding than those of faction because the partisan was less scrupulous: for factions were not formed to work within the existing system but to overthrow it, and derived their strength not from any religious sanction but from complicity in crime. Reasonable proposals from an adversary were met by the stronger faction with increased precautions and not with generosity. Revenge was prized more highly than self-preservation. Solemn agreements, if made, were made to meet an immediate difficulty and remained valid only until a better weapon presented itself; and the side that first ventured, when opportunity offered, to take its opponents off their guard enjoyed its revenge all the more for being accomplished by treachery, reckoning this to be the safer method and one which because it proceeded by guile would earn them the reputation of superior intelligence ... The root of all these evils was ambition and the lust for power: hence the violence of the conflict once they had embarked on it. The leaders on each side were armed with high-sounding slogans: the one faction claimed that they stood for social equality and the rights of the people, the other that they stood for order and tradition. Both claimed to have the good of the community at heart, while both aimed in fact at getting political control, and in their efforts to get it indulged in the worst excesses. Their acts of reprisal were even more savage, as they paid no regard to ordinary standards of justice or to the common good, but only to the factional caprice of the moment, and so, to satisfy the passions of the hour, were ready to pervert justice or to secure power by open violence ... (Thucydides, *Peloponnesian War* 3.82ff.)

### (iv) Hubris

**3.15** *Hubris* is often translated 'pride', and is used in this sense by, for example, professional literary critics. Its basic meaning for a Greek was 'aggression', 'violence'; and it came to mean an *unprovoked* assault on someone's person or status, with the express intention of *public humiliation* (cf. Demosthenes (*Against Meidias*) 21.180, where the essence of *hubris* is 'treating free men as slaves'). Here, a prosecutor, having outlined

3:11  A drunken brawl. Early 5th century.

his previous meetings with a gang of hooligans (whose leader was Konōn) relates the incident which led to the trial:

As we got to close quarters one of them, I don't know which, fell on my friend Phanostratos and pinioned him, while the defendant Konōn and his son fell on me, stripped me, tripped me up, pushed me into the mud and finally jumped on me and beat me so severely that my lip was split and my eyes closed, and when they left me I could neither stand nor speak. As I lay there I heard a lot of bad language from them, a great deal of it being foul abuse of the kind I should hesitate to repeat to you. But there is one thing I must tell you to show that this was assault (*hubris*) and prove the whole thing was his doing. He began to crow like a victorious cock, and the rest of the gang told him to flap his arms against his sides like wings. (Demosthenes (*Against Konōn* 54.7ff.)

Being beaten up was bad enough, but what clearly tipped the balance was Konōn's imitation of a triumphant cock over a fallen enemy. Here was an unprovoked assault, accompanied by intentional public degradation, for all to see. As a result, the prosecutor says, he almost brought a case for *hubris*, which carried a far stiffer penalty, than merely one for *aikeia* (assault and battery).

The point was that the pursuit of *timē* (*philotimia*) could be taken too far, as Demosthenes made clear:

I might indeed recall the money I have spent on trierarchies, on the ransom of prisoners-of-war and on other acts of generosity; but I pass over them in silence. My motives were never personal gain or ambition [*philotimia*] and I have steadfastly advocated a course which has made me unpopular, but which would be greatly to your advantage if you were to follow it. (Demosthenes (*On the Kherronēsos*) 8.70)

When a man overstepped the mark, he could easily become a *hubristēs* and as such incur the anger not only of his fellow men but also of the gods.

### (v) Restraints

**3.16** The Greeks seem to have had an almost endemic capacity for mutual annihilation and self-destruction and, if we may judge from their tragedies, appeared to realise it (cf. 7.40). It is easy to understand how a contest system of the sort described above could contribute to this disastrous characteristic, especially when even the young were involved. Here Demosthenes gives advice to a young boy:

Even if you are superior to the ordinary run of men, do not give up the effort to excel everyone else; let it be your ambition to be first in everything. To aim at this target brings more credit than respectable mediocrity. (Demosthenes (*On Love*) 61.52)

Nevertheless, this latent capacity for destruction was channelled, as we have already seen, into less harmful outlets, e.g. festivals, athletics, the law-courts, ostracism and the use of the lot to select state officials. The institution of democracy iself could be effective in diminishing and deflating one man's ambitions where they were perceived to run contrary to people's interests. Certainly it enabled the envious to take adequate revenge on the envied without (necessarily) violent consequences, especially in Athens (we have seen how *stasis* was more common elsewhere). Rationalism may also have been a restraining force; it could, after all, encourage people to see other grounds for decision-making than pure self-interest or respect for past practices.

**3.17** In all this it is possible to see a consistent counter-balance to the model of a contest as the best pattern for Greek values. This opposition can perhaps best be summed up in one word – *sōphrōn* (the noun form is *sōphrosunē*). It bears a wide range of meanings – 'prudent', 'discreet', 'sensible', 'chaste', 'law-abiding', 'modest', 'moderate', and 'disciplined'. At heart it implies restraint and acknowledgement of one's own limitations. Its force is perfectly captured by the two famous mottoes inscribed over the entrance to the temple of Apollo at Delphi: '*mēden agān*' 'nothing in excess' and '*gnōthi seauton*' 'know yourself'. To know oneself was to know what one could and *could not* do; it was to be constrained by the fact that one was human and not divine (and should not therefore attempt to challenge the gods, cf. 2.23); it was to realise that as a human being one had certain capacities, but *not* others. To do nothing in excess was part of the same picture.

Such styles of behaviour were as much accepted and praised as that of fierce competitiveness, and acted as a moderating influence upon latent aggression. The choruses of Greek tragedy, usually people of considerably lower status than those whom they advise (and so possibly a body of people with whom the general populace who watched the play could immediately identify) permanently urged this 'sensible' way upon kings and princes tempted, by their status, to push themselves to the limit. The tension between the two patterns of behaviour was a constantly recurring theme of Greek literature.

### (vi) Women and slaves

**3.18** In a standard work on Athenian law, the index has one entry under 'Women' – it is 'disabilities' (cf. 4.23ff.). The important point is that women and slaves were *not independent*: they had to rely on someone else for their existence and status. They were, in other words, incapable of competing. So too with the poor. A Greek defined 'wealth' as the condition in which he could live without working, 'poverty' as the condition in which he could only live by working. The latter condition removed his independence of action (cf. 7.14), especially if he was forced into the lowest category of work – working for *someone else*.

We can easily understand how dependent slaves were (cf. 4.62). As for free women, it is important to remember that they had little role outside the home (festivals in honour of the gods were an important exception, cf. 4.30), so had little or no opportunity to make identifiable friends and foes, and consequently were unable to reciprocate in a way that was obligatory for men (see 3.13). A woman's role lay, by definition, amongst her *philoi* in her own home.

**3.19** In general women were seen by the men who wrote about them not only as physically but also as morally, socially (cf. 4.20–22) and intellectually weaker. But there is an ambivalence about them. On the one hand, they were seen as the all-embracing archetypal source and providers of life, on the other as she-monsters of outrageous and devilish cunning (cf. the myth of Pandora at 2.9 and 2.58). When Klutaimēstra faced her son, the returning Orestes, knowing full well that he planned to kill her, her first reaction was to call for an axe with which to slaughter him, but a few seconds later she was appealing to him as his mother:

*Klutaimēstra*: What is the matter? What's this shouting in the palace?

*Servant*: I tell you the dead [i.e. Agamemnon's spirit] are slaughtering the living.

  *K*: Alas. You speak in riddles but I understand. We killed him [i.e. Agamemnon] treacherously and by treachery shall we die. Quickly, give me a battleaxe. It is the crisis now; will it be death or victory?
  (*Enter Orestes*)

*Orestes*: It is for you I am looking. I have dealt with him.

  *K*: Alas. My dearest strong Aigisthos, dead.

  *O*: You love your man? You shall lie in the same tomb; no chance for you to desert the dead.

  *K*: Hold your hand, son; see this breast, child, at which you slept and drew the milk that made you grow.        (Aeschylus, *Libation Bearers* 885ff.)

**3.20** It is difficult to say exactly why women should have been seen as

3:12  Zeus abducts Ganymede: divine sanction for an older man's love for a youth. C. 475–450.

such a potential danger. Perhaps one of the reasons may be that a woman had to cross lines of kinship in order to fulfil herself in marriage: she left one family, and was absorbed into another. Such outsiders could be seen as a dangerous threat to institutions as tightly knit as family, where the rules were made by men, and the descent of property was through the male line (cf. 4.21). Again, women were widely regarded as enjoying the sexual act more than men. Teiresias, the mythical prophet who had enjoyed the dubious pleasure of being both man and woman, was once asked who found more pleasure in making love, and replied that of the ten units of pleasure involved, the man got one and the woman nine. He was blinded for his pains by the goddess Hera, on the grounds that he had given away woman's great secret. Consequently, the Athenian male tended to feel threatened by any male outsiders in his home and would be commended for keeping a close watch on his wife (cf. 4.29). As Xenophon remarked, if one detected a fault in a herd of cattle, one would probably blame the herdsman, but if one detected a fault in a woman, there could be no possible doubt that the husband was to blame (cf. 4.23–31).

## *(vii) Homosexuality*

3.21 A Greek found it natural that one who enjoyed heterosexual relations might also enjoy homosexual relations. But by homosexual relations, a Greek generally meant pederasty. If our evidence is interpreted rightly, male homosexual relations were normally carried on between an older man and an adolescent boy.

Greek literature distinguished carefully between the *erastēs*, the active, older partner, and the *erōmenos* (or *paidika*), the youth whom the *erastēs* was trying to win. Greek pottery gives abundant evidence of a typical approach by an *erastēs* to a possible *erōmenos*: close conversations, then giving of gifts, handling of the *erōmenos*' body (particularly the testicles) and finally copulation, virtually always between the thighs. Greeks believed that, while the physical gratification enjoyed by the *erastēs* was intense, the *erōmenos* got (or should get) little or no physical pleasure from the advances of the older *erastēs* (so that while the *erastēs* was usually depicted as having an erection, the *erōmenos* never was). Again, Greeks tended to look down on the *erōmenos* who gave in to the *erastēs*' advances, though they naturally applauded the *erastēs* who got his way. (In the same way we might applaud an old man for having an affair with a young girl while at the same time feeling that the girl was throwing herself away.)

3.22 What pleasure or advantage could have accrued to the *erōmenos*

3:13 A man makes sexual advances towards a youth. Mid 6th century.

from this? In a society in which sexual relations with a woman were not necessarily regarded as anything other than a means of procreation or purely physical satisfaction (the latter widely available through prostitutes and slaves), an approach by an *erastēs* was one way in which a young man could feel wanted and valued for himself. Love from a woman, herself a dependent member of society, was perhaps not felt to be worth as much as love from a male, especially an older, wealthy, handsome, influential one. For all that, the *erōmenos* would only go so far. To allow anal penetration was, for a Greek male, to be treated like a woman, and therefore a degrading humiliation (cf. 3.18). It is interesting to note that Athenian citizens were deprived of full citizenship if convicted of male prostitution. Such an activity could be safely left to non-Athenians to practise in Athens.

**3.23** It would be quite wrong, however, to conclude that all Greeks practised both homosexual and heterosexual relationships. Homosexuality may have been a preserve of the wealthy and leisured rather than the normal Greek male, struggling to make a living from the land, and was probably confined to defined phases of the masculine life-cycle (there seem to have been few regular 'gays'). Certainly Aristophanes laughed as loud and brutally at 'queers' as any modern comedian. But there is no doubt that homosexuality was an important feature of Greek social, intellectual and, in Sparta, possibly even of political life (cf. H.I.10).

**3.24** In the following passage, Plato puts into the mouth of Alkibiades the story of Alkibiades' attempted seduction of Socrates. This gives us a first-hand picture of how an Athenian male would conduct an affair. There is a delightful irony at the heart of the story. Alkibiades was the golden boy of Athens – young, very handsome, very wealthy, highly successful and courted by all. Any Athenian male would have given his eye teeth to sleep with him. The irony is that it is the youthful Alkibiades who is attempting to seduce the older (and certainly uglier) Socrates – and failing (cf. H.I.46ff.).

As I was saying, we were alone together and I was enjoying the thought that we should soon plunge into the kind of talk a lover has when he is alone with his darling. Not a bit of it; he spent the day with me in his usual kind of talk and finally went off and left me. After that I asked him to come with me and exercise in the gymnasium, which he did, and I hoped to get somewhere. But though we exercised and wrestled together, often with no one else present, I need hardly tell you that I got no further. Finding I made no progress in this way, I decided to make a direct assault on the man and not give up my efforts but find out where I stood. So I invited him to dinner with me, for all the world as if I was the lover and he the darling. He did not accept in a hurry, but in the end I persuaded him. The first time he came he wanted to leave immediately after the meal, and I was ashamed and let him go. But I tried again and prolonged the conversation far into the night, and when he wanted to go I pretended it was too late and managed to force him to stay. So he lay down on the couch next to mine, on which he had dined. There was no one else sleeping in the room except the two of us, and so far the story could properly be told to anyone . . .

(*Alkibiades now offers himself to Socrates, but Socrates points out that physical beauty and internal goodness are different. Still . . .*)

After this exchange I reckoned that some of my shots had gone home, and I got up and without allowing him to say another word I wrapped my own cloak round him (it was winter) and lay down under his shabby garment, throwing my arms round his extraordinary and wonderful person. I lay there all night, and you cannot deny it, Socrates. But in spite of my doing so he defeated me, and despised and scorned and rejected all my youthful charm. And it was just in that charm that I thought I had something, gentlemen of the jury – for you are sitting in judgement on Socrates' disdain of me. For I swear by all the gods and goddesses that I got up next day without anything more happening than if I had been sleeping with my father or elder brother. (Plato, *Symposium* 217a ff.)

## Conclusion

3.25 Greeks had no conception of a god who placed an absolute value upon every individual (cf. 4.62). Nor did they think that everyone had an inalienable right to life, liberty and happiness, let alone property. 'Rights' (which we claim in great abundance nowadays because the state is regarded as the protector of individual freedoms) were limited by whatever laws were in force at the time. In general, the individual's needs were seen as wholly subordinate to those of the state. After all, in a radical democracy, the people *were* the state: it was not as if individuals were being tyrannised by some outside force (cf. 5.1ff.).

**3.26** One of the results of this was that Greeks tended to be uncomplicated in their view of human responsibility. What counted were not so much intentions (though these could, of course, be argued as relevant) as results. If one had argued in the Greek court that an individual should be excused killing his parents on the ground that he had had a disturbed upbringing, a Greek might well have seen that not as an excuse for acquitting him, but as an added *reason* for condemning him. Greeks tended not to confuse reasons with excuses.

This seems a harsh morality. But in a civilisation in which the opposite of freedom was not imprisonment but slavery, and in which existence was at best precarious, it is understandable. Modern states at war become more totalitarian than in peace. For all that, the most cursory reading of Homer or tragedy makes it clear that Greeks also placed a high value on mercy and pity. If we stress the harsher side of Greek values here, it is to draw attention to it. Christian values were six hundred years away, and Freudian understanding of human motivation some two thousand four hundred.

# 4
# *Athenian society*

## (1) The population of Athens

**4.1** Our word 'society' has a Latin root (*socius* 'an ally'). The nearest Greek equivalent was *koinōnia*, 'commonwealth' or 'community' (*koinos*, 'common', shared'). The way that Greek *poleis* (1.3) maintained their sense of political community was through strict and usually exclusive laws of citizenship.

**4.2** Citizenship was far more immediate and tangible to an ancient Athenian than it is to a citizen of, say, the United Kingdom today. No disgrace could be greater than being stripped of citizen rights (*atimia*, discussed at 3.12; 5.64). The Athenian lived in a state whose citizen body (as opposed to the total population of the state) probably never exceeded 50,000. Every year the Athenian citizen would expect to serve in the army or fleet. Every month he could congregate with several thousands of them in the *ekklēsia*; or he might be placed on the annual panel of 6,000 from which jurors for the popular courts were drawn at need. 50,000 is a tiny figure by our standards. But in the ancient Greek world, it meant that Athens had a far larger citizen population than any other of the hundreds of Greek states scattered from (in modern terms) Spain to South Russia.

**4.3** Besides, Athens was an exceptionally cosmopolitan city. An Athenian could observe thousands of temporary or permanent immigrants from other Greek cities or from non-Greek lands working around him, often doing exactly the same work as he and yet sharing none of his privileges of citizenship (cf. 4.67ff.). A final mark of the Athenian citizen's special status is that if he were to travel beyond the borders of his own *polis* he would at once find himself deprived of political rights and often dependent more on custom than on law for his protection and well-being.

**4.4** For these reasons an Athenian, like all his fellow Greeks, had an unusually strong sense of belonging to his own city. This feeling was reinforced by the myths that all Athenians were descended from Ion (cf. Ionians), son of Apollo, and that their ancestors had always lived in Attica. Over and above these myths Athens had citizenship laws that were strict even by Greek standards. After Pericles' citizenship law of 451 only men who had an Athenian mother as well as an Athenian father qualified as citizens. The thinking behind this new legal restriction, which was re-enacted in 403, is not entirely clear. But the law does nicely show how jealous Athenians had become of their extensive privileges as citizens of a democracy (cf. 3.2, 4.21).

**4.5** The Greek word *dēmokratia* is a compound, meaning literally the sovereign power (*kratos*) of the *dēmos*. How that sovereignty was exercised, and what is the range of meanings of *dēmos*, are matters to be discussed in Chapter 5. For present purposes *dēmos* stands for the people or citizen body as a whole. As we have seen, male gender and Athenian parentage on both sides became the first requirements for membership in that exclusive body. The other condition was enrolment at the age of eighteen on the register of the father's hereditary *dēmos* (see 4.16).

**4.6** Thus among the free population of Athens all women, whatever their status, and all males lacking the correct parentage were by definition excluded from citizenship. It was very exceptional indeed for a resident alien (*metoikos*, hence 'metic') or non-resident foreigner (*xenos*) (cf. 4.67) to be voted Athenian citizenship, and this would be a reward for some extraordinary service to the democracy. As for slaves, who were numerous and mainly non-Greek, they were without legally enforceable rights of any kind, private or public (4.62; 3.18). In short, only a fraction of the total population of the Athenian state enjoyed political rights under the democracy.

**4.7** Within the privileged citizen body, moreover, there were distinctions of economic class that affected political roles. From the time of Solon in the early sixth century the citizens were divided up into four census groups based on agricultural income for the purposes of distributing political power (cf. 5.26, 6.15). The growth of the democracy from the end of the sixth century made these divisions rather less important politically, but the influence wielded by the small number of very rich families in the top two groups remained strong. Besides, wealth determined the citizen's military role, and in ancient Greece political power went hand in glove with military function. Only the very wealthy could provide their own horses and serve in the cavalry (6.15); only the moderately wealthy could afford the equipment of a heavy-armed infantryman ('hoplite', see 6.17).

The poor majority necessarily served in a subordinate role in land warfare as light-armed skirmishers (6.18). However, as Athenian sea power became militarily crucial from the 480s onwards, the poor Athenians found themselves playing the leading military role in the state as rowers in the Athenian fleet. The fit between democracy and naval empire, as we shall see, was a tight one (cf. H.I.27).

4.8 Let us now turn to consider the size of the population of Attica, the 2,500 sq. km of territory that made up the *polis* of Athens. It is unfortunately impossible to give precise figures for either the total population or its three main components, the citizens (including women and children), metics and slaves. No ancient Greek state took regular overall population censuses. With one exception, to be noted shortly, our limited sources merely provide figures either in military contexts for (male) land troops or in political contexts for adult male citizens (see the table that follows). This explains the variations in the most sober modern estimates based on these inadequate sources.

## (i) Citizens

| Date | Source | Military numbers | | Total citizen (= adult male) population |
|------|--------|------------------|---|-----------------------------------------|
| 500 | Herodotus | | | 30,000 |
| 431 | Thucydides | 13,000 active 16,000* reserve 1,000 cavalry | } hoplites | |
| 411 | Lysias | 9,000 hoplites | | |
| 322 | Plutarch | | | 21,000 |
| | Diodoros | | | 31,000 |
| 317 | Ktesikles | | | 21,000 |
| | [Demosthenes] | | | 20,000 |

*This figure includes an unknown number of metics.

Our earliest figure for the total citizen population (adult males) is exceedingly unreliable, but it seems reasonable to assume that the hoplite population rose steeply from the early fifth century to the outbreak of the Peloponnesian War in 431, that it had fallen sharply by the time of the oligarchic counter-revolution of 411, and that it remained comparatively low during the fourth century. The steep rise in the fifth century reflects the general increase in prosperity, when the revenues of the Athenian state reached unparalleled heights and the opportunities for personal enrichment open to Athenians of all classes were greater than ever before or after. For example, many of the poor may have been able to reach the hoplite level through the acquisition of the land abroad that Athenian sea power made available. The figure of 9,000 hoplites for 411 seems rather low, but twenty years of war and the terrible plague of 430 and later had taken their toll of lives (see H.I. 36), and perhaps many Athenians had fallen below hoplite status through impoverishment.

### (ii) Metoikoi (s. metoikos)

**4.9** *Metoikoi* (see 4.6) are known from some seventy Greek states, but by far the largest absolute number resided in Athens, where they probably also formed the highest proportion of the total resident free population. The most reliable figure is that of 317, when 10,000 *metoikoi* (probably including a small number of independent women) were registered in an exceptional general census conducted after the democracy had been abolished by the Macedonians (in 322). The absolute number will almost certainly have been much higher a century earlier: an authority in the difficult field of ancient demography has recently argued that there were some 12,000 metic hoplites at the start of the Peloponnesian War and possibly even more who could not afford hoplite equipment. If this is right, *metoikoi* may in 431 have comprised about one-third of the free resident population of Attica.

### (iii) Slaves

**4.10** The size of the slave population is the hardest to assess. Our one preserved figure of 400,000 – also from the 317 census – is absurdly inflated, perhaps because the numerals were corrupted in the process of copying manuscripts. But it is impossible to say by how much it should be reduced, and hazardous to guess at orders of magnitude for other periods. For example, Thucydides reports that after 413 more than 20,000 slaves escaped to the Spartans in the last desperate phase of the Peloponnesian War and that the larger part of these runaways were skilled workers. There is some reason for thinking Thucydides' figure may be roughly accurate but no means of knowing what proportion of the total slave population, unskilled as well as skilled, female as well as male, old as well as young, these 'more than 20,000' represented. In general terms it seems fair to suggest that the slave population was at least as high as the adult male citizens and *metoikoi* combined, particularly if due allowance is made for the extensive use of slaves in agriculture as well as manufacture and domestic service (see below).

**4.11** With great caution the totals given in the table below may therefore be suggested for the three main groups of population in Attica at the two best documented points in time:

|  | 431 B.C. | 317 B.C. |
| --- | --- | --- |
| Adult male citizens | 50,000 | 21,000 |
| *Metoikoi* | 25,000 | 10,000 |
| Slaves | 100,000 | 50,000 |

To arrive at the total population of Attica, the figures for (adult male) citizens should be multiplied by about four to include the women and children of citizen families. The figures for *metoikoi* should be multiplied by a smaller factor, since at least some will have had families outside Attica. Slaves were normally not permitted to have families. The total in 431, then, would be of the order of 300,000–350,000, in 317 between 150,000 and 200,000. These made Athens the most populous Greek state, but the 431 total is about one-thirtieth the size of Greater London's present population (1983), and about one-thirty-eighth of the size of that of New York City.

## (2) Family and kinsmen

### (i) The oikos ('household')

**4.12** The typical family unit of the modern Western world has come to be the nuclear family consisting of the parents and a relatively small number of children. The ancient Athenians knew no such thing. In fact the Greeks did not even have a word for 'family'. Their nearest equivalent, *oikos*, means something more like our 'household' and has a far wider range of reference than our 'family'. It is vital to bear this crucial difference in mind throughout the following discussion, when it will sometimes be impossible to avoid using 'family' simply for convenience.

**4.13** The Athenians, particularly when contrasted with the other great Greek power of our period, the Spartans, had a reputation for being compulsive innovators. Yet in their family and kinship organisation they were almost neurotically conservative. The Athenian *oikos* of the fifth and fourth centuries would have seemed perfectly familiar to the original audiences of Homer. It based its wealth and permanence on family property held over many generations and on a close-knit and (to us) complicated kinship structure; and an Athenian's status as an Athenian depended, as we have seen, on his parentage and family connections. All this is nicely illustrated by the questions to which a man had to give satisfactory answers in order to hold office:

When they are checking qualifications they ask first: 'Who is your father, and what is your *dēmos*? Who was your father's father, and who was your mother, and her father and his *dēmos*?' Then they ask whether the candidate is enrolled in a cult of Apollo Patrōos and Zeus Herkeios, and where the shrines are, then whether he has family tombs and where they are; whether he treats his parents well . . . ([Aristotle], *Constitution of Athens* 55.3)

Moreover, the first official act of the chief civil official, the 'eponymous' *arkhōn*, was to proclaim that every Athenian 'shall hold and control until the end of the year such property as he held before [the *arkhōn*] took up his appointment'.

**4.14** As these quotations imply, the Athenian *oikos* extended beyond our nuclear family to include property. In the first instance that means land and the dwellings, storehouses and tombs built on it. But the *oikos* also embraced the instruments needed to work the land and service the property generally. Thus tools, animals and slaves ('animate tools' in Aristotle's unpleasantly accurate phrase) all fall within the definition of the *oikos*. At the head of this composite entity stood the *kurios*, the male master of the household who had in theory sovereign power over all its constituent elements. We shall return to his functions at the end of this section (cf. 4.16, 4.23).

**4.15** The Athenian *oikos* aimed to be economically self-sufficient (cf. 3.18). But socially and politically no *oikos* was an island nor would it have wished to be. All or almost all Athenian citizens would also belong to one of the primarily religious associations known as *phratriai* (see 2.40). These were literally 'blood-brotherhoods' (compare Latin *frater* from the same Indo-European root), but by the fifth century *phratria*-members were not all related to each other by blood. On the other hand, a group which was strictly made up of kinsmen was the *agkhisteia*, which embraced relatives to the degree of second cousins. This had legal importance in the areas of marriage, inheritance and vengeance. Over and above the *phratria* and *agkhisteia* groups, and standing in an uncertain relation to them, were the *genē* (s. *genos*), religious guild-groups with special rules of admission. The evidence is confusing, but it seems that relatively few and not necessarily aristocratic citizens belonged to a *genos* (often misleadingly translated as 'clan').

**4.16** By the fifth century the kinship or pseudo-kinship groups of *genos* and *phratria* had lost any political significance they may have had to the local units into which every Athenian *oikos* was grouped, the *dēmoi*. Under the dispensation of Kleisthenes there were, it seems, 139 *dēmoi* distributed among ten artificially created 'tribes' (see further H.I.11, 5.24). Where we use first names and surnames, an Athenian was identified in full by his own name, his patronymic (i.e. his father's name) and the name of his *dēmos*: for example, *Periklēs Xanthippou Kholargeus* (Pericles, son of Xanthippos, of the *dēmos* Kholargos).

Within the *kurieia* (protection, tutelage) of the *kurios* there fell any sons who had not yet attained the age of majority and all the women of the *oikos*. For women were treated in the eyes of the (male-created) law as perpetual minors, being first within the *kurieia* of their father or guardian, then within that of their husband (reverting to their father's on divorce or widowhood), and finally their son's if, as sometimes happened, he should take over the *kurieia* when he married and the father 'retired'. The *kurios* therefore had a twofold function. He represented all the females and the male minors of the *oikos* in legal and civic matters, and he was the present holder of ancestral property and estates.

## (ii) Legitimacy and property

**4.17** Real, that is landed, property was the basis of an Athenian's social status and political influence (cf. 1.10, 2.36). Land in Attica, except in the case of a special state exemption, could only legally be held by a legitimate

4:1 An *ostrakon* cast against Kleophon gives his patronymic (son of Kleippidēs) and his deme (Akharnai). Late 5th century.

Athenian citizen male. In almost all cases it passed by bequest from father to son, or by the nearest relationship in the male line through the family. An heir therefore had to be able to prove his legitimacy to secure title to landed property (cf. 2.40, 58).

4.18 In most cases, we must assume, succession to property passed off fairly smoothly, but several of the surviving fourth-century lawcourt speeches (especially those of Isaios, the leading probate lawyer of his time) concern disputed parentage and efforts by disgruntled relatives to discredit heirs. Since real property was the basic form of wealth, both sides had much to gain or lose, and it was worth paying for the best legal help. Part of the reason for the disputes was that the Athenians did not have birth certificates; they had no equivalent of London's Somerset House (the state registry of births). Nor were scientific methods of proof available to decide paternity. Instead, legitimacy and citizenship were most easily demonstrated to the satisfaction of a large citizen jury by proving registration in a *phratria* as an infant and in a *dēmos* at the age of majority.

4.19 One of the best examples of what could be involved is provided by a speech ([Demosthenes] (*Against Euboulides*) 57) written for a man who was voted off the register of his *dēmos* in 346/5; in that year, exceptionally, a general scrutiny of all *dēmos*-registers had been ordered presumably because there was reason to suspect that large numbers of men had somehow had themselves placed on the registers illegally. In order to prove his legitimacy and citizenship, the speaker has taken his case on appeal to a central Athenian court and seeks to show that both his father and his mother were true Athenians and that he had been legitimately entered on the register of his father's hereditary *dēmos* at the age of eighteen.

4.20 As witnesses of his father's legitimacy the speaker lists, first, five of his father's male kinsmen by birth and several of his male kinsmen by marriage (his father's female cousins' husbands); then his father's *phrateres* (fellow *phratria*-members), those with whom he shares his Apollo Patrōos and Zeus Herkeios and the same family tombs, and his father's fellow *dēmos*-members. With women, on the other hand, it was much harder to establish legitimacy, since they were not apparently enrolled in either *phratria* or *dēmos*. So the speaker cites, apart from a similar range of male kinsmen, only the *phrateres* and fellow *dēmos*-members of his mother's male kinsmen.

As for his own life history, he first calls witnesses to his mother's (second) marriage and then presents evidence of his induction into *phratria* and, most important, *dēmos*. He stresses that he had later been chosen priest of Herakles for the *dēmos* and indeed president of the *dēmos* (*dēmarkhos*) without his opponent's objecting to his legitimacy on either occasion. Finally, he sums up his claim to citizenship in terms of the answers required of candidates for public office at Athens (see 4.13). The stakes were appallingly high: if he lost, he would probably have been sold into slavery (cf. 2.33).

**4.21** Property was usually passed on by will, another potential source of inheritance disputes. It was almost unheard of to overlook sons, among whom the property would be divided up equally in accordance with general Greek custom; but if the sons were not of age, a guardian would be appointed to protect their interests. Daughters could not inherit in their own right, as we shall see. The state, in the person of the 'eponymous' *arkhōn*, took the closest interest in the welfare of children in guardianship, but this did not prevent guardians from being or being alleged to be fraudulent. The most celebrated instance of alleged fraud by guardians concerns Demosthenes, who made his debut in the courts to secure the large inheritance of which he claimed to have been unlawfully robbed.

A daughter could not technically be an heiress in the full sense, because women could not own and control property in their own right under Athenian law. A daughter who had no surviving brothers of the same father inherited only as an *epiklēros*, so called because she went with *klēros* or estate. That is, she acted as a passive instrument in the transfer of the estate to the nearest legitimate heir in the male line. The 'eponymous' *arkhōn* saw to it that she was properly married to her nearest relative (preferably related by birth rather than marriage) and that the property was duly passed on. If already married, the *epiklēros* might even be obliged to divorce her husband in order to marry the appropriate relative, although it was open to her father to adopt her son or some other male relative. This may seem extraordinary to our way of thinking, but it is simply the most striking illustration of the Athenians' fixed determination to keep property within the family and so preserve the number of functioning *oikoi*. In this way concentrations of property might be avoided and the social basis of the democracy maintained (cf. 7.63).

**4.22** The chief acknowledged purpose of Athenian marriage was, as we shall see, the procreation of legitimate children. Yet contradictory pressures operated on parents in a society without scientific birth control and where the death of children by disease or violence was far more likely than in our own. On the one hand, there was the risk of producing too many children, so that the property would be fragmented among the male heirs or depleted by dowries. On the other hand, if an Athenian father followed the advice of Hēsiod to have only one son, that son might die prematurely and leave the estate without an heir. Various responses to these pressures were open. Newborn infants might be exposed to die, a fate to which girls seem to have been more vulnerable than boys; or a son and heir might be adopted. In any event, the primary objective of reproduction was to secure the continuity of the *oikos* with all its social, religious, political and military implications.

### (iii) Women and marriage (cf. 3.18ff.)

**4.23** Betrothal and marriage continued the concern of the state and individual *kurioi* with property and legitimacy. The very word for betrothal, *egguē*, also means 'pledge' or 'security' and so emphasises the vital element of property in the transaction. The bride's *kurios* betrothed the girl to her prospective husband with the following formula: 'I give you this woman for the ploughing of legitimate children.' This ceremony took place in the presence of as many witnesses as possible to attest the girl's virginity and the size of her dowry. The girl, who might be betrothed at the age of five, had no say in the matter of her marriage, which was essentially a contract between the *kurioi* of two *oikoi*. Marriage at Athens did not go together with romantic love.

**4.24** Another difference from modern Western marriage is that Athenian marriage was a private contract and not registered with the state authorities; legal marriage was not constituted by a wedding ceremony and signing of the register. Instead it was a simple 'living together' (*sunoikein*), embarked upon as a private enterprise and considered valid from the moment the bride entered the house of her lord and master. This step was regularly taken when the girl was only about fourteen. The new wife brought with her a dowry, usually a sum of money. This was considered so important that a father might mortgage land to provide a dowry of suitable size. But the wife did not technically own her dowry. It remained the property of her father or guardian, and the control of how it was spent was in the hands of her husband. None the less, the provisions

4:2  A wedding procession makes its way to the new home. C. 540.

for the return of the dowry, for example on divorce, could afford some protection for the wife, or at least for her family whose property it really was. Divorce proceedings could be initiated by either party, but as usual in this male-dominated society it was easier for the husband to obtain a divorce.

**4.25** Not surprisingly, too, the 'double standard' that still exists in many countries today was in full force in Athens. While husbands were permitted to take concubines and mistresses and consort with prostitutes, sexual relations between a wife and a man to whom she was not married automatically counted as adultery; and a wife convicted of adultery was liable to cruel public humiliation. The practical reason for this was that the paternity of a child might be challenged by an enemy, but Athenian views on adultery also reflect the chauvinism of Athenian males. They considered the seduction of a woman a more heinous crime than rape, since seduction implied that the wife's affections had been turned away from her husband (cf. 3.20).

**4.26** One of the most vivid illustrations of the extremes to which an Athenian husband could go to preserve the legitimacy of his *oikos* is contained in a lawcourt speech delivered early in the fourth century. The speaker had been accused of murdering a man. His defence is that the homicide was justified because he had caught the man *in flagrante delicto* committing adultery with his wife in his own house:

When I decided to marry, Athenians, and brought a wife into my house, I was for some time disposed not to harass her but not to leave her too free to do just as she pleased. So I watched her as far as I could and paid attention to her as far as was reasonable. But when my child was born, thinking this the truest expression of the close tie between us, I began to trust her and I put all my resources at her disposal. At first, gentlemen, she was the best of wives – a clever housekeeper, thrifty and exact in her stewardship. It was my mother's death that was the origin of all my troubles. When she was carried out to burial, my wife went with the cortège, was seen by that man and eventually seduced. He used to wait for the slave-girl who went to market and, making propositions through her, brought about my wife's downfall. (Lysias (*Against Eratosthenes*) 1.6ff.)

**4.27** This passage has another point of interest. It was when she was attending her mother-in-law's funeral, outside the marital home, that the speaker's wife was seen by the alleged adulterer. Thereafter relations between the guilty pair had at first been carried on through an intermediary, the wife's servant-girl. Respectable wives, in other words, or at least the wives of wealthier men, should not, according to the Athenian social code, be as a rule seen in public. Their place was in the home, where we shall meet them again shortly. Only for funerals and festivals might they legitimately and without shame leave the house and play a social role in public (cf. 3.18). The speaker in the disputed citizenship case discussed earlier was considerably embarrassed at having to admit in court that his family was so poor his mother had to go to the market to sell ribbons: 'We do not live', he confesses, 'in the way we would like.'

**4.28** Passages like these have featured centrally in a long-running debate over what is too often called 'the position of women' in Athens. To pose the issue in these terms, however, involves dangerous ambiguities. For much depends on precisely which women we are talking about: daughters, sisters, or wives; wives as mothers or marriage partners; rich or poor, free or unfree women. Besides, this thorny question raises fundamental problems of method. The evidence available to us is almost entirely produced by and for men living in a male-dominated world and is expressed in the dominant language of men. Above all, perhaps, study of the 'woman question' in ancient Athens cannot help being affected by the impassioned debates over the status of women current in our own, also male-dominated, society. Caution therefore is the order of the day.

**4.29** Anyone who looks at all deeply into the social roles played by women in Athenian society (for the moment these remarks are confined to women of citizen status) is soon struck by an apparent paradox. In the private, enclosed and often secret world of the Athenian home, relations between men and women who are kindred can be warm, intimate and familiar. It is true that men and women occupy different physical spaces within the home and that the women are relegated to the back or upstairs parts, but in itself this is a sign not so much of contempt by the men as of

4:3  Women prepare oxen for sacrifice. C. 440.

their desire to protect the women from unwelcome contact with unrelated males; separateness did not necessarily imply inequality. But in the public world outside the home, by contrast, men alone have the opportunity to shine (except in one important area to be noted shortly) (cf. p. 60, section 45).

**4.30** The exception referred to has already been noted in a different context. It is the extraordinarily prominent role allotted to women in ritual. Athenian women acted as priestesses in more than forty major public cults, including that of the patron deity of the city, Athēnē Polias, and they played leading roles in the great religious processions (2.3, 19, 49). Listen to the female chorus in a play of Aristophanes:

When I was seven, I carried the sacred symbols; then at ten I was grinder of Athēnē's barley; then at the Brauronian festival of Artemis I was the Bear-girl in the saffron robe; and when I was grown up handsome, I carried the sacred basket, wearing a necklace of dried figs . . . (Aristophanes, *Lysistrata* 641ff.)

There were, moreover, festivals exclusively for women, most notably the cult of Dēmētēr at the Thesmophoria. Finally, in rites of passage – birth,

4:4  A young girl cradles a hare; she is a 'bear' in the service of Artemis at Brauron in Attica. 4th century.

initiation, marriage and death – women were indispensable, providing the element of continuity fundamental to the perpetuation of the *polis* and the maintenance of right relations between men and the gods.

**4.31** One more factor has to be taken into account: the role of women in myth. Here again, as with their role in ritual, what is striking is the women's prominence. But whereas in ritual the valuation of women is largely positive, in myth their functions and roles – as seen by men – are shot through with ambiguities and tensions (cf. 3.19). That is to say, male attitudes to Athenian women as revealed in the imaginative projections of myth show a deep sense of unease. They oscillate between the poles of fear, even revulsion, and of total dependence towards women (cf. 2.9–11).

Here perhaps lies the clue to explaining, so far as our limited and one-sided sources permit, the 'position' in society of Athenian citizen women. They are essential to the functioning and continuity of society and yet by their (alleged) potentially rampant sexuality and crossing of kinship lines they constantly threaten its male-dominated orderliness. In public – that is, in the strictly political arenas of the democracy – women are allotted no role whatsoever. They have no political rights and have to be represented at law by their male guardians. Where the public and private spheres overlap, in rituals performed outside the home, women are allowed a role, often indeed an important one. But the true sphere of Athenian citizen women, the sphere where their dependence on men was both most tangible and yet could be most attenuated, was the home.

### (iv) Home life

**4.32** Women of all classes were expected to live very different lives from their husbands. While the men met together in *ekklēsia*, lawcourts or *agora* to conduct the business of state, and spent much of their leisure with male friends or lovers in the wrestling-grounds, *stoas* or cool groves of the Academy or the Lykeion, their wives were supposed to spend nearly all of their lives inside their homes. Even in the evening when men brought friends home to dine, wives and daughters were not expected to join them. For a woman to dine with an unrelated man could be used in court as evidence that she was not a legitimate Athenian wife. The men's dining-room (*andrōn*) was a world apart from the women's quarters (*gunaikeion, gunaikōnitis*), and it was non-Athenian women or slaves brought in specially from outside the household who graced the ritualised male drinking-parties (*sumposia*) held in this room.

**4.33** Of course this account is a generalisation and draws the contrast

4:5 Savage women of myth: enraged Thracian women pursue and kill Orpheus. C. 480.

4:6 Drawn reconstruction of houses in 5th-century Athens.

too sharply. Above all, it does not adequately describe the lives of poor women, the wives and daughters of poor Athenians; and in Athenian terms the majority of Athenian citizens were more or less poor. Thus in both town and country wives must have worked alongside their husbands if they could not afford slaves. So, too, poor citizen women went shopping and fetched water from the public fountains – tasks otherwise performed by slaves. Poverty drove some women to act as wet-nurses, midwives or petty market traders. There is some reason for thinking that the women of rich men were more rigidly secluded than their poor sisters, partly for snobbish reasons; but even they will have been able to establish gossip relationships with neighbours and rub shoulders with other women at the public festivals. For all this, though, it remains true that the Athenian woman's place was in the home.

**4.34** From her earliest years she had been brought up to perform or supervise exclusively domestic tasks; this was woman's work. This passage illustrates the range of these supervisory duties in a well-off household; Iskhomakhos is addressing the wife whom he married when she was not yet fifteen:

Your business will be to stay indoors and help to despatch the servants who work outside, while supervising those who work indoors. You will receive incoming revenue and allocate it to any necessary expenditure, you will be responsible for any surplus and see that the allocation for the year's expenses is not spent in a month. When wool is delivered to you you will see that garments are made for those that need them, and take care that the dried grain is kept fit for consumption. And there is another of your duties which I'm afraid may seem to you rather thankless – you will have to see that any of the servants who is ill gets proper treatment. (Xenophon, *Oikonomikos* 7.35ff.)

A poor wife, of course, would have had to do all the work herself: the bringing up of children, the provision of food, the combing and spinning of wool, the weaving, and so on and so forth. Since all these were time-consuming, she will have enjoyed little or no leisure, unlike her husband. Indeed, it was of the essence of women's tasks that they be time-consuming, for to a suspicious male eye they could be seen as ways of keeping the women out of mischief.

4:7 A mother encourages her baby as it sits in its high chair. C. 440.

4:8 Women spin and weave at home. C. 540.

4:9 A mother teaches her daughter how to cook. Late 6th century.

**4.35** In general, males are presented as being aware of this convention of separation. In [Demosthenes] (*Against Euergos*) 47.34ff. the speaker, who was a trierarch, had not received the ship's gear from his predecessor (on trierarchy, see 6.42). He went round to the house of the previous trierarch, Theophemos, to demand the gear or its equivalent value. When refused, the speaker prepared to enter the house by force: but, as he was careful to point out to the courts, 'I had already ascertained that Theophemos was not married.' It was simply not done for a complete stranger to enter a house where a married woman was present. Later on, the speaker forcibly contrasts his behaviour with Theophemos', when Theophemos and his cronies swooped on the speaker's farm, in the presence of his wife and children and servants, and carried off everything he had. The speaker points out that even a neighbour, on seeing the attack, refused to enter the farm because the *kurios* was not there.

**4.36** This ideal of secluded industriousness is revealed in the design of the Athenian house. There was normally just the one entrance, and this gave on to the men's quarters from which the women were sometimes literally barred. Our evidence suggests that Greek houses, even those of the very rich, were not elaborate. Their few rooms had undecorated walls, there was little in the way of furniture or non-essential ornaments. Exceptions are known from the Attic countryside (cf. 1.37). But even so most Athenian women lived their lives in cramped, smelly and unhygienic surroundings. Food was also plain; the mainly vegetarian Greek diet seems to have been remarkably spare even by the standards of contemporary rural Greece (meat-eating was confined to sacrifices, see 2.30–3). Clothes, though, which (as today) carried many implications beyond the wealth suggested by the material, might be more elaborate. Vase paintings and the plays of Aristophanes attest many variations in pattern, colour and design.

### (v) Non-citizen women

**4.37** So far only citizen women, especially wives, have been under direct consideration. But, as remarked earlier, Athenian custom tolerated temporary or permanent liaisons with other women. These concubines (*pallakai*), courtesans (*hetairai*, literally 'companions') and prostitutes (*pornai*) would normally not be of Athenian birth. Alkibiades was notorious for not merely having numerous mistresses but also keeping concubines, slave and free, in addition to his aristocratic wife. Pericles, who was for a time Alkibiades' guardian, divorced his wife and formed a lasting union with Aspasia. But since she was a native of Milētos, it was only as a special mark of respect to Pericles that the Athenians granted citizenship to their son. (He was one of the generals executed after Arginoussai: see H.I.54–6 and 5.10.)

**4.38** Concubinage, though, had some legal status. Prostitution too was legalised and freely available – a fact which Aristophanes has to suppress in his *Lysistrata* for the sake of the plot (7.59). Prostitutes ranged in class and expensiveness from the brothel-girls of the Peiraieus, through the rather more sophisticated *aulos*-girls an Athenian might hire to enliven a male drinking-party (*sumposion*) in the *andrōn* (4.32), to the educated courtesans euphemistically known as *hetairai*.

The most amusing story concerning a *hetaira* in Athens is to be found in Xenophon's fictional *Memoirs of Socrates*. In an artful display of studied innocence Socrates, noting Theodote's wealth, gradually teases out of her its true source – her rich lovers. The passage incidentally lists the chief sources of wealth in Athens, in order of their importance:

Socrates asked 'Have you an estate, Theodote?' 'No.' 'Then perhaps you get your income from house-property'. 'No.' 'Well, does it come from some manufacturing business?' 'No.' 'Then what *do* you live on?' 'I live on the contributions of kind friends.' (Xenophon, *Memorabilia* 3.11.4)

4:10 The men of Athens enjoy the customary delights of a *sumposion*: wine, women and song. Early 5th century.

4:11 Three men barter for the sexual favours of the women. C. 480.

## (3) Education (cf. 7.15–31)

**4.39** *Hetairai* in Athens might be cultivated women possessing considerable literary or musical skills in addition to their physical charms. Athenian girls, on the other hand, seem typically to have been educated chiefly for purely manual and domestic tasks (though there are vase paintings showing scenes of girls reading and occasional references in the orators to women involved in small-scale financial transactions). So this account of Athenian education applies exclusively to boys and young men (cf. 7.15–16; 7.20ff.).

In Athens, as in almost all other Greek states with the notable exception of Sparta, education was a private affair, arranged and paid for by parents who were not legally compelled to have their children formally educated. Teachers were often of low status and badly paid: a characteristic of Theophrastos' Mean Man is to make deductions from the teacher's pay if the child is absent through illness. Schools were run from private houses or rooms attached to a public or private training-ground (*palaistra*) which could be used for physical education. Boys began to attend school from about the age of seven, or earlier if the family was rich.

**4.40** There were three main areas of education: basic literacy (and perhaps arithmetic), music, and physical education. Some schools offered training in all three, but parents might choose different teachers for the individual subjects. Basic literacy, which was greatly facilitated by the Greeks' invention of a fully phonetic alphabet script, was taught by the *grammatistēs*. Despite his low status, his job was fundamentally important, since many aspects of the democracy depended for their efficient functioning on at least a rudimentary knowledge of reading and writing. Once a boy could read he was set Homer and other poets, often to learn by heart and recite from memory. As Plato puts it:

When a boy knows his letters and is ready to proceed from the spoken to the written word, his teachers set him down at his desk and make him read the works of the great poets and learn them by heart; there he finds plenty of good advice, and many stories and much praise and glorification of great men of the past, which encourage him to admire and imitate them and to model himself on them. (Plato, *Protagoras* 325e–326a)

Monotonously repetitive exercises on wax tablets were used to practise writing, and some of the few vase paintings of school scenes show the teacher wielding a sandal to encourage the others. There were, nevertheless, Athenian illiterates. The most famous and probably apocryphal story concerns the one who asked Aristeides to write his own name on a pot-

4:12 A boy recites his lesson to his teacher in the presence of his guardian (*paidagōgos*). C. 490.

4:13 Two young men learn to play musical instruments, one the lyre, the other the double pipes. C. 480.

sherd to get him ostracised, because he was sick of hearing Aristeides constantly praised for being just (H.I.23).

**4.41** The music teacher instructed boys in singing and in playing the *aulos* or lyre. Perhaps not all children had a very extensive musical education, since Aristophanes represents the ability to play the lyre as a mark of the cultured gentleman. But music was certainly important to people at all levels of Athenian society. Plato, indeed, took its moral significance so seriously that he banned all but one of the musical modes from his utopian state. Music played a large part in many festivals, above all the Dionysia with its choral lyrics in tragedy and comedy and its contests between

4:14 Young men practise throwing the javelin and discus in the *palaistra*. A sponge and oil bottle hang in the background. C. 500.

choruses of both men and boys in the singing of dithyrambs (songs in honour of Dionysos). These choral contests point to the close connection between music and poetry at Athens; even narrative poetry like Homer's *Iliad* and *Odyssey* was recited to musical accompaniment. Equally close was the link between music and dancing: *khoros* is the Greek for 'a dance' as well as 'a chorus'. For the well-to-do musical entertainment was an integral part of the private symposium too (cf. 7.1, 35, 37; 4.38).

**4.42** Physical training was supervised by a *paidotribēs*, who gave instruction in running, long jump, throwing the javelin and discus, boxing and wrestling. Since Greek *poleis* depended for their survival on their citizen troops, physical skills and fitness were vital (cf. 6.28). For this purpose Athens provided public gymnasia (so called because the Greeks exercised there *gumnoi*, 'stark naked') in addition to the many *palaistrai*. These were general meeting-places and used for a variety of purposes besides physical exercise; Plato's Academy, for example, takes its name from its location within the gymnasium of Akademos (or Hekademos).

Physical training did not only have a utilitarian military end in view. Athletic excellence was one of the most important fields in which the Greeks expressed their essentially competitive value-system (see 3.1, 3.8). Greatest renown was accorded to the victors in the Panhellenic festivals, but not far behind these in prestige came the Panathenaic (All-Athenian) Games, which was the greatest of the local festivals (see 2.44, 2.49). During these celebrations, contests in honour of the gods were held, at first in running, but later in other sports and in music and poetry too. Contestants came from all over the far-flung Greek world, and the victors covered not only themselves but their cities in glory (3.9).

**4.43** At Athens the length of a child's formal education varied according to the means and outlook of his parents; there was no school-leaving age. In his pamphlet on the social system of Sparta, Xenophon assumes that children elsewhere were not normally educated beyond childhood; and though an Athenian by birth and upbringing, Xenophon praises Sparta to the skies for its comprehensive educational curriculum that was obligatory for boys from the age of seven right up to adulthood. What Xenophon keeps very quiet about was the almost exclusively physical and martial character of Spartan education. There was nothing corresponding to secondary, let alone higher, education in this state, because there was no need for it in a warrior society. But at Athens, especially after the Persian Wars, new social and political needs created the demand for new kinds of education, and the demand was satisfied by men known – often derogatorily – as 'sophists'.

**4.44** A *sophistēs* originally meant simply a sage or wise man; Herodotus refers to Solon (H.I.8) as a *sophistēs*, and Solon became a regular member of the elect Seven Sages of ancient Greece. But already by the end of the fifth century *sophistēs* had acquired the pejorative sense from which we derive our 'sophistical' and 'sophistry'. On this hostile view a sophist was a charlatan, a clever-clever verbal trickster whose stock-in-trade was to make the worse seem the better argument. To compound his felony (as the critics saw it) the sophist charged a fat fee to his pupils in return for corrupting their moral sense and turning them into immoral know-it-alls kicking over the traces of established convention.

Persuasion (*peithō*) is the nub of the matter. In an era of rapid political, economic and social change, political success no longer depended simply on a family name and glory won in battle but also, and above all, on the power of persuasive speech in *ekklēsia* and lawcourt. He who by skilful rhetoric could persuade mass audiences of Athenians to his viewpoint became a leader (*prostatēs*) of the Athenian democracy (cf. 7.16–19, 24–6).

**4.45** Our evidence on the sophists and their teaching is unfortunately very one-sided. It comes almost entirely from their opponents, especially Plato. Only a handful of fragments of original sophistic writings has survived verbatim from antiquity. Yet even Plato, for all his intellectual brilliance and verbal dexterity, cannot entirely hide the fact that the sophists' teaching filled a serious gap. In two of his dialogues the question of why the young have failed to match up to their famous fathers is explicitly raised in terms of their defective education. Indeed, Plato's own philosophical achievement is inexplicable unless the contribution of the sophists is taken into account.

**4.46** What the sophists provided was in effect a higher education for the sons of the rich. Though the sophists did not form a single school, the issue that lay at the heart of their teaching was *aretē*, 'goodness' or 'excellence'. The sophists claimed both to know what *aretē* was in any given field, whether politics, religion or private morality, and to be able to teach that *aretē* to their pupils. Their opponents claimed either, like Plato, that *aretē* was not teachable or, like Aristophanes in agreement with Plato, that their versions of *aretē* were immoral and wrong. It seemed to them and to many ordinary Athenians that the traditional view of morality – whereby universal standards of human behaviour were sanctioned by the gods – was threatened by the sophists' ability to present apparently convincing arguments on both sides of any moral issue.

**4.47** Almost all the sophists who taught in Athens were foreigners, men like Protagoras of Abdera and Hippias of Ēlis (a sophist of prodigious memory and learning). This is one reason why Aristophanes in his *Clouds* chose to attack Socrates as the representative of all the sophists, since Socrates was an Athenian citizen and so could be identified as a more immediate threat by an Athenian audience. Plato vehemently denied that his revered master was a sophist, partly on the technical ground that he did not accept pay from his pupils; but in the *Apology* (which purports to be the speech Socrates delivered in his defence at his trial in 399) Plato makes Socrates say that Aristophanes' play had influenced many Athenians. The charges against him were that he had corrupted the young and been unorthodox in religion, but the former was clearly the crucial one. Socrates' pupils had included the opportunistic Alkibiades and the openly traitorous Kritias (cf. 2.37 and H.I.57–8).

Socrates' condemnation did not mean the end of higher education in Athens. Far from it. At some time in the 390s Isokrates set up the first 'university' at Athens, essentially a school of advanced rhetoric, and his example was soon followed by Plato and his more philosophically based Academy. However, these institutes of higher learning no longer occupied the centre of the Athenian political stage in the way that the sophists had done, on occasions, during the latter part of the fifth century.

**4.48** Yet even if these institutions were not as central to the political life of Athens as individual thinkers had been in the fifth century, they still engaged fiercely in debates between themselves. Isokrates attacked both the sophists for their verbal quibbling and Plato for his 'head-in-the-clouds' attitude to philosophy, and dedicated his own school to the principle of utility in education. The debate is still with us. In the following passage (*c.* 370), Isokrates attacks philosophers for their useless speculations:

There are some who are very proud of their ability to formulate an absurd and paradoxical proposition and then make a tolerable defence of it. There are men who have spent their lives saying that it is impossible to make or to deny a false statement or to argue on both sides of the same question; there are others who maintain that courage and wisdom and justice are all the same, that we are not born with any of them but that they are all the concern of a single kind of knowledge; and there are still others who waste time on disputes which are quite useless and liable to get their pupils into trouble . . . They ought to give up this hairsplitting pedantry which pretends to find in verbal argument proof of absurdities which have in practice long been refuted, and turn to the real world and give their pupils instruction in the practicalities of public affairs and some expertise in them. They should remember that it is much better to be able to form a reasonable judgement about practical affairs than to have any amount of precise but useless knowledge, and that it is better to have a marginal superiority in affairs of importance than to excel in detailed knowledge of no consequence.

The truth is that they care for nothing except making money out of the young. This is what their so-called philosophy with its concern with disputation for its own sake can do. For the young, who give little thought to private or public affairs, particularly enjoy completely pointless argument. One can well forgive them for that, for they have always been inclined to extremes and taken in by startling novelties. (Isokrates, *Helen* 1ff.)

## (4) Work and slavery

**4.49** If we were to judge Athenian attitudes to work by those presented in the surviving literary sources, we would conclude that traditional agrarian values were still unchallenged in the fifth and fourth centuries. Wealth means agricultural wealth derived from the land, which guarantees social stability and status. Work means gentlemanly farming or the tilling of a peasant plot. Trade and manual craftsmanship are despised, being deemed suitable only for slaves, foreigners or the urban proletariat (cf. 1.10).

Here more than anywhere else the leisure-class bias of our sources can seriously mislead. These are long-standing upper-class attitudes, traceable as far back as Homer and Hēsiod. But they were intensified as political power swung away from the landed elite to the *dēmos* (in the sense of the mass of poor Athenians) and as slavery became ever more prevalent in agriculture and manufacture. It is unlikely that these values were entirely shared by those Athenians and non-Athenians who earned their living from manual crafts, petty retail trading and the host of other occupations necessary to the relatively large and complex society of Athens.

## (i) Farming

**4.50** At the outbreak of the Peloponnesian War, so Thucydides records, the majority of Athenians were still countrymen born and bred and had their homes in the rural districts of Attica. The following long years of warfare saw a demographic shift from country to city as the Spartans wreaked havoc on Athenian farmland, especially after their permanent occupation of Dekeleia north of Athens in 413. The plays of Aristophanes often bear witness to the sense of loss felt by the Athenian peasant farmer: as was pointed out at 1.21, he regarded his rural residence as nothing less than his *polis*.

**4.51** None the less, the Athenian economy remained unassailably rural at its base, and the pattern of widely dispersed landownership does not seem to have altered significantly throughout our period. The ideal of the self-sufficient farmer remained intact. This is a major reason why Athens was (as remarked in 3.14) largely free of the *stasis* (civil strife) that increasingly racked most other Greek states from the late fifth century onwards. By the standards of the subsequent Roman Empire even large estates were comparatively small. Athenian grandees tended to own properties in several different areas of Attica rather than add field to field in their hereditary *dēmos*. To run their estates they employed slave overseers in the manner recommended by Xenophon's Iskhomakhos, the ideal gentleman-farmer. The overseers supervised a work-force of slaves, but these were not organised in the large chain-gangs familiar from the American South. For the crops grown in Attica – above all, wheat and barley, the vine and the olive – did not demand large and concentrated labour-forces for their efficient production (see 1.9ff.).

**4.52** Smallholders produced less for the market than for their own *oikos* consumption. They could not afford so many slaves as their rich fellow citizens, but it would be a mistake to suppose that even relatively poor Athenians would not try to keep at least one slave for farm work. Mediterranean dry farming is cyclical, with short bursts of intensive energy at the times of ploughing, planting and harvesting interspersed with longish stretches of relative inactivity (cf. 1.11). It would therefore have been uneconomic for a smallholder to keep several slaves who had to be housed, fed and clothed even when not economically productive. But against this iron economic law must be set the fact that even one agricultural slave could on occasion provide his master with the leisure without which political activity would have been physically impossible. Participation by the largest possible numbers of citizens was of the essence of the Athenian democracy. In this sense the democracy was based on slave labour.

## (ii) Manufacture

4.53 In many if not most Greek oligarchies, where political rights depended on wealth, landownership was a requirement of full citizenship. In the Athenian democracy the links between landownership, citizenship and inherited property were not quite so tight; a proposal to make it so was put forward in 403 but rejected. Even landless men whose income came wholly from urban sources could hold the highest offices of state. This is what was meant when it was pointed out earlier in this chapter that under the democracy the four Solonian census groups based on agricultural income lost some of their political significance (4.7). But the proportion of such propertyless men was small.

The reactionary Plato saw in this separation between landownership and citizenship one of the characteristic evils of democratic government, and he goes on about the cobblers and other rude mechanicals whose votes in his view controlled the decisions of the *ekklēsia* and lawcourts. Undoubtedly the percentage of citizens who were craftsmen was highest in Athens, but, unlike Plato, we have to keep a sense of proportion.

4.54 The very word 'manufacture' may be misleading if it conjures up visions of large-scale industrial enterprises mass-producing goods for widespread distribution and consumption. When we consider the crafts in Athens, we must forget the Industrial Revolution and think ourselves back into a relatively primitive system of cottage industries employing small numbers of workers and operating at an almost unbelievably low level of technology; even the word 'system' may be inappropriate. One example

4:15 Ploughing and sowing. Early 6th century.

will perhaps sufficiently show the scale on which Athenian handicraft production operated. Throughout the fifth century, when Athenian potteries provided almost all the luxury tableware for the entire Greek world, it is reliably estimated that no more than 500 potters and painters were active in all.

Athenian manufacture, in other words, was carried on in small workshops. The two largest establishments of which we hear, which are among the largest known in all antiquity, employed respectively about 120 and about 50 (slave) workers. The typical Athenian craftsman, though, worked on his own or with a few slave assistants (no free man would work for another for a wage unless compelled to do so by poverty – cf. 3.18). There must have been hundreds if not thousands of artisans to satisfy the needs of a city the size of Athens, a city which boasted among other things complex architectural masterpieces like the Parthenon and had a regular demand for elaborately constructed ships of war. Yet these and other artefacts were produced by a multitude of individual specialists, not by large firms with a battery of mechanical aids at their disposal (see 7.64ff.).

### (iii) Trade

4.55 A great deal of modern discussion has been centred on the amount of trade conducted in and through Athens, the way that trade was organised, and the connection between trade and politics. Again, as with crafts, the wisest course is to think away modern notions such as trade cycles, balance of payments deficits and multinational shipping companies. Athenian trade – that is, the trade passing within and through

4:16  Making shoes to measure. Late 6th century.

Athenian territory which was by no means exclusively in the hands of
Athenian citizens – was economically speaking a relatively minor affair in
comparison with agriculture and was run on lines that seem to us not
merely simple but almost naive (cf. 1.11–13). The Athenian state, unlike a
modern state, took very little direct interest in, and certainly did not share
the modern preoccupation with, increasing exports. The major exception
to the rule of state indifference, the grain trade, is treated in the next chapter precisely because it is more a matter of politics than economics
(5.74ff.).

4.56 The Peiraieus is a natural emporium or trading centre for the
Aegean, and in the fifth century it became the centre of the commerce of the
entire eastern Mediterranean world (cf. 1.23, 32). Yet at the beginning of
the century Athens had no commercial port properly speaking, and her
naval harbour was the beach at Phaleron. By the middle of the fifth century
Peiraieus had become virtually a separate city, laid out on the grid plan by
Hippodamos of Milētos, linked to Athens by the Long Walls, and provided
with both commercial and naval harbours and the appropriate dock
facilities.

The Peiraieus handled a remarkable variety of goods. But these did not
all reach Athens simply through private commercial channels. The
anonymous Athenian pamphleteer (almost certainly not Xenophon) who
wrote in the early part of the Peloponnesian War rightly stresses the role
played in the exchange of goods and raw materials by Athenian sea power:

Where will a city rich in timber for ship-building dispose of its goods without the
agreement of the rulers of the sea? If a city is wealthy in iron, copper or flax, where
will it dispose of its goods without the consent of the rulers of the sea? But these are
just what I need for ships – wood from one, iron from another, and copper, flax,
and wax from others . . . Although I do nothing, I have all these products of the land
because of the sea, while no other city has two of them. ([Xenophon], *Constitution
of Athens* 2.11–12)

A passage from the comic poet Hermippos concentrates more on luxuries
than necessary imports:

From Kyrene stalks of silphium and hides of oxen,
From the Hellespont mackerel and salted fish of all kinds,
From Thessaly puddings and ribs of beef . . .
From the Syracusans pigs and cheese . . .
Those cities, those products. From Egypt rigging
For sails and papyrus, from Syria frankincense,
From glorious Crete cypress for the gods,
From Africa ivory in plenty at a price,

4:17  Chopping up a tunny fish. C. 470.

From Rhodes raisins and dried figs bringing sweet dreams,
From Euboia pears and well-fleeced apples,
From Phrygia slaves, . . .
From Pagasai servants with a brand-mark on them,
From the Paphlagonians Zeus' own acorns and glossy
Almonds, the adornments of a dinner,
From Phoenicia the fruit of the palm and fine flour,
From Carthage carpets and bright-coloured cushions.
                              (Quoted in) Athenaeus 1.27–8

4.57 Two points stand out from these passages: Athens' dependence on imports for such basics as shipbuilding timber (cf. 6.4, 36), and the fact that importation is assumed to be by sea. Both were constants of Athenian history. In the middle of the fourth century, when Athenian sea power was at a low ebb, Xenophon in a pamphlet entitled *Revenues* (*Poroi*) put forward a series of remarkable proposals by which, so he argued, Athens would be made enormously more attractive to foreign traders who would then be encouraged to settle as *metoikoi*. Thus Athens could be assured of a steady supply of necessary imports. The proposals were not adopted, partly because some of them would have blurred status distinctions between citizens and *metoikoi*. But the Athenians did take other measures to facilitate commerce and to ensure that the state took its share of the profits. (What they significantly did not do was anything to help the main Athenian exports of oil, wine and silver or to give preference to Athenian over foreign traders.)

4.58 They appointed market commissioners (*pōlētai*) to regulate transactions in Peiraieus and the *agora* of Athens. They auctioned out the right to collect the 2% tax on the value of goods entering and leaving the Peiraieus; in one year we happen to know that this tax yielded 36 talents (see 5.68–9). In cases of dispute involving traders there were special courts appointed, and a new kind of trial was established that had to be concluded within one month so that traders could be on their way as quickly as possible and avoid paying the compulsory metic tax (4.67). One type of lawsuit represented in the surviving speeches arose out of an Athenian innovation designed to encourage long-distance trade in goods of high value. The innovation is known as the bottomry loan and is worth spending a little time on.

4.59 For all its economic and strategic significance to Athens much Athenian trade was in the hands of non-Athenians – metics, foreigners and slaves. But Athenian citizens might own a cargo boat or they might finance trading. One way of financing it was through the bottomry loan (i.e. a loan made against a ship's cargo). This type of loan was made, at very high rates of interest (up to 120%!), to enable a trader to purchase a cargo. Loans rarely exceeded 2,000 drachmas and were for the duration of one trip only. If the cargo was carried safely to its destination and sold, the loan was repayable, with interest, but if for any reason the shipment failed to arrive (for the hazards of Mediterranean and Black Sea navigation, see 1.4–5, 1.15), the borrower owed nothing. This type of loan, which is first attested in 421, thus contained an element of insurance. Here we see the tiny seed of Lloyd's of London. We have no idea how extensively this method of financing trade was used, but we do know from lawcourt speeches that it was open to abuse by determined swindlers who might scuttle the ship and thereby hope to escape repayment of the loan. Here two crooks are caught in such an act (cf. 5.74–7):

The agreement was, as is usual in such affairs, that the money would be paid back on the ship's safe arrival; but in order to defraud their creditors they laid a plot to sink her. Accordingly Hegestratos, when they were two or three days on the outward voyage, went down by night into the hold and started to cut through the ship's bottom. Meanwhile Sdenothemis here remained on deck with the other passengers. But the others on board heard the noise Hegestratos was making and rushed below to prevent the damage being done in the hold. Hegestratos was caught in the act and anticipating punishment took to his heels, and when the others followed in pursuit jumped overboard, and because it was dark missed the ship's boat and was drowned. He was a bad man and he came to a bad end, very appropriately suffering himself the fate he had planned to inflict on others. His fellow conspirator and accomplice here at first pretended that he knew nothing of the attempted crime and was as alarmed as the rest of them; he tried to persuade the bow-officer and the crew to embark in the ship's boat and abandon the ship forthwith, on the ground that there was no hope of her staying afloat and that she would go down immediately. In this way their object would be achieved, the ship lost, and their creditors defrauded. But he was not successful because our agent on board opposed him and promised a large reward to the crew if the ship was saved, as by god's grace and the courage of the crew she was, and made a safe landfall in Kephallenia. (Demosthenes (*Against Sdenothemis*) 32.5)

**4.60** One striking feature of these and other speeches concerning Athenian trade is the high proportion of the named long-distance merchants (*emporoi*) who are neither Athenian citizens nor even resident aliens but foreigners; local retail traders (*kapēloi*), by contrast, were Athenians or *metoikoi*. The speeches cannot be taken as a representative sample of evidence, but they do support the strong impression given by our sources as a whole that trade overseas was not something an Athenian citizen would typically go in for and that, though it might yield handsome profits on occasion, it did not confer prestige on its practitioners. Similarly banking, which in any case was nothing like our own but consisted simply of money-lending and exchanging the currencies of different Greek states, was usually conducted by slaves.

**4.61** Finally, coinage. In a sense it is quite misleading to discuss coinage in the context of trade, since it was not invented to facilitate trade nor did it ever come to play the role in trade that bills of exchange do today. Still, after the invention of bronze coins of small denominations in the later fifth century coinage did occupy a more important place alongside traditional barter in small-scale local market exchange; and Athenian silver coins, which were worth what they weighed and were renowned for their purity,

4:18 Athenian silver coins of the 5th century: tetradrachm, drachma, triobol, trihemiobol, obol (one sixth of a drachma), hemiobol.

could always be exchanged outside Attica as bullion. Here is Xenophon again in his pamphlet, *Revenues*:

In the majority of cities traders must bring a return cargo with them, as the currency they use is not valid abroad; but at Athens most goods that are of use to anyone can be taken as return cargoes, and if one does not want to do this, one can export silver, an excellent commodity, since wherever one sells it one makes a profit on the original outlay. (Xenophon, *Poroi* 3.2)

### (iv) Slavery

**4.62** Slaves at Athens had an intimate though far from happy relationship with Athenian silver coinage. Almost all the miners who extracted the silver in gruelling conditions from the Laureion mines (perhaps as many as 40,000 at the peak) were slaves; and so too was the state official charged with testing the purity of the coinage (*dokimastēs*). Slaves have already been mentioned in several other contexts in this chapter – their numbers, and their employment in agriculture, manufacture and banking. This section aims to provide a brief general summary of their origins, status, functions and treatment in Athenian society.

Slavery as an institution was very rarely questioned in the ancient world (cf. 3.25). But characteristically one of those rare instances occurred at the height of the sophistic movement, when some enlightened spirits held that slavery was contrary to nature and, because it was based on force, morally wrong. They were very much out on a limb; even the writers of utopias could not imagine a world without slave labour. Aristotle spends the open-

4:19 A Thracian slave-girl with a jar on her head fetches water (cf. 1:11); note the tattoo marks on her arms and neck, a sign of her foreign origin. C. 475–450.

ing chapters of his *Politics* trying, not very successfully, to refute those unorthodox sophists and prove that slavery was natural (cf. 2.53).

**4.63** Force was the basis of the relationship between master and slave, whose rightless condition represented the extreme version of forced labour (cf. 3.18, 25). In some other Greek states, notably Sparta and Thessaly, there were large subject populations with restricted rights, whose status is best described as that of serfs. The chief difference between these populations and slaves at Athens is that the serfs enjoyed some kind of family life on the land that had once belonged to their ancestors. Slaves, in the sharpest possible contrast, had been uprooted from kith and kin in their native lands and transported forcibly to an alien environment. This extract from a document recording the compulsory sale of property belonging to men convicted of sacrilege in 415 well illustrates the equation of slave and outsider:

The property of Kephisodoros, (*metoikos*) living in Peiraieus: slaves – Thracian female, 165 drachmai; Thracian female, 135; Thracian male, 170; Syrian male, 240; Karian male, 105; Illyrian male, 161; Thracian female, 220; Thracian male, 115; Scythian male, 144; Illyrian male, 121; Kolkhian male, 153; Karian boy, 174; little Karian boy, 72; Syrian male, 301; Maltese (?) male, 151; Lydian female, 85.

This document, which gives the most detailed information on Athenian prices, suggests that by the end of the fifth century, when the slave trade had been firmly established for some two centuries, slaves were relatively cheap to buy in the Athenian slave-market. (A drachma was then the daily wage of a skilled worker.) This helps to explain the wide distribution of slave ownership in Athenian society. Most slaves came from the north and east – Thrace, the Danubian lands, Asia Minor. Warfare was the chief source: captives would be sold by their captors to slave-dealers and put on the markets of the Aegean (6.2). But some Thracians, according to Herodotus, actually sold their own children into slavery out of poverty. Other slaves were the victims of piracy, though under the Athenian empire piracy was much reduced in the Aegean. A few slaves at Athens were home-bred, but these were very much the exceptions.

**4.64** As a general principle a slave was by definition a man or a woman without enforceable legal rights. Slaves were chattels, mere property, of which their masters would dispose as they wished (cf. 4.14). Slaves therefore stood near or at the bottom of the social scale. Nevertheless, within the broad category of slaves distinctions of status existed. In the first place there was the distinction between public slaves like the *dokimastēs* and *hupēretēs* and private slaves such as the Laureion miners: the former group, which also included most famously the state police force of Scythian archers, was regarded as an elite. Also relatively privileged slaves were the skilled craftsmen who were either hired out by their masters or were actually set up by their masters in independent workshops in return for a percentage of their earnings. These skilled men might hope eventually to buy their freedom, though in general manumission does not seem to have been nearly as likely a prospect in Athens as it was to be for Roman slaves. Domestic slaves probably fared rather better than their agricultural counterparts and could in some cases strike up something of a personal relationship with their master or mistress. An adult male slave could be asked to look after the children, or be used to look after an old man (e.g. the blind Teiresias in Greek tragedy was traditionally accompanied by an adult male slave). Lowest of the low were the mine slaves, for whom death from their appalling conditions of work probably came as a blessed release (cf. H.I.15; 5.70).

**4.65** There were no specifically slave occupations, apart from that of policeman and perhaps miner and banker too. Otherwise Athenians and slaves might perform exactly the same tasks, sometimes side by side, as when dressing vines in rural Attica or fluting the columns of the Erekhtheion on the Athenian Acropolis. This explains why the Athenians, like other Greeks, on the whole judged a job less by the nature of the work than by whether the worker was self-employed or working for another (cf. 3.18). It was the mark of the truly free man, according to Aristotle, not to live for the sake of someone else. The word for a household slave, which was also used as a general word for slave (*oiketēs*), could be applied to a free domestic servant too.

**4.66** Slavery, to repeat, was basic to the Athenian democracy in that it gave even quite ordinary Athenians the leisure to participate in the political process. Its strictly economic significance is harder to fathom in the absence of the kind of statistical data a modern economist takes for granted. If our approximations for the population of Athens are of the right order of magnitude, slaves will have made up between one-quarter and one-third of the total (4.11). The greater part of Athenian production, in other words, will have been due to free not servile labour. It has been suggested that the level of production and the productivity of labour might have been higher if the Athenians had relied less on slaves, but it is not clear that slavery was the sole or even the main cause of the stagnation of Greek technology. It is not irrelevant that many of the major technological advances were applied not to peacetime industry but to warfare, which the Greeks regarded as a major means of production. Slavery to us (and to a tiny number of ancient Greeks) is a great evil. But in the final analysis it was the growth of slavery that permitted the growth of citizen freedom and democracy at Athens, two key aspects of 'the glory that was Greece' (4.52).

### (v) Metoikoi *and* xenoi *(foreigners)*

**4.67** Athenian citizenship laws, as we saw, were remarkably strict. Any non-Athenian, whether Greek or barbarian (non-Greek), was legally an alien and could only live in the state of Athens under special conditions. After residence of one month a foreigner was compelled to register as a *metoikos* and pay the tax of one drachma a month (*metoikion*). He or she had to have an Athenian patron (*prostatēs*), and though *metoikoi* had access to the courts, were admitted to theatres and festivals and could make a handsome living, there was never any doubt of the inferiority of metic status as such. Above all, *metoikoi* (with rare exceptions) suffered the crippling disability of not being allowed to own real property in Attica.

**4.68** Most Athenian *metoikoi* were probably quite humble people who for one reason or another found it easier to live in the broader compass of a large and cosmopolitan state like Athens than in their native lands (cf. 4.9). In 401–400 the Athenians voted rewards to those *metoikoi* who had helped in the overthrow two years earlier of the vicious Spartan-backed junta of the Thirty Tyrants (cf. H.I.57–8). Here are listed in the official document some of the honorands, some of whom are in all probability *metoikoi*, together with their often lowly occupations:

Khairedemos, a farmer; Leptines, a cook; Demetrios, a carpenter; Euphorion, a muleteer; Kephisodoros, a builder; Hegesias, a gardener; Epameinon, an ass-driver; [ . . . ]opos, an oil merchant; Glaukias (?), a farmer; [ . . . ], a nut seller; Dionysios (?), a farmer; Bendiphanes, a bath-maker (?); Emporion, a farmer; Paidikos, a baker; Sosias, a fuller; Psammis, a farmer; . . . Eukolion, a hired servant; Kallias, a statuette maker. (Austin/Vidal Naquet no. 70)

**4.69** But by far the most famous of the metic liberators stands at the very opposite end of the social spectrum, hobnobbing on equal terms with the Athenian aristocracy. This is Lysias, speech-writer extraordinary, who with his brother (murdered by the Thirty Tyrants) owned the shield factory with some 120 slave workers mentioned above (4.54). His father was from Syracuse and is said to have been invited by none other than Pericles, his friend, to take up residence in Athens. At the beginning of the *Republic* Plato portrays this distinguished and surely exceptional family of *metoikoi* at home in the Peiraieus (see 1.24). Evidently they have settled easily into

Athenian society. Men like these were bound to perform expensive public services (the *leitourgiai* discussed in 5.71) or, if rather less well-off, to serve as hoplites in the Athenian army (6.17).

**4.70** One other category of *metoikoi* deserves separate mention, that of the ex-slaves. When an Athenian slave was freed he did not, as in Rome, become a citizen but a *metoikos*. There were probably relatively few ex-slave *metoikoi* in the large metic population, but one – the exception to prove many rules – cannot be omitted from any survey of Athenian society. Pasion, who died about 370, began his career in Athens as a slave banker. By his master's will he was not only manumitted but he acquired the bank – and his master's widow as well. Thereafter as a *metoikos* he grew inordinately rich, owning not only the bank but a shield factory staffed no doubt by slave-workers. Diplomatically he disbursed large amounts of his wealth for the benefit of the Athenian people – so large that in return he was rewarded with a public grant of Athenian citizenship. On his death he bequeathed to his son landed estates worth 20 talents scattered in three *dēmoi*. He thus appears to come closest to the 'American dream' notion of the entrepreneur who rises from rags to riches and public esteem, and his career would seem to contradict traditional Athenian conceptions of rigid status boundaries. (His son Apollodoros, the speaker of the *Against Neaira* speech, presents himself as more Athenian than the Athenians in his moral and political outlook.) However, the main point is that Pasion was exceptional, indeed virtually unique. Most slaves and most *metoikoi* had no prospect of such elevation.

**4.71** Foreigners in Athens (*xenoi*, s. *xenos*) were by definition temporary residents: for example, statesmen or ambassadors on official business, aristocrats visiting their guest-friends, participants and spectators at the Panathenaic Games, passing merchants and so on. We can safely say that Athens welcomed more *xenoi*, Greek and non-Greek, than any other state, and welcomed them positively too. In this respect as in so many others Athens stands at the opposite pole to Sparta, who periodically conducted expulsions of *xenoi* (*xenēlasiai*) (p. 57, section 39).

One of the most interesting examples of Athenian tolerance towards *xenoi* may be seen in a state decree of 333, part of which runs as follows:

Since it has appeared that the merchants of Kition [in Cyprus] are making a legitimate request in asking the people for [the right] to acquire land on which they propose to erect a temple of Aphrodite, the people shall resolve to grant to the Kitian merchants [the right] to acquire land on which to erect their temple of Aphrodite, in the same way as the Egyptians have erected their temple of Isis. (LACTOR no. 9, inscription no. 16)

4:20  A doctor treats a patient while others wait. C. 470.

The establishment of foreign and, in the case of Isis, non-Greek cults on Athenian soil shows how varied and relatively open a society Athens had become (2.12).

### *(vi) Greek doctors* (cf. 7.10, 32)

**4.72** Greek doctors are a good example of a class of people who travelled widely in Greece. They were craftsmen, and they either travelled round from town to town, serving the country districts on their way, or set up shop in the big cities. The writer of a work ascribed to Hippocrates recommends that the good doctor pay careful attention to the environment of any new place he is visiting:

When a doctor moves to a town with which he is unfamiliar, he must consider its situation, its prevailing winds and its aspect. For a northern, southern, eastern or western aspect each has its own particular effects. He must bear these carefully in mind, as well as the water supply, which may be drawn from marshy ground, may be soft or hard and drawn from high and rocky ground, or again brackish and harsh. The soil may be barren and waterless or wooded and well-watered, hollow and humid or dry and cold. The inhabitants will have different life-styles; they may drink heavily, take a midday meal and be rather inactive, or take a lot of hard exercise, have a good appetite and drink little. ([Hippocrates], *Airs, Waters and Places*)

**4.73** For doctors who set up shop, the consulting-room was a meeting-place where rival methods of treatment could be discussed. Standards of practice were very variable. Some appear to have maintained very high standards in both practice and ethics, and treatises were written on how the good doctor should behave at all times, as the following extract shows:

The physician ought to have a certain flexibility; inflexibility repels both the sick and the healthy. He must keep a close watch on himself and not give himself away;

he must not gossip to laymen, but say no more than is necessary; to say too much is to expose his treatment to criticism.

Look out for your patients' misbehaviour. They often lie about taking the medicine you have prescribed. They won't take medicine they don't like, whether purges or tonics, and they sometimes die in consequence. They never confess what they have done, and the doctor gets the blame.

Carry out your treatment in a calm and orderly way, concealing most things from the patient, while you are treating him. If you have to give orders give them cheerfully and calmly, turning a deaf ear to any comments. Reproach your patient sharply and emphatically at times, and at others encourage him with concern and careful attention; but do not reveal anything about his present or future condition. Statements on the subject often cause a setback . . .

When you have made these arrangements and the necessary preparations for what is to be done, decide before you enter the sick man's room what treatment is needed. For what is needed is often not reasoned diagnosis but practical help. So you must predict the outcome from your previous experience; it makes a good impression and is pretty easy. When you do go in be careful how you sit and maintain your reserve. Be careful of your dress, be authoritative in what you say, but be brief, be reassuring and sympathetic, show care and reply to objections, meet any difficulties with calm assurance, forbid noise and disturbance, be ready to do what has to be done. ([Hippocrates], *Decorum* 7–13, excerpts)

At the same time, there were also drug-sellers, herbalists, users of magic spells and a fair sprinkling of charlatans too. We learn from the orator Antiphon of at least one case where death was due to the incompetence of the doctor, and [Hippocrates] comments that, although good doctors are in a minority, so, fortunately, are serious diseases.

**4.74** The good doctor was advised to arrange his shop, which would be open to the street, so as to obtain the best light for examining and operating, without exposing the patient to the glare of sunlight, and to ensure a supply of pure water and clean bandages. One picture shows two scenes from a doctor's consulting-room, the waiting patients and the doctor actually treating someone (4:20).

Doctors also went to treat patients elsewhere, as happened in the following incident when Ariston was beaten up by a gang of thugs:

It so happened, gentlemen of the jury, that Euxitheos of Kholleidai, a relation of mine who is here in court, and Meidias, who were on their way home after a dinner-party, came up with me when I was nearly home, followed me as I was carried to the bath and were present when the doctor arrived. I was so weak that they decided, in order to avoid carrying me the long distance from the bath to my house, that it would be best to take me to Meidias' house for the night. And they did so.

The immediate result of the blows and maltreatment to which I had been subjected was that I was reduced to the condition I have described to you and to which all the eye-witnesses whose evidence you have heard have testified. Subsequently, though my doctor said that the swellings on my face and my bruises did not give him any great anxiety, I suffered from continuous fever and severe body-pains, particularly in the ribs and abdomen, and was unable to take food. And indeed my doctor said that, if I had not had a spontaneous haemorrhage when the pain was at its worst and my attendants in despair, I should have died of internal suppuration; it was the haemorrhage that saved me. (Demosthenes (*Against Konōn*) 54. 9–10)

**4.75** For such visits the doctor was advised to have ready a portable medicine case, containing drugs and instruments for immediate use. Doctors acquired experience of dealing with wounds by serving on military expeditions, and the exercises on the *palaistra* ('wrestling-ground') provided much experience with setting broken bones and treating strains and dislocated joints.

**4.76** Fees were a matter for negotiation, but preferably not until the patient was on the mend. In large cities, public doctors were sometimes employed by the state to give free treatment to the poor. Such a post marked the peak of a career, and would be awarded on the reputation built up in private practice. We know that at Delphi a health tax was levied to pay the stipend of the public doctor.

## (5) Death, burial and the ancestors

**4.77** A prospective office-holder had to satisfy the state concerning his family tombs (see 4.13). Both cremation and inhumation burial were practised in fifth- and fourth-century Athens, the choice being left to family preference and external circumstances. In a land as little wooded as Attica cremation might be expensive, but the victims of the plague that struck Athens in 430 were necessarily cremated, in unruly heaps, and the invading Spartans withdrew from Attica when they saw the smoke arising from the funeral pyres (H.I.36).

The desire for proper burial at the hands of relatives and in one's native land was extremely strong. The plot of Sophocles' *Antigone*, where Antigone is forbidden by state decree to give due burial to a brother, will have struck a deep chord with the Athenian audience (2.25). Equally powerful was the concern to leave a good name among the living, to live on after death in vivid memory. Hence the conventional stress on honour (*timē*) and glory (*doxa*) in the funeral speeches (*epitaphioi*) delivered over the graves of dead warriors, such as Pericles' quoted on p. 56.

4:21 Divine healing was carried out by Asklepios, the god of medicine. 4th century.

**4.78** Pericles begins by speaking about the Athenians' ancestors, both their dim and distant ones and the immediately preceding generation who had created the radical democracy and the empire. He then eulogises the Athenians' present way of life and in particular their democratic ideals. Only now does he come to those who died in the first year of the Peloponnesian War and deliver himself of an unforgettable metaphor: (p. 59, section 43, ll. 17ff.). Finally, Pericles addresses the relatives of the dead. Their parents should not be downcast, he says, but rather uplifted by their good fortune in having had sons who died gloriously in the service of their country; their sons and brothers should strive to equal their fathers' and brothers' achievements, though this will be a near-impossible task.

**4.79** Memory of the dead was preserved by the performance of annual rites at the family tomb (cf. 1.31, 4.13). Some of these rites are poignantly rendered on Athenian vases, especially those designed to hold the special oil used. If a family could afford it, a gravestone or other grave-marker might be erected, and a suitable laudatory epitaph cut. The tomb itself also depended for its elaboration on the family's wealth. Funerals of the rich were liable to become the occasion of ostentatious expenditure, and attempts were made as early as the time of Solon to limit by law the amount that could be spent, the number of mourners in attendance and the extent of public demonstration of grief. The formal lament was restricted to the house and the graveside, and the funeral procession had to be held before dawn (cf. 3.3).

**4.80** On the day of the death the corpse was formally laid out (the

4:22   At her lying-in-state
(*prothesis*) a young woman is
mourned by a member of her
family who tears her long hair
and by an old slave-woman
who cradles the dead girl's
head. C. 470–460.

*prothesis*), usually in the house of the next of kin, by the close female relatives. The body was ritually bathed, anointed, dressed and garlanded, and laid on a bier. Friends and relatives came to pay their last respects, and women, dressed in black with their hair shorn, beat their breasts and sang a ritual lament; from antiquity to today this lament has been the prerogative of women in Greece. Since death was considered to pollute both house and mourners, a vessel containing spring water was placed outside the entrance to warn others of the pollution and to enable visitors to purify themselves on departure (cf. 2.35).

The funeral took place on the third day, before sunrise. The corpse, wrapped in a shroud and covered by a cloak, was carried to the graveyard in procession (*ekphora*). In cremation the body was burnt on a pyre and the ashes collected in a funerary urn. Burial took place either in the city cemeteries of Athens, which were sited outside the walls to avoid pollution, or on the family estates of the deceased in the countryside. Offerings were made at the grave, and libations of wine and oil poured. Then followed the funeral banquet.

**4.81** This description of course applies only to normal times. But in the chaos created by the Great Plague:

The funeral rites which had customarily been observed were disrupted and they buried their dead as best they could. Many had resort to the most shameless methods of burial, for lack of the necessary means and because so many deaths had already occurred in their households. They would anticipate the builders of a pyre, put their own dead on it and set it alight, or throw the corpse they were carrying on top of an already lighted pyre and leave it. (Thucydides, *Peloponnesian War* 2.52)

This awful scene Thucydides describes in the context of the general indifference to every rule of religion and law engendered by the plague.

**4.82** After the funeral, further rites were performed on the ninth day, and annually thereafter. Maintenance of the family tombs and the annual rites of the dead were the most solemn duties. This was partly for religious reasons. Although there was no 'orthodox' Athenian view on the afterlife, there was a widespread feeling that, unless the dead were properly disposed of and their graves properly tended, their aggrieved spirits might somehow escape to haunt the living like spectres (cf. 2.56). But possibly even stronger were motives that we would call social and political rather than religious. The great patriotic rallying cry to the Athenians at Salamis in 480 was to fight to free their land, the tombs of their ancestors and the shrines of the gods. It was these too which the country people of Attica were so loth to abandon in the face of the Spartan invasions during the Peloponnesian War (cf. 1.21). In the tombs of their ancestors the Athenians saw tangible witnesses of what bound them together as Athenians. So we return at the finish to the sense of community with which this chapter began (cf. 2.40).

4:23 The close affection of husband and wife is shown on this gravestone of Ktēsileos and Theano. C. 410.

4:24 A woman and boy bring offerings to a tomb. C. 450–425.

# 5
# *Athenian democracy and imperialism*

## (1) Theory and practice of democracy

**5.1** We are all democrats now, from the People's Democracies of the Soviet Bloc and China to the Western and Japanese democracies of the Free World. This makes it hard to appreciate that as recently as the eighteenth century 'democracy' was a dirty word, and even more difficult to think back to a time when there was no democracy anywhere in the world.

Democracy was an Athenian invention. It was traditionally ascribed to Kleisthenes (cf. H.I.11), but the reforms of 508/7 that go under his name were the result of forces beyond his individual control. Nor did the democracy spring from Kleisthenes' head fully formed. It continued to develop over the nearly two centuries of its existence from 508 to 322. Within this

5:1 Democracy places a wreath on the head of Dēmos, a personification of the people of Athens. 336.

period the democracy at Athens was twice interrupted, in 411 and 404, by oligarchic counter-revolutions fostered by the pressures of the Peloponnesian War (H.I.52; 57–8). Still, taken as a whole, the Athenian democracy represents one of the longest periods of popular self-government in human history, equalled among modern countries only by the United States.

5.2 That is a staggering achievement. It is important, though, to make a basic distinction between ancient democracy and the various modern versions of government that lay claim to the name. In antiquity government of the people by the people for the people was carried out directly by the citizens, whereas in modern democracies voters (who are not necessarily all citizens) elect representatives to take decisions on their behalf and have no direct access to political power on a day-to-day basis. Athens, in short, was a direct, not a representative, democracy.

5.3 One other point of terminology needs to be grasped firmly from the outset. The Athenians through Kleisthenes invented a system of democracy in 508/7, but the word 'democracy' was not invented until some time, perhaps more than a generation, later. Kleisthenes, in other words, could not have called himself a democrat even if he had wanted to. Instead, it seems that the contemporary description of his constitution was *isonomia*, equality under the law. This was an ideal that had obvious appeal for Athenians of all political hues, especially after the overthrow of tyranny, and carried no specific constitutional implications.

5.4 *Dēmokratia*, on the other hand, was ambiguous in a different and potentially explosive way. Literally it means the *kratos*, 'sovereign power', of the *dēmos*. But *dēmos* had a wide range of senses in fifth- and fourth-century Athens. It could mean the people as a whole, the entire adult male citizen body; *or* the common people, the poor majority of the citizen body, as opposed to the upper classes; *or* democracy as a constitution; *or* the democrats in contrast to those who favoured another form of government; *or* the democratic state of Athens; *or* the people of Athens in the *ekklēsia*; or, finally and rather confusingly, the local division, deme (see 4.16, 19ff.). Only the first two of these senses are relevant to the invention of the *dēmokratia*. Thus a supporter of the Kleisthenic system would naturally claim that it meant the rule of the people as a whole. But an opponent of the system, a conservative member of the Athenian upper class, for example, might well see it as the sectarian rule of the common people over their betters, the dictatorship of the proletariat.

5.5 The available evidence unfortunately does not reveal who invented the word *dēmokratia* nor when precisely it was coined. Aeschylus in his

*Suppliant Women* of (probably) 463 makes Theseus speak of the *dēmou kratousa kheir*, 'the sovereign hand of the *dēmos*', which may be a poetic equivalent; but *dēmokratia* itself is not found before Herodotus' *Histories* and [Xenophon's] *Constitution of Athens*, both of which were probably 'published' in the 420s. However, *dēmokratia* does not make an appearance in the passage of Herodotus where the relative merits of democracy and two other forms of government are discussed.

**5.6** The passage purports to be a debate between three Persian aristocrats in about 522. In actual fact it is wholly Greek in its inspiration (cf. P.1–2), and the original version of the debate on which Herodotus based his was probably not composed until well into the fifth century. The passage is also the earliest example of political theory in history. In Herodotus' Persian Debate the speakers argue respectively for democracy (rule by all, here called *isonomia*), oligarchy (rule by some, in this case the few rich and well-born), and monarchy (rule by one, here hereditary kingship):

Otanes recommended that the Persians should bring their political affairs into the open.

'I think', he said, 'we should no longer have a single monarch; this is neither an agreeable nor a good form of government. How can it admit of proper adjustment when it allows one man to do what he likes without being answerable for it? Even the best of men put in that position is bound to overstep the bounds of normality. The advantages he enjoys breed pride, and envy is deeply engrained in human nature [cf. 3.9]. A man with these two faults is wholly evil ... The worst feature of all is that he breaks down traditional law and custom, puts men to death without trial and subjects women to sexual violence. The rule of the people on the other hand has the most attractive of descriptions, rule by all (*isonomia*), and moreover does none of the things a monarch does. Offices are filled by lot, officials are answerable for what they do, and all questions are publicly debated. I propose therefore that we do away with monarchy and raise the people to power. For in the people everything is comprised.'

This was the opinion of Otanes. He was followed by Megabysdos, who recommended oligarchy: 'To be rid of the violence of a tyrant only to fall under the violence of an uncontrollable mob would be intolerable. A tyrant at least knows what he is doing, the people has no knowledge at all. How can it have, being uneducated and without sense of what is right and proper? It rushes mindlessly into public affairs like a river in flood. So leave democracy to the enemies of Persia, and let us give power to a chosen few of the best among us.'

This was the opinion of Megabysdos, and Dareios finally gave his in the following words: 'We have three alternatives before us, democracy, oligarchy and monarchy. The last of the three seems to me to be far the best. There can be nothing better than government by the best man. With his abilities his control of the people will be above criticism, and the measures he takes against wrongdoers will have maximum secrecy. In conclusion, I ask where did we get our present freedom from and who gave it to us? Was it from democracy or oligarchy or monarchy? My view is that as we were given our freedom by one man we should preserve that kind of constitution; and quite apart from this, it is never an improvement to change our ancestral laws and customs so long as they work well.' (Herodotus, *Histories* 3.80ff.)

5.7 Apart from a few passages in Thucydides there are hardly any surviving statements of democratic ideals. The reason is that almost without exception our sources are out of sympathy with or actively hostile towards the Athenian democracy. The less extreme critics preferred the moderate constitution of Kleisthenes to the radical democracy ushered in by the reforms of Ephialtes in 462 (see H.I.27, 5.27). The more extreme critics dishonestly called for a return to the 'democracy' of Solon (which was not a democracy at all) or of Kleisthenes, or openly advocated some form of oligarchy. Either way, democratic theory, such as it was, has to be reconstructed in reverse from the attacks of its critics, together with Aristotle's *Politics*. But its two chief elements are clear. These were the beliefs that democracy alone guaranteed true freedom and that it guaranteed equality (cf. 7.14).

5.8 A final point about the evidence. The best known or at least the most famous period of the democracy is the second half of the fifth century. Yet so far as the machinery of the democracy is concerned, by far the larger portion of the available source material – inscriptions as well as literary sources – comes from and relates to the fourth century. This matters because, as already pointed out, the democracy continued to develop. The democracy of the 320s that is described in some detail in [Aristotle's] *Constitution of Athens (Athēnaiōn Politeia)* was not the democracy of Pericles. Our picture of the democracy at any stage before the 320s must always contain an element of hypothesis.

## (2) The democracy in action

5.9 The structure and functioning of the Athenian direct democracy differed radically from those of our representative democracy. There were, for example, no government departments, no civil service, and only a limited archive system. Decisions were taken and executed directly by the Athenian People.

## (i) Two meetings of the ekklēsia (the Assembly)

**5.10** We begin with two accounts of the *ekklēsia*, a basic institution of the democracy, in action some seventy years apart. On each occasion Athens is at the crisis point of a war she is about to lose. Feelings are therefore running unusually high, and these meetings should not be taken as entirely typical. Neither of these accounts is from an unbiased source. They do nevertheless give a good impression of the immediacy of political proceedings in Athens and they introduce some of the most important features of the democracy.

In 406, towards the close of the Peloponnesian War, against the run of events Athens won the sea-battle of Arginoussai (H.I.55). Victory, however, was marred by the fact that Athenian survivors had not been picked up, and this had prompted Theramenes, a man of oligarchic sympathies, to institute proceedings against the overall commanders for dereliction of duty. An *ekklēsia* was held at which the commanders were permitted to speak, though more briefly than the law allowed, in their own defence. They claimed that rescue had been made impossible by a violent storm and they offered to produce witnesses to that effect.

With such arguments they were on the point of convincing the *ekklēsia*; many citizens were standing up and offering to go bail for them. However, it was decided that the matter should be adjourned to another meeting of the *ekklēsia*, for by then it was late and it would have been impossible to count votes, and that the *boulē* should draft a motion as to what sort of trial the men should have . . .

Then came the meeting of the *ekklēsia*, at which the *boulē* presented its motion on the proposals of Kallixenos [a supporter of Theramenes]: 'Resolved that, since speeches in accusation of the *stratēgoi* and speeches of the *stratēgoi* in their own defence have been heard at the previous *ekklēsia*, all the Athenians do now proceed to hold a ballot by tribes; that for each tribe there be two urns; that in each tribe a herald proclaim that whoever thinks the *stratēgoi* did wrong in failing to rescue those who won the victory in the naval battle shall cast his vote in the first urn; whoever thinks contrary, in the second urn; and that, if it be decided that they did wrong, they be punished with death and handed over to the Eleven and their property be confiscated, and a tithe thereof belong to the Goddess [*Athēnē*].'

. . . Next a summons was served on Kallixenos for having made an unconstitutional proposal; Euryptolemos . . . and a few others were the sponsors. Some of the People showed their approval, but the great mass shouted out that it was monstrous if the People were not allowed to do whatever they pleased . . . Then some of the *prutaneis* declared that they would not put the motion to the vote, since it was illegal. At this Kallixenos again mounted the rostrum and made the same complaint against them as had been made against Euryptolemos, and the crowd shouted that if they refused to put the motion to the vote they should be prosecuted.

This terrified the *prutaneis*, and all agreed to put the motion except Socrates . . . who said he would do nothing contrary to law.

Euryptolemos then rose and spoke in defence of the *stratēgoi* . . . After making this speech, he moved that the men should be tried in accordance with the decree of Kannōnos, each of them separately. The *boulē*'s motion, however, was that judgment should be passed on all of them together by a single vote. When there was a show of hands to decide between the rival motions, they decided at first in favour of Euryptolemos' proposal, but when Menekles alleged illegality under oath there was a fresh vote and the *boulē*'s motion was approved. They then voted on the eight *stratēgoi* who had taken part in the battle. The vote went against them, and the six who were in Athens were executed. Not long afterwards, however, the Athenians repented and voted that preliminary plaints be lodged against those who had deceived the People. (Xenophon, *Hellenika* 1.7.7–35)

**5.11** Sixty-seven years later, Athens was at war with King Philip II of Macedon (H.I.75, 81). Athens had once been an ally of Philip, by the terms of a peace which had been concluded between them in 346. But under the influence of Demosthenes, above all, the Athenians had been persuaded that Philip meant Athens harm and they had declared war on him again. One evening in November 339 news reached Athens that Philip had seized Elateia in central Greece and so was menacing Athens. This is how Demosthenes nine years later described the scene:

It was evening when the messenger arrived for the *prutaneis* with the news that Elateia had fallen. They were in the middle of supper but rose at once, cleared the stalls in the market-place and burnt the wicker screens, while others sent for the *stratēgoi* and summoned the trumpeter. The whole city was soon in an uproar.

At dawn next day the *prutaneis* summoned the *boulē* to the *bouleutērion* while you all made your way to the *ekklēsia*; the whole body of citizens had taken their places before the *boulē* could proceed to business or propose a motion. Subsequently, when the *boulē* had arrived and the *prutaneis* had reported the news they had received the messenger was introduced and told his tale; the herald then put the question 'Who wishes to speak?' No one came forward. He put the question again a number of times, but there was still no response, though all the *stratēgoi* were there and all the active politicians, and though our native land was crying aloud for someone to speak for her salvation. It was I who answered her call on that day, and came forward to address you. (Demosthenes (*On the Crown*) 18.169)

## (ii) Ekklēsia

**5.12** The two principal bodies involved in these emergencies were the *boulē* (Council of 500), with its subcommittee of *prutaneis* ('Presidents'), and the *ekklēsia* ('Assembly'). All state emergencies landed first in the lap

5:2  The Pnyx of Athens where the assembly (*ekklēsia*) met.

of the fifty *prutaneis* who lived at state expense in the *tholos* on 24-hour call. It was their duty to summon a meeting first of the full *boulē* of 500 and then, if necessary, of the *ekklēsia* (cf. 1.33, 35; p. 207).

**5.13** The *ekklēsia* when summoned (*ekklēsia* means a body that is 'called out') gathered on the Pnyx hill to the south-west of the *agora*, the civic centre of Athens (1.25, 29). Citizens over eighteen and duly enrolled on their deme register made up the *ekklēsia*, which was the decision-making organ of the democracy. In the fifth century the *ekklēsia* made laws as well as decisions of policy (*psēphismata*), but after the restoration of democracy in 403 the function of passing general laws (*nomoi*) was delegated to a smaller body of Lawmakers (*nomothetai*).

**5.14** Under the constitution of the 320s, as described by Aristotle, the *ekklēsia* held four stated meetings in each of the ten civil months. It is not known whether this prescribed number was already laid down in the fifth century. The first meeting of the four was called the sovereign (*kuria*) *ekklēsia*, at which the grain supply, national defence and the continuation of officials in office had always to be discussed. Emergency meetings could be called at need. The *ekklēsia* always met early in the day, emergency or not, and at least from the late fifth century onwards loiterers in the *agora* were herded in with a red-dyed rope by the state police force of 300 Scythian slaves who were in charge of public order. The credentials of the participants were checked, order was kept by the Scythians, purification offerings were made, a curse on traitors pronounced, and business began.

In his *Akharnians* of 425 Aristophanes, with typical comic licence, describes the start of an *ekklēsia* meeting from the viewpoint of a poor countryman who yearns for peace and return to his rural habitation:

There's a sovereign *ekklēsia* this morning and the Pnyx here is deserted. They're chattering in the *agora*, edging this way and that to avoid the red rope. Even the *prutaneis* aren't here yet either. They'll be late and then they'll come jostling each other for the front row like nobody's business, flooding down in throngs. But as for peace they don't care a damn for that. O my city, my city! And I'm always the first to come to the *ekklēsia* and take my place; and then when I'm alone, I groan and yawn and stretch, fart and don't know what to do, longing for peace, looking out over my *dēmos*. So now I have come quite prepared to shout and interrupt and slang the speakers if any of them says a single word other than on the subject of peace. But here are the *prutaneis* arriving – now that it's noon. (Aristophanes, *Akharnians* 17ff.).

**5.15** In the fifth century the chairman of the *prutaneis*, the *epistatēs*, was also chairman of the *ekklēsia*. The herald read out the agenda, and the people voted whether to discuss the items, as we saw in the trial of the *stratēgoi*. If they wished to do so, the herald proclaimed 'Who wishes to speak?' Speakers mounted the rostrum (*bēma*), and after the speeches a vote was taken by show of hands (hence Aeschylus' *dēmou kratousa kheir* (see 5.5)). In theory anyone could address the *ekklēsia*, but the matters to be discussed and voted upon had first to have been considered by the *boulē*, which in this respect acted at the *ekklēsia*'s steering committee.

**5.16** This was the *boulē*'s most basic function. Its prior deliberation (*probouleusis*) determined whether and in what form a matter was placed on the *ekklēsia*'s agenda in the shape of a proposal for discussion (*probouleuma*); an example appears in the Xenophon passage (5.10). But the *ekklēsia* was free to amend any proposal it objected to. Many decrees surviving on stone record amendments, which usually add minor details to a *probouleuma* approved by the *ekklēsia*. (The Athenians inscribed their decrees on stone (*stēlai*) to provide a permanent public record that any citizen might consult if he wished (cf. 1.35)). The *ekklēsia*, moreover, could demand that items be placed on the agenda of the next meeting. There was never any question of the *boulē*'s being able to dictate to the *ekklēsia*, which here as elsewhere was sovereign.

**5.17** Theoretically, as we have seen, all citizens could attend the *ekklēsia* and address it. But how many citizens would in practice attend, and who in fact spoke? The citizen population fluctuated in our period

5:3 *Ostraka* cast against Kimon and Themistokles in the 470s can be seen to have been inscribed on adjoining sherds of the same vase.

between about 20,000 and 50,000 (see 4.8). Yet in 411 it was claimed that no more than 5,000 had ever actually attended an *ekklēsia*, no matter how grave the business. True, it was in the interests of those making this claim to minimise the numbers alleged to attend, and the figure probably applies chiefly to wartime conditions when many citizens would be serving abroad; but there are reasons for thinking that 5,000 is not so very wide of the mark, at least for the fifth century. The Pnyx, as laid out in the fifth century, seems not to have been able to accommodate more than 6,000. (Ostracisms required a quorum of 6,000 voters, but these were held in the *agora*.) For an ordinary business meeting citizens would presumably not have been willing to make the long journey from outlying demes such as Sounion or Rhamnous and lose precious working time without financial compensation. Even urban dwellers seem to have needed the encouragement of the red-dyed rope.

5.18 In the fourth century, conditions were different. Around 400, pay for attendance at the *ekklēsia* was first introduced to compensate, partially, for loss of working time; by 392 it had been raised twice to three obols, and in Aristotle's day it was up to a drachma, with a drachma and a half for a sovereign *ekklēsia* (see 5.14). Between 400 and 330 the Pnyx area was enlarged to accommodate 6,500–8,500 citizens, and in 330 a massive enlargement enabled up to 13,000 or so to attend. Also in the fourth century we learn that certain measures, for example the ratification of a grant of honorary citizenship, required a quorum of 6,000. It seems therefore that in the fourth century, although the population was declining, 6,000 was a normal attendance figure, whereas in the fifth century it had been achieved only on exceptional occasions (the debate over the Sicilian Expedition, perhaps). Most of those who attended probably came from the city of Athens and Peiraieus rather than the country demes.

**5.19** Even 5,000, though, was a mass meeting, and the physical task of addressing it must have caused problems. Then again the essential quality of a speaker in the *ekklēsia* was persuasiveness based on knowledge and foresight, and, as the rise of sophistic education suggests, persuasiveness demanded rhetorical skill and not simply a stentorian voice (cf. 7.16–19). Moreover, during the fifth century the business of running not only home affairs but also an empire made the *ekklēsia*'s task of decision-making far more complex. So for all these reasons it is understandable if the ordinary Athenian did not normally respond to the herald's question 'Who wishes to speak?'

**5.20** Those Athenians who did respond would do so regularly and they became known as the *rhētores* (orators) or *hoi politeuomenoi* (the politicians). They were a definable group within the citizen body, though many of them are no more to us than names on an *ostrakon* (potsherd used for ostracism). In the fifth century the ten *stratēgoi* would frequently be *rhētores* as well as, or rather than, military and naval commanders; Pericles, for example, owed his influence with the *ekklēsia* in large part to his oratorical skills. But in the fourth century, the age of the specialist, a division of function hardened between *rhētores* like Demosthenes, who was never a *stratēgos*, and semi-professional commanders (cf. 6.24–5).

**5.21** *Rhētores* spoke in the *ekklēsia* as individuals or leaders of small groups of likeminded politicians. There were no political parties as we understand them in the direct democracy of Athens. Within these informal groupings certain men will have been the best speakers and hence their spokesmen. Aristocratic traditions still counted for something in leadership in the fifth century, but these became increasingly weakened. The career of Kleon, a non-aristocrat who made his fortune from slave-run manufacture rather than landowning, marks a turning-point (H.I.37). He and men like Hyperbolos, Androkles and Kleophon were labelled 'demagogues' by the more conservative Athenians such as the comic playwright Aristophanes. *Dēmagōgos* means literally 'leader of the *dēmos*', and since the Athenian democracy was at one level government by mass meeting they were an indispensable part of the democratic structure; Pericles was no less a 'demagogue' in this sense than Kleon. But by calling Kleon and others like him 'demagogues' Aristophanes meant to imply that they were mis-leaders of the People, who pandered to the *ekklēsia*'s baser whims. Thucydides, over-simplifying, laid the blame for Athens' defeat in the Peloponnesian War at the door of the 'demagogues'.

**5.22** Concerning the length of an *ekklēsia* meeting we are not well informed, but it seems that even normal (as opposed to emergency) meetings usually occupied less than a full day. Since the *ekklēsia*'s principal business was foreign policy, meetings would be shorter during the winter months outside the sailing season, and shorter still if rain stopped play. Comparative evidence from the Cantons of Switzerland today suggests that it is perfectly possible for 6,000 people, all with the right to speak, to discuss and vote, by a show of hands, on a dozen motions in the space of two to four hours. In practice, perhaps, votes in the Athenian *ekklēsia* were only counted if the decision was close or if, as may have happened in the trial of the *stratēgoi* in 406, a secret ballot by pebble (*psēphos*) was held.

### (iii) The boulē (Council of 500)

5.23 The way in which the *boulē* was recruited and operated shows the care the Athenians took to keep comparative amateurs in this body and so prevent its acquiring political power independent of the *ekklēsia*'s control. *Bouleutai* (s. *bouleutēs*) ('councillors') had to be Athenian citizens aged thirty or over. They served for one year at a time and could not serve more than twice in all. They sat in the Council House (*bouleutērion*) in the *agora*, except on annual festival days, and the public could observe their proceedings. Some time before 411, when the *boulē* was temporarily abolished by an oligarchic counter-revolution, pay was introduced for *bouleutai* in accordance with the democratic principle that no citizen should be debarred from participating in government by poverty. We do not know how much the pay then was, but it was probably not less than the three obols paid to jurymen (5.47).

5.24 The 500 consisted of fifty men from each of the ten 'tribes' (*phulai*), artificial divisions of the citizen body designed to ensure that citizens from all districts of Attica were equally represented. This tribal system was a democratic innovation by Kleisthenes and replaced the four ancient kinship tribes which had been dominated by leading aristocratic families (see H.I.5; 11). Candidates for the *boulē* were chosen by the democratic process of the lot at *dēmos* level, each *dēmos* being required to contribute a fixed number of *bouleutai*. The lowest number was three, the highest twenty-two, and it may be the case that in the smallest *dēmoi* practically every citizen will have had to have been a *bouleutēs* once in his life. The civil calendar was divided up into ten 'months'. Each of the ten tribes provided each month the fifty *prutaneis* (see 5.12); the tribe 'in prytany' was the one which had been appointed by lot to preside for that month. The *epistatēs* ('chairman') of the *prutaneis* was selected daily, again by lot, and could serve as such only once ever. There was therefore a better than

70% chance of each member of the *boulē* becoming *epistatēs*, since there were 35 or 36 days in each month of the civil calendar. On the day of the trial of the *stratēgoi* in 406 (5.10) it is possible that the *epistatēs* was none other than Socrates – remarkable if true, because his membership of the *boulē* at that time was the only public office he ever held in all his long adult life.

5.25 So far as our evidence goes, the *boulē*'s chief function was to be the steering committee of the *ekklēsia*. It could not initiate policy. Apart from preparing the *ekklēsia*'s agenda, it was essentially an administrative body, seeing to it that the decisions of the *ekklēsia* were duly carried out. The *boulē*, or rather its various boards and subcommittees (we know of about ten in Aristotle's day) therefore administered the necessary financial and other transactions and, together with the courts, exercised a general supervision of the responsible officials. One example will illustrate. Here is part of Aristotle's description of the *boulē*'s responsibility for Athens' major military arm, the navy (cf. 6.42):

The *boulē* is in charge of the completed triremes, the tackle stores and the ship-sheds, and builds new triremes . . . The triremes are constructed under the supervision of a board of ten members of the *boulē*. The *boulē* inspects all public build-

5:4 The interior of the *tholos* on the west side of the *agora*; it was here that the *prutaneis* lived during their presidency.

ings, and if it decides that someone has committed an offence, it reports him to the people, and hands him over to the jury court if they find him guilty. ([Aristotle], *Constitution of Athens* 46.1–2)

### (iv) The Areopagus (Areios Pagos, 'Crag of Arēs')

5.26 The Areopagus council, so named from the crag of Arēs between the Acropolis and the Pnyx where it had met from time immemorial, was the oldest permanent organ of the Athenian *polis*. It had in fact been the governing body under the aristocratic and oligarchic regimes that preceded the democracy. The nine *arkhontes*, who from the time of Solon were elected from his top two property groups (*pentakosiomedimnoi* and *hippeis*), automatically became members of the Areopagus after their year of office (H.I.5, 8). Before the reforms of Kleisthenes (who was *arkhōn* 525/4), the *arkhōn*ship had been the chief office of the Athenian state; but under the democracy its power and prestige were progressively diminished. The chief *arkhōn* continued to give his name to the civil year (for example, the year we call 403/2 was referred to by Athenians as 'the *arkhōn*ship of Eukleides'). But in 501 the new office of *stratēgos* began to take over some of the *arkhōn*'s functions (see 5.29); in 487 *arkhontes* ceased to be elected but were chosen instead by the democratic device of the lot; finally in 458/7 the *arkhōn*ship was thrown open to the third of

5:5   A model of some of the buildings on the west side of the *agora*, including (from left to right) the round *tholos*, the *bouleutērion* at the back and the Royal Stoa at the left. The temple of Hephaistos and Athēnē sits above on Market Hill.

Solon's property groupings, the *sdeugitai*, and in practice even the *thētes*, the lowest property grouping, could hold the office.

**5.27** This loss of prestige inevitably affected the Areopagus, whose position under the democracy became increasingly anomalous. It was a hangover from a past epoch, yet it retained some considerable political powers. It was 'guardian of the laws': that is, the body ultimately responsible for the Athenian law-code, and it held the scrutiny of officials after their term of office or their impeachment during their term. This anomaly was put right by the reforms of Ephialtes in 462/1 which created the radical democracy (as opposed to the moderate democracy of Kleisthenes). The powers of the Areopagus were redistributed among the *ekklēsia*, the *boulē* and the jury-courts (H.I.27). Ephialtes himself paid for his reforms with his life, but the reforms remained in force.

**5.28** Nostalgic conservatives like Isokrates attempted to boost its importance in the fourth century, but the strictly political power of the Areopagus was ended in 462/1. It has been argued that Aeschylus was among those who approved the reforms of Ephialtes; this is how he makes Athēnē speak at the trial of Orestes in his *Eumenides* of 458:

Hear now my ordinance, men of Attica, who pronounce judgment at this first trial ever held for bloodshed. Henceforth, even as now, this court of judges shall abide unto the people of Aigeus for ever. And . . . on this Crag of Arēs Reverence, in the hearts of my citizens, and Fear her kinsman shall withhold them from doing wrong . . . And I counsel my citizens to maintain and hold in reverence neither anarchy nor tyranny, nor to banish fear completely from the city. For who among men is righteous that fears nothing? Stand then in just awe of such majesty . . . This tribunal I do now establish, inviolable by lust of gain, august, quick to avenge, a guardian of the land, vigilant in defence of them that sleep. (Aeschylus, *Eumenides* 681ff.)

As this foundation myth was meant to show, after 462/1 the Areopagus retained its function as a court. In addition to cases of deliberate homicide (other forms of homicide were treated by the *ephetai*), it tried cases of arson and some forms of sacrilege. For example, it investigated the status of Phanō, illicitly married to the democracy's chief religious official; and it tried men accused of damaging the sacred olive trees, from whose fruit was pressed the special oil given in magnificent amphoras as prizes at the Panathenaia (2.49). In 403 the Areopagus was entrusted with the supervision of Athens' newly revised law-code in deference to the judicial experience of its members (see below for the judicial functions of the *arkhontes* after 462/1).

## (v) Officials (arkhai)

5.29 In the sixth century the *arkhontes* had been the senior officials of the Athenian state. But in 501 the Athenians created the new office of the ten *stratēgoi*, one from each of Kleisthenes' new tribes. A democratic innovation, it illustrates both the development and the character of the democracy. For some years its role in relation to the office of the war *arkhōn* (*polemarkhos*) was ambiguous, and this ambiguity was neatly and near-fatally exposed by the battle of Marathon in 490. Miltiades, the prime mover of Athens' famous victory, was a *stratēgos*, but the war *arkhōn* Kallimakhos still had an expensive memorial set up to him as if he had been in undisputed overall command of the army (H.I.13). It is not surprising therefore that the *arkhōn*ship was downgraded soon after Marathon, as we saw; and it was as *stratēgos* that Themistokles, Kimon and Pericles held sway over the *ekklēsia*.

5.30 With the Peloponnesian War, though, there came a further change. Athens' leading general, Demosthenes (not to be confused with the orator, his fourth-century namesake), was outshone in political leadership by the 'demagogues'. Kleon, it is true, did act as *stratēgos*, but at first almost by accident, and he never showed any real capacity for military command. (H.I.41). Nikias was almost the last to achieve success both as *stratēgos* and as politician. In the fourth century the distinction between the *stratēgoi* and the politicians became absolute, e.g. Demosthenes was never a *stratēgos*, and yet his authority over the *ekklēsia* and lawcourts was unparalleled, whereas Phokion was *stratēgos* forty-five times but had to bow to Demosthenes' policies.

5.31 Unlike almost all Athenian *arkhai* under the democracy, the *stratēgoi* were appointed by election (by the *ekklēsia*) and not by the lot. The Athenians had the sense not to sacrifice efficiency to democratic principle in an era when they were at war three years in every four. Besides, the *stratēgoi*, unlike all other *arkhai*, could hold office as often as the electorate wished and in successive years. Pericles, for example, was *stratēgos* fifteen times running between 443 and 429. If a *stratēgos* spoke in the *ekklēsia* he could expect to be listened to, but it was his speech, not his office, that decided whether or not his advice was accepted. If the policies he advocated proved unsuccessful, he would quickly lose the *ekklēsia*'s ear and perhaps his life. Being *stratēgos* could be a risky business; even the great Pericles was fined (and perhaps deposed from office) in 430 (cf. 3.9–10).

5.32 The fining of Pericles illustrates another cardinal principle of the democracy, that all officials should be responsible to the people. From highest to lowest all Athenian *arkhai* had to render accounts (*euthunai*) at the end of their usually annual term of office. The audit was held in two stages. First any financial accounts were examined by thirty Reckoners (*logistai*, a subcommittee of the *boulē*); then it was open to anyone who wished to prefer a charge of misconduct. In this way the Athenian people kept control of the executive and administrative branches of government.

5.33 It is therefore quite wrong to regard Pericles as the uncrowned king of Athens. On the other hand, he did exercise extraordinary and almost unparalleled ascendancy over the *ekklēsia* for a great many years, and this ascendancy needs explaining. It was partly due, as noted above, to his skilful oratory; but more especially it was because his policies consistently appealed to the majority of Athenians as being in their best interests. They did so mainly because Pericles was an unashamed imperialist, and naval imperialism benefited the Athenian masses (5.91). But it was equally crucial that Pericles' imperialist policies should work in practice. Pericles, too, would probably have had to struggle to maintain his ascendancy during the Peloponnesian War, as the fine imposed on him in 430 suggests. Other, non-democratic, forces were at work as well. For example, after the disaster to the Athenian fleet in Sicily had nearly brought Athens to its knees, there was an oligarchic *coup* in 411 organised by a number of aristocratic dining-societies known as *hetaireiai* (for *symposia*, cf. 4.32). So the picture is not one of uninterrupted democratic bliss.

5.34 With the exception of the *stratēgoi*, other high-ranking military officials, and the Hellēnotamiai (treasurers overseeing imperial expenditure in the fifth century), all officials were selected by lot (cf. 3.3). Only the *arkhōn*ship and the office of the Ten Treasurers of Athēnē had a property qualification attached to them, and even here the poorest Athenians could stand for the *arkhōn*ship (cf. 5.26). Otherwise the qualifications were that one should be thirty or over and a citizen of good standing. To test a candidate's standing he had to undergo a preliminary scrutiny (*dokimasia*). The beginning of the passage where Aristotle lists the questions put in the *dokimasia* has been quoted in 4.13; the remainder runs as follows:

... then [they ask] whether he treats his parents well, pays his taxes, and has performed the required military service. When these questions have been put, the candidate is required to call witnesses. When he has produced his witnesses, the question is put: 'Does anyone wish to bring a charge against this man?' If an accuser appears, the accusation and defence are heard, and then the matter is decided by show of hands in the *boulē* or (if the *boulē*'s decision is appealed against) by a ballot in the jury-court. If no accuser appears, the vote is held immediately. ([Aristotle], *Constitution of Athens 55.3–4*)

Candidates who survived this ordeal proceeded to take their oath of office standing on a block of stone (see 1.33).

5.35 Athens lacked a bureaucracy in the modern sense, but she made up for it somewhat by the relatively huge number of officials in post every year. In the second half of the fifth century, according to [Aristotle's] *Constitution of Athens*, there were 700 officials with domestic responsibilities and up to the same number whose duties lay outside Attica in the Athenian empire. This figure for fifth-century domestic officials has been thought too high, because Athens apparently had more in the fourth century and yet Aristotle lists only some 350 for his day. However, when the (incomplete) evidence of contemporary official inscriptions is taken into account, Aristotle's listing is seen to be only partial, and a recent study concludes that there may well have been 600 to 700 officials in his day. If we add in both those officials who were not technically described as *arkhai* (because they were not appointed directly by or responsible directly to the People) and the 500 *bouleutai*, then out of a citizen population of some 21,000 in the 320s no less than 5% would have held office in any one year – or some 8% of those of the required minimum age. The percentages would presumably have been smaller in 431 (almost twice as many officials but a population well over twice as large), but even greater in the last years of the Peloponnesian War. Athens was indeed a direct democracy and perfectly satisfies Aristotle's criterion of citizenship in a democracy, that all citizens should have the chance of filling *arkhai* in turn.

5.36 The titles and duties of all Athenian officials cannot be listed here; in any case, most were relatively minor and indeed part-time. But some were outstandingly important. Next to the *stratēgoi* in importance were the nine *arkhontes*. The 'eponymous' *arkhōn* dealt with state festivals and family matters, and gave his name to the year. The king *arkhōn* supervised the religious life of the city. The *polemarkhos*, despite his name, was after Ephialtes' reforms a civilian official in charge of lawsuits involving metics and foreigners (5.26–7). The other six *arkhontes*, known as *thesmothetai*, organised the state's administration of justice and themselves presided over the various jury-courts.

5.37 Below the *arkhontes* come 'the Eleven', officials responsible for executing legal punishments and maintaining the state prison (*desmōtērion*). To keep order in the city, they were assisted by the 300 Scythian archers, but the apprehension of criminals was largely left to pri-

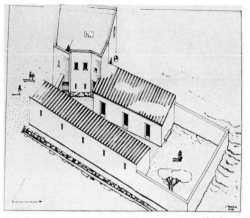

5:6  Drawn reconstruction of the state prison of Athens; it was here that Socrates was held.

vate individuals (5.48). Then there were the various treasurers, most notably the Hellēnotamiai and the Ten Treasurers of Athēnē already mentioned. Religious treasurers also included such important men as the *epistatai Eleusinothen*, who were the financial administrators of the Eleusinian Mysteries. Among the other treasurers we know, for example, of the Treasurers of the People, who managed the annual allowance made for public expenses like the publication of decrees. Especially important in the fourth century was the manager of the fund which enabled poor Athenians to attend festivals.

5.38 Of the minor officials we may mention the *astunomoi*, whose job was to see that streets and highways were kept clear and clean; the ten *agoranomoi*, who supervised markets, collecting fees from stallholders and checking for adulterated goods; the *metronomoi*, who checked weights and measures by the official standards in the Mint and the *tholos*; and finally the *grammateis*, who acted as secretaries to the *boulē*, the *ekklēsia*, and the *thesmothetai*.

In the absence of anything like a foreign office, diplomatic relations were conducted through heralds (*kērukes*) and envoys (*presbeis*). These important figures need a little further discussion.

### Heralds (kērux, pl. kērukes)

5.39 The *kērux* in Homeric times was an arm of the king, maintaining order at meetings, making proclamations, carrying messages, even serving

5:7 Athenian bronze weights, carrying inscriptions stating that they are official; further inscriptions and symbols (tortoise, shield and knucklebone) indicate their weights. C. 500.

5:8 An Athenian terracotta dry measure with an official stamp and the word *DĒMOSION* ('official') painted on it. 4th century.

wine at meals. He was felt to be under Hermes' protection. In classical Athens, the *kērux* continued to possess special status and was considered to be under divine protection. *Kērukes* were appointed by the *ekklēsia*, paid for out of the public funds and kept at the public expense. In general the presence of a *kērux* indicated that the state was acting in an official capacity. Their duties were wide-ranging. At home, they summoned and controlled meetings of both the *boulē* and *ekklēsia*, and were empowered to accompany official deputations (e.g. when the Eleven went to arrest someone). *Kērukes* could also be sent abroad on the authority of the *boulē* or the *ekklēsia*. In the following decree, they are being sent to ensure that Athens receives its proper tribute:

The *boulē* is to appoint eight *kērukes* to summon representatives from the cities, and ten *taktai* to list and assess the cities liable to tribute . . . The *kērukes* work under the orders of the *taktai* [for their route] and the *ekklēsia* [for what they are to say]. (M and L 69)

But note that they have power only to send a message, never to negotiate.
   **5.40** Abroad, the *kērux* had a vital role to play in the declaration and

cessation of combat. He declared war, he asked for a truce, he opened peace negotiations. In such situations, the *kērux* had to be able to rely upon the immunity which his office gave him. In general, this immunity was respected, since a *kērux* was under the protection of the gods. Any violation of his immunity could meet with divine vengeance.

## Envoys (presbeis, s. presbeutēs, *lit. 'elders'*)

**5.41** *Presbeis* themselves enjoyed no *specific* immunity, though as leading citizens they would almost certainly enjoy private ties as *xenoi* with citizens of the *polis* of their posting. Between states at war *kērukes* would normally be sent first to secure agreement for *presbeis* to be sent, which would impose a moral obligation on the receiving state, or an envoy might be led by a *kērux*, whose task would be to secure safe passage. It was a serious matter to mistreat *presbeis* and normally, even if their arrival was unwelcome or they were dismissed, they would expect simply to be given an ultimatum to leave.

*Presbeis* were often given power to negotiate within stated limits, and were generally important men in their own city. The word *presbeis* implies that they were originally the elders of the state (in Athens the minimum age was normally 50).

**5.42** Sparta regularly sent three *presbeis*, but the number sent by other states might vary, depending either on the importance attached to the mission or on the need for a variety of political views to be represented in the embassy. Serving on a diplomatic mission was a matter of prestige, and a service to the state in which one could take pride. *Presbeis* were selected by the state and given token public funds (1 drachma per day) for the journey, but considerable private expense was likely to be incurred, and even more likely to be recouped one way or another, e.g. by accepting bribes.

**5.43** But *presbeis* were not sacrosanct, as *kērukes* were. Here a sudden attack on the Peiraieus by Sphodrias, a Spartan commander in Boiotia (378), embarrasses the three Spartan *presbeis* who happen to be present in Athens (see H.I.67):

Now it happened that there were ambassadors of the Spartans in Athens at the house of Kallias, their diplomatic agent,* Etymokles, Aristolokhos, and Okyllos; and when the invasion was reported, the Athenians seized them and kept them under guard, believing that they too were concerned in the plot. But they were completely bewildered over the affair and said in their defence that if they had known

---

*The word is *proxenos* (see 5.95).

that an attempt was being made to seize Peiraieus, they would never have been so foolish as to put themselves in the power of the Athenians in the city, and, still less, at the house of their diplomatic agent, where they would most quickly be found. They said, further, that it would become clear to the Athenians also that the Spartan authority did not know of this attempt, either. As for Sphodrias, they said they were certain they would hear that he had been executed by the state. So they were judged to be ignorant of the affair and were released. (Xenophon, *Hellenika* 5.4.22)

### (vi) The jury-courts (dikastēria) and legal system

#### (a) Law and politics

**5.44** The *thesmothetai* were the six officials with overall responsibility for the conduct of justice at Athens (see 5.36). This was an extraordinarily exacting task, because the Athenians – not without cause – had an international reputation for love of going to law (cf. 1.27). The Athenian *dēmos* exercised its *kratos* not only in the *ekklēsia* but also, and increasingly in the fourth century, through the jury-courts.

**5.45** Aristotle in his *Politics* defined the citizen of a democracy as the man with a share in *krisis* and *arkhai*. The *arkhai* we have already discussed (see 5.35). By *krisis* Aristotle meant the power to deliver judgment in a court of law. This may come as a surprise to those readers brought up to disapprove of 'political' trials and the holding of 'political' prisoners. But in Athens, as in ancient Greece generally, there was neither in theory nor in practice any separation of powers. When the Athenian People became master of the courts, as [Aristotle] puts it, they became master of the constitution.

**5.46** In 594 Solon had established a popular court of appeal against the decisions of officials, which was called the Ēliaia. After the reforms of Ephialtes in 462/1 all the various jury-courts were known collectively as the Ēliaia, but now they were courts of first instance as well as appeal courts, and they were often referred to as *dikastēria*. This is because they were jury-courts staffed by jurors (*dikastai*) who numbered from 201 to 2,501 depending on the case. In the fifth century the juries were selected at need from an annual roll of 6,000 jurors, in the fourth century from those who put themselves forward. Strictly, though, 'jurors' is a misleading translation, because there were no judges in our sense and *dikastai* were both judge and jury.

**5.47** The jurors were paid for every day they sat. It has been estimated that, when allowance is made for festivals, *ekklēsiai* and so on, they might sit on between 150 and 200 days in the year (2.43). Payment was introduced by Pericles as a democratic measure and was at first only two obols a sitting. Kleon raised it to three, where it stayed, although this was only half, or less, of the daily wage of a skilled craftsman. Yet if we are to believe Aristophanes' extended satire on the courts, the *Wasps* of 422, elderly Athenians had a passion to serve in the Ēliaia. Here a slave describes his master's mania:

He loves it, this juror business; and he groans if he can't sit on the front bench. He doesn't get even a wink of sleep at night, but if in fact he does doze off just for a moment, his mind still flies through the night to the water-clock . . . And by god, if he saw any graffito by the doorway saying 'Dēmos is beautiful, the son of Pyrilampes', he would go and write by the side, 'The ballot-box is beautiful' . . .

Straight after supper he shouts for his shoes, and then off he goes to the court in the early hours and sleeps there, clinging to the column like a limpet. And through bad temper he awards the long line to all the defendants, and then comes home like a bee (5.61) . . . with wax plastered under his finger-nails. And because he's afraid that some day he may run short of voting-pebbles, he keeps a whole beach in his house. That's how mad he is . . . (Aristophanes, *Wasps* 87–112)

5:9 Reconstructed models of official water clocks for use in the Athenian lawcourts to time speakers. 4th century.

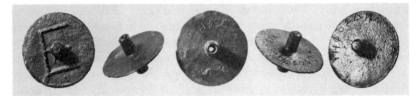

5:10  Athenian bronze ballots with a hollow hub for condemnation and a solid one for acquittal. Some carry the inscription *PSĒPHOS DĒMOSIA* ('official ballot') and a letter to indicate the court. 4th century.

**5.48** However much or little faith we put in Aristophanes' caricature, it is undoubted that the same kind of men applied for jury-service as attended the *ekklēsia*, which as we have seen, could on occasion act as a court. Speakers in the courts therefore often appeal to the jurors no less as citizens than as judges in a particular case. Besides, there was no Justice Department of Public Prosecutions in Athens, no 'case for the Crown', and no proper police force. If the state was wronged, or the community attacked, there was no state body to initiate proceedings for reparation or punishment in the courts. That was left to private initiative. The state depended on 'anyone willing' (*ho boulomenos*) to bring a case – a feature of Athenian justice that gave rise to the notorious *sukophantai* (see 5.63). So although the Athenians distinguished, as do modern courts, between private and public cases, all cases were brought by individuals. In private cases only the injured party could bring a suit, which was then called a *dikē* (murder – oddly, to our way of thinking – counted as a *dikē* in Athens, but cf. 3.13 on the role of the family). In public cases, on the other hand, 'anyone who wished' might issue a writ (*graphē*, so called because it had to be deposed in writing).

**5.49** The example of a particularly important public case, the *graphē paranomōn*, brings all these points together. This writ might be issued against any speaker in the *ekklēsia* who had introduced an allegedly unconstitutional proposal (cf. 5.10). It could be brought by anyone who wished and was intended originally as a constitutional safeguard against attacks on the democracy; its first attested use is in 415, a time of crisis and rumours of subversion (H.I.48–50). But it could also be employed as a weapon to attack a rival politician. In both these uses it went some way to replacing ostracism, which was abandoned in about 416. Once the writ had been issued, the motion, law or decree was suspended, and its proposer brought before a jury court. If the proposer was found guilty of unconstitutional behaviour, the law or decree was automatically cancelled, and the proposer fined (cf. 3.2).

**5.50** In a modern state a second chamber (such as the British House of Lords) generally reviews the decisions of the first chamber, and the Head of State has ultimate veto on acts of parliament. In Athens it was the People as jurors who sat in judgment on the decisions of the People in *ekklēsia*, and it was the proposer, not the decision, who stood to be condemned. Here again we see the cardinal democratic principle of accountability in operation, extended in this case to cover men who might hold no public office at the time. But this also meant that the *graphē paranomōn* could become ammunition in the raging competition for political success (cf. 3.2, 12). Consider the case of Apollodoros, son of Pasion.

**5.51** He had been selected by lot as a *bouleutēs* for 349/8, and in 348, at a moment of crisis in the war against Philip, he (in the words of Theomnestos):

brought forward in the *boulē* a bill and carried it as a *probouleuma* to the *ekklēsia*, proposing that the People should decide whether the funds remaining over from the state's expenditure should be used for military purposes or for public spectacles. For the laws prescribed that, in time of war, funds remaining over from state expenditures should be devoted to military purposes; and when the voting took place there was no one who opposed such use. Even now [late 340s], when the matter is mentioned anywhere, it is universally acknowledged that Apollodoros gave the best advice, and was unjustly treated. Your anger should therefore be directed against the man whose arguments deceived the jurors, and not against those he deceived.

This fellow Stephanos indicated the decree as illegal and took the matter to court. He produced false witnesses to slander Apollodoros saying that he had been a state debtor for twenty-five years, and by making all sorts of accusations that were extraneous to the incident he won a verdict against the decree. ([Demosthenes], (*Against Neaira*) 59.4–6)

This type of case carried no fixed penalty. So once the jury had found a man guilty, first the prosecution and then the defendant proposed alternative fines:

When the jurors were voting to fix the penalty, we begged Stephanos to compromise but he refused; he fixed the amount at fifteen talents with the object of depriving Apollodoros and his children of their civic rights, and causing my sister and all of us the extremest distress and deprivation. For the property of Apollodoros was not worth more than three talents, which made the payment of such a fine quite impossible. Yet failure to pay by the ninth prytany would have doubled the fine, and Apollodoros would have been registered as owing thirty talents to the

Treasury, his property would have been confiscated by the state and sold, and Apollodoros himself, his wife and children, and all of us would have been reduced to extreme destitution. What is more, his other daughter would have been unable to marry; for who would ever have married a girl without a dowry with a father in debt to the Treasury and without resources? . . . I remain therefore deeply grateful to the jurors in the case for refusing to let Apollodoros be ruined and fixing the fine at a talent, a sum he was able to pay, albeit with difficulty. ([Demosthenes], (*Against Neaira*) 59.6–8)

## (b) Trial by jury (the agōn)

5.52 Aristophanes' juror desperate for a conviction, Apollodoros threatened with economic and social ruin, the courts as an instrument for confounding political enemies – all this suggests colourful courtroom dramas. And indeed there were, mainly because of the absence of anything like the due procedure of a modern court. Socrates, in Plato's version of the defence speech he gave at his capital trial in 399, appealed to the jurors not to shout him down. There were no lawyers in the modern sense and the litigants had to speak on their own behalf, though the richer ones might commission a Lysias or a Demosthenes to write their speech for them. There were no strict rules of evidence, and no judge to enforce their observance even if there had been. Witnesses were not cross-examined. Jurors could not be directed on points of law except by the litigants, and they responded to appeals to their emotions and moral prejudices as much as to hard fact (which anyway was difficult to establish). Finally, trials had to be over the same day, and the jurors voted on the issue at once after listening to both sides; they did not retire to a sealed room for private deliberation away from the hurly-burly of the courtroom, let alone look for guidance on points of law from a judge.

5.53 In a system even more open-ended and unpredictable than our modern judicial systems, witnesses were of the highest importance, even though they were not cross-questioned (the lynch-pin of modern court cases). While we might think that impartial witnesses would carry more weight than partial ones, the Greeks were well aware of the importance of *philoi* and knew there was danger in trying to get evidence from someone you did not know, let alone from an *ekhthros* (3.13). The orator Isaios makes the point nicely:

You all know that when we are acting without concealment and need witnesses, we normally make use of our close relatives and intimate friends as witnesses of such actions; but for the unforeseen and unexpected we call on anyone who happens to be present. When evidence is needed in court we have to bring as witnesses persons who were actually present, whoever they are (Isaios, (*On the Estate of Pyrrhos*) 3.19)

**5.54** Further, evidence from slaves could only be accepted if it had been extracted under torture. Slaves, being after all only 'animate tools' (see 4.64), could not be expected to tell the truth without a little compulsion; and again, it was feared that excessive loyalty to, or hatred of, their master might bias their witness. Inasmuch as a slave was a valuable household effect, no master would willingly submit him to torture and possibly serious maiming. This may have had the effect of restricting evidence from such an 'unreliable' source.

**5.55** Against this apparent chaos must be set the extraordinary care taken, at least in the fourth century, to see that a case that ought to come to trial did come to trial and that the jurors were selected in such a way as to eliminate corruption (cf. 5.63). The aggrieved party first presented his opponent with his claim in front of witnesses. Misunderstandings might be smoothed out at this stage. If not, private arbitrators were called in. Both parties agreed on a panel of arbitrators and their terms of reference, and contracted to stand by their decision, which had judicial force. At any stage in a private suit the parties could go to arbitration.

**5.56** If both these methods failed, a summons was served. The aggrieved party visited the *agora*, confirmed (to his satisfaction at least) that the law displayed there supported his case and found out when his type of case was due to be heard. The summons was served orally and the defendant was told before witnesses to present himself to the appropriate *arkhōn* or judicial board on a stated day. On that day the *arkhōn* decided whether the case was actionable; if it was, the plaint was formally deposed in writing, though the accused could lodge official objection. A down payment was made by both parties against costs, which the loser paid in full after the trial. A day was fixed for the hearing by the *arkhōn*, and a copy of the plaint was displayed publicly in the *agora*.

**5.57** The preliminary hearing took the form of a public arbitration, the arbitrator being a citizen beyond military age who was selected by lot. Both sides swore an oath that their case was correct and presented their supporting evidence. If a decision was reached at this stage, it was binding and the case was closed. If not, all the evidence was sealed up in a box (it would be read out in court) and could not be added to later. The box was deposited with the *arkhōn* and the matter submitted to public jurisdiction in a jury court.

**5.58** The care taken over the selection of juries was mainly intended to prevent bribery. This too was the chief reason why Athenian juries were by our standards so enormous. The citizens placed on the jurymen's roll for the year swore to abide by the laws, and each received a ticket with his name on entitling him to serve (the *pinakion*). Jurors for a particular trial were chosen at the last minute by an allotment machine (*klērotērion*), which selected jurors at random and distributed them to courts at random. There was of course no guarantee that a juror would be selected to serve. Once selected, and now armed with a lettered ball drawn from an urn, the juror proceeded to the court marked with the corresponding letter. There he handed in his *pinakion*, which he would get back, together with his pay, at the end of the session. In exchange he was given a short rod (*baktērion*) with paint of a certain colour on it, another device for making sure he went to the right court. Inside the courtroom he received yet another token, this time one enabling him to draw his pay.

**5.59** After this remarkably complicated rigmarole the trial itself may seem a laughably informal affair. So it may not be totally inappropriate if we return to Aristophanes' *Wasps* to sit in on a mock trial. As ever with Aristophanes' fantasy, the humour depends largely on his staying in close touch with everyday reality; and together with the first-hand material unearthed by archaeologists in the *agora*, Aristophanes provides us with much of our evidence for the equipment of a jury court. This is the scenario in *Wasps*.

**5.60** An absurd courtroom has been set up in the home of Philokleon ('Kleon-lover'). His son has agreed to pay him, the sole juror, his usual fee. Philokleon first cries for a railing to separate the jury from the public (we have some evidence that crowds gathered round the open courts and reacted as strongly as the jurors). His son then goes to fetch the lists of impending cases displayed in the *agora*, while Philokleon improvises voting urns with large bowls and presses into service a chamber-pot as a water-clock to regulate the length of speeches. Prayers follow. The son

5:11 An Athenian bronze identity ticket (*pinakion*) with which a citizen eligible for jury service was enabled to enter the court. 4th century.

5:12 Voters place their ballots in jars. C. 470.

announces: 'If any juror is outside, let him come in, since once we've started we won't admit him.' The charge is read, and the speeches begin.

Here we break away from the play: the defendants are dogs and need help to speak. In a real case the litigants would deliver their appeals to the jury, producing written evidence and calling for the relevant laws to be read out. Philokleon then proceeds to vote and, by mistake, acquits the defendant. In our earlier quotation we saw Philokleon clutching his voting-pebble; in the fourth century, bronze ballots were specially made and many of these have been found in the north-east and south-west of the *agora*. The verdict was reached by secret ballot. The jurors placed their ballot in the acquittal or the condemnation urn.

**5.61** If the verdict was 'guilty', and the penalty not a fixed one, as in the cases of Apollodoros (5.51) and Socrates (5.52), then the jurors had to vote again on the punishment. The slave describes Philokleon going home with wax all over his finger-nails (5.47). This is because Philokleon had been voting on the punishment by scratching a wax-covered tablet known as a 'tablet for fines'. A long line in the wax was a vote for the stiffer sentence, a short one for the lighter; Philokleon always went for the heavier sentence.

**5.62** In a *dikē* enforcement of the verdict was left to the individual concerned. Repeated refusal to settle could lead to further suits and eventual loss of full citizen rights (*atimia*, see 5.65, 3.12). If the convicted man refused to pay a fine, the successful litigant was allowed to seize property to the stated amount of the fine (cf. 4.35). The *arkhōn* who presided at the trial was bound to see that the jury's decision was enforced if he could, since he was accountable to the People at the end of his term of office. Even so, enforcement was often difficult in practice. Judgment in a *graphē* and sentences of death were attended to by officers of the state (5.37).

### (c) The Sukophantai

5.63 The Athenians' reputation for litigiousness was unjustified to the extent that they took great trouble to make sure whether or not a dispute ought to come to court. On the other hand, the fact that in *graphai* it was left up to 'anyone willing' to bring a suit did leave the door open to abuse. Towards the end of the fifth century it began to be felt that there were too many men who brought prosecutions, not out of public spirit, but either to curry favour with their political masters or to make a dishonourable living out of the financial rewards of winning a case. Such men became known as *sukophantai* (derivation uncertain), and Aristophanes portrays them, no doubt with comic distortion, in several plays. Here is a scene from his last, *Ploutos* (*Wealth*), of 388:

Just Man:  How do you live then, and what on, if you don't *do* anything?
Sukophantēs:  I am a supervisor of public affairs; private affairs too. Everything.
    J.M.:  You? Who put you on to that game?
      S.:  I do it because I enjoy it.
    J.M.:  And you call yourself a good citizen, you who break into people's homes and get yourself loathed for meddling with things that are none of your business?
      S.:  So serving my country to the best of my ability is none of my business, you moron?
    J.M.:  Then serving one's country means playing the busybody?
      S.:  Giving one's support to the established laws and stepping in to prevent offences being committed: that's service to one's country.
    J.M.:  But hasn't the state put jurors on the job precisely for that purpose?
      S.:  But who is to bring the charges?
    J.M.:  Anyone who is willing.
      S.:  Well it's I who am willing. So the government of the country falls to me.
(Aristophanes, *Ploutos* 906ff.)

Typical charges brought by *sukophantai* include information laid against a man who had not paid a fine or a denunciation of illegal trading practices. Their victims had either to face trial or pay blackmail. Measures were taken to deter *sukophantai*; for example, if they failed to get as much as one-fifth of the jury's votes or abandoned a prosecution after starting it, they were liable to a stiff fine and lost the right to bring similar cases again (a form of *atimia*). However, the evidence as a whole suggests that the Athenians had great difficulty in making these measures effective.

## (d) Loss of full citizen rights (atimia)

**5.64** *Sukophantai* and many other features of the Athenian legal system may well strike the modern reader as incredible. The Athenians themselves, however, were inordinately proud of their respect for law and justice. As the Athenian founder-hero Theseus puts it to the Theban Kreon in Sophocles' *Oedipus at Kolonos*: 'You have come into a *polis* that cultivates justice and sanctions nothing without law' (cf. 7.17). To get the Athenian legal system into perspective, we should consider how far the developed system of the later fifth and fourth centuries had travelled away from its much rougher origins. The law concerned with *atimia* brings this out particularly sharply.

**5.65** *Atimia* means literally deprivation of *timē* or acclaim (cf. 3.12). In the sixth and early fifth centuries to be in a state of *atimia* (*atimos*) was equivalent to being an outlaw: the *atimos* man could be killed or robbed of his property without the possibility of legal redress. Prudence therefore dictated that he exile himself from Attica. By the end of the fifth century outlawry had become distinguished from *atimia*, and the latter was the less severe penalty of the two. Thus those citizens who were found guilty of sacrilege in 415 were sentenced to outlawry, not *atimia*; they were executed unless they fled abroad in time, their property was confiscated by the state and sold at public auction (H.I.49).

5:13 A fragment of one of the Attic *stēlai* which record the sale of the property confiscated from Alkibiades and others after they had been found guilty of sacrilege in 415.

**5.66** *Atimia*, on the other hand, did not necessarily entail loss of property or the need to go into exile. All the same, it was the stiffest penalty handed out by the courts short of exile or death, and in its extreme form amounted to political death. For the totally disenfranchised man could not speak in *ekklēsia* or lawcourt, hold any public office, act as *bouleutēs* or juror, or enter either temples or the *agora*. Anyone who saw an *atimos* man in a prohibited place could arrest him on the spot and present him to the Eleven or the *thesmothetai*. Disenfranchisement, moreover, was normally for life, and in particularly grave cases could be applied to the offender's descendants too. Even so this was a considerable advance on the law of the jungle.

**5.67** In 415 Andokides suffered partial disenfranchisement for being implicated in the profanation of the Eleusinian Mysteries. This sentence was revoked under the extraordinary general amnesty of 403, the first recorded in human history, but in 399 Andokides found himself in the courts again. Here he lists some of the offences for which *atimia* was the specified punishment:

Those who owed money to the treasury, all those who had failed to pass their *euthunai*, or were guilty of disobeying court orders, or had lost public lawsuits or had summary fines imposed on them, or after buying tax-collecting privileges had failed to pay the agreed sum, or after acting as guarantors for the treasury had failed to pay: all these had to pay during the ninth prytany or their debts were doubled and their possessions sold. This was one form of *atimia*, but another consisted of those whose persons were disenfranchised, but who retained and enjoyed possession of their property. In this second group were those convicted of embezzlement or bribery. These and their descendants were to be disenfranchised. All those who deserted their post or were convicted of evading military service or cowardice in the field or avoiding a naval battle or throwing away their shield, or were convicted three times of giving false testimony or claiming falsely to have witnessed a summons, or who misused their parents – all these had their persons disenfranchised, but kept their property. Others again were disenfranchised . . . not totally but partially: for example, soldiers who . . . had stayed in the city at the time of the Four Hundred (411) . . . were not permitted to speak in the *ekklēsia* of the *dēmos* or be *bouleutai* . . . Others did not have the right to prosecute publicly, others to lay information before an official. For others the specification was not to sail to the Hellespont or to Ionia, for others [like Andokides himself] not to enter the *agora*. (Andokides (*On the Mysteries*) 1.73–6)

In short, the *atimia* legislation neatly illustrates the inextricable connection between politics and the law with which we began this section.

## (vii) State finance

### (a) Income and expenditure

**5.68** The Athenian state derived its regular income from several sources, not least from court fees and fines. The state did not have a budget in the modern sense, but, though evidence is scrappy, it is possible to calculate roughly its annual revenues. In 431 it seems that internal and external revenues together amounted to about 1,000 talents, whereas in 355 internal revenue had plummeted to 130 talents per annum, about one-quarter of the 431 figure. Apart from the courts, internal income was derived from harbour and market dues, taxes on metics, rents from mining concessions and other leases controlled by the *pōlētai* (sellers), and a host of lesser sources. The chief source of external revenue in the fifth century was imperial tribute, but this was abolished in 405 and never successfully replaced in the fourth century.

State income was used above all to provide pay to citizens serving in a public capacity. Expenditure increased markedly after it was first introduced in about 460 to pay jurors. There was also pay for service as *bouleutēs* or official, for military service as hoplite or rower, for attendance at the *ekklēsia* and certain festivals. Large items of expenditure, apart from the building of triremes or temples, fell on the shoulders of individual rich men, as we shall see.

**5.69** Two examples will illustrate the processes whereby the state derived its internal income. The Peiraieus, as we saw (4.56), became the most important commercial centre of the eastern Mediterranean. It acted not only as the import–export centre for Athens but also as a clearing-house for goods passing to and from other states. Not unnaturally Athens sought to tap this commerce for her own benefit, and one of the chief ways she did so was to sell to the highest bidder the right to collect the 2% tax levied on the value of goods going into or out of Peiraieus. Again some of our most detailed information is contained in Andokides' speech *On the Mysteries*, but it has to be remembered that he was addressing a jury:

Agyrrhios, that honest man you know well, had been for two years the chief farmer of the 2% tax. He had won the right to collect it for thirty talents . . . [He and his associates], having made a profit of six talents and seeing what a profitable business they were on to, formed a syndicate, bought off rivals by giving them a share in the profits and again offered thirty talents for the tax. As no one was putting in a rival bid, I came forward before the *boulē* and outbid them, purchasing the right to collect the tax for thirty-six talents . . . So, thanks to me, these men were prevented from sharing out among themselves six talents of money that was rightfully yours. (Andokides (*On the Mysteries*) 1.133–4)

**5.70** For our second example we look to the leasing of the silver mines in the Laureion district of south-east Attica. There had been mining here since as far back as the Bronze Age, but production first acquired national significance for Athens in the late sixth and early fifth centuries (by then the mines were state property, cf. H.I.15). Evidence for the way the mines were worked in the fifth century is scanty, though we know that the labour was provided overwhelmingly by slaves and that some of the richest Athenians had mining interests. But for the fourth century we have the evidence of inscriptions as well as literary sources. Aristotle specifies that the *pōlētai* leased out the mines and ratified concessions granted by the *boulē*. Here is an extract from the only completely surviving annual record, for 367/6. The lessees are all citizens:

*Pōlētai* in the arkhōnship of Polysdelos

Polyeuktos of the deme Lamptrai, Deinias of the deme Erkhia, Theaios of the deme Paiania, Theotimos of the deme Phrearrhoi, Aristogenes of the deme Iphistiadai, Glaukos of the deme Lakiadai, Kephisokles of the deme Peiraieus, Nikokles of the deme Anaphlystos, with, as secretary, Exekestos of the deme Kothokidai ...

In the first prytany, that of Hippothontis, [the following] mines were leased: Dexiakon in the Glen at the Look-Out, of which the boundaries are on all sides [the property of] Nikias of the deme Kydantidai, lessee Kallias of Sphettos: 20 drachmai. Diakon at Laureion, of which the boundaries are to the east the lands of Exopios, to the west the mountain, lessee Epiteles of the deme Kerameis: 20 drachmai. (*Hesperia* 10 (1941), 14ff.)

*(b)* Leitourgiai *(liturgies) and* eisphorai *(war-taxes)*

**5.71** The modern reader will have immediately spotted that there was no direct tax on income. Instead, the state imposed a form of taxation on the rich, and in emergencies it made capital levies on property.

A *leitourgia* meant originally a service performed voluntarily for the community, but under the Athenian democracy 'liturgies' were compulsory for those who owned a certain amount of property. They fell into two main categories: the trierarchy and festival liturgies. A trierarch was assigned to a state trireme (see 6.41–2), which for one year he had to keep in good order, man with a crew (paid in theory by the state, but times were hard in the fourth century) and command. A festival *leitourgia* involved the selection, financing and training of teams competing in the athletic, dramatic or musical contests at Athens' many religious festivals (7.35).

(There seem to have been nearly a hundred festival *leitourgiai* to be performed each year.) Here is a part of a lawcourt speech delivered in about 400 which clearly illustrates the wide range and potential expense of *leitourgiai*:

I passed my *dokimasia* to become a citizen in the *arkhōn*ship of Theopompos (411/ 10). I was then appointed a producer (*khorēgos*) for tragedy and spent thirty mnas. Two months later I won first prize at the Thargēlia with a men's dithyrambic chorus, having spent 2,000 drachmas. In the *arkhōn*ship of Glaukippos (410/9) I spent 8,000 drachmas on Pyrrhic dancers at the Great Panathenaia, and I won first prize as *khorēgos* with a men's dithyrambic chorus at the Dionysia, spending 5,000 drachmas including the cost of dedicating the tripod. In the *arkhōn*ship of Diokles (409/8) I spent 300 drachmas on a cyclic chorus at the Little Panathenaia.

Meanwhile I was trierarch for seven years and spent six talents, and . . . twice paid *eisphorai*, on one occasion thirty mnas, on the other 4,000 drachmas.

Directly after sailing back to Athens, in the *arkhōn*ship of Alexias (405/4), I served as producer of a gymnastic display (*gumnasiarkhos*) at the Prometheia and won first prize, having spent twelve mnas. Afterwards I was appointed *khorēgos* for a boys' chorus and spent over fifteen mnas. Next, in the *arkhōn*ship of Eukleides (403/2) I won first prize as *khorēgos* for a comedy by Kephisodoros and spent sixteen mnas including the cost of dedicating the equipment. Then at the Little Panathenaia I was a producer for boy Pyrrhic dancers and spent seven mnas.

I have won first prize in a trireme race off Sounion, at a cost of fifteen mnas; not to mention leading delegations to festivals and paying for the Arrhephoria and other such items, which together have cost me more than thirty mnas. (Lysias (*On a Bribery Charge*) 21.1ff.)

**5.72** This speaker, who is defending himself on a charge of embezzlement and so is liable to *atimia*, is not a typical liturgist. The 10½ talents he has spent in ten years represent more than four times the legally required minimum, and, as he expressly tells the jury, he has overspent to build up credit with the People. Presumably his exceptional wealth (perhaps 20 to 30 talents) or political record left him open to accusation in the courts. For the average liturgist, it seems, *leitourgiai* became an increasing burden in the fourth century, especially the trierarchy. This was reformed in 357 to spread the load more equitably (see 6.46), but without notable success.

If a man wanted to avoid a *leitourgia*, he could find another man richer than himself and yet doing less than his share of *leitourgiai* and challenge him either to perform the *leitourgia* in his place or carry out an exchange of property with him; if the property of the man who was challenged really was of less value, he would not mind the exchange.

**5.73** *Eisphorai*, emergency war-taxes, were perhaps first levied in the early part of the Peloponnesian War. In the fourth century, when there was no imperial tribute and Athenian state finances grew steadily more precarious, *eisphorai* became increasingly frequent, and in 378/7 citizens liable to pay them were grouped into tax-syndicates (*summoriai*) (6.46) to make payment more regular and efficient. However, the speeches of Demosthenes are replete with calls to the citizens to do their patriotic duty in the struggle against Philip by paying the *eisphorai* they owed, so the system seems in practice to have been far less successful than hoped.

## (viii) The grain supply

5.74 Another matter of life and death which was not handled as well as was desirable in the fourth century was the grain supply. Grain, that is wheat and barley, together with the vine and the olive, form the 'Mediterranean triad' of dietary staples (1.9, 12). Yet though the cultivable 20% of Attica's surface area was well suited to the vine and the olive, it did not favour barley or, even more importantly, wheat. From Attica's own resources, it has been estimated, a maximum of only about 75,000 people could be fed annually, including a maximum urban population of 10,000. But if our approximate calculations were correct (4.8), the total population of Attica was four times this maximum figure in 431, and more than twice as great a century later. The shortfall in locally produced grain had to be made up somehow by overseas supplies (cf. 1.20).

5.75 Greek states had experienced severe population pressure as early as the eighth century and responded by exporting surplus population to all points of the compass (cf. H.I.4). Those who emigrated to the northern shore of the Black Sea found themselves beyond the olive line, but in compensation they had access to the richest wheatlands of Europe, the black-earth region of the Ukraine and Crimea. Probably already by the end of the eighth century a trade in wheat from the Black Sea to mainland Greece had begun. As Athens' urban population grew markedly in the fifth century, so did its dependence on imported grain, and the need to control the grain trade became paramount. Fortunately, the instrument of control was ready to hand, the Athenian navy (6.31ff.), and an intimate connection developed between imperialism and the grain supply (4.59).

5.76 In the fifth century, therefore, Athenian naval power somewhat masks from us the extent of Athens' reliance on grain from abroad; but it does not do so entirely. In 445 the Athenians were happy to receive a gift of Egyptian grain from an Egyptian king, and in 405 it was the cutting of Athens' Black Sea wheat supply that finally forced her capitulation to

Sparta. However, in the fourth century Athenian dependence was revealed in all its nakedness. Since naval power was at first a thing of the past and later exercised only fitfully at best, other devices for influencing the grain trade had to be employed.

The evidence that grain was the most essential import of Athens is considerable. The 2% tax on imports and exports at the Peiraieus (5.69) was so administered that the duty on grain was farmed separately from that on other goods. Supervision of the grain trade was entrusted, not to the *agoranomoi*, but to a special board of grain inspectors. This board oversaw prices, making sure that millers and bakers did not make undue profits. Even more strikingly, the grain trade was the only branch of foreign commerce which was treated as a strictly political matter.

5.77 In the time of Aristotle, and probably for some time before, the grain supply was a statutory item on the agenda of the sovereign *ekklēsia* of each month. One of the decisions taken by the *ekklēsia* to safeguard the supply so far as was in their power is highly revealing of Athens' weakness in the fourth century. Instead of ordering petty northern rulers around, Athens now had to kowtow to those who controlled the point of supply. So the *ekklēsia* voted Leukon, ruler of the Kimmerian Bosporos (the Crimea), honorary citizenship, together with freedom from the taxation to which Athenian citizens were liable. Here in 355/4 Demosthenes refers to Leukon's reciprocal benefaction to Athens:

> You know that we are more dependent than anyone else on imported grain. Our imports from the Black Sea are equal to those from all other sources. There is nothing surprising in this. Not only is it the area of highest production but Leukon, who controls it, has granted exemption from dues to shippers bound for Athens and announced that they are to have priority of lading . . .
>
> Consider what this amounts to. He exacts dues of a thirtieth on all grain exports. We import from him about 400,000 *medimnoi* – the figure can be checked from the records of the grain-commissioners. So for each 300,000 *medimnoi* he makes us a free gift of 10,000 *medimnoi*, and on the balance of 100,000 one of roughly 3,000 . . .
>
> Two years ago when there was a general shortage of grain, he supplied your needs so generously that you were left with a surplus worth fifteen talents.
> (Demosthenes (*Against Leptines*) 20.30–3)

Following the death of Leukon in 349/8, Athens in 346 confirmed the privileges for his three sons, and the handsome decree recording this grant survives. Additionally, the Athenians legislated to protect their grain supply, for example by making it a capital crime for anyone resident in Athens to ship grain to any harbour other than Peiraieus.

5:14  The start of an Attic inscription honouring the three sons of Leukon in 346; the sons are portrayed in the relief carving that heads the inscription.

## (3) Athenian imperialism

### *(i) League and empire*

**5.78** Had the Athenians who created the empire a century before been able to read the decree in favour of Leukon's sons, they would have been appalled at the way Athens was obliged to grovel before petty rulers (3.2). In their day it had been Athens who, thanks to her naval power, cracked the whip. It had not, however, always been so. Only a generation before the Persian Wars of 480–79 Athens had not been a force in the land. Sparta had intervened in Athenian affairs four times within a decade, and in 499 the Athenians had been able to send a mere twenty ships to aid their fellow Ionians in revolt from the mighty Persian Empire (H.I.12). The real turning-point in Athens' military fortunes came with the naval victories of Salamis and Mykale (H.I.18, 20).

**5.79** Thereafter Sparta was no longer the undisputed leader of Hellas. In 478 divided opinions in Sparta over whether or not to continue the war against Persia prompted some of the more powerful Greek islands and cities on the west coast of Asia Minor to request Athens to assume the leadership. This Athens readily did, but rather than simply take over direction of the existing alliance (known by modern scholars as the Hellenic League) Athens created instead an entirely new one, which is usually now called the Delian League (see map 4 ; cf. H.I.22–4).

**5.80** In winter 478/7 representatives of Greek states met on the sacred isle of Dēlos in the centre of the Aegean to swear oaths of alliance. They swore to have the same friends and enemies, that is, they concluded an offensive and defensive alliance; and they dropped lumps of iron into the sea and swore not to desert the alliance before they rose again to the surface: the alliance, in other words, was to be eternal. Formally all allies were of equal status, but in fact the predominance of Athens was clear-cut from the start. In the first place, the allies did not all swear oaths of alliance to each other, but each ally swore individually to have the same friends and enemies as Athens, and Aristeides reciprocated the oaths on Athens' behalf. Athens was to be recognised as *hēgemōn* (leader).

**5.81** The aims of the alliance were threefold: to liberate the Aegean from the remains of Persian control; to ravage the lands of the Great King of Persia in reprisal for the damage Xerxes' invasion had inflicted on Greece; and to guarantee permanent security for the Greeks against any renewed attempt by the Persians to restore their control. Given the geography of the area, the alliance was inevitably going to be a primarily naval one, unlike the land-based Peloponnesian League of which Sparta was *hēgemōn*. Since naval warfare was incomparably more expensive than hoplite warfare, the Delian League allies would have to pay more towards the cost of the alliance, either by contributing ships or by making a cash payment.

The dominant position of Athens becomes even clearer at this stage. It was Athens who decided which allied states were to contribute ships and which money, and what amount of each. It was Athens who provided the commanders-in-chief of the alliance from among the ten *stratēgoi* and also its treasurers, the Hellēnotamiai (literally 'Treasurers of the Greeks'); these officers were selected by and answerable to the Athenian People, not the allies as a whole. The treasury of the alliance, however, was to be kept on Dēlos (H.I.23). Provision was also made for there to be regular congresses of the allies on Dēlos. In practice most allies, being relatively small fry, would tend to vote the way the *hēgemōn* wished. In short, a better name than Delian league would be 'Aegean Treaty Organisation' or 'the Dēlos Pact Powers' (for tribute-list, see H.I. p. 22).

**5.82** At first, so far as we know, no complaint was voiced publicly against Athens' dominance of the alliance. The tribute in ships or cash was not apparently felt to be unduly burdensome, and, since Athens contributed by far the largest number of ships of any ally and had won great respect by her resistance to the Persians, her leadership was thought to be justified. Within fifteen years, however, the important ship-contributing island states of Naxos and Thasos had tried to secede from the Delian League (H.I.26), and disaffection with Athens increased markedly in the late 450s and early 440s. Athens in return tightened her control on the alliance. League congresses ceased to be held, the treasury was removed from Dēlos to Athens in 454, and allies like Naxos and Thasos were forced to remain within the alliance and punished severely for what the Athenians regarded, strictly correctly, as revolt. By the beginning of the Peloponnesian War, Thucydides reports, Athens was so unpopular that most Greeks wanted Sparta to win. Even if Thucydides was exaggerating (as he almost certainly was), the nature of the relationship between Athens and her allies in 431 was not what it had been in 478/7 (H.I.33–4).

5.83 Most scholars describe the change in terms of the transformation of the Delian League into the Athenian empire (*arkhē*). There is some basis for this description. For example, around 450 the Athenians begin to refer to the allies as 'the cities which the Athenians rule [*arkhousi*]'; about the same time we first hear of Athenian interference in the constitutions of the allied states and the installation of Athenian garrisons and governors; and no less important was Athens' decision now to appropriate allied land for Athenian settlements that could also act as informal garrison towns. However, to speak of the transformation of the Delian League into an Athenian empire around the middle of the fifth century is to obscure the crucial point made above in describing the foundation of the alliance (cf. H.I.27). Athens was from the start unquestionably the *hēgemōn*, the dominant partner, and since Greek competitive values were as firmly entrenched in interstate relations as elsewhere in Greek life (3.1, 14) a predominance of power tended to be translated into a relationship of rule. The earliest League offensives were of more benefit to Athens than to the alliance as a whole, and they set the pattern for the future. By the time Naxos tried to secede in 470 Thucydides rightly treats the League as being already in effect the Athenian empire.

## (ii) The economics of Empire

5.84 Thucydides is our main literary source for the empire, but his account of its earlier years is very incomplete. Athens decided which states should contribute ships, and which cash, but we are not told how many states were involved in all nor how many contributed ships as opposed to cash. All we know for certain is that the number of ship-contributors declined, partly because the expense was found too onerous, partly because Athens deprived revolted allies of their fleets as a punishment.

5.85 The obligation to contribute ships was apparently found burdensome mainly because of the cost of manning, equipping and running them. Pay alone for the crew of one trireme cost one talent a month in 431; even if it was only half that fifty years earlier, it was still far more expensive to contribute in this way than to make a straight cash payment to Athens. By comparison, the cash tribute (*phoros*) seems at first to have been a mild imposition. But as time went on, even this tribute was found irksome, and not only for purely economic reasons. The very word *phoros* acquired unpleasant overtones of subservience, since Athens could be regarded as using it to build up a predominantly Athenian fleet with which to increase her control of the allies.

5.86 A crisis seems to have been reached in the early 440s. In 460 Athens had launched a large expedition to Egypt to aid a native ruler in rebellion from the Persian empire (H.I.25). The expedition proved a major disaster, and it was in its wake that the League treasury was moved to the security of Athens. Following the Egyptian disaster there appears to have been widespread disaffection within the alliance, and the allies' feelings will not have been calmed by Athens' failure to dislodge the Phoenicians (who provided the Persians' chief naval arm in the Mediterranean) from Cyprus. Early in the 440s, most scholars believe, Athens concluded peace with Persia, the Peace of Kallias.

5.87 This peace was an honourable, even a glorious achievement from Athens' viewpoint, but it seems to have increased the reluctance of some allies to pay tribute. Their reluctance will have been aggravated by the Athenians' decision to devote the enormous surplus built up from nearly thirty years of tribute to rebuilding the temples and monuments of the Athenian Acropolis destroyed by the Persians in 480 and 479. This decision to divert the allies' money from its original objectives to the glorification of Athens was questionable, and Athens tried to conciliate them by treating them as honorary colonists of Athens and involving them intimately in the Great Panathenaia and Dionysia festivals.

5.88 Signs of allied disgruntlement are visible in the Tribute Lists. The record for one whole year, perhaps 449/8, is missing, and in the following year many payments are partial or simply absent. The Athenian *ekklēsia* therefore passed a decree designed to tighten up tribute collection, probably in 447. Here is an extract from the best preserved part of the decree, as reconstructed by modern scholars; the decree was proposed on the motion of Kleinias, probably the father of Alkibiades and a political associate of Pericles:

The *boulē*, the governors in the cities (*arkhontes*) and the inspectors (*episkopoi*) shall see to it that the tribute payments be collected each year and be brought to Athens. Identification seals shall be made for the cities, so that it will be impossible that fraud be committed by those bringing the tribute payments. And after the city has inscribed in an account book whatever tribute payment it is sending, and has set its seal to it, let it be sent off to Athens. Let those bringing it give up the account book in the *boulē*, to be read at the same time as they are paying in the tribute money. And let the *prutaneis*, after the Dionysia, summon an *ekklēsia* for the Hellēnotamiai to make known to the Athenians which of the cities paid the tribute money in full and which fell short . . . (M and L 46 = Fornara 98)

**5.89** In 431 Athens' reserve fund, despite the expenditure on the Acropolis building programme and the heavy cost of putting down the revolt of Samos in 440/39 (H.I.33), stood at the gigantic figure of 6,000 talents. The annual external income from the tribute, from indemnities such as that imposed on Samos, and from other sources amounted to 600 talents. With reason did Pericles stress Athens' financial preparedness for the coming war. Five years later, however, the demands of war, not of course against the Persians as originally envisaged, were proving unmanageable. A similar decree to that of Kleinias was passed by the Athenians, making it a treasonable offence to impede the collection of tribute; and in 425 the assessment of tribute was at least doubled, bringing it up to perhaps as much as 1,460 talents per annum. But difficulties over collection persisted, and after the disastrously costly Sicilian Expedition of 415/13 (H.I.48–50) the tribute was abolished in favour of a 5% tax on all trade within the empire. This proved to be a temporary expedient, though, and by 410 tribute had been reimposed, only to be abolished for ever in 405 by the Spartans.

The burden of tribute payment fell chiefly on the shoulders of rich allies, who probably had little love for the Athenian democracy anyway. It comes as no surprise therefore that payment of tribute came increasingly to be resented. Poor allies, on the other hand, might possibly welcome the Athenian empire on economic grounds, since it provided employment as rowers, dockers and so on, and opportunities for booty. However, economically speaking it was the Athenians who collectively profited most from their empire.

**5.90** Rich Athenians might not be in sympathy with the radical democracy, but even oligarchs will have basked in the reflected glory of Athens' power and did not object to imperialism as such. Besides, it was they who filled many of the top jobs in the empire, and there were many top jobs to fill: Aristotle says that up to 700 officials were employed abroad in the second half of the fifth century, more for its size than in the Roman empire. It seems too that under the cloak of empire rich Athenians were able to enrich themselves further by acquiring land illegally in subject territories; the richest Athenian of whom we happen to know (he was convicted of sacrilege in 415 and his property sold at public auction) owned tracts of property in Euboia and elsewhere outside Attica. Finally, the tribute and other imperial revenues somewhat lightened the tax burden on the Athenian rich, and this may have helped to conciliate some of them to the democracy.

5.91 The real beneficiaries of the empire, though, were the Athenian poor, especially the *thētes*. Thanks to the Athenian navy, whose ships they played a large part in rowing, Athens had a reasonably assured grain supply. Indeed, Athenian power was such that Athenian officials called 'Guardians of the Hellespont' (*Hellēspontophulakes*) were able to control where Black Sea wheat went. The growth of the empire meant an increase in jobs, not just in the fleet, but in the dockyards, in the manufacture of arms and other necessities, and in public works. Some Athenians too – perhaps as many as 10,000 in all – benefited from the land they received abroad, whether as cleruchs (*klēroukhoi*) or colonists (*apoikoi*), the difference between these being that cleruchs retained their Athenian citizenship. Here is part of the decree establishing a colony at Brea in Thrace, probably in about 445:

> Land-distributors (*geōnomoi*) shall be elected, ten in number, one from each tribe. These are to distribute the land. Demokleides shall establish the colony at his discretion as best he can. The sacred precincts which have been reserved for the gods shall be left as they are, and others shall not be consecrated. A cow and a panoply shall be brought to the Great Panathenaia and to the Dionysia a *phallos*. If anyone wages a campaign against the territory of the settlers, aid shall be despatched by the cities as swiftly as possible as prescribed by the agreements . . . (M and L 49 = Fornara 100)

There follows an amendment, in which it is specified that the colonists shall be drawn from the two lowest census groups of the citizen population.

### (iii) The politics of empire

5.92 In view of its economic benefits it was small wonder that virtually to a man the Athenians approved the empire. For the allies, however, it was a mixed blessing or a positive curse from the political point of view.

5:15–16  The artistic influence exerted by Athens in the later 5th century can be seen by comparing a detail of horsemen from the Parthenon frieze (*c.* 440) (top) with the riders from a Lykian sarcophagus of the late 4th century found in the ancient royal necropolis of Sidon.

Poor allies, as suggested above, may well have welcomed the empire for its economic advantages. But they also stood to benefit politically. Democracy was the rule of the majority, and the majority in Greek terms was poor. Athens, being a democracy, naturally had an interest in promoting democracy within the empire, if only for the practical reason that a democratic ally was likely to be more loyal than an oligarchic ally. On the other hand, we should not suppose that Athens deliberately went out of her way on principle to create democracy throughout the alliance, since this would only have alienated further the rich men who traditionally formed the governing class of oligarchic states and who paid the tribute. Rather, Athens tolerated oligarchy, at least in the larger allied states like Milētos and Samos, unless and until civil strife arose in the allied state or the state tried to defect from the alliance. Then Athens would intervene on the side of the democrats and of democracy. However, even a democratic ally would not have wished in an ideal world to be subject to Athens. It was a case of setting off this loss of the political freedom that was so dear to a Greek against the even less desirable alternative of Persian and/or oligarchic control.

5.93 Perhaps even the most fervent Athenian imperialist would not have denied that the empire infringed two cardinal principles of political sovereignty, autonomy (*autonomia*) and independence (*eleutheria*). But he would have claimed that the infringement was necessary in order to make the alliance an effective anti-Persian instrument. Two surviving decrees illustrate Athenian thinking and the forms imperial interference might take. First, here is an extract from the regulations Athens prescribed for the Asiatic Greek city of Erythrai, probably in 453/2:

Among the Erythraians lots shall be drawn for a *boulē* of 120 men. The men allotted the office shall undergo scrutiny in the Erythraian Council. No one shall be allowed to serve as a member of the *boulē* who is less than thirty years old. Prosecution shall lie against those found guilty, and they shall not be *bouleutai* for the space of four years. The allotment shall be carried out and the establishment of the *boulē* effected for the present by the Inspectors (*episkopoi*) and the Garrison Commander (*phrourarkhos*), in future by the *boulē* and the Garrison Commander . . . (*IG* I³ 14 = Fornara 71)

There follows the *boulē*'s oath of allegiance, in which there is a reference to 'those who fled to the Medes'; presumably it was these Persian sympathisers whose collusion had occasioned Athens' intervention and the establishment of a democratic *boulē*. The garrison was not necessarily forced on Erythrai. It could have been welcomed as a temporary safeguard of the new democracy against any Persian-backed attempt to subvert it.

**5.94** In 446 Athens was faced with a crisis at the tail-end of the so-called First Peloponnesian War. The cities of the island of Euboia, which was an important station on the grain route, revolted (H.I.32). Athenian reaction was severe. One city, Histiaia, was utterly depopulated and settled with Athenian colonists. Eretria and Khalkis, the two principal cities, were treated more leniently – but not much more, as this part of the decree recording regulations for Khalkis in 446/5 reveals:

The Khalkidians shall take the following oath: 'I shall not rebel against the *dēmos* of the Athenians either by artifice or by device of any kind either by word or by deed. Nor shall I follow anyone in rebellion and if anyone does rebel, I shall denounce him to the Athenians. I shall pay the tribute to the Athenians which I persuade them to assess, and as an ally I shall be the best and truest possible. And I shall assist the *dēmos* of the Athenians and defend them if anyone does injury to the *dēmos* of the Athenians, and I shall obey the *dēmos* of the Athenians.' This oath shall be taken by the Khalkidian adults, all without exception. Whoever does not take the oath is to be deprived of his citizen rights and his property shall be confiscated, and Olympian Zeus [in Khalkis] shall receive the tithe consecrated from his property.

There follows a record of Athens' chilly response to the Khalkidians' pleas for concessions. The decree as preserved concludes with the following amendment:

The legal processes of punishment shall be in the hands of the Khalkidians, as regards their own citizens in Khalkis, just as they are in Athens for the Athenians, except when the penalty involved is exile, death or loss of citizen rights. In regard to these, appeal shall lie in Athens, in the Ēliaia of the *thesmothetai*, in accordance with the decree of the *dēmos*. (M and L 52 = Fornara 103)

The imperialistic tone of this document is unmistakable and wholly in keeping with the fact that at just this time Athens concluded the Thirty Years' Peace by which Sparta in effect formally recognised the Athenian empire. Particularly important in the document is the extension of Athens' control of Khalkis' internal affairs to the sphere of jurisdiction; law and politics, as stressed earlier, went hand-in-hand. Not all trials, however, were to be transferred from Khalkis to the Athenian jury-courts, but only those carrying the penalty of death, exile or *atimia*. The aim of this transfer was to prevent the unjust condemnation of Khalkidian friends of Athens and the unjust acquittal of Athens' enemies. The penalties, and not the offences, are specified in order to prevent evasion in Khalkis – for example, the accusation of a friend of Athens on a trumped-up charge of homicide that carried the death penalty.

**5.95** This was not all Athens did to encourage its friends. Apart from installing democratic constitutions and garrisons and instituting legal safeguards, Athens took steps to protect and honour the democratic leaders upon whom the duty of representing Athens' interests in the allied cities chiefly fell. Here is a good example of a proxeny-decree, whereby the Athenians in about 450 made Akheloion a *proxenos* or a kind of honorary consul of the Athenians:

Akheloion is to be *proxenos* and benefactor of the Athenians: and if Akheloion is wronged by anyone, he can prosecute them at Athens in the court of the *polemarkhos*, and he is not to pay court-fees except for five drachmas . . . If anyone kills Akheloion or one of his sons in one of the cities which the Athenians rule, the city is to owe a fine of five talents, as if one of the Athenians were to die, and vengeance is to be taken against this person as if an Athenian had died. (*SEG* 10.23)

It is noteworthy that the phrase 'the cities which the Athenians rule' makes its earliest appearances in honorific decrees like this, not in the regulatory decrees such as those for Erythrai and Khalkis. Later, Athens was not so diplomatic.

**5.96** One final example of the politics of imperialism will illustrate both Athens' imperialistic mentality and at the same time the limits of Athenian imperial power. Somewhere between 450 and 446 (probably) Athens issued the so-called Coinage Decree, which sought to impose on the cities of the empire the use of Athenian coins, weights and measures to the exclusion of all others. The decree, which survives only in fragments of copies scattered over the area of Athenian domination, has no very obvious economic significance for Athens. So the true significance of the decree is political: Athens aimed further to diminish her allies' sovereignty by removing their right to strike coins bearing their city's badge. However, as the archaeological evidence shows, the coinages of the allies were not all brought to a halt after 446. For whatever reasons, the decree was never fully enforced.

### (iv) Athenian imperialism in the fourth century

**5.97** The Peloponnesian War, as we have seen, proved enormously expensive for the Athenians. But not even the desperate resort to the iron reserve of 1,000 talents set aside in 431 was able to counteract the combination of Athenian mistakes, allied defections and Persian aid that eventually won the war for the Spartans. By 404 Athens no longer ruled any other cities, and her own was ruled by a pro-Spartan oligarchic junta backed up by a Spartan garrison (H.I.57). Sparta had deprived Athens of her last shreds of empire by levelling her walls with the ground and reducing her fleet to a token twelve ships. The desire for empire, however, remained strong at Athens, especially of course among the landless poor, and within a remarkably short space of time the democracy (restored in 403) was up to its old tricks (H.I.58).

5.98 The refortification of the Peiraieus was begun in 395/4, and more or less completed a few years later thanks, ironically, to a gift of Persian money. Despite this gift, Athens allied herself in 390 to a revolted Persian vassal, and over the next couple of years the rejuvenated Athenian fleet began to act in a manner noticeably reminiscent of the fifth-century empire; for example, a toll-station was established at Byzantium (cf. H.I.63). Persia was naturally alarmed, and it was once more with Persian money that the Spartans were again able to cut off Athens' corn supply at the Hellespont in 387. By the King's Peace of 386 (H.I.64), to which all Greeks were formally party, Sparta was in effect recognised as *hēgemōn* of the Greek world outside Asia. Sparta, however, grossly abused her position, giving Athens the chance to reassert herself as leader of an alliance ostensibly designed for mutual protection against Sparta's infringements of the King's Peace.

This alliance, which was founded in 378/7, is generally known today as the Second Athenian League (or Confederacy) (H.I.68). The text of the prospectus by which Athens sought to attract allies is preserved on a magnificent monument. Since most members of the League had also been subjects of Athens' fifth-century empire, the promises made by the Athenians in the prospectus are the best possible clues to what they and the allies thought had gone wrong there:

If any of the Greeks or of the barbarians living in Europe or of the islanders who are not subject to the Great King wishes to be an ally of the Athenians and their allies, he may be – remaining free and independent, being governed under whatever constitution he wishes, without receiving a garrison or submitting to a governor or paying tribute . . . For those who make alliance with the Athenians and their allies, the People shall renounce whatever Athenian possessions whether public or private there may be in the territory of those who make the alliance, and shall give them guarantee of this. If there are in Athens *stēlai* [inscribed pillars] unfavourable to any of the cities which makes alliance with Athens, the *boulē* in office shall have authority to demolish them.

From the *arkhōn*ship of Nausinikos it shall be illegal for any Athenian to own either publicly or privately, by purchase or by mortgage or in any other way whatever, any house or land in the territory of the allies. If anyone does buy, acquire or take out a mortgage on such property in any way, any of the allies who wishes may report him to the *sunedroi* [delegates] of the allies: the delegates shall sell the property and give half the proceeds to the informer, while the other half shall be the common property of the allies. (Tod 123 = Rhodes 1, lines 15–45)

5.99 However, as the allies quickly discovered, the road to imperialism is paved with good intentions. The Athenians did not collect tribute (*phoros*), but by 373 they were levying 'contributions' (*suntaxeis*) which only a sophist, perhaps, could have distinguished from tribute. No Athenians were settled on the territory of those allies whose names are listed on the monument after the text of the prospectus, but after 373 Athens did establish cleruchies, for example, on the island of Samos. In the late 360s Athens infringed the autonomy of the island of Keos; and by the 350s governors and garrisons were to be found in some member states of the alliance. The allies' delegates had their own permanent and separate congress (*sunedrion*) at Athens, but this had no independent power over Athens' decisions.

The Social War (revolt by some important allies) of 357/5 (H.I.73) can be seen as signalling the demise of Athens' revived imperialism. The Confederacy remained notionally in existence until 338, and Athens remained the leading naval power in the Aegean, but these were not enough to forestall the domination of Greece by Philip of Macedon (H.I.75ff.). Athenian imperialism died on the battlefield of Khaironeia (H.I.81), and Athenian democracy soon followed, being terminated by Macedonian edict in 322 (H.I.85).

# 6
# *Athens at war*

## Introduction

**6.1** In the Western world, declared international war has not been experienced since 1945, a longer period of 'peace' than any it has ever experienced. When it does come again, it will be a matter of high technology quite as much as complex strategy and simple human courage; if nuclear, destruction will be appalling. Civil war, in the United Kingdom, is known only in Ireland. War is fought by professionals, who make their living out of it, and financed by governments, who allocate expenditure raised by taxes on it. There is a substantial body of opinion opposed to war, especially nuclear war, on moral grounds. International conflict can arise for economic as much as for political reasons.

**6.2** For fifth-century Greeks, war was a permanent condition of life, fought almost annually, on land by those who could afford to equip themselves appropriately, and at sea with the help of wealthy individuals who could afford to pay for the upkeep of a ship. Battles were for the most part fought against other Greeks, never for purely economic reasons, rarely to gain territory (only to hold it and reclaim frontiers), usually to assert political dominance over others (cf. Ireland today). Major conflicts were fairly rare occurrences. Far more common, and perhaps more to be feared, was ravaging – the systematic destruction of food supplies. No Greek objected to war on moral grounds: to reject the idea of conflict with external enemies would have seemed perfectly incredible to societies whose internal social relationships were defined in terms of *philoi* and *ekhthroi* (cf. 3.1, 13), and who knew that defeat could mean slavery for the whole population (4.63). Standing armies and standing navies were anathema to Greeks, who could not afford them anyway but who, on principle, saw them as an ever-present threat to their own independence (in modern states, the first move in any coup is to win the army's support).

6:1 Victory puts the finishing touches to a trophy covered in captured arms and armour. Mid 5th century.

**6.3** Again, in ancient Greece, the whole life of the army – before the march, on the march, before and after conflict – was accompanied by religious rituals. Each army had its own seers (*mantis* – see 2.19) who, to judge by the number of times they prevented military commanders from engaging when they wanted to, were no mere yes-men. Divination before battle (*ta hiera*), and blood-sacrifice (*ta sphagia*) as the army marched to fight were standard practice (6.14), and often stopped proceedings (cf. Herodotus, *Histories* 9.37–61 and see 2.20). Nikias' belief in his *manteis* at Syracuse may well have caused the destruction of the Athenian army there. When armies marched to battle, they sang paeans, hymns to avert evils; if they won, they erected a *tropaion* ('trophy', literally the place where the rout started, the 'turning-point') as a thank-offering to the god as well as the tangible, visible proof of victory (see 3.9).

**6.4** Athens' power depended largely on her fleet. It is difficult for us to envisage what it must have meant to have built and maintained a fleet of between 200 and 400 triremes. With about 200 people on board each boat, where did Athens get the population to man them? (Mercenaries, obviously (6.35).) And how feed them? (Greeks could not take food with them.) Where did she get the wood to build such a huge fleet? With 170 rowers, a fleet of 200 ships requires 34,000 oars; we still have not reckoned with the wood to build the ship itself, the canvas for sails, the ropes, the bronze fitments for the rams (these at least were kept and reused when the ship itself was taken out of service). The answer is that Macedon and the north were major suppliers of wood, where Athens' relations with the kings resembled that of the Western world to the oil sheikhs, so vital was wood to Athens' ambitions (cf. 4.57; 1.7). Again, maintaining the fleet (hulls rot if kept in the water too long, split if left on land too long) was a major headache. There are therefore serious logistical questions to bear in mind when we consider the Greeks at war (4.56; 6.40–5).

### War and peace

6.5 From 497–338, Athens was at war for three years out of four, and Greek states in general regarded periods of peace more as respite from inevitable war than as the normal state of affairs. In the fifth century 'truces' were made for limited periods only. Sparta and Athens, for instance, made a thirty-year peace in 446, and more than a generation was not to be thought of. In the fourth century dreams of a more abiding state of peace found expression in talk of 'peace', something more positive than the mere cessation of war implied by 'truces', and the so-called Common Peaces (H.I.64), made to ensure peace and goodwill amongst all the Greeks, had no time limits. But the dreams were vain. In 375, to express jubilation over the end of hostilities with Sparta, the Athenians erected an altar to peace and every year from then on there were sacrifices made to

6:2 Weapons from the field of Marathon (cf. HI:8), including a bone-hilted sword from the infantry, and arrowheads and a lead sling bullet from the light-armed troops.

this abstract deity, but by 373 they were at war again. War was central to Greek life (H.I.85).

6.6 Most Athenian wars were in large degree naval and it was in naval warfare that Athens excelled. On land her record was far from glorious. If one excepts the battle of Marathon (H.I.13), Athens on her own never won a major land battle nor as part of a larger army ever played a leading part in gaining victory. The real warriors on land were (until the rise of the Macedonians under Philip) the Spartans and the Boiotians, and it is to their battles that we must look for enlightenment. Yet what they did well, Athens did less well, but not differently, and there is no harm in treating Greek land warfare as uniform. When it comes to the sea, Athens can without rival speak for herself.

## Land warfare

6.7 War was constant, but major battles were rare. Between 479 and 404, Sparta, the dominant power on land in that period, fought only four major land battles, and Thucydides had only two, the battles of Dēlion (424, H.I.42) and [First] Mantineia (418, H.I.46) to describe. In the fourth century, Boiotian supremacy was established by a mere two major engagements, Leuktra (371, H.I.70–1) and [Second] Mantineia (362, H.I.71–2). For the rest, warfare was a matter of minor operations such as skirmishing and ravaging, which sounds to our ears somewhat trivial. It was not so to the Greeks.

### Ravaging

6.8 Greece was a poor country. Most states lived off home-grown produce (unlike Athens), so that hostile ravaging was very much to be feared, and invasions took place when the corn was ripe. The Greek word for ravaging was 'cutting'. Cereal crops were cut (and presumably consumed by the invading army or burned), vines likewise, and trees ring-barked (i.e. a strip of bark cut off right round the trunk), to look like whipped slaves (Aristophanes, *Peace*, 747). The economic effects of such ravaging must have been severe, even if in the later years of the Peloponnesian War it seemed minor compared to the systematic plundering of the Athenian countryside. Athens, however, did not depend on Attica alone and could endure (cf. 1.20, 4.57ff.). Other states must have suffered greatly. Ravaging, so casually reported again and again by the historians, was a major disaster for those who endured it, and in thinking about Greek warfare we must not forget that warfare was for the most part damage and destruction of the enemy's means of maintaining life.

'Minor operations' too were not negligible and we must not belittle their importance. But inevitably, when we think of Greek warfare, we think of formal battle, not the discharge of weapons at a distance which is what the Greek word for skirmishing means, but hand-to-hand conflict.

## Major battles

6.9 Let us begin with Thucydides' accounts of the two major battles he had to describe. First, the battle of [First] Mantineia in 418 between Sparta and a coalition consisting of Argos, Mantineia and Athens (see H.I.46).

### *[First] Mantineia 418*

(66) The next day the Argives and their allies formed up in battle order, ready for the enemy. The Spartans, returning from the water to their old camp by the temple of Herakles, found themselves at close quarters with the enemy already drawn up for battle and advancing from the hill. This caused them greater alarm than any other occasion on record. There was little time for preparation, and they formed ranks in haste, under the orders of Agis. For it is their rule that when a king is in command all orders are given by him. He instructs the *polemarkhoi*, they give the word to the *lokhagoi*, they to the *pentēkontēres*, they in turn to the *enōmotia*. All necessary orders are passed on through the same channels and quickly reach the ranks. For almost the whole Spartan army with a few exceptions consists of officers serving under officers and responsibility for seeing that orders are carried out is widely delegated... [*Thucydides now describes the formation and estimates sizes.*]

(69) Before they actually engaged, the generals on either side spoke a few words of encouragement . . . The Spartans meanwhile sang war-songs and exchanged words of individual encouragement reminding each other of their proven courage and well aware that long training in action is more effective than a few words of encouragement however well delivered.

(70) After this they joined battle, the Argives and their allies advancing with vigour and fury, the Spartans slowly to the sound of pipes, a standing institution in their army, not for religious reasons but to make them advance evenly, keeping time, without breaking ranks as large armies are apt to do at the moment of impact. (71) As they were approaching each other, Agis decided on the following manoeuvre. All armies have a common tendency as they go into action; they get pushed out towards the right, and overlap the enemy left with their own right wing, because each man seeks protection for his own uncovered right-hand side from the shield of his right-hand neighbour, thinking that the more closely the shields are locked the safer he will be. The man primarily responsible is the man on the

extreme right of the front line, who keeps trying to keep his own unarmed side away from the enemy; the rest follow him with the same motive. On the present occasion the Mantineians far outflanked the Skiritai, and the Spartans and Tegeans outflanked the Athenians still further, their force being correspondingly larger. Agis was afraid that his left would be surrounded, and that the Mantineians were outflanking it too far; he therefore ordered the Skiritai and the Brasideioi to move out of their position in the line and level up the front with the Mantineians, while he passed word to the two generals Hipponoidas and Aristokles to move two companies from the right wing to fill the gap, thinking he had men to spare on his right and that he would strengthen the line facing the Mantineians . . . (73) The flight and retreat however was pressed neither hard nor long. The Spartans fight long and stubbornly until they have routed the enemy, but that once done their pursuit is short and brief.

(74) That, or something very much like it, was the course of the battle, which was the greatest that had occurred for a long time among the Greeks and involved the most famous of their cities. The Spartans took up a position in front of the enemy dead, and proceeded at once to set up a trophy and strip the bodies of the fallen. Their own dead they took up and carried to Tegea, where they buried them; the enemy dead they gave back under truce. The Argives, Orneatai and Kleonaioi lost seven hundred killed, the Mantineians two hundred, the Athenians and men of Aiginē two hundred with both generals. On the Spartan side the allies suffered no losses worth mentioning; of the Spartans themselves it was reported that three hundred were killed, but the true figure was difficult to find out. (Thucydides, *Peloponnesian War* 5.66–74)

This battle, the best documented in Greek military history, is in many ways revealing.

### (a) The size of the armies

The question of the Spartan numbers at Mantineia is one of the most hotly debated, but even if Thucydides' calculations are, as some would have it, wrong by half, there could hardly have been many more than 17,000–20,000 in all engaged that day. Yet Thucydides spoke of it as 'the greatest . . . for a long time'. Armies were, by our standards, small. Only when the Greeks united, as against the Persians at Plataia, for example, or against Philip at Khaironeia, were very much greater numbers of men involved.

### (b) The numbers of fatal casualties

6.10 On the Spartan side there were alleged to have been 'about 300', on the other side 1,100 in all, a discrepancy at first surprising. But it is typical. The main strength of Greek armies, the hoplite (to whom we shall come shortly) was generally well protected (see 6.17) and in direct conflict

6:3  A young man binds the head of a wounded companion. C. 530.

only a few were killed (e.g. at Plataia (H.I.19), according to Herodotus, '91 Spartans, 16 Tegeans, 52 Athenians'). It was in the rout that most of the fatal casualties occurred: this explains the large numbers of dead on the Argive side. Of course there must have been many a man lamed or maimed, although historians rarely allude to them, but in general fatal casualties were not great.

## (c) Other aspects of hoplite warfare

**6.11** The Spartans were drawn up, on average, eight deep, the normal formation in fifth-century warfare; the cavalry was placed on the wings – again normal, for reasons to be discussed; the Spartan 'waggons', casually mentioned in (72), were probably normal, for armies needed supplies and replacements for damaged equipment and if the Spartans found waggons convenient, no doubt others did too. In all this the battle of Mantineia is revealingly typical.

**6.12** On the other hand, we must remember that the Spartans, who fought at Mantineia, were professionals in an age of amateurs. Thucydides saw fit to describe their method of transmitting orders, plain sense to us but worth reporting to the Greeks. The Spartans were better trained in every way. Others received and needed harangues to excite valour; the Spartans with professionals' confidence in their well-practised powers needed no reminding but sang their familiar martial songs. Their opponents advanced to battle in unrestrained fashion; the Spartans advanced with slow and measured tread to the sound of the *aulos*, thus keeping their distances and their alignment. But nothing better demonstrates the superiority of their military training than the difficult tactical manoeuvre that King Agis ordered during the very advance. Only for a highly practised army was such a move to be conceived. In crimson raiment and with flowing locks, bearing polished shields with Λ for Lakedaimonioi, the Spartans' official name plain to see, they were the terror of Greece. No wonder that many did not dare to close with them. We must not think that the Spartan army was as other armies were (cf. P.7).

## *Dēlion*

6.13 Let us turn to Thucydides' other great battle, the battle of Dēlion in 424 (H.I.42). The Athenian general, Hippokrates, had led out the full Athenian army into Boiotia to join with another general, Demosthenes, coming from the west, in a two-pronged attack. The venture miscarried and Hippokrates, having fortified a temple at Dēlion, set out to return home. The full Boiotian army prepared to attack him. Their general, Pagondas, harangued them. Hippokrates passed along his army, exhorting the Athenians to valour. But he was cut short by the Boiotian advance.

(93) When the approach of the Boiotians was reported to Hippokrates at Dēlion, he sent orders to his army to take up battle formation, and shortly afterwards joined them himself, leaving three hundred cavalry at Dēlion to guard the place from attack and to watch for a chance of attacking the Boiotians during the battle. The Boiotians posted a detachment to deal with these, and when they were ready appeared over the crest of the hill, grounded their arms and halted in their pre-determined order. They numbered seven thousand hoplites, ten thousand and more light-armed troops, a thousand horse and five hundred peltasts. On the right wing were those from Thebes and district; in the centre the Haliartioi, Koronaioi, Kopaiēs and other lake-side dwellers: on the left the Thespiēs, Tanagraioi, and Orkhomenioi. The cavalry and light troops were on the wings. The Thebans were drawn up twenty-five shields deep, the rest as they pleased. So much for the Thebans. (94) The Athenian hoplites were drawn up eight shields deep, their numbers were about equal to the Boiotians, and their cavalry was on the wings. The Athenians had no regular light-armed troops present on this occasion nor did the city possess any. Those who had joined the invasion far outnumbered the enemy, but were for the most part unarmed; they were a general expedition of foreign residents and citizens, and as they had been the first to start home very few were present . . . [*Hippokrates now encourages his army.*]

(96) These were Hippokrates' words of encouragement, but he only got half-way down the line when he had to break off as the Boiotians, after a few more hurried words from Pagondas, struck up the paean and advanced down the hill. The Athenians advanced to meet them and closed at a run. The wings of neither army came to blows, being held up by water-courses. The rest fought stubbornly,

shield thrusting against shield. The Boiotian left, as far as the centre, was worsted by the Athenians, the Thespiēs being particularly hard-pressed. The troops next to them in the line gave way, they were encircled in a narrow space and cut down in hand-to-hand fighting. Some of the Athenians were confused by the encircling movement and mistakenly killed each other. The Boiotians were thus worsted in this part of the field and retreated towards the fighting, but on the right wing where the Thebans were, they got the better of the Athenians, pushed them back slowly at first and followed them up. It so happened also that Pagondas, seeing his left was in trouble, sent two squadrons of cavalry round under the hill where they could not be seen, and their sudden appearance caused the victorious Athenian wing to panic, thinking that another army was advancing against them. What with this and the Theban pressure and breakthrough on the right the whole Athenian army took flight. (Thucydides, *Peloponnesian War* 4.93–6)

Here again characteristic features assert themselves, the depth of the Athenians, the cavalry posted on each flank. The interesting detail about the battle being joined late in the day suggests that normally battles began early enough to allow a long time for the fighting. But one hesitates to generalise much from this battle. The Boiotians were twenty-five deep, a striking innovation. The Athenian light-armed had been withdrawn, and although Thucydides suggests that they would have been of little use had they stayed, we get no idea of how they would have been used and the geography of the battlefield prevented the very large force of Boiotian light-armed showing themselves.

### Athenians and Syracusans

**6.14** One other engagement, admittedly minor, which Thucydides described, can be taken into account. It is the battle fought by the Athenians against the Syracusans and their allies outside the city of Syracuse in winter 415/14 (cf. H.I.48–50).

(69) The engagement started with a preliminary skirmish between the stone-throwers, slingers and archers, in which, as usually happens with light-armed troops, fortunes varied. Then the priests brought out the usual victims for sacrifice and the trumpeters sounded the charge for the hoplites, who advanced . . .

(70) When battle was joined, for a long time neither side gave way. Meanwhile a thunderstorm broke, with thunder, lightning and heavy rain, which added to the fears of the Syracusans, who were in battle for the first time and had little experience of war, though the more experienced Athenians put it down to the time of year and were more alarmed by the continued resistance of the army. The Argives were the first to push back the Syracusan left, the Athenians followed on their part of the front, and Syracusan resistance elsewhere was then broken and flight ensued. The

Athenians did not press the pursuit far, being prevented by the numerous Syracusan cavalry, who were still undefeated and attacked their hoplites and drove any they saw pursuing in advance of the rest; but they did follow up the fugitives so far as it was safe to do so in close formation. They then withdrew and set up a trophy. (Thucydides, *Peloponnesian War* 6.69–70)

First, the light-armed troops skirmished before the battle but had no real part in it and Thucydides dismisses them somewhat contemptuously. Then in the battle proper there was a long hand-to-hand combat and at a later stage when the Syracusans had begun to fare less well it came to 'shoving', i.e. with overlapping shields the Athenians and their allies pushed back the Syracusans. These latter then fled and the Syracusan cavalry came into play for the first time (although the Athenians had none) in preventing the Athenian pursuit. In this battle the three elements of the fifth-century army show themselves distinctly enough, viz. cavalry, hoplites, and light-armed, and it is time to describe them and their armament.

## Economics of service

**6.15** Since the state did not fully provide arms and armour, the three kinds (cavalry, hoplites and light-armed) represent different economic classes. Keeping horses was then as now an expensive business, and the cavalry (*hippeis*) were the richest men in the state, never more than 1,200 at Athens, by the middle of the fourth century considerably fewer. Hoplite equipment too was not cheap, and the hoplite class was at Athens drawn from the third of Solon's property classes (H.I.8, 5.26), the so-called *sdeugitai*, in origin men rich enough to own a yoke of oxen. Finally, the poorest citizens, the so-called *thētes*, were liable for service in the light-armed, the *psiloi* (literally, 'bare'). All citizens were liable for military service of some sort from the ages of 18 to 60 (1.11).

## Cavalry

**6.16** Cavalry proper, i.e., men who fought on horseback, were a late development in the Greek world. Earlier, the richest citizens had ridden to battle, but dismounted to fight, and the name of the Spartan *hippeis* (cavalry) who fought as the king's bodyguard at Mantineia (see 6.9), was a survival of what had once been general. Cavalry was in due course to come into its own, but in the fifth century its use was, and had to be, limited to the very subsidiary roles it fulfilled in the battles Thucydides described. The cavalryman carried only a spear, and since the stirrup had not been

invented he was equally likely to fall off if he missed or be pushed off it he
hit too firmly or if struck himself. In addition, the horses of southern
Greece seem to have been rather a puny breed (cf. 1.13). So frontal assault
on a line of hoplites would have been worse than useless.

### Hoplites

**6.17** The hoplite was, therefore, the main strength of Greek armies in
the fifth century. He was well protected, principally by a round shield a
metre wide (the so-called *hoplon*, whence the name), a helmet, a
breastplate or a corslet, and greaves. His principal weapon was the spear;
hence Aeschylus in his tragedy *Persians* 147ff. represented the conflict of
spear and bow. But the hoplite also carried a short, single-edged, curving
sword for emergencies, to be used as we see represented on vases, in a
downward hack. A hoplite would often be accompanied by a slave to carry
his equipment for him (H.I.7).

### Light-armed

**6.18** As to the light-armed in the fifth century, we are less well informed.
As will be seen, they came to play a very important part in warfare, and this
development began in the 420s, but as Thucydides remarked in his account
of the battle of Dēlion (6.13), as late as 424 Athens had no regular constituted units of light-armed. Their function was to discharge missiles

6:4  A hoplite's equipment: breastplate, helmet, bronze shield, sword; only the
spear and greaves are missing. Early 5th century.

6:5 Hoplites fasten on their armour; one warrior takes his shield from its wrappings. C. 480.

6:6 The warrior on the right brings his sword down on his opponent in a downward hack. Late 6th century.

6:7 A slinger. C. 470.

(stones, javelins, arrows) from a distance, but they were more of a nuisance to the enemy than a serious danger (but cf. H.I.39).

### Hand-to-hand fighting

**6.19** We must now face the awkward question of what exactly happened in the hand-to-hand fighting. From vase paintings we can see how the spear was used. It was raised above the shoulder and aimed at the hoplite's most vulnerable point, the gap between helmet and breastplate. But that is all we can say for certain. The common notion that a hoplite battle was in essentials a huge pushing match has problems. Certainly there was a concerted shoving (*ōthismos*) at some stage of the battle; and there must be some point in the measured advance to battle, controlled by an *aulos*-player, the concerted lines with overlapping shields, the great depth of soldiers (see 6.12). Yet at Plataia, according to Herodotus (*Histories* 9.67), there was a 'fierce battle for a long time until they came to shoving', just as in the battle outside Syracuse in 415 in the hand-to-hand battle the two sides long resisted each other and the shoving came later(see 6.14). What then was happening before the shoving? Or perhaps these passages refer to the time when one side actually succeeded in pushing the other back? Differing views have been advanced and it is best to resign ourselves to confessing that we do not really know what happened in 'fierce battle for a long time'. It was one of those matters too plain to a Greek historian to seem to need explanation.

Neither of the major battles described by Thucydides can, for various reasons, be regarded as wholly typical, so much must remain supposition and speculation. However, it will be generally conceded that in this early period battles were almost entirely hoplite affairs, that once the two phalanxes joined battle, they fought it out, the generals having done their bit in engaging the armies, and there was nothing more to be done. The use of reserves or unusual tactics had no part.

### New developments in Greek warfare

**6.20** Yet great wars stimulate innovation and experiment and the long-drawn Peloponnesian War set in motion a century of dramatic development in the art of warfare. The future lay with the specialised use of specialist arms and with the ever-increasing professionalisation of military practice. Then came the experience of Greek fighting barbarian in Persia and in Thrace, and when the Corinthian War began in 395 Greek warfare was well on the way to its grand finale, the battle of Khaironeia (H.I.81).

### (i) Lekhaion 390 (H.I.63): the peltast

**6.21** It will be best to start with one of the most celebrated events of Greek arms, the disaster at Lekhaion in 390, when a mercenary force of peltasts (special light-armed troops (6.18)) under the command of the Athenian general Iphikrates, cut to pieces a division of the Spartan army near Corinth. Here is the account of Xenophon:

(13) The generals in Corinth, Kallias the son of Hipponikos who commanded the Athenian hoplites, and Iphikrates who commanded the peltasts, when they saw that the Spartans were few in number and unescorted by peltasts or cavalry, decided that it was safe enough to attack them with their own peltasts. If they marched along the road, they could be attacked on their unprotected side with javelins and destroyed; and if they turned in pursuit it would be easy enough for the peltasts with their light equipment to get away from hoplites. (14) Kallias drew up his hoplites close to the city and Iphikrates with his peltasts attacked the Spartan regiment. Under this assault by javelin some of the Spartans were wounded and some killed, and the shield-bearers were ordered to pick them up and carry them to Lekhaion; and they were the only men in the regiment to get away safely. The general then ordered the first ten year-groups to drive off their assailants. (15) They went after them, but failed to catch any of them. They were hoplites chasing peltasts who had a javelin throw's start, and Iphikrates had given orders that they were to retire before the hoplites got to grips with them. Besides, the hoplites became scattered in their efforts at pursuit, and when they turned to retire Iphikrates' men wheeled round and attacked them again, some from the front and some from the flank, running along to expose their unprotected side. In the first pursuit nine or ten of the peltasts' javelins struck home, which encouraged them to attack still more boldly. (16) As the Spartans continued to suffer casualties, their general ordered the first fifteen year-groups to the attack and pursuit. But when they turned to retire they suffered more casualties than before. They had already lost all their best men, when the cavalry appeared and they attempted a joint pursuit. The peltasts turned to run, but the cavalry mismanaged their attack. Instead of pressing their pursuit till they had inflicted casualties they kept a continuous front with the hoplites both in advance and retreat. The Spartans continued to pursue the same tactics with the same result, becoming fewer and less resolute while their assailants became bolder and more numerous. (17) At last in desperation they formed up on a small hill, about half a mile from the sea and two miles from Lekhaion. The men of Lekhaion, when they saw them, embarked in small boats and sailed along till they were opposite the hill. The Spartans were already desperate; they were suffering acutely and being killed without being able to retaliate, and

when they finally saw the hoplites coming up they broke and ran. Some plunged into the sea and a few managed to escape to Lekhaion with the cavalry; but in the whole engagement and in the subsequent flight about two hundred and fifty of them were killed. (Xenophon, *Hellenika* 4.5.13–17)

The peltasts, so named from the small, light, wicker-work shield they carried (the *peltē*), were by contrast with the hoplite highly mobile, operating by hit-and-run tactics, on this occasion hurling their javelins and retiring before the Spartan hoplites could get to them. In itself the engagement had no important influence on the course of the war. Two hundred and fifty Spartans in all were killed; only three hundred and fifty survived. The disaster was the clearest demonstration that the long dominance of the hoplite could be effectively challenged.

6.22 The demonstration was clear but not really surprising. Peltasts had long been familiar to the Greeks. But the real emergence of the light-armed as a specialist arm with specialised uses was in the operations based on the headland of Pylos in Messenia (425), in which Demosthenes, arguably Athens' greatest general in the fifth century, alerted to the importance of the light-armed by the rough handling his own hoplites had received in Aitolia the previous year, assembled a huge force of light-armed for his attack on the Spartan hoplites, unwisely placed on the adjacent island of Sphakteria (Thucydides, *Peloponnesian War* 4.32ff.; cf. H.I.41–2). Demosthenes killed or captured every Spartan on the island. The day of the specialist was dawning. Through the later years of the Peloponnesian War we hear of the light-armed, especially peltasts, ever more frequently.

6:8 A Thracian peltast dressed in a heavy cloak and carrying the characteristic small crescent-shaped shield (*peltē*). Early 5th century.

## (ii) The cavalry

**6.23** The success of the light-armed signalled the beginning of the end for hoplite dominance, but more important in the long run was the rise of the cavalry. As already noticed, in the fifth century the cavalry play an insignificant and largely subsidiary part. But at the battle of Khaironeia in 338 it was the Macedonian cavalry, under the command of the youthful Alexander, which delivered the fatal blow to the Greek army. The full development was largely due to Philip who had at his disposal a people long habituated to fighting on horseback. But notable landmarks in this development were the two great battles of the Theban military genius, Epameinondas. At the battle of Leuktra in 371 the Boiotian cavalry were used to play an integral part in his plan for the battle; while they fought the Spartan cavalry, the Boiotians advanced, under cover as it were, and began the attack on one flank. At the battle of [Second] Mantineia in 362 Epameinondas used his cavalry in conjunction with infantry to 'ram' part of the opposing line. The cavalry were, in short, already coming into their own.

6:9 A public funerary monument showing a cavalry engagement. The inscription which accompanies it records that 'those who died at Corinth and in Boiotia' in 394 have their names listed below.

Thus the fourth century was the age of specialists and specialised arms, and the Macedonian army had units appropriate to every situation. It was also the age of the professional, in all spheres, but in none more than in the art of war.

### Fourth-century professionalism: Thebes and Macedon

**6.24** In the fifth century, as already remarked, the Spartans were the professionals in an age of amateurs. But as early as [First] Mantineia, others had begun to copy them. The 1,000 picked Argive troops, who were stationed separately from the regular Argive companies and who fought with considerable effect against the Spartan left wing when most of their countrymen did not dare even to endure combat, were, as the historian Diodoros commented, 'admirably trained in the business of war'. The Spartan monopoly was beginning to slip. In the fourth century they were equalled or outdone by the Theban 'Sacred Band' of three hundred, who fought heroically on the battlefield of Leuktra and died to a man, it is said, at Khaironeia. Here again, however, the supreme professionals were the Macedonian army, and despite the attempts of Greeks to adjust to the new age they were surpassed by Philip, his 'Companion Foot' and his 'Companion Cavalry'. But the Greeks did try, and one sign of this professionalism was the emergence of the mercenary. In an age when warfare was continuous through summers and winters and increasingly complex, no city could do without them.

### *Generalship*

**6.25** Nowhere is the new professionalism more plain than in the sphere of generalship. The illustrious mercenary generals of the age, Iphikrates, Timotheos, Khabrias, Khares, to name a few, unlike Pericles, Nikias and Alkibiades in the preceding century, confined themselves to war and left politics to mere politicians (5.29ff.). Theory too developed and professional teachers of the military art are to be found, men like Dionysodoros, an Athenian whom we meet in Xenophon's *Memorabilia* 3.1.1, professing 'to teach how to be a general', or that curious figure the Boiotian Phalinos, the 'expert on tactics and arms-drill' who turns up in the service of the King of Persia in 401 (Xenophon, *Anabasis* 2.1.7). Indeed a military literature began to be in vogue (7.21).

**6.26** The fourth century is indeed the age of the professional soldier, but there was one portent, in the fifth century. The general Demosthenes was no politician and was fairly constantly engaged in the military service of Athens (5.30). Both in tactics and in strategy, he was an innovator. By contrast the greatest general of free Greece, Epameinondas, was, like Pericles, both politician and soldier, but in the latter role he was a supreme professional, in the sense that he thought about war and planned war to better effect than any of his predecessors.

The battle of Leuktra in 371 is his masterpiece (H.I.70–1).

(10) As there was level ground between the two armies, the Spartans stationed their cavalry in front of their phalanx and the Thebans stationed theirs opposite them. (11) The Theban cavalry was in good training as a result of their wars against the Orkhomenioi and Thespiës, but the Spartan cavalry at that particular time was in poor shape. (12) As far as the infantry is concerned, the Spartans are said to have drawn up each half-company three files abreast, so that their phalanx was not more than twelve deep. The Thebans on the other hand were drawn up not less than fifty shields deep, reckoning that if they defeated those around the king the rest would be easy.

(13) When Kleombrotos the Spartan began the advance, and before his troops were aware that he had done so, the cavalry had already joined battle and the Spartans had been quickly worsted. In their flight they ran into their own hoplites, who were at the same time attacked by the Thebans. None the less the troops round Kleombrotos at first had the best of the fighting . . . (14) But Deinon the *polemarkhos* was killed and Sphodrias one of the king's council and his son Kleonymos fell also; the king's hoplites and the troops known as the 'Polemarkhos' Own' were pushed back by the massed weight of the Thebans, and when they saw their right wing thus forced back the Spartan left turned and fled. (Xenophon, *Hellenika* 6.4.10–14)

The most important point is that the battle was fought and won, not by two colliding lines of hoplites, but by a concentration of force on the Boiotian left flank, whereas one normally sought to win on the right. The Thebans were drawn up fifty deep, a startling fact, however one interprets

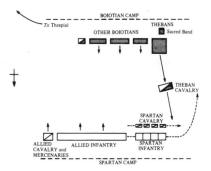

6:10  Possible schematic reconstruction of the battle of Leuktra, 371. The initial position of the Sacred Band is uncertain.

it (although at Dēlion the Thebans were twenty-five deep (see 6.13): so someone in Thebes in the fifth century was conceiving of new ways of war), and only the Thebans of the allied army actually fought. Further, when the Spartans sought to outflank the Thebans the 'Sacred Band' was sent in to prevent them; thus the general Epameinondas continued to control the battle after it had been joined. He had thought out and trained his men for new methods of war.

**6.27** Epameinondas' other great battle is [Second] Mantineia (362, H.I.71–2). One anecdote concerning its victor is worth mention, for it graphically illuminates the succession of the great professional soldiers. It concerns the death of Epameinondas on the battlefield. He was carried from the field with a spear through his chest, and the doctors declared that when it was pulled out he would die.

First he summoned his shield-bearer and asked 'Did you save my shield?' He said 'Yes' and held the shield before Epameinondas' eyes. Then he asked 'Who has won?' The boy said 'The Boiotians'. 'Then it's time to die. Pull out the spear.' His friends there cried out in protest and one of them in tears said 'You die without a son and heir, Epameinondas.' 'I do, by God, but I leave two daughters, my Victory of Leuktra and my Victory of Mantineia.' The spear was pulled out, and he calmly died. (Diodoros 15.87)

Two daughters indeed: and a suitor was at hand, Philip of Macedon. He took what they had to teach him, and the battle of Khaironeia was the result, the climax of Greek warfare on land.

### Athens in the fourth century

**6.28** From this picture of military development the Athenians are, generally, conspicuously absent. For the most part their professional generals in the fourth century, in so far as they fought on land, used mercenary troops. How much then did land warfare impinge on Athenian lives? The Boiotians under Epameinondas trained with no less zeal than the Spartans, from whom they wrested the primacy. The Macedonians under Philip did the same. By contrast, the city of Athens, Xenophon declared (*Memorabilia* 3.12), had 'no public training in military matters'. But Athenians did have their share in battles, and the truth would appear to be that on coming of age, i.e. becoming an *ephēbos*, young Athenians did two years' service in the 'Scouts' (or 'Rangers') (*peripoloi*) and received training, and after that it was left to individuals to keep themselves ready for war, which they did. (The conversation in Plato's dialogue, *Lakhes*,

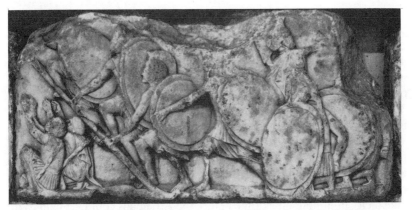

6:11 Soldiers attempt to storm a city they have been besieging. C. 400.

which discusses the nature of courage (cf. 7.30), was occasioned by the sight of a famous teacher of hoplite fighting.) So, after their own fashion, which may not have been all that different from the general practice, they trained (cf. 4.42).

## Siegecraft

6.29 Athens acquired a considerable reputation in siegecraft, and in the late 460s the Spartans called on the city for help in the siege of the Messenian stronghold, Ithome (H.I.30). Generally, in the fifth century the only really effective way of taking a city was by circumvallation, i.e. putting a wall around it and starving it into submission. There were devices. We hear of Pericles using a battering-ram and 'tortoise-shell' of shields (which acted as a platform from which to scale walls) in the siege of Samos in 440 (H.I.33) and of Spartans using siege-engines against Plataia (Thucydides, *Peloponnesian War* 2.71ff.; H.I.35), but it was all rather ineffective. It took Pericles nine months to reduce Samos and the Spartans two years to reduce Plataia, which was manned in the earlier stages of the siege by 480 men, in the later by less than 240. The operations round Syracuse in 414 and 413 typified the age (H.I.48, 50). The best the Athenians could think of was to try and wall the city off from harbour to sea and let time and hunger do their worst.

6.30 The stalemate was broken by non-Greek ingenuity and energy. In the wars of the Carthaginians against the Greeks in Sicily in the last decade of the fifth century cities were taken by assault. We hear of rams and mounds, of wheeled towers and mines, and, whether it was a Greek invention or a Carthaginian, we shortly encounter for the first time in the service of Dionysios of Syracuse the 'catapult', a weapon that discharged arrows at defenders of walls, rather like a cross-bow. The best indication of the new state of affairs is provided by what survives of the military handbook of the Arkadian Aineias, the so-called Tactician, published in the early 350s. In it is much advice about how to defend cities against rams and mines and the like, but not a word about circumvallation.

In this development Athens played her part. The general Timotheos took Samos by assault in 366/5 and a string of Thracian cities thereafter. But the real master of the art was Philip of Macedon. Eleven cities are recorded as falling to him, but what is so striking is his speed. He could take a city in double-quick time before the Athenians could get help to it. Cities were no longer secure. The end of the city-state was at hand.

### Sea warfare

#### (i) *Triremes and their crews*

**6.31** Throughout the classical period one sort of warship was almost universal, the trireme (the *triērēs* in Greek (cf. 1.15)). It was a long, slender ship (the dimensions attested by the fourth-century remains of the ship-sheds at the Peiraieus were 35–37 m by 3.5 m) with a low draught, an 'overgrown racing eight'. Its chief armament was the ram which was an extension of the keel. There were 170 rowers, in three superimposed

6:12  Two warships with boar-shaped prows. C. 530.

banks, 27 on each side in the lowest, the so-called *thalamitai*, likewise 27 in the middle, the *sdugitai*, and 31 on each side in the top bank, the *thranitai*, who sat on benches above the gunwhale and rowed by means of an out-rigger (and since their oars were rowed at the sharpest angle to the water, their task was the most strenuous, and was rewarded with a higher rate of pay). Above the level of the *thranitai* a deck ran from stem to stern on which the marines travelled and fought. The ship was commanded by a trierarch who had under him a steersman (*kubernētēs*), a rowing officer (*keleustēs*), a bow officer (*prōrātēs*) (whose function was mainly to keep watch), a quartermaster, and others including a ship's carpenter, an *aulos*-player to pipe the time for the rowers, and four archers. In all there were two hundred men.

**6.32** The trireme carried masts, and on a long voyage it was possible to exploit a favourable wind. Nor did all the rowers row all the time except in battle. There was no room on board for eating or sleeping, and the trireme, generally speaking, had to be beached at night for crews to eat and sleep (cf. 1.15). The account given by Xenophon of the voyage of Iphikrates round the Peloponnese illuminates normal practice; Iphikrates was in a hurry and wanted to train his crews at the same time, but one can infer what was normal from Xenophon's account:

When Iphikrates began his voyage round the Peloponnese, he took with him all the equipment he needed for a naval battle. He left his large sails at home, as if he was sailing to battle, and made very little use of his small sails even when the wind was

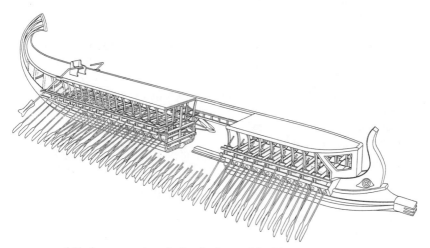

6:13  A cutaway view of a Greek trireme of the 5th century.

favourable. By proceeding under oars in this way he made his crews fitter and his ships faster. And when the expedition was due for its morning or evening meal at any particular place, he would order the leading ships back, turn the line round again to face the land and make them race at a signal for the shore ... Again, if they were taking a meal on hostile territory, he set the usual sentries on land but he also raised his ships' masts and had men keeping watch from the top of them. They had a far wider view from their point of vantage than they would have had from ground level ... On daylight voyages he trained them to form line ahead or line abreast at a signal, so that in the course of their voyage they had practised and become skilled at the manoeuvres needed in a naval battle before they reached the area of sea which they supposed to be in enemy control. (Xenophon, *Hellenika* 6.2.27–30)

One point, which does not emerge from this account of Xenophon, was of great importance: the trireme was so light that it could not be used in really rough weather (cf. 1.15). This meant that naval operations were, generally speaking, not possible in winter, nor in the bad weather caused by the Etesian winds (see 1.4–5). They were a constant limiting factor in naval strategy.

### (ii) Athenian expertise

### (a) Training

6.33 It is important to realise that in only moderately rough weather a great deal of skill and training was necessary if the trireme was to be at its most effective. This is the principal reason why the Athenians were so successful. The demands of naval empire in the fifth century and of their attempts to recover it in the fourth kept them constantly at sea. Others had fleets for short periods; for the rest of the time their naval activity was very limited. Athens was constantly at sea and her naval expertise remained very high (cf. 5.75).

6.34 The favourite tactical manoeuvre, the *diekplous*, was particularly demanding. In it a ship would pass through the enemy line, swing round and attack the enemy either by ramming it broadside or by shearing off its oars. Speed of movement, speed in turning, and accuracy in attack were essential and not easily acquired. Steering was particularly a matter for skill, which is partly why the steersman, the *kubernētēs*, was in many ways the key man. (When Alkibiades went off on a small mission in 407 he left the whole Athenian fleet at Samos under the command of his steersman.) But all the crew needed to be skilled at their tasks. Consider, for example, the control needed for a trireme to execute a high-speed turn of the sort described in 6.39.

## (b) Mercenaries

6.35 It was not, of course, the case that all Athenians could row well. There was a celebrated moment in 411 when the whole Athenian people rushed down to the Peiraieus, manned the ships, and presented a spectacle of far from well-trained seamanship (Thucydides, *Peloponnesian War* 8.95). But many lived by rowing. In the *Akharnians* Aristophanes refers to 'the *thranitai* folk (key rowers, see 6.31) the city savers', and Aristotle in the *Politics* attributed the rise of democracy to 'the naval throng'. But to a large extent the Athenian navy was mercenary. 'The Athenian naval power is hired rather than their own' the Corinthians asserted in 432 and Pericles' reply, while declaring that Athens could man the fleet herself if necessary, conceded the point (Thucydides, *Peloponnesian War* 1.121–40). It was in fact a source of strength. A fleet of sixty ships required over 10,000 rowers. If Athens had had to rely solely on her citizens and resident aliens, the *metoikoi*, she would never have been able to man the large fleets she constantly did.

## (c) The Peiraieus

6.36 The Peiraieus was the centre of the Aegean. To it came everyone who wanted a job as a rower, as well as all the supplies necessary for seafaring of every kind – rope and tar, timber and leather and so on. It was the prerequisite for naval power. As Xenophon remarked in the *Poroi*, in the mid-350s, the Peiraieus was inevitable for Greek seafarers (cf. 4.56–7). No wonder that Athens, navally speaking, led the world.

## (iii) The development of naval warfare

6.37 In the discussion of land warfare it was necessary to emphasise the constant development of the art of war. In the case of sea warfare we are confronted by the apparent contrary. Naval tactics remained virtually unchanged, as far as we know, from the start of the Peloponnesian War to the bitter defeat of the Athenian navy and the end of Athens as a naval power at the battle of Amorgos in 322 (6.49). What development there was had come much earlier. The Persian fleet which fought the Greeks at Artemision and Salamis in 480 (H.I.17–18) consisted of ships rather unlike triremes, being decked all over, higher, lighter and carrying more than thirty marines. At that stage the Phoenicians, fighting on the Persian side, excelled the Greeks in seamanship and their aim, amply fulfilled at Artemision, was to sail through the Greek line, turn, come alongside and send their marines aboard. In the confined waters of the bay of Salamis

6:14   The Peiraieus, the port of Athens.

their seamanship was frustrated and the heavier Greek ships won the battle *by ramming*. This was to be the method of the future, yet in 480 the Greeks could only see the battle as a freak bit of luck. For when in the early 460s Kimon sailed out to confront a grand Persian naval and land force at the battle of the Eurymedon (H.I.25), he fully decked his ships and loaded them with marines in the Phoenician manner and as late as 433 many Greeks, though not the Athenians, were still fighting in the same old-fashioned way. Thucydides' account of the battle of Sybota makes this plain.

As soon as the signals were given, the ships on both sides came to close quarters and fighting began. Both sides had many hoplites on deck, as well as a number of archers and javelineers, for they were still using old-fashioned tactics owing to their inexperience. The battle was obstinately fought, but without corresponding skill, being more like a land engagement fought at sea. Once they had grappled with each other they found it difficult to disengage because of the number of vessels involved and their crowding together; they relied for victory mainly on the hoplites on deck, who stood and fought while the ships remained stationary. There was no attempt at the manoeuvre of breaking the line; courage and brute force played a greater part than skill. Confusion reigned throughout the battle and there was tumult everywhere. (Thucydides, *Peloponnesian War* 1.49)

**6.38** But in the naval operations of the Athenian Phormion at the mouth of the Gulf of Corinth in 429 the Corinthians came up against the new naval tactics of the Athenians and were clearly terrified (H.I.39):

(83) Phormion watched the Corinthian fleet as they coasted along out of the gulf, intending to attack them in the open sea. But the Corinthians and their allies had to put to sea with no thought of fighting, their object being the transport of troops to Akarnania; and they assumed that the Athenians with their twenty ships would not venture to attack their own forty-seven. However, as they sailed along their own coast they saw the Athenians sailing parallel to them, and when they tried to cross from Patrai in Akhaia to the opposite mainland they noticed them again sailing from Khalkis and the Euenos river to meet them. They failed to give them the slip by putting out at night, and so were compelled to fight in mid-passage . . . The Peloponnesians drew their ships up in a circle, as large as they could make it without allowing the enemy passage between the vessels, whose prows faced outwards and sterns inwards. The lighter craft of the expedition were placed inside the circle together with five of their fastest ships ready to sally out at short notice to meet any enemy attack.

(84) The Athenians drew up in line ahead and sailed round and round them, gradually forcing the circle to contract by sailing very close and pretending to attack, though Phormion had given orders that no attack was to be made till he gave the signal. He expected that they would not be able to keep formation, as they would on land, and that the warships and the lighter craft would foul each other and fall into confusion, while the wind which usually got up towards evening and for which he was waiting during the manoeuvre, would complete their disorder in no time. He judged that he could pick his own time for the attack, as his ships were the more manoeuvreable, and that the best moment was when the wind rose. When the wind did rise the Peloponnesian ships were already crowded together, and what

6:15 Athēnē holds a ship's stern (*aphlaston*) as a sign of an Athenian naval victory, perhaps at Salamis. C. 480.

with the wind and their own light craft were soon in confusion. The warships fouled each other and the crews tried to push them free with poles, shouting and swearing and struggling with each other; the noise made it impossible to hear the orders of the ships' captains and the helmsmen, and the rough water prevented the inexperienced crews from clearing their oars and made it more difficult for the helmsmen to control their vessels. At this moment Phormion gave the signal and the Athenians attacked. They first sank the ship of one of the enemy commanders, and then went on to disable any ship they came across; in the confusion the enemy's resistance was completely broken and they fled to Patrai and Dyme in Akhaia. (Thucydides, *Peloponnesian War* 2.83–4)

**6.39** In this first engagement the forty-seven Peloponnesian ships were still equipped in the old-fashioned way seen at Sybota, and forming up in a circle for fear of the Athenian *diekplous*, they were driven together in confusion by the Athenians circling round them. For the second engagement the Spartans called for new ships to be built, more apt to the new ways of war, and a fleet of seventy-seven was assembled. The Athenians still had only twenty, but the Peloponnesian fleet was afraid to face them in open sea. In the speech of the Spartan commander before the battle, arguments were put to diminish fear of Athenian experience and skill and, although some of the Athenian ships were caught within the narrow waters of the gulf and suffered, in the end it was Athenian experience and skill that took the real credit:

(90) When the Peloponnesians saw Phormion sailing along inside the gulf, in line ahead and close inshore, which was just what they wanted, at a given signal they all turned to port and bore down with all speed in line abreast on the Athenians, hoping to cut the whole squadron off. The eleven leading ships evaded the Peloponnesian wing and its turning movement and escaped into open water, but the rest were caught, driven ashore as they tried to escape, and disabled; any of the crews who failed to swim ashore were killed . . .

(91) Meanwhile their twenty ships from the right wing were chasing the eleven Athenian ships which had evaded the turning movement and reached the open sea. The Athenians, with the exception of one ship, outdistanced them and made good their escape to Naupaktos, and drawing up by the temple of Apollo, with prows seaward, prepared to defend themselves against a Peloponnesian attack. The Peloponnesians came up later, singing a paean of victory as they advanced. A long way ahead of the rest was a Leukadian ship pursuing the one Athenian straggler. There happened to be a merchant ship anchored off shore, and the Athenian ship outwitted the pursuit by sailing round this merchantman, ramming its pursuer amidships and sinking it. This unlikely and unexpected exploit caused panic among the Peloponnesians, who had fallen out of formation in the excitement of victory, and some of them stopped rowing so as to lose way till the others came up

(a very dangerous thing to do with the Athenians so close), while others, not knowing the coast, ran aground in the shallows. (92) When they saw what had happened the Athenians plucked up courage, and at a single word of command fell on the enemy with a cheer. They, because of their mistakes and the disorder into which they had fallen, after a brief resistance made off for Panormos, from which they had originally put out. The Athenians pursued them and captured six of the ships nearest to them, and recovered those of their own which had been disabled close inshore when the action began and taken in tow. Of the crews they killed some and took others prisoner. (Thucydides, *Peloponnesian War* 2.90–2)

In short, after the battle of Sybota the Peloponnesians slowly but at length saw the light; the Athenians had for quite some time past held the torch. For Athens the perfection of the use of the trireme had come before the Peloponnesian War, and that is why for over a century there is no development in the art of naval warfare.

## (iv) The Athenian naval system

6.40 There was not much change in the Athenian naval system either. Our knowledge is chiefly derived from a speech delivered by Apollodoros in [Demosthenes], *Against Polykles* 50. In it we see the Athenian navy at a time of particular stress in the late 360s. The supply of rowing labour in the Peiraieus roughly matched the regular demand and when in autumn 362 the call came for yet more ships, exceptional measures had to be taken. Moreover Apollodoros was an extravagant young man (4.70) and spent more on his ship and his crew than he could reasonably expect his successor to take over lightly. A sober appraisal of the situation behind the speech shows that essentially the organisation of the fleet was no different in any respect from that pertaining in 415 when the great armada set out for Sicily, a matter on which we are well informed by Thucydides:

The fleet had been equipped at great expense both by the trierarchs and from public funds. Public funds paid each member of the crews at the rate of a drachma a day besides providing sixty warships and forty troopships with picked petty officers; the trierarchs added a bonus to the public payment for the *thranitai* and petty officers and spared no expense on figureheads and other gear, rivalling each other in the provision of vessels which would be outstanding both in appearance and speed. The land forces were picked from the best muster-rolls and individuals competed keenly in the quality of their arms and other equipment . . . Indeed the total outlay found by the city amounted to an enormous sum, if you reckon up the private expenses of individuals serving in the forces as well as public expenditure by the state. Public expenditure included funds already expended as well as moneys in the hands of the generals for the expenses of the expedition, private expenditure both what individuals had laid out on their equipment and what the trierarchs had already incurred on their ships and were likely to incur in the future; to this should be added the provision individuals were likely to have made by way of journey money for a long campaign quite apart from its cost to the state, and what soldiers and merchants took with them with a view to trade . . .

When the ships were manned and everything they meant to take was on board, the trumpet gave the signal for silence and the prayers customary before putting to sea were offered, not ship by ship but all together, conducted by a herald, and officers and crew throughout the whole force mixed and poured libations from gold and silver cups. The crowds on shore joined in the prayers, both citizens and those who wished them well. And when the paean had been sung and the libations poured, they put to sea, sailing out first in line ahead and then racing to Aiginē. (Thucydides, *Peloponnesian War* 6.31)

### (a) Trierarchy and syntrierarchy

**6.41** Trierarchy was a form of military service (a *leitourgia*, see 5.71) which all men of the necessary minimum wealth were obliged to undertake. Its functions were primarily financial. (For although the trierarch shared the danger of service, the knowledge and experience necessary for naval operations lay, as had already been remarked, with the *kubernētēs* (6.34).) It certainly was costly. Although the city provided the ship, paid the crew, and made the naval equipment in the dockyards available for trierarchs to draw, the trierarch found it expedient to have his own equipment, especially things as vital as ropes, and to hire as expert a set of officers as he could. Because it was so costly in the later years of the Peloponnesian War when Athens was much impoverished, there were not enough sufficiently rich men of military age to take the duty on, and the 'syntrierarchy' was introduced, whereby the cost was shared by two men, each of whom served in person for six months, since a trierarchy lasted for a full twelve months from the day it commenced.

**6.42** Equipping involved providing two classes of gear, wooden and hanging. The wooden gear, a set of oars, a mast, steering-oars, ladders, sail-yards and poles, was kept in the ship-shed, where the ship was kept when not at sea. The hanging gear, sails, sail-tackle, ropes, anchors and some other items, were kept in the gear-store. Many of the ship-sheds were situated in the harbour of Sdea, while the gear-stores were probably mainly in the main harbour, Kantharos. Thus the preparation of an expedition would necessitate someone bringing the ship, with the wooden gear, round from Sdea to the quay in Kantharos, where the ship's hanging gear would be loaded (not all of it, as ordinary sails were not taken into battle) (5.25).

**6.43** The ship would then be manned. The crews would know which ship they belonged to as they would have practised together – manoeuvring the ship in battle required timing and experience which could only be gained by regular sessions. They would come with their *tropōtēr* (a leather thong for tying the oar to the pin against which it worked) and *hupēresion* (a cushion, perhaps tallowed underneath for sliding back and forth at the oar). It seems that the oars were placed on a rack on board while the ship was being manned, and that the amount of pay due to the trierarch for distribution to the sailors was calculated on a count of hands (the lower banks of rowers would have to stick their hands through the oar-ports, giving an opportunity for cheating if one of the crew was absent).

**6.44** In the performance of other *leitourgiai*, for instance the staging of a play at one of the great dramatic festivals, the wealthiest citizens vied with each other in their munificence. The trierarchy was no exception. Often the trierarch would spend more than was strictly necessary in order to ensure that he had the best officers and rowers.

**6.45** A conscientious trierarch would have had the added incentive of receiving a crown or garland if he could get his ship first to the quay. Some members of the *boulē* would be on the quay to see that preparations went smoothly. Their task would, of course, have been doubly difficult at night, when the Peiraieus would have to be lighted by torches, unless there was a moon. When the ships were ready, the trierarchs would offer libations to the gods, and then the *keleustēs* on a signal from the trierarch or *kubernētēs* would give the order to get under way.

At the end of service, the trierarch had to ensure that all state equipment was handed on in good order (cf. the incident at 4.35).

## (b) Summoriai

**6.46** Syntrierarchy was a satisfactory enough system in a city so lacking in a bureaucracy, and in principle it served Athens perfectly well. But in the fourth century the city was much poorer than in the fifth, and pay for the sailors became irregular and was rarely complete. As the city approached the nadir of its financial condition in the mid-350s, a law, at first sight revolutionary, was passed, the law of Periandros of 357. By it no longer was the obligation to pay linked to the obligation to serve. From now on even elderly grey-beards like Isokrates, long past the age of military service, were obliged to pay a share. Boards (*summoriai*) were formed, consisting of up to sixteen persons, to which the duty of financing a trireme was assigned. The system did not long satisfy. In 340 Demosthenes succeeded in passing a law, whereby financial liability was more equitably shared (5.73).

## (c) The success of the system

**6.47** It was remarked in the discussion of land warfare that the fourth century was the age of the professional. Did this show itself in naval matters? The law of Periandros did seem to open the door to the professional, making it possible for a man devoted to the sea to be hired by a *summoria*, but since the law was primarily financial, it might be thought to have let in the professional by accident by a back door. This is illusion. The separation of payment and service had already begun, and Periandros merely gave legal approval to what was increasingly fact. At the battle of Peparethos in 361 there were quite a number of trierarchs who had hired out their trierarchies. Characteristically the Athenians rounded on them and blamed them for the defeat. But it went on, as Demosthenes' speech (*On the Crown of the Trierarchy*) 51 shows. Where there was room for it, professionalism asserted itself, but the real advances had been made back in the days of Pericles. The perfection of the navy was one of his greatest achievements.

**6.48** In theory, the system was not perfect. It took time to get a fleet out to sea, precious time in which the city's cause might be lost. But what was the alternative? A standing navy with rowers and trierarchs ready to leave within the hour would have cost more than the city-state of Athens probably in the fifth century and certainly in the fourth could have afforded. Again, a standing navy in the Peiraieus would have been no use in the north once the Etesians had begun to blow, and a standing navy would have brought the city's fortunes to a standstill. It was better to devote resources as they did, to keeping up the supply of new ships. Ships that are waterlogged and leak do not, as Nikias found at Syracuse (Thucydides, *Peloponnesian War* 7.12), move as fast as new ships. In the navy lists of the fourth century, which are a prime source of information about the Athenian navy, we are at first astonished to find how many ships the city possessed; between 357/6 and 353/2, a period when Athens was financially at her lowest, the number of triremes increased from 283 to 349. But such expenditure was inevitable if Athens was to maintain her naval primacy, and far more important than a standing navy (cf. 6.2).

**6.49** The system worked. There was no competition. But once the Macedonian Alexander had captured the naval bases of the Persian empire in Phoenicia in 332, the writing was on the wall, for Alexander now had control of the mighty Phoenician fleet. At the battle of Amorgos in 322 the largest Athenian fleet ever to take part in a battle after the Persian Wars, 170 ships, faced the Macedonian, Kleitos, with 240. At the end of the day Athens' naval glory became a matter of history. Kleitos 'trident in hand, had himself proclaimed Poseidon'. Certainly the god of the sea had withdrawn his favour from Athens.

# 7
# *The intellectual world*

## (1) Background to the classical achievement

### *(i) The production of Greek literature*

**7.1** In all societies people tell stories and sing songs. It is reasonable to assume that traditional stories (or myths) had been told for centuries before the first Greek literature emerged, though no Brothers Grimm collected them. We know of myths partly through the Greek poets' use of them and partly through the collections made by much later compilers (e.g. the second-century Athenian Apollodoros). The first identifiable literature of the Western world is Homer's epics *Iliad* and *Odyssey* (eighth century?), the stories of the wrath of Achilles during the Trojan War and the return of Odysseus to his home after it; and the first songs we know of (but words only, not music) are those of the poet Arkhilokhos, who served the Muses and the god of war, as he says, around the islands of the eastern Aegean *c.* 650, and of Alkman, writing songs for choral recitation in Sparta at about the same time. It is easy to assume that Greek literature 'began' then, but stories must have been recited and songs sung to musical accompaniment for thousands of years before that. Greek literature seems to us to 'begin' in the eighth century simply because it was then that the Greeks learned the art of writing.

**7.2** The Greeks developed their own, unique, system of writing in the middle of the eighth century from the Phoenicians. Phoenicians, in common with other literate cultures of the time, used symbols to represent consonantal sounds (cf. Hebrew). The Greeks invented the first fully phonetic alphabet, i.e. one with symbols representing consonants *and vowels*, and took over some of the Phoenician letter forms and names, e.g.:

| א aleph | A alpha |
|---------|---------|
| ﬡ beth | B beta |
| ᴧ gimel | Γ gamma |
| ᴧ daleth | Δ delta |

7.3 If our evidence is rightly interpreted, writing was in fairly wide-spread use in Greece by the beginning of the seventh century. Over the years of its development, many different alphabets were invented to serve local needs, but the main features of all writing that survives on inscriptions and poetry from the time are that it was in capital letters, with no gaps between words and no punctuation, and sometimes written backwards, right to left, sometimes alternately right–left, left–right (*boustrophēdon*, like an 'ox turning' up and down a field). Spelling too was variable. For example, fifth-century Athenians could use o for o (o), ω (ō), or ου (ou); and ε for ε (e), η (ē), or ει (ei). In 403, Athens agreed to adopt an Ionic alphabet which gradually became standard throughout the Greek world, and it is from this agreed alphabet (through its Roman adaptation) that our system of writing has developed (though punctuation, gaps between words and minuscule writing did not become standard till the ninth century A.D.).

7.4 In our world, prose is the main medium of written communication, but in all ancient societies the first writing was in verse, not prose, and, apart from formal state decrees, the first prose in Greece was not written till the sixth century. Virtually all the earliest philosopher-scientists wrote in verse, and poets were seen rather as teachers, practical men of business, wise men and scientists than inspired visionaries. In the fifth century, even Homer could be used as a military training manual (P.10)!

7.5 The story of how the literature of the Greeks has survived to this day is a fascinating one. All we can do here is to offer the barest outline. The vast majority of Greek literature survives because it was copied and recopied down the ages. But recopying texts by hand (and excerpting for e.g. school use) had soon left many texts in a state of chaos, and in the third century the Greek scholars gathered at the Museum of Alexandria in Egypt (by then the intellectual centre of the world after the demise of Athens) decided to produce a 'best text' of all surviving Greek literature. It is from these texts that all our texts ultimately derive. What the Alexandrians did not edit does not survive, unless we are lucky enough to dig it out of the desert. The Romans, soon to be masters of the Mediterranean, were captivated by Greek culture and ensured that its products continued to be copied (selectively) for individuals, schools and libraries. The collapse of

7:1  Fragments of Sappho's poetry written on papyrus. 2nd century A.D.

the Roman Empire in the fifth century A.D. in the West, and the stagnation of monasteries and anti-pagan feeling in the East, left the Greek heritage hanging by a thread, but in the ninth century A.D., there was a revival of learning, when Greek literature was 'rediscovered' and began to be copied again, and virtually everything that survived through till then is with us today. Our most tantalising loss from this time is that of early Greek lyric poetry. Because of its frequently risqué nature, the Church did not look kindly on it, so that it was simply not recopied. What we have has survived in quotations, anthologies and been recovered from the desert sands. This is all the more infuriating when we know that virtually the sole female voice of the ancient Greek world, the sixth-century poetess from Lesbos, Sappho, had her works gathered into some nine books of verse. All we have to show for it is one complete poem, stanzas from a few others, and odd scraps of quotations and fragments. It is as if all that survived of Yeats was what there is in the *Oxford Dictionary of Quotations*.

### (ii) Discounting the gods: myth, philosophy and medicine

7.6 Already in the Homeric epics we can see signs of that peculiarly Greek attitude to the world which marks Greek thought out as crucially different from any other. If the versions we have of Greek myth have not been too radically reinterpreted by fifth-century writers, the signs are there as well. The differences are best brought out by contrast. First, read the myth of the house of Pelops quoted at 7.40 (and cf. the stories of Prometheus at 2.9). Now consider the following myth of the Bororo of Brazil:

Long ago a young man called Geriguiaguiatugo followed his mother into the forest, where she was going to collect special leaves for the initiation of young men after puberty. He raped her, and his father, discovering by a trick that his son was the culprit, sent him on a deadly mission to fetch various kinds of ceremonial rattle from the lake of souls. The young man's grandmother advises him to enlist the help of a humming-bird, which obtains for him the object of his quest. Other missions aided by other kinds of bird are also successful, so that eventually his father takes him on a parrot-hunting expedition and strands him half-way up a cliff, hanging on only by a magic stick given him by his grandmother. Father goes away, but son manages to climb the cliff. On the isolated plateau above he kills lizards and hangs some of them round his belt as a store of food; but they go rotten, and their smell makes the young man faint, then attracts vultures who devour his posterior as well as the maggoty lizards. The sated vultures turn friendly and convey him to the foot of the cliff. The young man is now hungry again, but the wild fruits he eats go straight through him, devoid as he now is of a fundament. Remembering a tale of his grandmother's, he fashions a new posterior out of a kind of mashed potato. He returns to his village, which he finds abandoned; but eventually discovers his family, after taking the form (according to the main version) of a lizard. He appears to his grandmother in his own shape; during the night a terrible storm extinguishes all the fires except hers; the other women, including the father's new wife, come for embers the next day. Father pretends that nothing has happened between him and his son, but the son turns into a stag and casts him with his antlers into a lake, where the father is devoured by cannibal piranha fish. His lungs rise to the surface and become the origin of a special kind of floating leaf. The young man then kills his mother and his father's second wife. (Taken from G.S. Kirk, *Myth: its meaning and functions* 64–5)

It is obvious what the difference is. In strongest contrast with the (to us) insane behaviour of the characters in the Brazilian myth, Greek myths are largely populated by human heroes behaving in humanly intelligible ways, and (in general) there is little or nothing of the grotesque, the absurd and the fantastic which so characterise the myth of Geriguiaguiatugo (though how far this is due to the literary nature of Greek myth is uncertain). This insistence that the world should make sense in human terms and that it could be explained without recourse to the supernatural is the hallmark of all the best Greek thinkers.

7.7 This important truth is emphasised by a brief glance at the earliest Greek philosophers. Greeks invented philosophy, but the first Greek philosophers were more what we should call 'natural scientists'. They

7:2  A goat-legged and goat-horned Pan is worshipped along with Hermes and the Nymphs. 4th century.

asked the extraordinary question 'Where did the world come from and what is it made of?' It is extraordinary because it implies that the universe must be humanly comprehensible, i.e. rational, and therefore explicable in rational terms. For example, the first philosopher, Thales of Milētos (*c.* 580) pronounced that the guiding principle (*arkhē*) behind everything was water, a most subtle guess (consider how it can take liquid, solid and gaseous forms). He explained earthquakes by saying that since the world rested on water, earthquakes occurred when the water was disturbed by the wind. He was wrong, but the important observation to make is that he did not say they were caused by the god of earthquakes, Poseidon. Other early thinkers proposed other *arkhai*. Parmenides (*c.* 480), an eastern Greek who moved to Elaia in Italy, nearly destroyed this form of speculation by denying that change was possible – since how could 'water' change to 'not-water'? It either *was* or *was not* water: it could not be both. So change (and all its associations, e.g. movement) was not possible. To the natural objection that one was moving every waking moment of one's life, Parmenides devastatingly replied that this simply proved that the senses were unreliable guides to the real nature of the world and should not be trusted. This appalling revelation had radical repercussions for Greek thought. To meet Parmenides' objections, one school of thought tentatively proposed an 'atomic' theory of the universe, i.e. that matter consisted of minute indivisible particles *below* the level of perception, which did not of themselves change, but merely regrouped themselves to make the different shapes, sizes, textures, tastes of the world we experience.

7.8 This simplified account of one of a number of running debates amongst early thinkers reveals their strengths and weaknesses. On the credit side, there was no dogma. Everything was open to question. There was no authority, religious or political, telling them what to think. On the debit side, much Greek thought tended to be, on the model of mathematics, axiomatic. That is, on the basis of a number of unquestioned assumptions, Greek thinkers constructed a model of the universe without recourse to anything other than observations and pure logic, and when Greeks did experiment, it was generally to demonstrate rather than prove a hypothesis. But there is evidence (from e.g. medicine) that they understood the importance of the principle of verification (this becomes increasingly true in the fourth century onwards): and if we are surprised by the lack of experimentation amongst the early philosophers, we should take into account the nature of the questions they were asking and the means of observation open to them: what sort of experiment could they possibly do to prove a theory of the origin of the universe? All the same, while the Greeks started a process which in time would make empirical research the basis of Western intellectual enquiry, they were only in a limited sense 'scientific' themselves and tended generally towards large-scale, abstract speculation throughout the classical and Hellenistic period.

7.9 One powerful analytical tool was repeatedly used by these early (and later) thinkers to help them get a grip on the problem: argument from analogy. This is an argument in which the phenomenon to be explained is likened to a similar phenomenon already understood, and the one is used to cast light on the other (the frequent use of similes by Homer, a comparable literary device, suggests the technique was particularly congenial to Greek thought). For example, Anaximandros describes the order of the cosmos in terms of an equilibrium caused by opposed substances which make up the cosmos 'paying the penalty and recompensing one another for their injustice': an image taken from the rule of law in the human world.

Another way in which early thinkers got a grip on problems was to see the world and its constituent parts in terms of opposites: hot and cold, wet and dry, light and dark, and so on. They believed that 'most human things go in pairs' (attributed by Aristotle to Alkmaion), and we can see in later Greek thought a tendency to look for oppositions (two of the most common particles in the Greek language are *men* and *de* – meaning 'on the one hand . . . on the other hand'). The Greeks made a clear distinction between body and mind, and psychiatrists have been trying to join the two back together ever since.

7.10 But medicine, as we have said, is something of an exception. The

Greeks invented the discipline of medicine, removing it from the realm of quackery, charlatanism and magic and making its foundation empirical observation. In the early fifth century Alkmaion of Kroton (in South Italy), head of a famous medical school, was said to have dissected the eye. This is almost certainly not the case, but he may have drawn his important conclusions about the path of the optic nerve into the brain, and located the brain as the centre of thought, through experimental dissection of animals and the treatment of war wounds. This empirical trend was to develop from then on (cf. 4.72).

7.11 Speculation was not restricted to the natural world. Some of the most independent and original observations were made by early thinkers about the gods, many of them striking at the heart of the conventional, 'Homeric' view (cf. 2.66). Xenophanes, an Ionian (*c.* 570–470), quite explicitly attacked Homer and satirised the way in which he represented gods as men (anthropomorphism):

Homer and Hēsiod have attributed to the gods everything that among men earns shame and abuse – theft, adultery and mutual deceit. (fr. 11)

Men think the gods are born and have clothes and voices and bodies like their own. (fr. 14)

If oxen and lions and horses had hands like men and could draw and make works of art, horses would make gods like horses and oxen like oxen and each would draw pictures of the gods as if they had bodies like their own. (fr. 15)

7:3 A sacrificial offering is made at an altar to the god Apollo whose statue in human form stands on a pillar. C. 430.

Herakleitos condemned both ritual purification after murder and praying to statues (cf. 2.26):

They purify themselves vainly with blood when they are suffering from blood-pollution, as if someone who had stepped into mud were to try and wash it off with mud. Anyone who noticed him do this would think him mad. And they pray to the images of the gods, which is like trying to have a conversation with a house; for they do not know the true nature of gods and heroes. (fr. 5)

7.12 It is important to remember that none of these early Greek thinkers were Athenians. Most of them came from the Ionian coast and its adjacent islands as a result of their ancestors' migrations from the tenth century on. If we look for a reason why speculation of the sort discussed above should have originated there, it is difficult to resist the conclusion that the contact between Greek and Near Eastern culture was a stimulus. (Cf. the Near Eastern impact on Greek art at 7.68ff.)

7.13 One other point needs to be stressed. Greek intellectuals had the leisure to speculate because they were generally wealthy aristocrats, whose freedom was created by slaves (cf. 4.52, 66). They were in no way representative of the 'average' Athenian, who regarded their speculations with as much suspicion as we might regard the following passage in which a modern scientist 'describes' the beginnings of the world:

The temperature of the universe is 100,000 million degrees Kelvin ($10^{11}$ °K). The universe is simpler and easier to describe than it ever will be again. It is filled with an undifferentiated soup of matter and radiation, each particle of which collides very rapidly with the other particles . . . Since the temperature of the universe falls in inverse proportion to its size, the circumference at the time of the first frame was less than at present by the ratio of the temperature then ($10^{11}$ °K) to the present temperature (3 °K); this gives a first-frame circumference of about 4 light years. (Weinberg)

Note the thoroughly Greek image in the third sentence: in the beginning there was *soup* (cf. 7.59).

### (2) Fifth-century Athens

7.14 The intellectual achievement of classical Greece was built on the extraordinary work of the preceding centuries. In mathematics, rhetoric, history, ethics, politics, linguistics, logic, and then in the more scientific disciplines (medicine, biology and physics), thinkers of the stature of Protagoras, Hippocrates, Socrates, Plato, and Aristotle, constructed systematic disciplines which were to be held valid for thousands of years; and in the arts, the tragedians, sculptors and architects (cf. 7.74) created works of such excellence that they were to be of lasting significance. Whatever the reasons for this sudden burst of powerful intellectual activity, one cannot separate the achievements of the Athenians, at least, from their political institutions (cf. H.I.27–8). Democracy could only have been invented in an atmosphere in which people as a whole felt a strong sense of their own independence of judgement and as a result demanded the right to control their own destinies, and this sense of freedom accords well with what we have seen of the early Ionian philosophers and doctors, who attempted to explain the world in humanly intelligible terms (cf. 7.76). Most of all, the early thinkers conducted their speculations in an atmosphere of critical debate, in which issues were not settled by diktat, but by their capacity to convince free, thinking men of the correctness of their views (cf. 3.16). With this background firmly in mind, we can now turn to fifth-century Athens.

### (i) The written word and the spoken word

7.15 In the fifth century, literacy would seem to have been fairly widespread amongst male Athenians living in Athens, since otherwise there can have been little point in displaying laws, notices of lawsuits or lists for military service in the *agora* (cf. 1.35). Literacy was probably less common in country areas. As for girls, we can only guess. Possibly only the wealthy minority were literate. There was certainly a book trade of sorts in fifth-century Athens (Socrates in his defence speech claims one could buy a copy

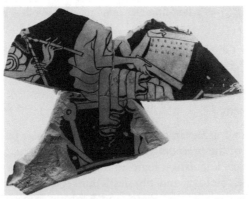

7:4  A youth reads from a scroll, but the painter has aligned the letters at right angles to what was usual. Early 5th century.

of Anaxagoras' work in the *agora* for about a drachma), but we know nothing of the size of the book market (H.I.59; 7.60 – oracles).

**7.16** Far more important than the written was the spoken word. Where we read books, Athenians listened to live recitations, when a poet or historian or scientist would stand up and address an audience (in public or private). Where we read news or see it, through newspapers or television, the Athenians heard it. We read reports of governmental proceedings, but Athenians took part in them actively and listened to debates in the *ekklēsia* (cf. 5.19ff.). We have legal contracts and documents, but Athenians relied on oaths (cf. 2.27) and witnesses (evidence was written down to be read out in court (cf. 5.53)). Thus few Athenians actually *read* Homer. They learnt his poetry at school, and heard professional recitations, given by rhapsodes in competition at festivals (2.47). No doubt they were acquainted with the works of other poets in the same way. No living poet 'published' his work in our sense of the word. A tragedian like Sophocles had his plays performed, and it is unlikely that most Athenians would have read again a play they had seen. They relied on revivals, or productions elsewhere in Attica, for plays they had missed (cf. 7.35).

**7.17** Since active political life and the power to influence decisions meant joining in debates in massed gatherings (*ekklēsia*, *boulē* and law-courts, cf. 1.35), the ability to speak persuasively was of paramount importance (cf. 5.19). Where a Homeric hero, or a sixth-century leader, needed to persuade a small group of acquaintances to adopt a particular course of action, his fifth-century Athenian counterpart faced an audience of several thousand, the majority complete strangers, who were by no means bound even to listen to, let alone accept, what he said (cf. the debate at 5.10). Consequently, a successful speaker had not only to propose

7:5 A professional reciter (*rhapsōidos*) stands on a dais and holds his staff as he performs. C. 490–480.

policies in a way that would be understood and acceptable, he had to know how to catch his audience's attention in the first place and hold it. *Peithō*, 'persuasion', the ability to make someone acquiesce peacefully, became something of a watchword of the day, and its influence was felt not only in the assembly and courts but on the stage and in higher education too. It was felt to be typical of a lawful, civilised, as against a barbarian, society, and was frequently contrasted with *dolos* (treachery, deceit) and *bia* (force, violence) in Greek literature (but cf. p. 95, last paragraph).

**7.18** It was in the democratic *polis* of Syracuse that, according to tradition, the very first handbooks of rhetorical technique were produced, by Teisias and Korax, in the 460s. These collections of notes soon reached Athens, so that by the end of the fifth century anyone could have got hold of the basic principles of public speaking. The notes were written for the lawcourts, but must have had relevance to speaking in the *ekklēsia* too. Plato in his *Phaidros* gives us some idea what the handbook must have contained:

*Socrates*:  In the first place a speech must begin with an 'Introduction'. That's the sort of technical term you mean, isn't it?

*Phaidros*:  Yes.

*Socrates*:  That is followed by a 'statement of the facts' and 'evidence from witnesses'; thirdly there is 'indirect evidence' and fourthly 'arguments from probability'; and I think our expert friend from Byzantium would want to add the further niceties of 'confirmation' and 'additional confirmation'.

*Phaidros*:  You mean the good Theodoros?

*Socrates*:  Of course.                                    (Plato, *Phaidros* 266d)

**7.19** In 427 the famous Sicilian sophist and orator Gorgias came on an embassy to Athens, and Athenians were given the first taste of his extraordinary prose style – rhythmical, rhyming, obsessed with antithesis and parallelism, even down to equalising the number of syllables in parallel clauses. Something of its manic effect can be gained from the following translation of an essay in which Gorgias is defending Helen's reputation:

If, then, the eye of Helen, charmed by Paris's beauty, gave to her soul excitement and amorous incitement, what wonder? How could one who was weaker, repel and expel him who, being divine, had power divine? If it was physical diversion and psychical perversion, we should not execrate it as reprehensible, but deprecate it as indefensible. For it came to whom it came by fortuitous insinuations, not by judicious resolutions; by erotic compulsions, not by despotic machinations.

How then is it fair to blame Helen who, whether by love captivated or by word persuaded, or by violence dominated, or by divine necessity subjugated, did what she did, and is completely absolved from blame?

By this discourse I have freed a woman from evil reputation; I have kept the promise which I made in the beginning; I have essayed to dispose of the injustice of defamation and the folly of allegation; I have prayed to compose a lucubration for Helen's adulation and my own delectation. (Gorgias, *Helen* 19)

Gorgias saw rhetoric as a form of magic. It gave the speakers the means to stir the passions, to work on the emotions and convince the mind. Fortunately, Gorgias' style was never taken seriously in its pure form (2.48).

In one sense we must not be deceived by all this. It is not as if oratory was invented in the fifth century. One-third of Homer is speeches, many brilliant works of persuasion. What happened in the fifth century was that the technique of effective persuasion was elucidated for the first time. A previously unconscious skill now became available for anyone to learn. But to be effective, rhetoric had to teach what to say as well as how to say it. The rise of rhetoric and the sharpening of the skills of argumentation went hand in hand. It was also recognised that such skills could be dangerous. The teaching of rhetoric was outlawed during the oligarchic coup of 404.

## (ii) The sophists (cf. 4.39–48)

7.20 To provide higher education in the cultural centre of the Mediterranean was obviously a juicy prospect to private teachers, and in the fifth century they flocked to Athens. Many were known primarily as teachers of rhetoric so it is hard not to connect their arrival in Athens with the development of radical democracy (cf. H.I.27) and the need for the wealthy young future leaders of the day to develop appropriate skills of persuasion.

These teachers are generally lumped together under the title of 'sophists', but though Plato (who hated them) has given the word a bad name, many of them were men of the highest intellectual distinction. They developed and taught their own specialities and grappled in their own way with largely the same questions that Socrates, Plato and later Aristotle faced.

7.21 The sophists undoubtedly helped to create a demand for education, but they also came when there was an unfulfilled need for it. They taught a vast variety of subjects – from astronomy and law through to mathematics and rhetoric. It is in large measure due to the sophists that subjects such as grammar, logic, ethics, politics, physics and metaphysics first emerged as separate entities and in that age of technical treatises and specialisations in all fields, the fourth century, began to be defined, to develop a terminology, to be taught and to take shape as disciplines. The important point is that the sophists were at the fore of a movement to make man, not the physical world, the centre of intellectual debate. If their main preoccupation was to describe how man could be most successful in life, rather than with scrupulously argued questions of right and wrong of the sort that Socrates and Plato posed, they should not be blamed for it. It was, after all, their job, if they were to get pupils.

7.22 Much work was going on in other fields at this time too. If our sources can be trusted, technical manuals were written by Sophocles on tragedy, by Iktinos on the Parthenon, by Polykleitos on the symmetry of the human body and by Hippodamos (who designed the layout of the Peiraeus) on town planning. Rudimentary experimental work in sciences may also have been going on, if we wish so to interpret the evidence of Aristophanes' *Clouds*. When the rustic Strepsiades is introduced into Socrates' private school (*phrontistērion* or 'think tank'), he finds all sorts of extraordinary devices cluttering up the place:

*Strepsiades*: [*examining some of the objects in the* phrontistērion] Tell me, what on earth are these?
*Student*: This is astronomy.
*Streps.*: And this?
*Student*: Geometry.
*Streps.*: And what is the use of it?
*Student*: It is for land measurement.
*Streps.*: For a new settlement?
*Student*: For any land whatever.
*Streps.*: That's a smart dodge. What a useful democratic device.
*Student*: And here we have a map of the world. This is Athens . . .
*Streps.*: Come off it. I don't believe you. Where are the juries?

(Aristophanes, *Clouds* 200ff.)

These cosmic models (celestial globes? star maps? compasses? maps?) are an important feature of the play, where the association between the new thought and its various trappings is constantly being made. It suggests that the use of models and apparatus, generally seen as a later, post-Aristotelian device, was understood well enough in fifth-century Athens to be made the subject of comic humour.

### (iii) Styles of argument and intellectual concerns

#### (a) Mathematics and the real world

7.23 Pythagoras of Samos (*c.* 525), who, to escape the tyranny of Polykrates, tyrant of Samos, fled to Kroton in South Italy and there set up a school which taught a whole way of life, made an important series of observations about the relationship between the natural world and numbers. The most famous of these is the way in which musical intervals can be expressed in terms of numerical ratios. This led Pythagoreans to suggest that 'number' might lie at the heart of reality, and so began the movement which was to give understanding of nature a mathematical foundation.

To the Greek mind the lure of mathematics was its precision, and Plato for one saw in mathematics a perfection which did not exist elsewhere in this imperfect world: it worked through expressible but unchanging and apparently eternal laws. The Greeks desired to categorise the problems of existence with the precision of mathematics. But the Greeks were well aware that even mathematics was not wholly rational. For example, they knew that the hypotenuse of a right-angled triangle whose base and perpendicular = 1 (see diagram) was $\sqrt{2}$ and that $\sqrt{2}$ *could not be mathematically expressed*. Yet it was real, tangible and apparently measurable.

They were also deeply disturbed by the problem of infinities. Zeno (*c.* 450) pointed out that if you kept on cutting a line in half, you would continue to do so infinitely. How therefore could a line have finite length? He expressed this in another way – the paradox of Achilles and the tortoise. If Achilles gave a tortoise a 20 metres' start, Achilles could never catch it. For while Achilles ran the 20 m, the tortoise would run 1 m; while Achilles ran the 1 m, the tortoise would run 1 cm; while Achilles ran 1 cm, the tortoise would run 0.1 cm; while Achilles . . . and so on. So even in the 'pure' world of mathematics, there were irrationalities.

*(b) The power of words*

**7.24** Verbal paradoxes intrigued Greeks just as much as mathematical ones. The mere use of words seemed able entirely to distort perceptions of reality in the most bewildering way (cf. Zeno's paradox above). One particular problem was that of negative statements, e.g. if falsehood consists of saying something that *is not so*, does not that imply *saying nothing*? Hence the notorious sophistic paradox that it is impossible to *speak falsely*. These problems, and that of the nature of language, have continued to haunt logic and philosophy and become prominent again in the modern twentieth-century movement. Here Plato parodies such arguments. The sophist Euthydemos 'proves' to Socrates ('I') that his father is not his father (the 'Patroklos' referred to in the first line is Socrates' half-brother):

*Euthydemos*: And Patroklos is your brother?
*Socrates*: He is; we have the same mother but not the same father.
E: Then he is both your brother and not your brother.
S: Our fathers are different as I've said. His father is Khairedemos, mine Sophroniskos.
E: But Sophroniskos and Khairedemos are both fathers.
S: Of course, one mine and one his.
E: Then Khairedemos isn't the same as 'father'.
S: He's not the same as *my* father.
E: So he is 'father' and not the same as 'father'. Or are you the same as 'stone'?
S: I don't think I am, but I expect you will prove I am.
E: Then are you different from 'stone'?
S: Yes, different.
E: And if you are different from 'stone' you aren't a stone, any more than if you are different from gold you are golden.
S: That's so.
E: So Khairedemos not being the same as 'father', isn't a father.
S: It looks as if he can't be a father.          (Plato, *Euthydemos* 297e)

Another problem concerned the relationship between a word and its meaning. In what sense does a word 'tell' us about the object it applies to? Plato's *Kratylos* is concerned with this fundamental question:

The name Zeus is like a sentence: we divide it in half and some use one half, some the other, some calling him [in the accusative case] *Sdēna* and some *Dia*. The two forms when put together express the nature of the god which is just what we say a name should be able to do. For Zeus is the chief author of life [*sdēn* = 'to live'] to all the rest of us, being lord and king of all. So this god is rightly named, *through* [*dia* = 'through'] whom all things have life. (Plato, *Kratylos* 396a)

### (c) Human psychology

7.25 Greeks were as interested in the patterns of human behaviour as in the patterns of the universe (cf. 7.40–1 and the interaction of myth and Greek understanding of human behaviour on the tragic stage). After all, sophists could only claim to teach techniques of persuasion if they had reasons for believing that human behaviour could be predicted. Two sorts of argument, one for predicting human behaviour, the other for proposing successful ways of behaving, were very common. The argument from probability, which may have been invented by Teisias and Korax (see 7.18), used common experience to suggest how people would behave or had in fact behaved, e.g. 'The defendant was drunk: is it likely or probable that a drunk man would be so foolish as to try to negotiate a difficult gangplank from a rocking ship to the shore?' The paradigm, an example of approved past behaviour, was quoted to offer a model for the present, on the pattern 'X behaved like this; so ought you.' This is especially common in Homer. Here the historian Thucydides puts into the mouths of some Athenian ambassadors a justification for their demand that the people of the island of Mēlos should become subject to Athens:

> Our claims and our actions are entirely consistent with men's beliefs about the gods and with the principles which govern their own conduct to each other. Of the gods we believe and of men we know that by a universal and necessary natural law they rule wherever they have the power. We did not make this law nor were we the first to take advantage of it. We found it already in force and we shall leave it to operate in perpetuity for our successors; all we are doing is to make use of it in the full knowledge that you yourselves and anyone else who enjoyed the same power as we have would act in precisely the same way. (Thucydides, *Peloponnesian War* 5.105)

Thucydides himself believed that human nature was such that, given similar conditions, humans would behave in largely the same way (*Peloponnesian War* 1.22) (cf. 7.34).

The sophists were particularly interested in the origins of human society. They developed the theory that early man found survival difficult because of wild animals, illness and lack of food and so was spurred on pragmatic grounds to invent *tekhnai* ('skills, the results of applied intelligence') like hunting, medicine and agriculture in order to survive. But men were still at risk from other men. So social compacts were formed, giving rise to *philia* ('making common cause with another', cf. *philos*), for example, and *peithō* ('getting someone to acquiesce peacefully' cf. 7.17). These utilitarian practices became enshrined in time into a moral code, giving rise to constraints such as *aidōs* ('respect for others') and *dikē* ('justice'). From these beginnings fully civilised societies, characterised by laws, religious observances and democratic practices, were able to develop. But the basis of the sophists' view of man's development was ultimately utilitarian, and this fact reflects the enlightened self-interest and ethically relativistic view of many sophists, against which Plato and Socrates reacted so strongly (7.29ff.).

### (d) Arguing both sides of the case

7.26 It was the great sophist Protagoras who first claimed that there were two sides to every question, and that to be successful, one should be able to argue both cases. The following extraordinary extract (certainly not by Protagoras) will give some idea of the extremes to which this could be taken. It may well be typical of the sort of manual of argumentation which was available in late fifth-century Athens:

So sickness is bad for the sick, but good for the doctor: death is bad for the dead, but good for the undertakers and monumental masons: a good harvest is good for the farmers, but bad for the grain-traders: shipwrecks are bad for the shipowners, but good for the shipbuilder: when iron is blunted and worn away it is bad for others but good for the blacksmith: when pottery is broken it is bad for others but good for the potter: when shoes wear out and fall to pieces it is bad for others but good for the cobbler: in athletics victory in the quarter mile is good for the victor but bad for the losers. (*Dissoi Logoi* 1.3)

The importance of this method of argument lies in its inherent implication that all cases have two sides, i.e. nothing is absolute, it all depends on the circumstances. When extended to the sphere of moral values, it was a short step to Protagoras' famous dictum 'Man is the measure of all things', and thence to the assertion that there were no higher authorities to whom one could appeal to determine what was right and wrong. This struck many Greeks as a highly dangerous step to take.

*(e) Evidence*

7.27 In general there was an increasing interest among Greeks in what sort of evidence was acceptable to prove or disprove a case. Giving a rational account of an illness and assessing the value of evidence adduced formed an important part, for example, of medical casework, and this principle was easily extended to other spheres of human life (political and moral, for example). Here Thucydides discusses how he gathered the evidence for his history:

But on the whole I think that anyone who accepts the narrative which I have based on the proofs cited can do so with confidence. The poets are not to be trusted because they elaborate and exaggerate, and the prose writers prefer the entertainment of their readers to the truth; their facts cannot be checked because of the passage of time and are legend rather than reliable history. My own narrative is based on the clearest evidence that can be expected considering the antiquity of the events . . . not on a casual enquiry nor on my personal opinion, but partly on my own experience and partly by following up as closely as I could the accounts of eyewitnesses. This last process was a difficult one because the accounts of eyewitnesses differed according to memory and partiality. (Thucydides, *Peloponnesian War* 1.22)

## (f) Nomos *and* phusis

**7.28** Debates were fiercely joined on a number of topics which still remain important. The Greeks endlessly debated the nature of justice and the relationship between it and written law; the nature of right and wrong, and where expediency fitted in; the nature of power and the rights that the stronger held over the weaker; and, most famous of all, the relationship between *nomos* and *phusis* – or, to put it simply, the question 'Is there an absolute right and wrong in any situation, or does it depend on the circumstances?'

*Nomos* means 'law', 'custom', 'convention', 'inherited ideals', 'received wisdom', 'what we all acknowledge to be the case'; *phusis* means 'nature', 'the natural world', 'reality'. Herodotus puts the issue at its sharpest in the following story:

If anyone were to offer men the opportunity to make from all the customs in the world what seemed to them the best selection, everyone would after careful consideration choose his own; for everyone considers his own customs far the best. So no-one except a madman would make fun of such things. There is ample evidence that this is the common opinion of mankind about their customs. A particular piece of evidence is this: when Dareios was King of Persia he summoned certain Greeks who were at his court and asked them how much he would have to pay them to eat the bodies of their dead fathers. They replied that there was no sum for which they would do such a thing. Later he summoned certain Indians of a tribe called Callatians, who do eat their parents' bodies, and asked them in the presence of the Greeks, through an interpreter so that the Greeks understood what was being said, how much they would have to be paid to burn their fathers' dead bodies. They cried aloud and told him not to utter such blasphemy. Such is custom and Pindar was in my opinion right when he wrote that 'Custom is King of all'. (Herodotus, *Histories* 3.38)

The argument was easily extended. Did the gods exist in reality, or only by convention? Did states exist in reality or only by convention? Were human races naturally, or only conventionally, divided? Should one man control another, or one nation control another nation, because it was natural, or only because it was convention?

These questions seemed to many Athenians to strike at the very heart of morality, and when many thinkers started to call into question the existence of the gods as well (see 7.11), the stage was set for a long and at times bitter intellectual debate which rages still today. We must now put the alternative point of view, that represented by Socrates.

## (iv) Socrates

**7.29** Socrates never wrote a word, but he was the key figure in changing the direction of Greek philosophy away from cosmology to man's position in the world. What we know of him comes from the greatest of his disciples, Plato; from Xenophon, soldier and country gentleman who wrote memoirs of him; and from Aristophanes' comedy *The Clouds*. He was part of the same intellectual movement which produced the sophists, and many Athenians thought of him as a sophist. The Socrates of Aristophanes' *Clouds* is a composite figure – all 'modern' movements rolled into one – but one element is the sophist and Plato represents him in discussion with them. Yet as Plato again makes clear there is a sharp contrast between them. Briefly, the sophists were interested in success, in giving their pupils techniques, especially in the art of speaking (see 7.16ff.; 4.46) that would enable them to get on in the world. Socrates, in contrast, was interested in morals, in what I must do to be good. Xenophon brings out this moral preoccupation, and Aristotle describes him in a brief phrase as 'concerned with the moral virtues'.

**7.30** But Socrates was a great arguer and concerned with both clarity and precision of thought, and Aristotle goes on to attribute to him the systematic use of 'inductive argument and general definition'. One must beware of the modern associations of the word 'induction', and 'argument from example' is a better translation. The following passage from the *Lakhes* is an excellent illustration. The argument 'leads you on' (the literal meaning of the Greek word for 'induction') by observation of particular instances to understand the general characteristics of the class of actions or objects being considered. And so of course to a 'general definition'. Socrates was looking for precision and definite standards. If you want to be good or brave you must first know what goodness or bravery is; so, in a sense, goodness *is* knowledge and it should be possible to be as *precise* about moral virtue as a carpenter is about what makes a good chair. Socrates pursued his general definition in *dialogue* with others, and the word 'dialectic' (which Plato was to use as a term for philosophy) is derived from the Greek word for dialogue. (Plato invented the dialogue as a literary form: it was the closest he could get to dialectical argument on the page.)

All these points are illustrated in the following passage in which Socrates and a famous general discuss the definition of bravery:

*Socrates*:  Very well: let us take as an example the brave man you have mentioned, the man who keeps his position in the line and fights the enemy.

*Lakhes*: Yes, he is a brave man.

*Socrates*: I agree. But what about a man who fights the enemy not by keeping position but by retreating?

*Lakhes*: What do you mean, retreating?

*Socrates*: I'm thinking of the Scythians who are said to fight by withdrawing as much as by pursuing . . . For I wanted to get your opinion not only of bravery in the hoplite line, but also in cavalry engagements and in all forms of fighting; and indeed of bravery not only in fighting but also at sea, and in the face of illness and poverty and public affairs. And there is bravery not only in face of pain and fear, but also of desire and pleasure, both fearsome to fight against whether by attack or retreat – for some men are brave in these encounters, aren't they, Lakhes?

*Lakhes*: Yes, certainly.

*Socrates*: Then all these are examples of bravery, only some men show it in pleasure, some in pain, some in desire, some in danger. And there are others who show cowardice in the same circumstances.

*Lakhes*: Yes.

*Socrates*: Now what I want to know was just *what* each of these two qualities *is*. So try again and tell me first, what is this common characteristic of courage which they all share? Do you understand now what I mean?

*Lakhes*: I'm afraid I don't. (Plato, *Lakhes* 191a)

7.31 Exactly what Socrates himself believed we cannot with certainty extract from our sources, and we should do well to remember that (as with Christ) there is virtually no criticism from ancient sources (Aristophanes' comedy *Clouds* is an important exception). Plato shows him as arguing against the relativism and scepticism which characterised much of sophistic thought and looking for a precision about definitions of moral virtues of the sort that existed in the technical world. He was looking for some kind of stable reality and standard behind the confusion of perceptions and standards in the world of common experience. Here Socrates describes his methods to Theaitetos:

*Socrates*: My art of midwifery is concerned with men and not women and I am concerned with minds in travail, not bodies. And the most important thing about my art is its ability to test fully whether the mind of the young man is giving birth to a mere image and a falsehood or to a legitimate truth. For there is another point which I have in common with the mid-wives – I cannot myself give birth to wisdom, and the criticism which has so often been made of me, that though I ask questions of others I have no contribution to make myself because I have no wisdom in me, is quite true. The reason is that god compels me to be midwife but forbids me to give birth. So I am myself quite without wisdom nor has my mind produced any original thought; but those who keep my company, though at first some of them may appear quite ignorant, if god wills, in due course make what both they and others think is marvellous progress. This is clearly not because of anything they have learned from me but because they have made many marvellous discoveries of themselves and given birth to them. But the delivery of them is my work and the god's . . .

Now the reason why I have rehearsed all this at length to you, my dear Theaitetos, is that I suspect that – as you think yourself – you are in labour with some thought you have conceived. So put yourself in my hands, remembering I am a midwife's son and practised in her craft, and answer my questions as best you can.        (Plato, *Theaitētos* 150b)

There is no doubt at all that Plato's picture of Socrates as the epitome of the goodness (*aretē*) he so ardently sought to define has been of enormous influence on the history of Western philosophy. He was portrayed as the uncompromising searcher after truth, who would allow no consideration of person or position of influence to stand in the way (but cf. Aristophanes' very different picture in *Clouds*). It cost Socrates his life (H.I.59). Put on trial on a charge of corrupting the young (cf. Alkibiades' attraction to him at 3.24) and introducing new gods, he was found guilty and, refusing the option of going into exile, was executed with hemlock (cf. 4.47). Nevertheless, it is arguable that the sophists' achievement was as important as Socrates', and that it was they no less than Socrates who laid the groundwork for Plato's, and later Aristotle's, work.

### (v) Medicine and history

### (a) Medicine (cf. on doctors, 4.72ff.)

7.32 The Greeks were the first people we know of to turn medicine into something approaching a scientific discipline (cf. on Alkmaion 7.10). The leading advocate of 'rational' medicine was Hippocrates from the island of Kōs. He established a medical 'school' there, and virtually all medical treatises of the fifth and fourth centuries were ascribed to him. The passage taken from *On the Sacred Disease* (epilepsy) at 2.18 illustrates the stand Hippocratic doctors took against magical cures. It continued:

The so-called sacred disease is due to the same causes as all other diseases, to bodily intake and waste, to cold and sun and constant atmosphere and weather changes. These are all 'divine' and there is no need to put this disease in a class by itself and regard it as more 'divine' than all others; all are equally divine and human. But each disease has its own particular nature and characteristics, and none is hopeless or insusceptible to treatment. ([Hippocrates], *On the Sacred Disease* 2ff.)

The weakness of Greek medicine was (as one can see from the above) in diagnosis. Without a real understanding of how the body worked, Hippocratic doctors resorted to cures calculated to restore an imagined 'balance' to the elements of which the body was composed (cf. 7.9), by such means as dieting, exercising, blood-letting, surgery and purgative drugs. Their strength was in prognosis, i.e. the careful observation of the course a disease took, so that if similar symptoms arose, doctors could predict what would ensue. This gave confidence to patients (an important consideration for doctors, who on the whole acted privately and had to win patients), and alerted them to the periods when their help would be most needed. Their understanding of anatomy came from surgical work (especially dealing with war wounds) and by analogy from animal dissection. Dissection of humans was taboo (cf. Greek reverence for the dead, 4.77), although such dissection, and probably even vivisection too, were practised briefly in the very different cultural atmosphere of the Alexandrian Museum in Egypt in the third century.

In all this, the 'rationalistic' doctors were in constant conflict with the temple doctors at, for example, the shrine of Asklepios at Epidauros, who dealt out magical cures through dreams, snake-bites and so on (cf. 2.4). Hippocratic doctors did not displace temple doctors, but debate between the two different styles of cure, the one rational, the other supernatural, was fiercely joined in the effort to win patients (cf. 7.17 on *peithō* in public life, and 3.2 on Greek competitiveness). The importance of the Hippocratic argument for the future of medicine lay in its refusal to sanction divine or mystical reasons and cures for illness, and in its realisation of a distinction between genuine cause and merely associated side-effects of illnesses.

## (b) History

7.33 Besides turning their interest towards questions of the nature of the world and man's place within it, Greeks also considered afresh their past and in the process invented history (*historia* means 'research', 'enquiry'). Before this happened, Greek interest in the past was satisfied by myths, epics, family stories and trees, and lists of 'eponymous' officials (it was common to express the year as 'in the *arkhon*ship of X'), to which they turned to settle questions of e.g. cult practices, territorial disputes and the right to exercise power. When the Greeks through colonisation came into contact with other peoples and places, there was a need for a rudimentary form of *Blue Guide* for settlers, a need fulfilled by writers called *logographoi*, who described places geographically, intimated local customs and filled in with a little 'background'. History began here, and perhaps the first historical statement we possess is that of Hekataios from Milētos, a late sixth-century *logographos* who constructed a map of the world and wrote a commentary to accompany it, who at one stage comments 'What I write here is the account I believe to be true. The Greeks tell many stories on the topic which are (in my opinion) absurd.' But the key figure, the 'father of *historia*' ('enquiry') (Cicero), was Herodotus from Halikarnassos (died *c.* 430). His *History of the Persian Wars* (490–479; see H.I.12ff.) was an extremely daring venture. In the first place, he took it upon himself to ask the questions 'Why?' and 'How?' in relation to events many generations ago. In the second place, he integrated into his work the history, culture and customs of peoples from all over the Mediterranean (e.g. Egyptians, Scythians, Babylonians) who had come into contact with the two great powers, Greece and Persia, involved in the final conflict. In the process he developed an important historical attitude: that evidence should, as far as possible, be ascertained by personal enquiry and research. Here was the start of a scientific approach to the past. The result goes beyond the *logographoi* to the extent that, while there is still much fascinating local detail and description of place and custom, Herodotus perceives an overall pattern to human affairs beyond the individual and the

7:6  Herakles scatters the African henchmen of the Egyptian king Busiris whose custom it was to sacrifice strangers. Note the emphasis on foreign features and un-Greek circumcision. C. 470.

7:7 An aged negro well observed by an Athenian artist. C. 500.

particular – the permanent rise and fall of the powerful. At the last count, Herodotus does see this as the consequence of supernatural intervention in human affairs, but there is nonetheless much discounting of the gods *en route* and the influence of Ionian thinkers is strong (7.6–13).

7.34 Thucydides, the Athenian historian who died *c*. 400, took Herodotus' concept and narrowed it. He chose as his subject the contemporary conflict known as the Second Peloponnesian War between Athens and Sparta (see H.I.33ff.); he cut out ethnography, 'romance', conversations and local colour of the sort still evident in Herodotus; he focused on the military and political aspects of the war (though he was well aware of the importance of domestic and economic factors); he started the annalistic tradition of historical writing by analysing the war year by year; he applied extremely rigorous standards for testing evidence (see 7.27); and, in contrast to Herodotus, he 'ministered to man's knowledge of man' in his history by excluding the gods entirely from his own exposition. He acknowledged, of course, that men's belief in the gods affected the way they behaved, but he did not himself believe that the gods were actually responsible for history: man was. In one vitally important point Thucydides agreed with Herodotus, that the historian was in a unique position to see the patterns to history. For Thucydides, the pattern was what we might call 'behavioural'. Men behave in certain ways under certain pressures, so that if similar events occur again, the intelligent man will be able to foresee them (cf. his recipe for how people behave during revolution at 3.14, and cf. 7.25 on Greek interest in human behaviour). For all that, Thucydides acknowledged that *tukhē*, blind chance, was the great unknowable factor, although he insisted it was not a divine visitation.

Even Pericles, Thucydides' prime example of the man who could read the future, could not have foreseen the plague which devastated Athens in 430 and carried him off as well (see H.I.36–7). It was not merely coincidence that Thucydides places his description of the plague *immediately* after Pericles' famous statement about the greatness of Athens – the Funeral Speech (see pp. 56–61). (Cf. how Phormion foresees events at p. 269 (84).)

### (vi) Tragedy and comedy

#### (a) Introduction

7.35 Comedies and tragedies were put on in Athens at specific times of the year, to celebrate festivals of Dionysos (though 'community carnival' may be a better term than 'festival', cf. 2.41). These festivals were called the Lenaia (in January), and the Dionysia (in March). As well as being elements of a religious occasion (cf. 2.46–7), the plays were intensely competitive since the best work of tragedy and comedy was awarded a much coveted prize (judged by 10 judges, one from each of ten tribes (*phulai*)). The plays were staged at the theatre of Dionysos in Athens, just below the Acropolis (the theatre, not in its fifth-century state but as adapted by the Romans, still exists in ruined form), and could be attended by *c.* 14,000 people (cf. 1.29). It is uncertain whether women and children were present at them.

Although the plays were only put on once in Athens, they could be taken round rural festivals and thus 'revived'. Despite the apparent lack of scope for actors (the idea of a play having a 'run' was, of course, completely alien to Greeks, whose plays were annual events to celebrate festivals of Dionysos), there were professional actors in the fifth century, and the services of the best actors were much sought after by playwrights. The playwrights directed, choreographed and wrote the music for their work, and at first acted in them. It may even have been that Sophocles and Euripides could write for actors of their choice. But by the fourth century, playwrights probably had no choice in their selection of a lead actor. The 'eponymous' *arkhōn* assigned a wealthy citizen to bear the expense of the play, as part of a state liturgy (the *khorēgia*). He (*khorēgos* = 'manager') paid for the musicians and the chorus (and its training in singing and dancing), stage sets, costumes and so on (cf. on *leitourgiai*, 5.71).

7.36 For the comic festival at the Dionysia, five single plays by five different playwrights were entered in competition against each other. For the tragic festival, three playwrights entered four plays each: three tragedies followed by a lighter 'satyr' play. In the early days the three tragedies were often fairly tightly connected in subject-matter and formed a 'trilogy'. Aeschylus' *Oresteia* (the story of the death of Agamemnon at the hands of his wife Klutaimēstra, the return of their son Orestes to take revenge on her and Orestes' trial on a murder charge and acquittal at Athens), is the only group of three plays we have, and is a 'trilogy' of this sort. Later on, the plays were more loosely connected, by continuity or contrast of *mood* rather than subject matter (e.g. Euripides' *Iphigeneia at Aulis* and *Bacchae* were written for production together). The only certain example of the 'trilogy' form like *Oresteia* is Euripides' plays of 415, all centred on Troy but examining the war from radically different angles and moods. They are *Alexandros*, in which it is revealed that Paris, exposed as an infant and assumed dead, is in fact living as a shepherd in the mountains; *Palamēdēs*, a story of treachery and intrigue in the Greek camp outside Troy; and *Trojan Women* (the only play of the 'trilogy' we possess in full), the sack of Troy and departure of its womenfolk into slavery. It is a very great loss that we have no more groups of plays, since our understanding of the single plays we do possess would be enormously enhanced if we could see them in their original programme setting.

We only possess six plays of Aeschylus (525–456) (*Prometheus* is probably not by him), seven of Sophocles (496–406) and nineteen of Euripides (485–406). But we have records of the titles of *c.* 80 plays by Aeschylus (with an uncertain number of firsts), 123 by Sophocles (24 firsts) and 92 by Euripides (6 firsts). A 'first' meant that the group of four plays had won the competition, so that of Sophocles' 123 plays, 96 were successful.

## (b) Tragedy: origins and form

**7.37** The first tragedy that we possess in full is Aeschylus' *Persians* produced in 472, but its development as a form is as obscure to us as it was to the fourth-century Greeks. It seems that Athenians invented tragedy, so in a sense, tragedy is the uniquely *Athenian* contribution to Western culture. What tragedy (*tragōidia*) means is disputed. It could mean 'song of goats' (i.e. of men dressed up as goats) so that the proto-tragedy was a form of satyr play. But satyrs are not goats, and according to depictions on vase paintings, the first satyr plays began to be produced about 520, considerably later than Thespis, the traditional inventor of tragedy (*c.* 535). There is also a linguistic difficulty. The word most commonly used for 'tragedy' in the fifth century was not *tragōidia*, but *tragōidoi* (pl.), a word which referred to the human participants in tragedy, probably the chorus. Now this word cannot mean 'goats who sing'; it can only mean 'singers who

7:8  A pipe-player accompanies a dance by actors dressed up as satyrs, complete with masks and trunks. They formed the chorus in a satyr-play and are assembling an elaborate throne. C. 470.

have something to do with a goat'. This meaning fits better with a second explanation in antiquity, that *tragōidia* meant 'song for the prize of a goat', or 'song at the sacrifice of a goat' (goats were certainly sacrificed to Dionysos, as to other gods). Sacrifice was the climax of the festival (cf. 2.28, 45). The pleasure of the festival and the death of an animal, returned back to the gods in a complicated ritual to ensure that animals would continue to be available as food (cf. 2.28), were part of the same ceremony: life was affirmed through death. This made sense in the context of the worship of Dionysos (cf. 2.57); and the image of sacrifice as slaughter, not only of animals but also of humans, runs through tragedy (e.g. Aeschylus' *Agamemnon*, and cf. Euripides' *Bacchae*, especially the scene in which the god Dionysos dresses Pentheus up in woman's clothes and leads him off to the mountains where the Bacchic woman will 'sacrifice' him; the whole scene is chillingly close to the ceremony of preparing an animal for slaughter). So it may be that sacrifice rather than satyrs is at the heart of tragedy. Still others, ignoring goat songs, connected tragedy with fertility festivals (since, *inter alia*, Dionysos was god of everything living), and it may be that choral songs and dances in honour of Dionysos (of the sort that survive in celebration of gods from seventh-century lyric poetry) formed the original core. It may be that the chorus leader (*koruphaios*, called *exarkhos* when applied to early non-dramatic choral song) took a more dynamic role by singing against the chorus, so that a conflict could develop, and that, in time, other individual chorus members joined in, to form the nucleus of a dramatic performance. This explanation would, at any rate, help to

7:9  Six young men dance towards a tomb that is decked with ribbons and sprays. A bearded figure stands behind, or rises through, the structure. This may show a theatrical performance. C. 500–490.

7:10  Two actors prepare for a performance of a tragedy: on the left one actor holds a mask and is to play Dionysos, on the right the other is a masked member of the chorus of maenads. C. 460–450.

account for the very special form of the tragedy: a chorus (the personnel consisted of 12 or 15 members), and no more than three individual actors (who had to divide amongst themselves all the speaking parts of the play), while the heart of the play was a contest, a conflict between opposing forces (cf. 3.2). The chorus (and increasingly during the fifth century the actors also) sang and danced those parts of tragedy written in lyric metres but the details of the music and movement which were so vital a part of the spectacle are lost to us. All we have are the words. Originally Greek tragedy was far more like an opera than what we would call a play (4.41).

### (c) Myth in tragedy

**7.38** Given the Dionysiac origins of tragedy, it may strike us as odd that very few plays seem to have been about Dionysos. Nevertheless, the themes of the plays were nearly always taken from mythology (Aeschylus' *Persians*, our very first extant tragedy, is a unique exception among plays that survive in that its subject is a historical one, the defeat of the Persians at Salamis in 480 and the reception of the news at the Persian court. But we know of two 'historical' plays by Phrynikhos (*Fall of Milētos* ?492, *Phoinissai* (about Salamis) ?476), so perhaps such 'historical' plays were more common in the early fifth century). Drawing on myth and legend relieved the playwright, faced with the problem of writing three tragedies and a satyr-play each year if he wished to compete annually (which would represent an impossible burden to a modern playwright), of the problem of inventing plots.

**7.39** We are tempted to say that this must have made tragedy predictable. If the play was about Oedipus, or Agamemnon, surely everyone knew what was going to happen? This seems an odd criticism when going to see yet another production of a well-known play is an integral part of Western culture, and that is the point: interpretation is, if not all, a great deal. For example, Aeschylus, Sophocles and Euripides all wrote a tragedy about the return of Orestes to take revenge upon Klutaimēstra (Aeschylus' *Libation Bearers* (part of the *Oresteia* trilogy), and Sophocles' and Euripides' *Ēlektra*). The audience doubtless knew that Klutaimēstra would be killed by Orestes at the end of the play, but the handling, perspective and point of view of each are differentiated extremely sharply. In Aeschylus' *Libation Bearers*, the whole of the first half of the play is taken up with the rather perfunctory meeting of Orestes and his sister Ēlektra and the lament at Agamemnon's tomb. Ēlektra then disappears entirely. The deed is done and Orestes is pursued off-stage by Klutaimēstra's avenging Furies. In Sophocles, Ēlektra is the focal point of the whole play, the encounter with Orestes is postponed and enormously elaborated, and Orestes is almost a tool of personal revenge in her hands. For Euripides, Ēlektra has been married off to a peasant farmer, and the scene is set not in the palace but in the farmer's hut, to which Klutaimēstra has to come in order to be dispatched. No Furies appear at the end of Sophocles' play; in Euripides', the twin gods Kastor and Pollux tie the ends up neatly. In other words, the playwright's imaginations were so rich and subtle that each of their plays represented to the audience a wholly fresh experience.

7.40 Myth to a Greek was, at one level, his history: Agamemnon, Oedipus, Hekabe *were* his past. But myth was not merely 'history'. As we have seen (2.9–11), one of the functions of myth is to make sense of the way the world is, and that is why Greek myth dealt almost exclusively with issues of the highest importance to Greeks and made of them a generally 'coherent ethical structure, imbued with violent human feelings' (B. Vickers, *Towards Greek Tragedy*) – particularly, the relationship of gods with men (cf. 2.22–3), the preservation of human decency (man-slaughter, guest–host relationships, trust and betrayal) and most of all the stability of the *oikos*, particularly when this was threatened by sexual crimes, mistreatment of parents, murder, revenge. Here, for example, is a version of the myth of the House of Atreus, subject of many Greek tragedies (of which Aeschylus' *Oresteia* is our most important surviving example): Tantalos is punished for testing to see if the gods would eat human flesh by serving his son Pelops to them at a feast. Pelops is restored to life and decides to win the hand of Hippodameia, daughter of King Oinomaos. To do that, he must defeat Oinomaos in a chariot race (punish-ment for failure is death). He enlists the help of Oinomaos' charioteer Myrtilos, promising him as a reward the first night with Hippodameia. Myrtilos replaces the wooden lynch-pins of Oinomaos' chariot with wax, and Oinomaos is killed. Pelops wins the race but does not fulfil his promise to Myrtilos, flinging him over a cliff instead. Pelops has two sons, Atreus and Thyestes. Thyestes commits adultery with Atreus' wife and to punish him, Atreus serves up all but one of Thyestes' children to him in a pie (Aigisthos survives). Atreus' son Agamemnon has to sacrifice his own child Iphigeneia in order to get a favourable wind for the expedition to sail to Troy to win back Helen for his brother Menelaos and restore the family honour. When Agamemnon returns, his wife Klutaimēstra has married Aigisthos and slaughters Agamemnon in revenge for his sacrifice of Iphigeneia. But Agamemnon's surviving son Orestes returns to take his due revenge on Klutaimēstra.

The most obvious point to make is that myth gave Greeks their sense of what it was to be *Greek*, since in myth they were confronted with the basis for their moral and ethical understanding (cf. 2.9). The authority of tragedy stems from the conviction of the tragedian that he is handling topics which lie at the very heart of his own understanding of the human condition (cf. tragedy and art, 7.72). The power of tragedy lies in the way

7:11  Agamemnon, enmeshed in a net, falls before the onslaught of Aigisthos.
C. 470.

7:12  It is now Aigisthos who falls before Agamemnon's son, Orestes, while
Klutaimēstra rushes forward with an axe to help her lover before being killed
herself. C. 470.

in which the tragedians, wielding an astonishingly sophisticated dramatic
skill, subjected this powerful and emotional material to a questioning
examination which at times threatened to destroy that understanding (cf.
2.24).

   **7.41** If we ask why this should have been so, we cannot divorce the
answer from the social and intellectual climate of fifth-century Athens,

particularly from the invention of democracy and the insistence that the world should be humanly intelligible (cf. 7.6). It is significant that, of all the titles of Greek tragedy to have come down to us (nearly 1,000), only a couple feature the names of gods, and in only a few of the plays did the gods appear on stage in anything other than a very restricted role. However important the gods were in Greek tragedy (and they were), man was always there at the centre.

7.42 Greek tragedy was, then, a highly contemporary art form. It is even possible to find in it references to democracy and contemporary constitutional and political problems (cf. 5.28). Some find overt criticism of Athenian imperialism in Euripides' *Trojan Women* (see 7.36), produced a year after the Athenian subjugation of Mēlos (see H.I.47). Others have seen a connection between the plague in *Oedipus Tyrannus* and the great plague of Athens (see H.I.36).) But its true contemporaneity is not to be found here. The plays are not political or social commentaries. They were up-to-date in the way the tragedians brought to bear on myths the whole intellectual armoury of Athens: the new techniques of argument, the understanding of human psychology, the debates about the nature of the gods, the *nomos–phusis* controversy outlined above. Here are two examples, both from Euripides, which exploited the possibilities presented by the interaction of myth with contemporary understanding of the world. Here Hekabe, queen of Troy, whose city has been captured by the Greeks and is about to be destroyed, argues that Helen should not be spared by her husband Menelaos now that he has her back in his grip again. Helen has just pleaded her case and, like a skilful advocate, Hekabe answers her point by point. Paris, who took Helen back to Troy, is Hekabe's son:

But, say you, the goddess of Love herself went with my son to Menelaos' palace. What an absurd suggestion. Couldn't she have stayed quietly in heaven and transported you and your home town Amyklai to Troy without having to stir herself?

The fact is that my son Paris is extremely good-looking; one look at him and your mind was all Love. Men call all their silly infatuations Love, and Love and mad Lust begin the same way. You saw him gorgeously dressed, glittering with foreign gold, quite unlike anything you were used to in poor provincial Argos, and you went mad about him. Once rid of Sparta, so you thought, and in a Troy flowing with gold, expense could flow freely, and away from the constrictions of Menelaos' palace luxury and insolence would be unrestrained.

So much for that. And you say my son brought you here by force. Did any Spartan notice it? Did you cry rape? And when you came to Troy with the Greeks in hot pursuit, and battle was joined, if you heard the Greeks were winning then you were full of Menelaos' praise – a great lover and rival who would bring my son to grief; but if fortune favoured the Trojans, no more was heard of Menelaos. You kept your eye on the main chance; loyalty counted for nothing, your concern was to be on the winning side.

Then there's that tale of ropes let down from the battlements and you an unwilling prisoner. Who found you in a suicide noose or sharpening a sword as any honest woman would have done, pining for her lost husband? What is more I often urged you to go. 'Daughter,' I would say, 'leave us. There are other women for my sons to marry. I will help you to escape to the Greek ships and stop this war between them and us.' But not a bit of it. You were queening it in Paris' house and liked the homage of us barbarians which flattered your pride. And to crown it all you have dolled yourself up for your husband and dare to face him openly, you abominable bitch. You ought to crawl in rags to him, trembling with fear, with shaven head, ashamed at last of your evil doing. (Euripides, *Trojan Women* 983ff.)

**7.43** In the following passage, Euripides uses his knowledge of psychology to depict how the maddened Agaue, queen of Thebes, who holds in her hands, unknown to herself, the head of her son Pentheus whom she has killed (she believes it to be a lion, caught in a hunt), is brought to her senses by her father Kadmos (cf. 2.57):

*Kadmos:*   Oh grief immeasurable, sight that eyes cannot bear to see, death inflicted by your unhappy hands. A fair sacrifice it is you lay before the gods, and call Thebes and me to join the feast. I weep for your suffering first, and then my own . . .

*Agaue:*   How old men complain and scowl! I wish my son was as good a hunter as his mother, and went hunting wild beasts with the young men of

7:13   Maenads carry the dismembered remains of King Pentheus. Here there is no reference to a theatrical performance. C. 500.

Thebes. All he can do is to fight the gods. You must correct him, father. Call him here, someone, to see his mother's happy triumph.

*Kadmos*: Alas, alas. How terrible your grief will be when you know what you have done. And if you remain unknowing, as you are, happy you will hardly be but at least you will not know your wretchedness.

*Agaue*: But what is wrong? What reason is there for wretchedness?

*Kadmos*: Look child, turn your eye skyward.

*Agaue*: I see the sky. But why do you want me to look at it?

*Kadmos*: Has it its usual look, or do you see a change?

*Agaue*: It seems brighter and clearer than before.

*Kadmos*: And is your mind still in its former confusion?

*Agaue*: I don't know what you mean. But my mind is somehow clearing, and my former mood is changing.

*Kadmos*: Could you listen now and give a clear reply?

*Agaue*: Yes: but I have forgotten what you last said to me.

*Kadmos*: To whose house did you go when you married?

*Agaue*: You gave me to Ekhion, one of the Sown Warriors, so they said.

*Kadmos*: And who was the son born to him?

*Agaue*: Pentheus, born of our union.

*Kadmos*: And whose head is it that you hold in your arms?

7:14 The presence of a pipe-player shows that the painter had a theatrical performance in mind. The maenad is to be thought of as an actor taking part in a tragedy. C. 470–460.

*Agaue:*  It is a lion's, as my fellow huntresses told me.
*Kadmos:*  Look straight at it – that's easy enough to do.
*[Agaue screams in horror]*
*Agaue:*  What is it I see? What have I in my hands?
*Kadmos:*  Look closely at it and make sure.
*Agaue:*  Oh deadly sight, oh misery.
*Kadmos:*  Does it look like a lion's head?
*Agaue:*  No, no. It's Pentheus' head in these unhappy hands.
*Kadmos:*  Tears have been shed for him before you knew.
*Agaue:*  Who killed him? How did he come into my hands?
*Kadmos:*  The bitter truth dawns at an ill moment.   (Euripides, *Bacchae* 1244ff.)

7.44 At the same time, the very nature of the material with which the tragedians dealt and the skill with which they worked it ensured that tragedy was as much an emotional as an intellectual experience. Tragedy confronted the deepest questions of human existence and challenged the spectators to make sense of the human suffering not of any ordinary man but of the greatest figures of Greek myth, heroes who (by any normal standards cf. 3.9–10) should have had the world at their feet (and perhaps for a while did) but who now found themselves utterly destroyed. It is their human greatness which makes their predicament so agonising; were their roots not so deep, their uprooting would not be so tragic (cf. 2.22–3).

7.45 Finally, the emotional impact of the plays was considerably increased by the distance created between play and spectators not only by the myths themselves, but also by the formal appearance of the actors (with their masks and stylised clothing: see 7.51) and the strict maintenance of the dramatic illusion. In contrast with comedy, which continually involves the audience, it is arguable that nowhere in Greek tragedy was the audience directly addressed. The writer never referred to himself, nor the actors nor the theatre. The audience was not 'there' as far as the tragedy itself was concerned. Aloof, dignified, distanced, Greek tragedy engaged the emotions of the community in its probing of the deepest human questions.

### (d) Different approaches to Greek tragedy

7.46 Greek tragedy as we have it spans the period from 472 (Aeschylus' *Persians*) to 402 (Sophocles' *Oedipus at Kolonos*, posthumously produced). In that time, profound changes had come over the form. In early tragedy, the role of the chorus was very pronounced; there were only two actors; and the action could be at times highly formalised. There was sometimes little sense of personal interaction between actors and chorus.

Consider the following rather distant and ritualised exchange between the Persian queen Atossa and the chorus. She enquires about Athens' whereabouts and power:

*Atossa*: But tell me, friends, where is this Athens reported to be?
*Chorus*: In the far west, where the Sun-god's rays grow dim and set.
*Atossa*: But why should my son be so anxious to make it his prey?
*Chorus*: Athens won, all Greece would be subject to him.
*Atossa*: Has it so plentiful a supply of fighting men?
*Chorus*: It has, and has inflicted much damage on the Persians.
*Atossa*: What else has it? Are its people wealthy?
*Chorus*: There is a spring of silver which the earth treasures for them.
*Atossa*: Have they the bow-stretching arrow in their hands?
*Chorus*: They have not. They carry spears for close fighting and are equipped with shields.
*Atossa*: What leader and commander have they?
*Chorus*: They are no man's slave and take no man's orders.
*Atossa*: How then can they withstand invading enemies?
*Chorus*: So well that they destroyed Dareios' great and splendid army.
*Atossa*: Dread words to those whose sons are with the army now.
*Chorus*: Soon, I think, you will know the full truth. This man is surely a Persian courier bringing news, good or bad. (Aeschylus, *Persians* 230ff.)

**7.47** The form of this dialogue – single-line exchanges known as 'stichomythia' – is traditional. Other playwrights turned it to quite different use and gave it a quite different tone, especially when a third actor was added. Compare the famous scene in Sophocles' *Oedipus Tyrannus* where Oedipus questions the old shepherd (who knows that Oedipus killed his father King Laios and married his mother, but clearly does not want Oedipus to know) in the presence of a messenger with news from Corinth. The shepherd had long ago given the baby Oedipus to this same Corinthian, though the shepherd had been instructed to expose the baby, so it would die. The Corinthian does not know the significance of Oedipus' questions and cannot understand the shepherd's reluctance:

*Oedipus*: Though I have never met him, I guess, my friends, that I see the shepherd whom we have been looking for all this time. He is an old man, like our friend here, and I recognise those who are bringing him as my servants. But you may have seen him before and so have the advantage of me.
*Chorus*: Yes, I know him. He was one of Laios' most trusty shepherds.
[*Enter shepherd, attended*]
*Oedipus*: My first question is for you, my Corinthian friend. Is this the man you mean?

*Corinthian*: Yes, he is the man before you.

*Oedipus*: Come then, old man, look at me and answer my questions. Were you in Laios' service?

*Shepherd*: I was a slave of his, born and bred in his household.

*Oedipus*: What was your occupation and way of life?

*Shepherd*: For most of my life I was a shepherd.

*Oedipus*: In what part of the country did you mostly spend your time?

*Shepherd*: In Kithairon – or its neighbourhood.

*Oedipus*: Do you remember having seen this man in those parts?

*Shepherd*: Doing what? What man do you mean?

*Oedipus*: This man here; have you ever met him?

*Shepherd*: I can't say I remember him at first sight.

*Corinthian*: That's not surprising. But I will revive the memory of what he has forgotten. I am sure he remembers the days when we were neighbours in Kithairon, he with two flocks, I with one, for three grazing seasons, spring to autumn; when winter came I would drive my flocks home to Corinth and he to Laios' folds. Is that what happened? Am I right?

*Shepherd*: True enough, though it's long ago.

*Corinthian*: Come then, tell me, do you remember giving me a baby to bring up as my own child?

*Shepherd*: What do you mean? Why this question?

*Corinthian*: Because, my friend, here stands that one-time child.

*Shepherd*: Damnation take you – hold your tongue.

*Oedipus*: Don't abuse him, old man; your words call for more abuse than his.

*Shepherd*: But best of masters, how have I offended?

*Oedipus*: By not telling me of the child about whom he is asking.

*Shepherd*: He does not know what he is talking about; his words are vain.

*Oedipus*: If you will not answer a request, torture will make you speak.

*Shepherd*: No, no, for God's sake; don't hurt an old man.

*Oedipus*: Pinion his arms, someone, at once.

*Shepherd*: Oh misery, why? What do you want to know?

*Oedipus*: That child he asks about – did you give it to him?

*Shepherd*: I did – and I wish I had died that day.

*Oedipus*: And die you will unless you tell me the truth.

*Shepherd*: And if I do, ruin is still more certain.

*Oedipus*: The fellow still evades my questions.

*Shepherd*: No, no. I said before that I gave it to him.

*Oedipus*: Where did it come from? Was it yours or someone else's?

*Shepherd*: Not mine; I had it from another.

*Oedipus*: From whom? What was its home?

*Shepherd*: For god's love, master, question me no more.

*Oedipus*: If I have to ask again, you die.

*Shepherd*: Very well – it was a child from Laios' house.

*Oedipus*: A slave, or one of his own family?

*Shepherd*: Oh misery: I am on the brink of telling the awful truth.
*Oedipus*: And I of hearing it – yet it must be heard.
*Shepherd*: It was said to be his own child. But your wife within can best tell you that.
*Oedipus*: Did she give it you?
*Shepherd*: Yes, my lord.
*Oedipus*: And what were you to do?
*Shepherd*: To kill it.
*Oedipus*: Wretched woman – her own child.
*Shepherd*: She did it in fear of evil prophecies.
*Oedipus*: What prophecies?
*Shepherd*: Prophecies which said it would kill its own father.
*Oedipus*: Then why did you give it to this old man here?
*Shepherd*: In pity, master, thinking he would take it away to his own country. And he rescued it indeed, but for what a terrible fate. For if you are that child, you were born to misfortune.
*Oedipus*: Ah God, ah God: all come true and known! Let this be the last time I see the light of day. Cursed in my parents, cursed in my marriage, cursed in the blood I have shed!         (Sophocles, *Oedipus Tyrannus* 1110ff.)

This almost intimate exchange conveys a sense of the engagement of the total personality of all three characters, as they respond emotionally to the twists and turns of the gradual revelation of the truth. This shows how a single dramatic form, which was a traditional part of Greek tragedy from first to last, could be used for different purposes in different hands (it is not a matter of 'early incompetence' vs. 'later sophistication', but of dramatic intention). The exchanges between Pentheus and the god Dionysos in Euripides' *Bacchae* 810ff. illustrate another use: the god formal and correct, the man a tool in his hands, the whole highly emotionally charged (cf. 2.57).

7.48 Human character too was handled differently. In Aeschylus, the major characters tended to be distanced, powerful, archetypal figures. In Sophocles, the action characteristically moved around great individual heroes faced with the contradictions of a past of glory and a present of shame (cf. 3.10). With Euripides, generalisation is more difficult. His range seems greater, and he has the disconcerting habit of exploring 'realistic' situations in highly stylised forms. For example, the earthy nurse of Euripides' *Hippolytos* inhabits the same world as the austere and rhetorical Hippolytos himself. To point up extremes, the great hero Menelaos here verges on the comic (on his return from Troy, he has been swept ashore on a hostile Egyptian coast):

*Menelaos*: Hi there! Come to the door: this is a cry for help.

*Old Woman*:  Who's that knocking? Don't stand there disturbing the bosses. Go away; you'll get killed if you don't – you're a Greek and we have no dealings with Greeks.

*Menelaos*:  Come off it, old girl. Keep a civil tongue in your head. I'll do what you say, but do unbolt the door.

[*She opens the door*]

*Old Woman*:  Be off. My orders are to admit no Greeks.

*Menelaos*:  Here, hands off, no shoving.

*Old Woman*:   You've only yourself to blame if you won't listen to what I say.

*Menelaos*:  Take a message to your master –

*Old Woman*:  He won't be pleased to hear it.

*Menelaos*:  I've been shipwrecked, and you have to be kind to shipwrecked sailors.

*Old Woman*:  Be off, and knock on someone else's door.

*Menelaos*:  I won't. I'm coming in. Do what I tell you.

*Old Woman*:  You're a nuisance. You'll be thrown out soon.

*Menelaos*:  Hell! I wish I had my army here.

*Old Woman*:  You may impress them, but you don't impress me.

*Menelaos*:  God, what humiliating treatment!

*Old Woman*:  Tears in the eyes? What are you crying for?

*Menelaos*:  At the thought of my past happiness.

*Old Woman*:  Well, run away and weep on some friendly shoulder.

*Menelaos*:  Where am I anyway? Whose palace is this?

*Old Woman*:  It's Proteus' palace, and you're in Egypt.

*Menelaos*:  Egypt! What a wretched place to have got to.

(Euripides, *Helen* 435–61)

Contrast this with Medeia in Euripides' *Medeia* 1021ff., where she wrestles with her heart whether to kill her children or not. The writing is highly stylised, yet she is in the grip of the most primitive feelings which reduce her almost to emotional paralysis.

7.49 Finally, while the role of the chorus did change considerably between Aeschylus and late Euripides, it is important to stress that the element of singing and dancing, for which the chorus was largely responsible, did not disappear. This element became transferred, especially in Euripides' hands, from the chorus to the individual. In Euripides, there were far more solo arias than in previous tragedy. Euripides, in other words, continued to experiment with different ways of creating emotional impact through music and dance on the stage.

*(e) Production and acting*

7.50 There is much dispute about what the theatre looked like in the fifth century. Certainly there was the large circular dancing area (sixty feet across at Epidauros), the *orkhēstra*, where the chorus moved and danced and sang; and almost certainly there was a low raised stage at the back, on which the actors moved (they also used the *orkhēstra*) and behind which was a long, flat-roofed building (*skēnē*, which could stand for a palace or hut or tent, and be used as the actors' dressing-rooms). This building probably had a single door in the middle of it. There were also entrances along the sides, called *eisodoi* or *parodoi* (see the diagram). Sophocles is said to have introduced 'scene painting' (perspective sets along the front of the *skēnē*, which could be replaced as needed).

7.51 Actors and chorus wore all-over face masks (including hair) and dramatic, highly coloured costumes. Roles could be identified by the masks and costumes worn (a Greek audience would know at once who was 'king', who 'messenger'), but clearly the onus on actors was very great. Wearing a mask, the actor could not express emotions by facial expression. The audience stretched back up the theatre a very long way (and in the open air), so that the small intimate gesture and the subtle whisper (especially behind a mask) would be entirely lost on them. For all the excellence of the acoustics of the theatres, acting had to be 'big', using

7:15 An air view of the theatre at Epidauros. The theatre was built in the late 4th century.

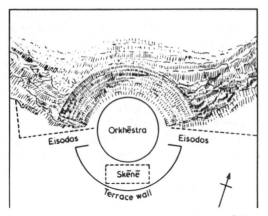

7:16   A suggested plan of the 5th-century theatre of Dionysos in Athens.

expansive gestures (especially since it is often difficult to tell *which* of a number of masked actors is speaking) with clear and audible enunciation. Likewise, the words had to carry much of the weight of a play. New characters were usually introduced by what others said about them ('Look! Here comes Menelaos'). Emotions were verbally expressed ('I weep' etc.). Extraordinary versatility was also demanded of actors. Given that the playwright was only allowed three, any one actor could be called upon to play a great number of roles. For example, in Sophocles' *Antigone*, one of the actors had to play Antigone's young sister Ismene, a guard, Antigone's lover Haimon, an old prophet Teiresias, and Haimon's mother Eurydike.

7.52 The main stumbling-block to our appreciation of the plays is that all we have are words on the page. We have no stage instructions, except what the characters themselves tell us. We have almost no idea at all what the singing and dancing sounded or looked like. (There are even doubts about the assignation of parts to characters, since manuscripts give us lists of *dramatis personae* but do not actually say who is speaking at any one time, merely marking a *change* of speaker by a dash.) Consequently, we have lost entirely any sense of the spectacle – the colour, dash, movement, music – of tragedy. But at least we have the words, and these can tell us a great deal. We can appreciate the agony of the predicaments with which characters are faced, and enjoy the power of the rhetoric in which the great debates (*agōn*) are expressed. Production can bring out clearly the Greek playwright's suggestive use of stage implements and stage actions to carry significance and reinforce the spoken word. Oedipus, for example, at the start of *Oedipus Tyrannus* comes out of the palace to be supplicated by the people of Thebes as the only man to whom the city can turn in its hour of need: he is king of Thebes, honoured by all, almost a god. At the end he *is led* back into the palace, against his will and express plea, blinded, cursed, almost an object, having found out who he really is, that he had married his own mother and killed his own father. Visually, the contrast between the two states at the beginning and end of the play could not be more clearly indicated, but it is difficult to appreciate it unless you actually go to a production, or develop the capacity to 'see' a play as you read it. As for stage implements, in Sophocles' *Philoktetes*, the possession of Philoktetes' magic bow (which is what Odysseus and Neoptolemos are out to get) expresses visually the dramatic stiuggle for mastery with which the play is concerned.

## (f) Comedy

**7.53** It may be that at the Dionysia, a day's tragic fare (i.e. trilogy + satyr play) was followed by one of the comedies which was being judged in the comic competition. If so, the audience was in for a most extraordinary experience. From the distant world of myth, and a performance which did not acknowledge their presence, the audience was thrown headlong into a fantastic and wholly contemporary comic world, where actors and chorus handled any issue of the day – literary, intellectual, political, personal, social – and where the audience itself would be the butt of the jokes as much as the characters and issues on stage, in language as extreme (and, where necessary, as obscene) as the action.

## (g) Old Comedy and Aristophanes' precursors

**7.54** The Alexandrians (see 7.5) divided Attic comedy into three types: Old Comedy (*c.* 450–380), Middle (380–320) and New (after 320). We know the names of about fifty writers of Old Comedy, but the only complete plays we possess are those of Aristophanes (*c.* 445–*c.* 385). We have eleven complete plays by him, which span the length of his career (the first, *Akharnians*, was produced in 425 and the last *Ploutos* (*Wealth*), in 388). They were preserved not necessarily because later readers saw anything especially fine in them as comedy, but because of their pure Attic language.

The origins of comedy (*kōmōidia*, 'song to do with a *kōmōs*' ('group revel')) are obscure, but are probably to be found in choral revels in Dionysos' honour, perhaps in a phallic ritual, to which episodes became attached. There is really no need to seek its origins in Dorian or Sicilian farce, as some scholars have done, since all elements of Attic comedy can be shown to have perfectly feasible origins in Attica.

**7.55** Comedy was 'given a chorus' (i.e. became a state-financed part of festivals in Athens) in 486 at the Dionysia and *c.* 445 at the Lenaia. In his comedy *Knights* (517ff.), Aristophanes talks scathingly about early comic writers. He cites Magnes who won eleven victories in all (a record) but lacked satirical power; then Kratinos (*fl.* 450–420), who had become a pathetic drunkard falling apart at the seams; and finally, Krates, renowned for his refinement. From surviving fragments of the work of Kratinos and Krates, we can see the major influences upon Attic comedy and Aristophanes. Magnes, we may guess, developed the comic element of the *kōmos* of men dressed as animals; Kratinos may have been the key figure in the development of comedy as drama in which politics and social grievances could be publicly aired. He was renowned for his ferocious obscenity and his plays often burlesqued mythology (he would take a common myth and use it to criticise contemporary politicians e.g. his *Dionysalexandros*, in which an analogy is drawn between Helen and Paris and Pericles and his mistress Aspasia). He also criticised and parodied current literary fashions, as Aristophanes was to do in, for example, *Frogs* and *Thesmophoriasdousai*. Krates (who won his first victory probably in 450) was said to have given up invective and to have developed a better plot structure.

**7.56** Common to all Old Comedy seems to have been the general struc-

7:17  To the accompaniment of pipes mounted dancers act out a traditional element in Greek comic performances: the animal masquerade that is to be found over a century later in Aristophanes. C. 550.

ture (see 7.58) and a number of traditions and subjects of attack. There were two main features: first, Old Comedy was relentlessly political, i.e. it existed and flourished within the framework of the small, tightly-knit, radically democratic *polis* (Old Comedy's power declined when the fifth-century *polis* system started to change); secondly, whatever its forms and themes and characters, it always began with a contemporary human predicament. As for technique, literary parody and burlesque of mythology were common. Dionysos, Odysseus and the Cyclops were characters in the comedies of more than one playwright, and Euripides and Socrates were often depicted as typical 'intellectuals'. Amongst politicians, Pericles (with his mistress Aspasia) was most frequently attacked, and of the intellectuals, Pericles' associates Anaxagoras and Lampon came under continual fire. Nostalgic looking back to the 'golden age' of the past seems to have been a common theme. Common, too, were the all-male actors (this gave piquancy to plays like Aristophanes' *Lysistrata*, where most of the characters were women); the grotesque costumes (padded stomachs and rumps, leather *phallos*, exaggerated but life-like masks: it is likely that the actor playing Socrates in *Clouds* wore a recognisable mask); the three-actor rule (four speaking parts are needed in some places); and the chorus.

Aristophanes' achievement was to have taken all the traditions and techniques that his precursors offered (though some he rejected, e.g. mythological burlesque) and, combining them with his own sensitivity to contemporary issues (e.g. the war, the sophists, literary fashions, politicians) and sharp eye for the absurd, to have produced a brand new confection whose sheer range and variety (from the downright obscene to the elegant lyrical) make it almost undefinable.

*(h) Aristophanes' career*

7.57 Aristophanes must have been born *c.* 445, and his first play *Banqueters* (lost) was produced in 427 in his teens. Normally, the playwright produced it, but in this case, as with *Babylonians* and *Akharnians*, Aristophanes gave it to Kallistratos to produce, for reasons (possibly) of youth or diffidence. This play came second. There then followed an extraordinary run, for a young playwright: *Babylonians* (lost) 426 (probably 1st), *Akharnians* 425 (1st), *Knights* 424 (1st). The sequence was broken by *Clouds* 423 (3rd), a result which so shocked Aristophanes that he rewrote it (though it was never reproduced) and it is this rewritten version that we possess. Then came *Wasps* 422 (2nd) and *Peace* 421 (2nd). Already these early plays prefigured what was to come. The theme of *Banqueters* was the new education. A father brought up two sons differently, one in the new, one in the old, education, and the results were observed. *Clouds* was to pick up this theme (cf. 4.47). *Babylonians*, whose main theme was the relationship between a central power and her subject allies, brought the wrath of Kleon (cf. H.I.37) down on Aristophanes' head. He (unsuccessfully) prosecuted Aristophanes for bringing Athens into disrepute with this play (cf. 4.71 and Athenian openness). Aristophanes did not forget, and his next four plays poured a torrent of vicious abuse on his head, the most violent of all being *Knights*, in which Kleon was the central figure. Personal rivalries also played their part. In *Clouds*, Aristophanes claimed that the contemporary comic playwright Eupolis (449–412) had cribbed some material from *Knights* for his play *Marikas*; Eupolis replied that he had helped Aristophanes write *Knights* – and for free. Again Aristophanes had accused Kratinos in *Knights* of being a drunken has-been (see 7.55). Kratinos responded with *Flask* in 423, with himself as the main character (a drunken has-been) in conflict with his wife Kōmōidia. Kōmōidia was shown complaining about his relations with the slut Methē ('drink') and the pretty little boy Oiniskos ('little wine'). Kratinos excused himself on the grounds that only the drunkard could produce anything worthwhile. The audience agreed, and he won first prize – sweet revenge, since Aristophanes came last with *Clouds*!

So rivalry was intense amongst these comic playwrights (cf. 3.2), and their hatreds could last (e.g. Aristophanes' hatred of Kleon). That comedy was not without its effects on the politicians may be judged from the fact that comedy was suspended between 440 and 437, and perhaps also in 415.

### (i) The structure of Old Comedy

7.58 Old Comedy is rather like pantomime in that there are recurring dramatic moments which the audience have come to expect (e.g. the spectacular entry of the chorus) and typical routines which always occur somewhere (e.g. comic monologues, slapstick, patter songs) as well as traditional costumes (e.g. the actors wearing the *phallos*). The traditional structure of Old Comedy was as follows:

1 The prologue: the actors come in, and, in a series of often irrelevant and farcical routines, introduce the plot and themselves and prepare for the entry of the chorus.
2 The *parodos*: this is the long-awaited and often highly spectacular entry of the chorus (e.g. a chorus of birds in *Birds* and clouds in *Clouds*). It is normally the signal for the start of the main action, out of which a conflict

develops, often between actors on the one side and the chorus on the other.

3 The *agōn* ('conflict'): this is a traditional, stylised form of alternating speeches and songs which always include a *pnigos* (a tongue-twisting, breath-taking *tour de force* in the shape of a patter song).

4 The *parabasis*: the chorus comes forward and gives what purports to be serious political advice, frequently entirely unconnected with anything in the play.

5 Various farcical scenes and self-contained sketches in which the consequences of the *agōn* are worked out.

6 The *exodos*: the 'departure', in which events reach a climax, often involving celebrations, or a wedding, to hail the end of the dispute.

But just as characteristic as the formal structure of Aristophanes' plays is the nature of the plots. They usually follow this sort of pattern: (1) a great and fantastic idea is put forward (the more outrageous the better), frequently involving salvation for oneself, one's family or the whole of Greece. The originator of this idea becomes the hero(ine). (2) The idea is advanced and after a series of minor setbacks, the main struggle takes place, after which the 'great idea' is realised. (3) The consequences of the success of the 'great idea' are worked out.

*(j) The art of Aristophanes* (for *Wasps*, see 5.47, 5.59ff.)

7.59 In common with other playwrights of Old Comedy, Aristophanes sacrificed all consistency of e.g. character, logic, time, place to the needs of the moment and the episode. Thus *Lysistrata* is about a sex-strike by wives against their husbands, to bring about an end to the war: yet all their husbands are at the battle-front! Secondly, fantasy was an important ingredient of his art. In *Birds*, Euelpides and Peisetairos escape from Athens and found a new city, with none of its vices, in the clouds above, amongst the birds of the air, and call it Cloudcuckooland (Nephelo-kokkugia); in *Peace*, Trygaios harnesses a dung beetle and soars up to heaven to bring Peace back to earth. Thirdly, Aristophanes presented people and ideas in forms which made them laughable *in the eyes of the common man*. Thus in *Clouds* Socrates is a typical 'intellectual', dealing in all the sort of claptrap which the common man might be expected to foist on him, whether it bore any relation to the truth or not (cf. on Socrates 7.29, and on misunderstanding intellectuals at 7.13). Fourthly, Aristophanes had a keen ear for verbal dexterity. His language was (as far as we can tell) colloquial, but it was shot through with parody of and allusions to any discipline he cared to abuse (e.g. he freely uses medical and tragic diction, the language of decrees and prophecies, philosophical jargon and rhetorical tricks), as well as rich in invented words, outrageous puns and extended alliteration. He was especially adept at parodying tragedy and tragic diction. Does this imply that the audience, in order to understand the parody, was acutely aware of the nuances of tragedy? Probably not. *Frogs*, for example, reaches its climax with a contest between Aeschylus and Euripides about who wrote the best tragedy. It is full of allusions to their plays and parody of their language (especially Euripides'), but the actors could easily have signalled parody by their use of tone and gesture, and the quotations themselves might have been well-known enough for the average man to pick up. Again, Aristophanes' language was rich in obscenity and outrageously inventive in metaphors for the sexual parts and act, e.g. metaphors for the male organ include: eel, finger, dried fig, acorn, chickpea, soup-ladle, oar, handle, rope, peg, ram, pole, goad, beam, wing, tail, sparrow. Outside the Ionian iambic poetry of Arkhilokhos (7.1) and cult practices (especially in worship of Dionysos or Dēmētēr), such obscenity is found only in Old Comedy. This obscenity, which brought social taboos out into the open and made public fun of them (contrast modern pornography, which encourages retreat into a private fantasy world), added great emphasis and power to Aristophanes' attacks on people, ridiculing, exposing and degrading them. In the following passage, an old hag takes advantage of a new law passed by the women in parliament – that if a young man wants to make love to his girl, he must make love to an old woman first. Observe the pleasing combination of lyricism and filth.

*Girl*:  Come here my dear,
Come here, come here
And spend all the night in my bed with me.
For my head it just whirls
At your beautiful curls
And I'm wholly on fire
With the strangest desire.
Love, give me relief from my torment and grief
And make sure that you bring him to bed with me.

*Boy*:  Oh open, my dear,
Your door and come here
Or I'll fall on your doorstep and lie there.
Oh why *am* I so mad about you, dear, oh why?
For what I am longing to do is to lie
Head nicely at rest on your bosom
And hands caressing your dear little bottom.

Love, give me relief from my torment and grief
And make sure that you bring her to bed with me.

That's really a very moderate expression
Of all the torment I suffer from my passion.
So open the door and give me a kiss,
As it is you are simply tormenting me.
You're the song in my heart,
My treasure, my bliss,
My sweet honey-bee,
My love and my flower
My delicate luxury miss.

*Hag*: Hi! Who's knocking? Are you looking for me?
*Boy*: Not likely.
*Hag*: You knocked on my door.
*Boy*: Damn me if I did.
*Hag*: Who are you looking for with that torch?
*Boy*: Someone from Wankborough.
*Hag*: Who?
*Boy*: Not the screwdriver whom you are perhaps expecting.
*Hag*: Well you've got to do me whether you want or not.
*Boy*: But we're not dealing with the over-sixties now. We're leaving them till later and trying the under-twenties.
*Hag*: That was under the old regime, love. Now you must take us on first.
*Boy*: But the rule is you can take your choice.
*Hag*: Oh no you can't. It's table d'hôte, not à la carte.
*Boy*: You don't understand. I've got a girl to knock here.
*Hag*: But you've got to knock at my door first.
*Boy*: We don't want soiled goods.
*Hag*: Oh I know I'm desirable. Are you surprised to find me out of doors? Come on, give us a kiss.
*Boy*: No, no: I'm afraid of your lover.
*Hag*: Who?
*Boy*: The best of artists.
*Hag*: And who's that?
*Boy*: The undertaker's man. Be off in case he sees you.
*Hag*: I know what you want.
*Boy*: And I know what you want.
*Hag*: I vow by Aphrodite, whose devotee I am, that I will not let you go.
*Boy*: You are mad.
*Hag*: Nonsense. I'll get you to bed yet.

(Aristophanes, *Ekklēsiasdousai* 952ff.)

**7.60** Finally, Aristophanes had an enviable capacity to integrate effortlessly the fantastic plot on stage with contemporary life. His characters did not step outside themselves to make topical allusions; instead they drew the subjects of their allusions (people, places, events, issues) into the plot. Thus when Dikaiopolis at the start of *Akharnians* laments the Athenians' refusal to take seriously the question of ending the war (see 5.14), he alludes to real people and real occasions, yet the plot itself is outrageously absurd – one man's fight to forge a personal peace-treaty with Sparta. In *Birds*, Peisetairos is founding a new city in the clouds (Cloudcuckooland), but finds the usual charlatans coming to make some money. First is a soothsayer (cf. 2.19):

*Peisetairos*: Eh? Who are you?
*Soothsayer*: A soothsayer.
    *Pei.*: Get lost.
      *S.*: O think not lightly, friend, of things divine; you see, I've an oracle of Bakis, bearing on your Cloudcuckoolands.
    *Pei.*: Eh? then why did you not soothsay that before I founded my city here?
      *S.*: The Force forbade me.
    *Pei.*: Well, well, there's nowt like hearing what it says.
      *S.*: 'Nay, but if once grey crows and wolves shall be banding together
           Out in the midway space, twixt Corinth and Sikyon, dwelling, – '
    *Pei.*: But what in the world have I to do with Corinth?
      *S.*: Bakis is riddling: Bakis means the Air.
           'First to Pandora offer a white-fleeced ram for a victim.
           Next, who first shall arrive my verses prophetic expounding,
           Give him a brand-new cloak and a pair of excellent sandals.'
    *Pei.*: Are sandals in it?
      *S.*: Take the book and see.
           'Give him moreover a cup and fill his hands with the inwards.'
    *Pei.*: Are inwards in it?
      *S.*: Take the book and see.
           'Youth, divinely inspired, if thou dost as I bid, thou shalt surely
           Soar in the clouds as an Eagle; refuse, and thou ne'er shalt become an
           Eagle, or even a dove, or a woodpecker tapping the oak-tree.'
    *Pei.*: Is all that in it?
      *S.*: Take the book and see.
    *Pei.*: Well well! How unlike your oracle is to mine, which from Apollo's words I copied out:
           'But if a cheat, an impostor, presume to appear uninvited,
           Troubling the sacred rites, and lusting to taste of the inwards,
           Hit him betwixt the ribs with all your force . . . '
      *S.*: You must be joking . . .
    *Pei.*: Take the book and see.
           'See that ye spare not the rogue, though he soar in the clouds as an Eagle,

Yea, be he Lampon* himself or even the great Diopeithes*.'
    *S.*: Is all that in it?
*Pei.*: Take the book and see. Get out!
[*Strikes him*]
    *S.*: Aagh!
*Pei.*: Take that! Now get out of here and soothsay somewhere else.
                              (Aristophanes, *Birds* 959ff. (Rogers, adapted))

## (k) Aristophanes' views

7.61 Aristophanes generally pulled no punches and took no hostages. It is true he never called for a change in the radical democratic constitution of fifth-century Athens, nor did he (in his surviving work) seriously attack public figures such as Nikias or Alkibiades; likewise, many subjects natural for satirical abuse in our society (e.g. industrial management and unions; administrative hush-ups; tax swindles; educational scandals) did not exist in Aristophanes' time. But apart from these, all was grist to his mill: the audience, the gods, politicians, intellectuals, homosexuals, jurors, bureaucrats, students, the military. In all this, his purpose was to win first prize; but the appeal to his audience, which included farmers, city men, the poor, sailors, soldiers, the successful, and the disillusioned, the educated and the illiterate, surely resided in the *hope* he gave them. Aristophanes' heroes like Dikaiopolis were all little people of no importance, but still individuals who felt passionately about something probably close to the heart of the audience and who made heroic efforts to achieve their ends – usually successfully. In the strongly competitive world of Athenian society (cf. 3.8), this reassertion of the little man's will to win and to overcome his superiors must have been as reassuring as the discomfiture of the high and mighty (cf. on Kleon 7.57).

7.62 But where did Aristophanes stand in all this? It is extremely difficult to disentangle his views. His aim was to make people laugh and to win a prize. There is no reason why anything he said should reflect anything other than this end and the audience's prejudices. On the other hand, the *parabasis* of his plays did contain what is apparently serious advice (though frequently this is purely generalised, on a 'good of all mankind' level, rarely does it seem contentious, and often it is interspersed with jokes as well). Again, there are constant themes running through this work which may suggest to us that we can define some of his serious concerns.

Here Aristophanes reminds the Athenians how they had granted freedom to those slaves who had fought at the battle of Arginoussai and urges

*Famous seers.

them to grant a pardon to those who had been deprived of their rights for their 'one mishap' in becoming involved in the oligarchic coup of 411. Phrynikhos had played a major part in the coup. Plataia had been admitted to Athenian citizenship after its destruction in 427 (H.I.35, 52, 55).

> Well it suits the holy Chorus evermore with counsel wise
> To exhort and teach the city; this we therefore now advise –
> End the townsmen's apprehensions; equalise the rights of all;
> If by Phrynikhos's wrestlings some perchance sustained a fall,
> Yet to these 'tis surely open, having put away their sin,
> For their slips and vacillations pardon at your hands to win.
> Give your brethren back their franchise. Sin and shame it were that slaves,
> Who have once with stern devotion fought your battle on the waves [i.e. Arginoussai],
> Should be straightway lords and masters, yea 'Plataians' fully blown –
> Not that this deserves our censure; there I praise you; there alone
> Has the city, in her anguish, policy and wisdom shown –
> Nay but these, of old accustomed on our ships to fight and win
> (They, their fathers too before them), these our very kith and kin,
> You should likewise, when they ask you, pardon for their single sin.
> O by nature best and wisest, O relax your jealous ire,
> Let us all the world as kinsfolk, and as citizens acquire,
> All who on our ships will battle well and bravely by our side.
> If we make our city haughty, narrowing her with senseless pride,
> Now when she is rocked and reeling in the cradles of the sea,
> Here again will after ages deem we acted brainlessly.
>
> (Aristophanes, *Frogs* 686ff. (Rogers))

First and foremost we may say Aristophanes loved Athens. But though he never attacked the principle of the radical democracy, he did resent what he saw as the misuse of power by people like Kleon and he despised the *dēmos* when it encouraged such 'unworthy' individuals (cf. H.I.37; 5.21). Again, he wanted an end to the Peloponnesian War but only if it brought glory to his beloved city: he was no 'peace-at-all-costs' poet. So much seems fairly clear. When it comes to his frequent attacks on e.g. intellectuals and jurors, it is more difficult to decide. Perhaps he saw such trends and institutions as symptomatic of some vague and indefinable threat to the solidity and moral fibre of the Athenian people. Certainly, in Plato's *Symposium* Aristophanes sits most comfortably discoursing among the leading intellectuals of the day (including Socrates), which suggests that Plato wished us to suppose that Aristophanes did not have an ineradicable prejudice against everything new.

7:18 Terracotta figurines giving some of the typical characters of 4th-century Athenian comedy.

## (l) Later comedy

7.63 Aristophanes' later plays are not like his earlier ones. His last play, *Ploutos* (*Wealth*), lacks almost entirely the outrageousness of insult, fantasy and obscenity so characteristic of earlier work. The reason must lie in what was happening at Athens (7.56). By the end of the fifth century, the heroic days were gone. The gradual dissolution of the *polis* system (6.30), culminating in the destruction of the democracy by the Macedonians (see 5.99) in 322, had an important effect on the style of comedy to which the people were able to respond. The period we call Middle Comedy (380–320) is almost entirely undocumented, but by the time of what we call New Comedy (320 onwards), of which we have substantial work by the Athenian Menander, Greek comedy was an entirely different animal: language was plain, typical of ordinary conversation; lyrics were confined to song and dance routines between the acts (the chorus had no part in the plot of the play at all and the playwright merely wrote 'choral song' as a stage direction at the act-divisions, so that none of the songs survives); instead of the formal structure of Old Comedy, there was a five-act unit; the grossness of Old Comedy costume was modified in favour of more decency; and, most important of all, the plays moved from the disorganised, fantastic, obscene (but in many ways fundamentally serious) chaos of Aristophanes to a world where ordinary human affairs, played out by carefully drawn, ordinary human characters, held the stage. It was a world which we recognise as the origin of drawing-room comedy or the comedy of manners, where humour arises from misunderstandings and 'double-takes'. It is this style of comedy (which reached Western Europe through its Roman adaptations), not that of Aristophanes, which was to have such an important effect on the development of European comedy. The plays of Molière and *The Importance of Being Earnest* are in direct line of succession from Menander (cf. Euripides' *Helen*, 7.48).

Here is a typical extract from New Comedy. In it Farmer Knemon (the bad-tempered old man of the title, *Dyskolos*), after a life of surliness, has fallen down a well and is rescued in the nick of time. He abandons his responsibilities to his son Gorgias, who is to ensure that he marries off Knemon's daughter Myrrhine to someone suitable. Gorgias ensures that Sostratos, the leisurely, aristocratic young neighbour who is in love with Myrrhine but has been going through hell trying to win her (e.g. pretending to be a farm-worker) should be the groom (cf. 4.21).

*Knemon*: What's the matter, young man? Whether I die now – I'm in a bad way and think I shall – or whether I survive, I adopt you as my son; so consider my whole estate yours. As for my daughter Myrrhine, I make you her guardian. Find her a husband. Even if I get well again I could never find one for her myself – not to satisfy me. If I do live, let me live as I like. Take things over and run them as you like – thank god you have some sense, and you are the proper guardian for your sister. Divide the property in half – give her one half for dowry, keep the other half and look after your sister and me.

   Now help me lie down, Myrrhine. Talking more than necessary is no occupation for a man, I reckon. But there's one thing I'd like you to know, son. I'd like to say a few words about myself and my ways. If everyone was like me there would be no law-courts, no imprisonment, no war. Everyone would have enough and be satisfied. But I guess people like things better as they are. Carry on then, this cantankerous old malcontent will soon be out of your way.

*Gorgias*: Thank you, father, for all that. But you must help us to find a husband for the girl as quick as we can, if you agree.

*Knemon*: Look, I've told you what I want. For goodness' sake, don't bother me.

*Gorgias*: There's someone here who wants to meet you.

*Knemon*: No, no, for God's sake.

*Gorgias*: He wants to marry the girl.

*Knemon*: That's nothing to do with me now.

*Gorgias*: But it's the man who helped rescue you.

*Knemon*: Who's he?

*Gorgias*: There he is. Here, Sostratos!

*Knemon*: He's nicely sunburnt. Is he a farmer?

*Gorgias*: He certainly is. He's tough, not the sort you find idling round all day.
*Knemon*: Very well; give her to him. Carry me indoors.

(Menander, *Dyskolos* 729ff.)

That is an example of typical New Comedy moralising, and humour based on character. For more slapstick humour, involving cooks (traditional figures of fun in New Comedy) who are trying to borrow some utensils from Knemon, see *Dyskolos* 441ff.

## Greek art

### (i) Art and society

7.64 The Greeks had no word for 'art' in our sense. Their nearest word was *tekhnē*, which meant 'skill' or 'workmanship'. The artist was a master *craftsman*, and he worked according to the demands of his customers, whether the requirement was a vase with appropriate scenes for a wedding, or the pediment sculpture for a temple which was to illustrate some scene from myth. In the matter of kind there was no difference between a mason and a sculptor, nor between potter and vase painter. But the craftsman was not anonymous. He proudly signed his name beside that of his patron on many sculptures, and in sixth-century and later Athens, signed his potting or painting of a vase. By the fourth century painters and sculptors were famous men, and a considerable literary tradition grew up in later times concerning artists and their achievements.

7.65 Since most Greek art and literature was for public consumption, it had to meet public approval. Pheidias the sculptor hid behind the door to hear the public's comments on his statue of Zeus and then made changes accordingly; tragic and comic writers hoped to win the first prize at the public festivals in which they were competing; lyric poets like Pindar hoped to win commissions to celebrate important public occasions. If we can draw any inferences from the art and literature which was successful, we can conclude first that Greek artists had a powerful sense of the tradition within which they worked, and valued neither experimentation nor self-expression *as such*. What counted was the persuasiveness of the result (cf. on *peithō* 7.17), and its ability to impress the viewer or hearer. Secondly, it was an almost universal ancient view that art, especially poetry and sculpture, was a form of *mimēsis*, 'imitation' of life, and that one should judge it by the extent to which it made the recipient more or less virtuous. Shoddy and ill-disciplined work was despised. Since art was a *tekhnē*, Greeks were no more concerned with the artist's 'sincerity' than we are with our dentist's: what was important was that the result 'worked'. Thus while Greek artists and writers did experiment, with extraordinary results, experimentation was always firmly grafted onto the trunk of the tradition; and the artist usually had one eye firmly on public opinion (cf. 3.1ff.; 3.26).

### (ii) The beginnings: 800–700

**7.66** The beginnings of Greek art had its roots in a world which had suffered a profound shock four centuries earlier. Mycenean civilisation had been swept away, and Greece was only just beginning to recover sufficient stability to achieve new things, to 'look forward' (cf. H.I.3ff.).

Protogeometric and Geometric art had provided a slow transition through those centuries, and the first signs of figurative and representational art appear at its end. For example, in the eighth-century cemetery of Athens the graves of the well-to-do were marked by monumental vases (no stone sculpture existed as yet) – a wide-mouthed mixing bowl for wine for men, and a tall storage jar for women. These great vases, more than

7:19 Geometric grave marker with a scene of a *prothesis* – the body lying in state on the bier. C. 750.

three feet high, stood above the graves as memorials to the dead. They bore highly stylised scenes showing one stage in the funeral (Fig. 7:19), and sometimes a scene of warfare, on land or at sea. These 'pictures' were an astonishing achievement for they depicted a recognisable, unambiguous activity, although severely limited by the schematic technique. The artist was at great pains to make precise the relationship of all the figures to each other, and to show the 'reality' of the objects. However, this Geometric art was severely limited by its use of solid silhouette, for there was no detail and no means of showing overlapping or interlocking relationship between the figures.

7.67 From this newly confident world we also have model horses and bronze warriors which were made in great numbers for dedication to the gods in their sanctuaries but all on a small scale and in solid metal or clay. (As yet there was no sculpture or monumental architecture of the type which we identify as the main Greek achievement.) But these vigorous studies are full of life and freshness, and show the beginnings of the break-up of the Geometric forms (Fig. 7:20). They also showed the first depiction of scenes from myth and epic.

### (iii) 'Orientalising' period: change and innovation 700–600

7.68 From the East, where highly skilled craftsmen worked in a wide variety of materials, sophisticated metal work, ivories, jewellery, and richly decorated fabrics poured into Greece. They had an immense influence on Greek art. But Greek artists took over only what they could use, and recast or built anew on what they had borrowed. The series of small ivory figures from the same cemetery as the great vases above shows us this

7:20 A bronze statuette moulded from a clay original of a hunter with a dog slaying a lion. Late 8th century.

7:21 Ivory girl from the Dipylon cemetery, Athens. *C.* 730.

principle in action. From one tusk of ivory (itself an exotic new material from the Orient) a Greek craftsman carved a series of figures of standing naked girls (Fig. 7:21). By their nudity, as well as their material, they betray their eastern inspiration, and the smaller figures, from the narrowing end of the tusk, show eastern superficiality. But the largest figure has a formal quality, both restrained and instinct with life, which is quite different and new. This is the Greek transformation in action.

### (a) Development of drawing

7.69 Oriental models also inspired the development of true drawing, with outline used to flesh out the figures, and internal detail shown. This new style is called 'Orientalising' and it carries within it the seeds of the whole development of Western painting. The powerful group of Odysseus blinding the Cyclops shows how ambitious the artists had become by the middle of the seventh century (Fig. 7:22). Work in other material, like jewellery, ivory and bronze was by now highly skilled.

### (b) Sculpture

7.70 Influence from another part of the East was responsible for the next exciting development. Greek mercenaries and traders found their way to Egypt about the middle of the seventh century and the impact of the massive stone sculpture and architecture which they saw in Egypt was immediate and lasting. In particular the over-life-size figures of men who step forwards, dominating the space around them, impressed the Greeks. Here they saw man's power and abilities symbolised in a uniquely idealised

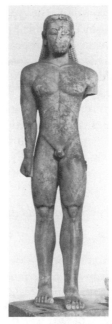

7:22 Protoattic amphora by
the Polyphemos Painter.
C. 660.

7:23 Over-life-size marble
statue of a young man
('*kouros*') from the Temple of
Poseidon at Sounion in Attica.
C. 580.

way. They very soon located sources of hard stone in Greece itself, and
using stone-working techniques adopted from the Egyptians made their
first marble statues (Fig. 7:23). No feeble imitations these, but bold, skil-
fully worked interpretations of the scheme, which seem to strive to create
a permanent, distanced ideal.

## (c) Temples

7.71 The other important stimulus from Egypt was towards building
temples in stone, with stone columns supporting projecting roofs over the
central *naos* (the house of the deity itself). Temples already existed in
Greece – elongated, over-elaborated mud-brick cottages – with a central
internal row of supporting columns which obstructed the view of the
divine image (Fig. 7:24). But the proportions of the new stone temples
were startlingly different. Now the pitched roof was *tiled*; the upper works
of the roof, at the top of and above wall level, became the focus for

sculptural decoration. The type of temple building is immediately recognisable to us since its gabled pediment and colonnaded façade is still a powerful influence in European architecture. However, the figures actually carved in the triangular pediment of the temple at Kerkyra show how early the building is (Fig. 7:25).

The Greeks had therefore, by the sixth century, established their main fields of artistic creativity. The seventh century, the 'Orientalising period', had been one of experimentation and bold adventure and new techniques – with, in its second half, influence from Egypt in stone-working and temple-building. Concurrently, writing was becoming common, and the intellectual revolution discussed at 7.6ff. was gathering momentum.

### (iv) Archaic period: consolidation 600–500

#### (a) Vase painting

7.72 The sixth century saw the full flowering of the Archaic style, in which formalism and patterning combined with a developing sensitivity to the depiction of human feelings. Vase painting, especially in Athens, developed from the lively figures of such painters as Sophilos (the first real 'name' in vase painting) (Fig. 7:26) – to sophisticated work like that of the great potter and painter, Exekias. His compositions depicted scenes charged with emotion and showed the turning-point of a tragic action for

7:24 Drawing of a reconstructed model temple from Perachora. C. 750–720.

7:25 A Gorgon – the central figure from the pediment of the Temple of Artemis, Kerkyra. C. 580.

7:26  *Dinos* (wine-mixing bowl on a
stand) by Sophilos. C. 570.

7:27  Achilles killing
Penthesileia on an amphora
signed by Exekias as maker.
C. 540.

the first time, e.g. the depiction of the death of Penthesileia, her face
upturned to meet Achilles' glance (Fig. 7:27). Such paintings, full of moral
feeling, looked forward to Attic tragedy of the next century (cf. 7.40). But
the technique used on these vases, which is called 'black-figure', with
figures silhouetted in black glaze, and details incised on that, was inflex-
ible, and could not accept brushwork. A new technique was tried out, with
the glaze colours reversed, and black used as a background, while the
figures were left in the red of the clay body. This allowed ample scope for
painting detail, and from about 530 this new technique, called 'red-figure',
allowed the development of anatomical studies of bodies in ambitious,
turning poses and the exploration of muscular structure (see Sleep and
Death struggling to lift the body of Sarpedon (Fig. 7:28)). With this new
realism, the Archaic style began to be left behind.

### (b) Sculpture

7.73  In sculpture, some of the most delightful work to survive from
Greece belongs to the sixth century. The fine series of free-standing

7:28 Sleep and Death (so named above their heads) struggle to lift the body of Sarpedon on an early red-figure *kalyx kratēr* by Euphronios. C. 510.

sculptures from the Acropolis of Athens charts the development of sculpture in this period. They show the combination of archaic formalism and sensitivity at their most potent. Instead of standing as powerful abstractions (7.70) of man's capabilities, these sculptures seem to feel and think. One example must suffice to illustrate this feeling of interior existence achieved within a formal framework (Fig. 7:29).

From sacred buildings we now have a growing number of sculptural groups, both in low relief and in the round. A pediment group from the Acropolis showed Athēnē (patron goddess of Athens) battling against giants. One giant is awkwardly balanced in the tension and weight of conflict. It is a bold attempt (Fig. 7:30). By the end of the sixth century, however, the fine sculptures from the Temple of Aphaia on the island of Aiginē showed figures in the round in movement and tension – in both active life, and agonised death, although there was still a certain stiffness (Fig. 7:31). And the standing figures of youths, the *kouroi*, which had continued to develop since their introduction to Greece (7.70), now revealed an understanding of internal structure: the weight of the body is all on one foot, and hips and torso are shifted sideways to accommodate this (Fig. 7:32).

7:29  Marble statue of a young girl ('*kore*') wearing a *peplos*. C. 530.

**7.74** A new realism, then, was already developing in Archaic art by 500: developed outer form combined with sensitivity to inner bodily structure, which took precedence over the decorative surface patterning of the Archaic style. At the same time, mental states began to be expressed. But the aftermath of the Persian invasions (H.I.13ff.), with the almost total destruction of the Acropolis and its temples and sculptures thrown down (1.31, 34), put an end to this Archaic formalism for ever. The new 'classical' style which emerged was at first sober and restrained, perhaps (after the Persian Wars) reflecting contempt for Eastern decoration and awareness of human frailty. But the wars also bred confidence in fifth-century artists, and in both sculpture and in painting the pace of development and innovation started to quicken. Increasing Greek confidence in man's intellectual capacities and interest in human motivation (7.6, 14) must have had their influence upon the artist's work.

### (v) Classical period – idealism and reality

#### (a) Sculpture

**7.75** In original sculpture (i.e. not Roman copies) the (reconstructed) pediment from the Temple of Zeus at Olympia shows groups of figures

7:30  Marble giant from an Acropolis pediment. C. 520.

7:31  A fallen warrior from the East Pediment of the Temple of Aphaia, Aigine.
C. 490.

7:32 The Kritian boy – marble statue about half life size. C. 490–480.

united in intense movement, and conveys struggle (intellectual and physical) and pathos (Fig. 7:33). It leads us on to the highest achievement of classical art which survives to us – the sculptures belonging to the temple of Athēnē Parthenos, built at Athens between 447 and 432, under the direction of the sculptor Pheidias (Fig. 7:34) (cf. 1.34). The most impressive are the (now battered) figures from the pediments (the Elgin marbles, in the British Museum in London). These show a new understanding of form. It is our great loss that the complete arrangement of sculptures is destroyed. Look at the reclining male nude (a river god) with a sense both of the weight of lax muscle and of the structures *beneath* the skin which we have not seen before (Fig. 7:35). The comparable female figures are massive and heavily draped, and it is the treatment of the drapery which hints at the body beneath, and points forward to the expressionist use of drapery in later sculpture (Fig. 7:36). (See 7.79.)

7.76 The frieze on the temple, part of the Elgin marbles in London, which depicted the procession known as the Great Panathenaia (see 2.49) was no less significant. Not only was the work of the highest skill in design and execution (Pheidias' responsibility), but it was also the first temple sculpture to show not only gods and heroes but also *men*, and men celebrating a human festival. True, the men were particularly beautiful,

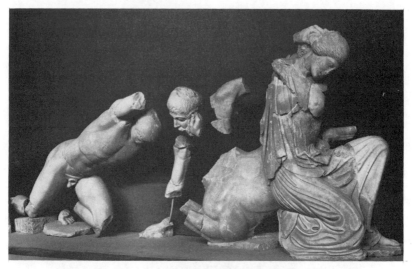

7:33  Marble group of a struggling lapith, Centaur and girl, from the west pediment of the Temple of Zeus at Olympia. C. 460.

7:34  The west front of the Parthenon, viewed from inside the propylaia – the entrance gates. C. 440.

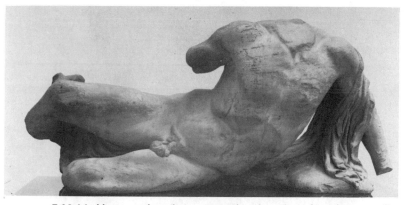

7:35 Marble statue of a reclining river god, perhaps Ilisos, from the west pediment of the Parthenon. 438–432.

7:36 Iris, the messenger of the gods, starting in fright – marble statue from the west pediment of the Parthenon. 438–432.

7:37 Horsemen taking part in
the Panathenaic procession.
Part of a marble slab from the
north frieze of the Parthenon.
C. 447–438.

7:38 Bronze statue of a nude
warrior, from Riace in
Calabria, southern Italy.
C. 450.

7:39 Red-figure cup by the Brygos Painter, showing the sack of Troy. C. 490.

almost idealised, but they were still human. In this sculpture, the Greek capacity to reconcile the human with the divine reached a climax. It was a search in which thinkers and writers had also been engaged (cf. 7.6). If, as has recently been suggested, the horsemen riding in the procession (Fig. 7:37) represented the 192 Greeks who died at Marathon and had now been heroised, we can link them with two of the finest bronzes ever recovered (most bronzes were melted down long ago). These, possibly executed by Pheidias, may well have represented heroes of Marathon. They clearly show the powerful presence, as of a living being, with weight and muscular tension realistically rendered, which workers in bronze could create (Fig. 7:38).

### (b) Painting

7.77 Throughout this period (late Archaic and early Classical) Attic red-figure pottery (in particular the vases associated with drinking wine – the amphora, mixing bowl, cups and dippers) are decorated with acutely observed scenes of everyday life. (See the illustrations in *Reading Greek*.) The same artists also created grand set pieces, such as the Brygos Painter's rendering of the Sack of Troy on a drinking cup (Fig. 7:39). But it is now that we hear for the first time of masterpieces of composition in wall painting on a scale similar to sculptural groups, and worthy of consideration as major works of art. (Witness the second-century A.D. Greek traveller Pausanias' enthusiastic description of the paintings by Polygnotos at Delphi and Athens). These were on walls, or wooden panels, and were used to decorate buildings. Unfortunately, no examples survive to us from the fifth century. However, certain vase paintings, on a *white* background, use natural colours, and give some idea of the new effects, with a delicate style of drawing used to deploy figures in a three-dimensional sense in the beginnings of a landscape (Fig. 7:40). Examples of red-figure vase painting at this time also reflect these new experiments in perspective. See the Niobid Painter's vase, with figures disposed on a staggered background, to give a new impression of depth and immanence within the landscape (Fig. 7:41). However, by the time of the Meidias painter at the end of the century, such ambitious attempts to turn the whole vase surface into three-dimensional 'theatres' are overwhelming in their effect (Fig. 7:42). By the end of the fifth-century vase painting at Athens no longer led the Greek world.

### (c) Temples

7.78 Athens then was a major centre for artistic creation in the fifth century. Thucydides, writing late in the second half of the fifth century,

7:40 A white-ground lekythos from Eretria, showing a dead youth and his companions at the tomb. Late 5th century.

remarks that to judge by the comparable surviving monuments in Sparta and Athens, coming generations would think Athens much more powerful than she was and Sparta much less. So Athens was unusually well adorned with art and architecture, while Sparta was little more than a collection of small villages. The Acropolis building scheme, begun by Pericles with the Parthenon in 447, was continued through the rest of the century and was by no means the only focus for replanning and for prestigious buildings in Athens (see, for example, the Peiraieus, the *agora* to the north of the Acropolis, the Odeion on the south slope of the Acropolis (1.31–6, 2.38–9). Other buildings erected on the Acropolis perfectly complement the Parthenon. The Propylaia, the formal gateway to the sacred enclosure, is an austere and masculine foil. (It bears no sculpture.) On the other hand, the Erekhtheion, with its elaborate decoration and its use of the Ionic order, which is lighter and more feminine, complements the Parthenon while in no way rivalling it. Only the statuesque girls of the porch which faces the Parthenon, the so-called Karyatids, mirror the monumental style of the pediment sculptures (Fig. 7:43). The final building on the Acropolis, the tiny temple of Athēnē Nikē ('Victorious') which perches on the bastion outside the entrance gates, was protected by a fine balustrade. This bore

7:41 Theseus and Peirithous in the Underworld, on a *kalyx kratēr* by the Niobid Painter. C. 460.

figures of winged victories in gracious, stately movement (Fig. 7:44). The proportions of these buildings, the sculpture they bore, and the relationship between them, all witness to the confident poise of the classical moment. The figures show a reserved superiority, an ideal presence which is almost superhuman, verging on the divine. There are no personal oddities, no depiction of the extremes of age or youth, though youths and older men do appear, and no hint of emotion – either joy or fear. However, the bald-headed self-portrait which Pheidias included on the shield of Athēnē caused a scandal, and (we are told) prosecution for impiety. For it impinged on the ideal and sullied the divine plane with a hint of the temporality of mortal existence (5.87).

### (vi) The fourth century

### (a) Sculpture

**7.79** Change was not uniform during the fourth century. The grave monument of Dexileos, for example, dated to 394, kept the restrained

7:42  Red-figure water jar (*hudria*) decorted by the Meidias Painter, showing the rape of the daughters of Leukippos by the Dioskouroi (Kastor and Pollux). C. 410.

7:43  Marble porch of the Erekhtheion, with Karyatids supporting the roof. C. 420.

7:44 Two victories bringing a bull to sacrifice on a marble relief slab from the balustrade of the Temple of Athene Nike on the Acropolis. C. 410–407.

idealism of the classical style, and must have been executed by a sculptor who had been trained on the Acropolis scheme (Fig. 7:45). But the Ilisos monument, made some forty years later, gave a clear indication of change. Here there is an un-classical sense of immediacy, and of individual personality – the dead man looks directly at us (Fig. 7:46). The style of the great sculptor Skopas is visible here.

Notwithstanding this new immediacy and realism, the pursuit of ideal beauty continued. Great sculptors like Praxiteles of Athens continued to develop the study of a standing figure in tension and balance, and in the 'ideal' mode. Look at the sinuous stance of the bronze boy, which is in the style of Praxiteles and valuable for being an original in bronze (Fig. 7:47). When complete, the figure leant against a pillar or a tree, and held a tray (?) in the left hand. To Praxiteles also belongs the achievement of establishing the female nude as a worthy subject for serious sculpture, although the inhabitants of Kōs, who had originally commissioned the Aphrodite, were too shocked when they saw her naked to accept her (Fig. 7:48). The bolder Knidians benefited, and built a special shrine for the statue which allowed her to be viewed from all four sides. But already there began to be an underlying contradiction, which became increasingly hard

7:45  The grave monument of Dexileōs, killed fighting the Corinthians in 394, from the Kerameikos.

to reconcile. The realism which the fourth century so admired contradicts the pursuit of ideal forms. For instance, the statue was so realistically feminine that, so the story went, someone attempted to make love to it. There is already a sense of unreality about these ideal depictions, which stems from the new ability to create portraits. The portraits of Alexander the Great show the range of solutions, from ideal to realistic, to the problem of portraying an individual (Fig. 7:52; p. 54). Henceforth, the creation of an 'ideal' art takes new paths.

### (b) New centres of patronage

7.80 Athens in the fourth century still produced great artists, but hers was no longer the wealth and power to be patron to great projects. In the middle of the century, it was Mausolos' funeral monument in Halikarnassos which attracted the greatest sculptors of the Greek world. Artists and skilled craftsmen moved to other new centres like the Macedonian court, where wealth was allied with a desire for everything Greek.

*(c) Painting*

**7.81** Painters and mosaicists were also finding work in Macedonia, as witness the new tombs unearthed at Vergina (the old capital, see Fig. 7:49) and the magnificent floors from the palace at Pella (the new capital). Painting now saw the final development of three-dimensional depiction: shadows were used to give substance to limbs and bodies, and they even fell across other objects or figures (see the Pella mosaic of the Hunt (Fig. 7:50)). This usage implies that the figures had a strictly positioned relationship to each other 'inside' the pictorial space. They were no longer balanced, like a flat frieze of 'cut-out' figures, along the edge of it.

A fine combination of painter's and mosaicist's art is the so-called Alexander mosaic. Found at Pompeii, it is a mosaic copy of a late fourth-century painting. Alexander and Dareios are shown poised at the moment

7:46 Marble grave monument found near the Ilisos. C. 350.

7:47 Bronze statue of a young man, from a wreck found off Marathon in northern Attica. C. 340.

7:48  Aphrodite of Knidos by Praxiteles. This is a Roman copy of the marble original which was made *c*. 350.

7:49  A painting from a tomb in the Great Tumulus at Vergina, Macedonia, showing the rape of Persephone by Hades. *C*. 350.

of crisis – world power is about to shift to the victor and their glances meet across the field of battle (Fig. 7:51). Here figures were shown in a complex mass of interrelationships which defined them in three-dimensional space. The smell of fear, the sound of horses screaming in pain, the groans of the dying, all these come through from the flat surface. The effect of such a picture is illustrated beautifully by the little poem in the Greek Anthology:

> Calpurnius, our favourite braggart soldier,
> Strayed into an art gallery, and there
> Ran into a mural of the Trojan War.
> He goggled
>      swooned
>          crying 'I yield
> O comrade Trojans, belov'd of the War God.'
> We brought him to. He asked where he was wounded,
> And insisted on paying ransom to the wall.
>
> (Lucilius, 11.211, trans. by Dudley Fitts)

7:50 The Stag Hunt Mosaic in pebbles from Pella, Macedonia, showing the use of shadow to define form, signed by the artist Gnosis. C. 300.

**7.82** This is the new realism in action, with the power to convince us of its existence in the real world. Apelles' grapes won a competition for the most 'real' painting by luring a bird from the sky to peck at them. Painting now rivals sculpture as a major art.

This magnificent work provides an apt ending to our survey of Greek art, for the world which came into being with Alexander's defeat of Dareios in 332 was a very different one from the old Greece. Before, there had been numerous, small city-states, each in fierce rivalry with its neighbours, each in pursuit of the ideal of excellence. Now there were huge, wealthy kingdoms, with great urban centres: the art required by the royal courts and by the new bourgeoisie was very different from that of the old world. State propaganda, and the particularities of home life and the domestic scene, stimulated the growth of divergent uses of art, much more akin to our own multi-faceted world.

7:51  The Alexander Mosaic, found at Pompeii in the House of the Faun, showing Alexander defeating Dareios at the Battle of Issos. This is a copy of a Greek painting of *c.* 300.

7:52  Detail of the Alexander Mosaic, showing Alexander riding Bucephalus.

# Postscript: other worlds

**P.1** This book has been unashamedly Athenocentric because Athens *was* the most important *polis*, and not merely because more evidence about it has survived than about any other contemporary *polis*. But the temptation to see everything through Athenian spectacles is overwhelming. If we had a history of the Greek world written, say, by a fifth-century Spartan, we would have a very different view indeed of the Athenian achievement. In this postscript, we look at what the Athenians and other Greeks thought about two real worlds (Persia and Sparta) and one imaginary world (Homer) to point up Greek prejudices about other people. In this way, we get a somewhat different angle on the Greek mentality. Herodotus, for example, records in his *Histories* the customs of hundreds of peoples living all around the Mediterranean. In a sense, he tells us more about Greeks than barbarians. Consider his view of the marriage customs of Enetoi, and compare it with 4.23ff.:

Once a year in each village the girls of age to marry were collected all together into one place; while the men stood round them in a circle. Then a herald called up the girls one by one, and offered them for sale. He began with the most beautiful. When she was sold for no small sum of money, he offered for sale the one who came next to her in beauty. All of them were sold to be wives. The richest of the Babylonians who wished to wed bid against each other for the loveliest girls, while the humbler wife-seekers, who were indifferent about beauty, took the more homely girls with marriage-portions. For the custom was that when the herald had gone through the whole number of the beautiful girls, he should then call up the ugliest – a cripple, if there chanced to be one – and offer her to the men, asking who would agree to take her with the smallest marriage-portion. And the man who offered to take the smallest sum had her assigned to him. The marriage-portions were furnished by the money paid for the beautiful girls, and thus the fairer girls portioned out the uglier. No one was allowed to give his daughter in marriage to the man of his choice, nor might any one carry away the girl whom he had purchased without agreeing really and truly to make her his wife; if, however, it turned out that they did not agree, the money might be paid back. All who liked might come even from distant villages and bid for the women. This was the best of all their customs, but it has now fallen into disuse. They have lately hit upon a very different plan to save their girls from violence, and prevent their being torn from them and carried to distant cities, which is to bring up their daughters to be prostitutes. This is now done by all the poorer of the common people. (Herodotus, *Histories* 1.196)

What Herodotus considers good and bad about this custom emerges very clearly between the lines, and so this passage gives a fascinating view of Greek priorities (cf. 7.28 on customs).

## (a) Persia

**P.2** Greeks regarded non-Greek speakers as *barbaroi*, because their language sounded to them like unintelligible 'bar-bar' noises. Greeks were proud of their language, culture and (most of all) their freedom. In particular, they drew distinctions between Greek and barbarian ways of doing things; for example, Greek reliance upon argument, laws and justice self-imposed by a free people as against barbarian reliance upon force, anarchy and injustice imposed on a servile population. In this respect, not unlike ourselves, Greeks were tempted to see other people through Greek-coloured spectacles, representing them as Greeks liked to think them to be (cf. 5.6). For example, the Greeks saw the Persian defeat at Marathon (see H.I.13) as an event of world-shattering significance. For Persia it was, no doubt, an annoyance, but typical of many they had to endure on the fringes of their vast empire, and one which could be rectified in time. It was easy for a Greek to see the wealthy Persia as an example of luxuriating decadence, a vast servile empire, which had grown fat and lazy and was ready for the taking at any time by the hardy, freedom-loving Greek. In fact, the Persian empire was an extraordinary achievement.

**P.3** It had emerged in a very short space of time after 550 and, from being a vassal province in the south of the empire of the Medes, the Persians became rulers of the Near East, defeating in turn the Medes, the Lydians under Croesus, the dependent Greek towns of Ionia, the Babylonians and (in the 520s) Egypt. The story of the growth of the Persian empire is sketched by Herodotus in the opening books of his *Histories*.

**P.4** Generally, the empire was stable and well-governed. The Persians well understood the difficulties of ruling so many people over such a large area. Consequently, they allowed a measure of autonomy among their subject people even though the local Persian governor, the satrap, had final authority. Nor were satraps always subject to strong central control, though the Persian king had his channels of communication, particularly his 'Royal Eyes' and 'Royal Ears', officials who reported back the latest developments in the satrapies. So that armies and messengers could move at speed, a series of paved roads was built, the most impressive being the famous 'Royal Road' running from the capital Susa in southern Persia to Sardis. In their dealings with the Greek cities of Ionia, the Persians generally encouraged the establishment of local Greek *turannoi* ('tyrants', i.e. single rulers) favourable to themselves (cf. Dareios at 5.6). Greeks resented these *turannoi*, but probably overplayed their wickedness. Persia was also able to learn from its subjects. Persian culture may have given the appearance of being primitive in comparison with others in the Near East, but they soon learnt from their Babylonian and Greek subjects.

**P.5** If earlier Greeks had dismissed Persians as *barbaroi*, the Persian Wars set the seal on their contempt for the mightiest empire of the East. Marathon became a highlight of Greek folklore. The Marathōnomakhai ('fighters at Marathon') were seen as the ideal for an Athenian warrior. The victory 'proved' the superiority of Greek over barbarian, and the huge Persian invasion force (whose numbers could not be exaggerated too highly) showed all the weakness of servile, barbarian military organisation compared with the tight discipline of the free hoplite and, by extension, 'demonstrated' the inferiority of barbarian warriors, politics and society. Ten years after Marathon the Persians returned in vengeful spirit under Xerxes, son of the previous king Dareios. The invasion furnished Greeks with further legends of heroic Greek resistance against arrogant barbarian aggressors – Leonidas and the Spartans fighting to the death at Thermopylai, the defeat of the Persian (i.e. Phoenician) fleet at Salamis, and the story of the gods thwarting Xerxes in his outrageously ambitious plans, beyond what man should hope to attain (see Herodotus, *Histories* 7–9; H.I.13–19).

**P.6** But though the fifth century vaunted Greece's superiority over the Persians, the Persians were little affected. Their empire was far too large to be seriously damaged by these setbacks. Satrapies, the great king, his court and the way of life the Greeks imagined so decadent, continued. So too did Persian gold, and Greek individuals and cities found this lure hard to resist. Successive Persian kings welcomed Greek exiles, some of whom, like the Athenian Themistokles and the Spartan Pausanias, had been instrumental

in repelling the Persian invaders at Salamis and Plataia but found Persian
influence hard to resist. When Athens and Sparta met in the Peloponnesian
War in 431, Arkhidamos, a Spartan king, tried to enlist Persian support.
He failed, but after the disastrous Sicilian expedition, both Athens and
Sparta sought Persian wealth to build and rebuild their fleets (e.g. H.I.51).

## (2) Sparta

**P.7** If the fifth-century Greeks imposed an image of their own choosing
upon the Persians, the image which Greeks had of Sparta was as much
Sparta's doing as anyone else's (cf. 4.43). By the fifth century Sparta was
a legend already, characterised by two features – its austerity (cf. 'spartan'
in English) and its secrecy (cf. 'laconic' in English; Lakōnia was the area of
the Peloponnese inhabited by the Spartans). To most other Greeks, Sparta
was a secret society wholly closed to them (cf. 4.71). There was some truth
in this. In gaining control of the territory they inhabited (from, say, the
tenth century onwards) the Spartans had reduced to slavery a far greater
number of people than there were actual Spartans (they may have been
outnumbered six to one by their Greek slave – called 'helot' – population).
Consequently they lived in permanent fear of a helot revolt and had, over
the years, consciously developed a social system (which they ascribed to
their legendary lawgiver Lykourgos) which trained men for little else than
war: all their effort went into channelling Greek competitive spirit (see 3.1)
into military virtue. This was the main reason why the Spartan land army
was the most feared in Greece (cf. 6.11–12).

**P.8** The reason why the Spartan legend persisted was largely because it
was so appealing to certain Greeks (especially Athenians like Kritias and
Plato), who compared the anarchic Athenian democracy with the
(apparent) good order and stability of Spartan society. Lykourgos' laws
regulated life at every point and seemed to give Sparta a sense of controlled
direction and solidity quite alien to wildly fluctuating democracies. Plato
in particular, with a true intellectual's instinct for telling people what to
do, sketches a picture of the ideal state in his *Republic* which has remarkable similarity to Sparta at many points, e.g. the Guardians (Plato's super-
rulers) must eat frugally, regulate their sex lives, expose children born with
defects, eat in communal messes, avoid wealth, not journey abroad, abide
by the constitution, and so on, all features of Lykourgos' laws (cf. 4.43).

**P.9** Naturally there were exceptions but these only proved the rule.
Herodotus draws a neat contrast between the archetypal Spartan who
obeys his rulers, eschews cowardice and fights to the death (Leonidas at

Thermopylai, cf. H.I.17) and Pausanias, who played a leading part in defeating the Persians at Plataia (H.I.19) but afterwards plotted against his own country and met a degrading end. There was bound to be the occasional runt in the litter, but the Spartan legend persisted.

## (3) Homer

**P.10** How much hard history there is in Homer's two epic poems the *Iliad* and the *Odyssey* is a matter of dispute, but there is no doubt that the world the poems present is essentially one of the imagination. Nevertheless, myths were history to the Greeks, and when Homer appealed to the Muses for inspiration, he was appealing for the *facts*: he claimed to get the story right. So Homer's audience were probably disposed to believe him.

What is extraordinary about Homer, however, is that his poems became the heart of Greek education. Aeschylus said his tragedies were 'slices from Homer's banquet'. Homer was constantly quoted in Greek literature as the arbiter on matters ranging from social etiquette to historical boundary disputes. What was it about Homer's world which struck such deep chords in Greek minds?

**P.11** The point is that Homer's world fostered Greek prejudices about the way their world really *was* (partly, of course, because Homer helped to shape it: not for nothing did Plato call Homer 'the educator of the Greeks'). First, it was a world of recognised rules of behaviour on the battlefield (*Iliad*) and in host–stranger relationships (*Odyssey*) which guaranteed security and therefore underpinned civilisation (cf. 2.24). Secondly, it was a world not merely of physical violence but also of verbal excellence. Achilles, the greatest Greek fighter, was trained to be 'a speaker of words and a doer of deeds' (*Iliad* 9.443), and a third of Homer is taken up with people talking to each other. Greeks placed a high premium on *peithō*, the ability to persuade by argument rather than force (cf. 7.17), and saw this as an essential ingredient of freedom and civilisation. Thirdly, it was a world where men knew their place, and stepped out of it at their peril. Great men got great rewards; upstarts like the soldier Thersites who started arguing with his commanders got a thump over the back for his pains (to universal approval: *Iliad* 2.211ff.); men could have close commerce with the gods (cf. 2.62), but only if they were worthy of it, and to rise above their station and challenge the gods was to take an incalculable risk. Fourthly, it was a world of intense personal conflict and rivalry (cf. 3.5ff.), where *timē* (honour) was permanently at stake, but behind the struggle was a world of peace and security which the heroes were fighting to win back for themselves (a world which surfaces in, for example, the similes, descriptions of the home life of dead warriors, and Achilles' shield in *Iliad* 18, engraved with scenes of peace and happiness). Fifth-century Greeks lived a life full of opposing contrary tensions, involving not only rivals but external enemies and the forces of nature and the mysterious gods, and yearned for peace (cf. 6.5). Homer's world must, in this respect, have ·seemed very real.

**P.12** As a result, Homer's world seemed to fit so perfectly into the Greeks' perceptions that it was not surprising if Homer became far more than a repository of moral and ethical truth. In matters of religious, naval and military practice, Homer was taken as an acknowledged authority. In Plato's dialogue *Ion*, the rhapsode Ion is driven to claim that, because he has mastered Homer, he must have mastered all the best tactical advice there was, and was therefore the finest *stratēgos* in Greece!

# GLOSSARY OF TERMS
# (WITH GREEK ALPHABET)

**Alphabet and simplified pronunciation**

| *Minuscule* | | *Transliteration* | *Capitals* |
|---|---|---|---|
| α | (alpha) pronounced 'c*u*p' or 'c*a*lm' | a | A |
| β | (beta) pronounced 'b' as in English | b | B |
| γ | (gamma) a hard 'g', like '*g*ot' | g | Γ |
| δ | (delta) a clean 'd', like '*d*ot' | d | Δ |
| ε | (epsilon) short 'e', like 'p*e*t' | e | E |
| ζ | (zeta) like 'wi*sd*om' | sd | Z |
| η | (eta) pronounced as in 'h*air*' | ē | H |
| θ | (theta) – blow a hard 't' ('*t*are') | th | Θ |
| ι | (iota) like 'b*ea*d' or like 'b*i*n' | i | I |
| κ | (kappa) a clean 'k' like 's*k*in' | k | K |
| λ | (lambda) like '*l*ock' | l | Λ |
| μ | (mu) like '*m*ock' | m | M |
| ν | (nu) like '*n*et' | n | N |
| ξ | (xi) like 'bo*x*' | x | Ξ |
| o | (omicron) a short 'o', like 'p*o*t' | o | O |
| π | (pi) a clean 'p', like 's*p*ot' | p | Π |
| ϱ | (rho) a rolled 'r', like '*rr*at' | r | P |
| σ ς | (sigma) a soft 's', like '*s*ing' | s | Σ |
| τ | (tau) a clean 't', like '*t*ing' | t | T |
| υ | (upsilon) French 'l*u*ne' or German 'M*ü*ller' | u | Y |
| φ | (phi) – blow a hard 'p', like '*p*ool' | ph | Φ |
| χ | (khi) – blow a hard 'c', like '*c*ool' | kh | X |
| ψ | (psi) as in 'la*ps*e' | ps | Ψ |
| ω | (omega) like 's*aw*' | ō | Ω |

*Note*: 'clean' indicates no 'h' sound; 'blow hard' indicates plenty of 'h' aspiration (e.g. φ as in 'top-*h*ole'). Greek words have accents which indicate change in pitch (´ = higher, ` = lower, ^ = higher, then lower). They are best ignored.

**Diphthongs and double consonants**

|  | Transliteration |
|---|---|
| αι as in 'h*i*gh' | ai |
| αυ as in 'h*ow*' | au |
| ει as in 'fianc*ée*' | ei |
| ευ (pronounce both elements *separately*) | eu |
| οι as in 'b*oy*' | oi |
| ου as in 't*oo*' | ou |
| γγ as in 'fi*n*ger' | gg |

Dwell on all double consonants, e.g. ττ as 'ra*t-t*rap', λλ as 'who*ll*y' etc.

**Sigma and iota subscript**

Observe that ς is used at the *end* of words, while σ is used elsewhere (see next example). Sometimes ι is printed *underneath* a preceding α (ᾳ), η (ῃ) and ω (ῳ). Transliterations are ai, ēi, ōi.

**Breathings**

ʽ above a vowel indicates the presence of an 'h' sound: ʼ above a vowel indicates the absence of 'h' sound, e.g.

ὅσος = 'hosos'
οἷος = 'oios'

**Names, institutions and terms**

Academy Ἀκάδημος (Akadēmos, or possibly Hekadēmos): a grove of Athens, where Plato (*c.* 385) established a school.

Achilles Ἀχιλλεύς (Akhilleus): Greece's greatest fighter at Troy. Subject of Homer's *Iliad*, when he withdrew from the fighting, to return only when his companion Patroklos had been killed by the Trojan Hektor. Achilles killed Hektor, only later releasing the body to Hektor's father Priam, king of Troy.

Acropolis Ἀκρόπολις: lit. 'the top of the city', usually the high spot of a town where temples and final defences were built. In Athens, it was where the temple of Athēnē, the Parthenon, and the temple of Erekhtheus, the Erekhtheion (and others) were built. The Parthenon served as the Athenians' treasury.

Aeschylus Αἴσχυλος (Aiskhulos) *c.* 525–459: Athenian tragedian, most famous for our sole surviving trilogy, *Oresteia*, the story of Agamemnon's murder by his wife Klutaimēstra after his return from Troy, and subsequent revenge by his son Orestes.

Agamemnon Ἀγαμέμνων: leader of Greek expedition to Troy, who sacrificed his daughter Iphigeneia to get the wind for the journey. Quarrelled with Achilles. Murdered on his return home by his wife Klutaimēstra.

*agōn* ἀγών: trial, contest, struggle (cf. 'agony'). Used of any contest e.g. at law, the

Olympic games, between playwrights competing for prizes at festivals, to describe the central struggle in a comedy, etc.

*agora* ἀγορά: lit. 'gathering-place'. Came to mean the market-place and civic centre of any town.

Agoraios ἀγοραῖος: 'of the *agora*', a title used for gods in their capacity as protector of the *agora* of Athens.

*agoranomoi* ἀγορανόμοι: in Athens, there were 5 for the city, 5 for the Peiraieus. Collected market dues, checked quality and weight of goods.

Alkibiades Ἀλκιβιάδης *c.* 450–404: Athenian general and statesman, close associate of Pericles and Socrates. Wealthy, handsome, enigmatic figure; accused of complicity in the mutilation of the Hermai; joined the Spartan side briefly during the Peloponnesian War, but returned to Athens later. Later he was rejected again, and died at the hands of a lesser satrap.

Andokides Ἀνδοκίδης *c.* 440–390: Athenian politician and speech-writer. Implicated in the Hermai incident and wrote and delivered a speech *On the Mysteries* at a later date, which is an important source of information about it. Spent much time out of Athens because of the incident.

Anthestēria: festival in honour of Dionysos.

Antiphon Ἀντιφῶν *c.* 480–410: Athenian speech-writer and politician, who came to the fore during the oligarchic coup of 411, but was later executed.

Aphrodite Ἀφροδίτη: goddess of love.

Apollo Ἀπόλλων (Apollon 'the destroyer'): god of prophecy (his major shrine was at Delphi), medicine and music.

Areopagus Ἄρειος πάγος (Āreios Pagos, 'Crag of Arēs'): Athens' most ancient council, consisting of ex-*arkhontes*. It once held great power, but in the fifth century it oversaw religious functions and had jurisdiction in murder trials.

Arēs Ἄρης: god of war.

*aretē* ἀρετή: manliness, courage; then it came to mean goodness, excellence, virtue – in general, what is admirable in a man or thing.

Aristeides Ἀριστείδης (nicknamed 'the Just'): Athenian statesman and soldier. Fought at Marathon, Salamis and Plataia. Fixed the contribution for each state in the Delian league to make.

Aristophanes Ἀριστοφάνης (*c.* 445–*c.* 385): greatest Athenian comic playwright. Eleven of his 40 or so plays survive, including *Wasps* (about the law-courts), *Akharnians* (where Dikaiopolis ends the Peloponnesian War for *himself* by making a personal truce with the Spartans), *Frogs* (literary criticism of Aeschylus and Euripides) and *Lysistrata* (a sex-strike by the women to end the war). Much obscenity, social and political comment.

Aristotle Ἀριστοτέλης (Aristotelēs) 384–322: born in Stageira (Khalkidike). Joined Plato's Academy. Settled eventually in Athens and founded his own school, the Lykeion (Lyceum), a great research centre. Aristotle wrote works on physics, metaphysics, zoology, ethics, politics, rhetoric, poetics, logic, astronomy. Probably the single most influential figure of the ancient world.

*arkhē* (pl. *arkhaī*) ἀρχή (ἀρχαί): official state position; Athenian empire; guiding philosophical principle. Generally, rule, control or beginning.

*arkhōn* (pl. *arkhontes*) ἄρχων (ἄρχοντες): there were 9 *arkhontes* in all. They were chosen by lot annually, and joined the Areopagus at the end of their term of office. Originally the leading officers of state, after the sixth century they were left with mainly religious and judicial functions. The 'king' *arkhōn* presided over the Areopagus, and was in charge of homicide and impiety cases; the *polemarkhos* (originally the war *arkhōn*) was in charge of non-Athenians resident in Athens; the 'eponymous' *arkhōn* (so-called as the year was named after him) was in charge of family property disputes, inheritance etc., especially orphans and heiresses. For the other six *arkhontes*, see *thesmothetai*.

Athenaeus *c*.200 A.D.: his account of a cultured conversation over dinner spans 15 books and is an invaluable source of information. He cites *c*. 1,250 authors and quotes *c*. 10,000 lines of verse, much of it not extant from any other source.

Athēnē ᾽Αθήνη: goddess of the arts, and crafts, of war (frequently depicted in full armour), and patron goddess of Athens. The Parthenon (so called after *parthenos*, virgin) was dedicated to her. Ten Treasurers controlled the payments to the goddess.

*atimia* ἀτιμία: dishonour, disenfranchisement, i.e. loss of some or all civic rights.

*aulos* αὐλός: a sort of pipe whose sound was produced by means of a double reed (rather like an oboe). Generally, a player played two at once. Provided the music for dramatic performances, accompanied personal poetry and kept lines of hoplites in step.

Boulaios βουλαῖος: 'of the *boulē*', often used of a god in his capacity as overseer of the *boulē*'s decisions.

*boulē* βουλή: council (of 500: see *bouleutai*). Open to all citizens over 30. It met daily (except for holidays) and had the vital task of preparing the agenda for the *ekklēsia*, presiding over it, and seeing that its decisions were carried out. It oversaw state officials and finance.

*bouleutai* βουλευταί: members of the *boulē* (councillors). There were 500 of them, 50 from each *phulē*, selected by lot. They served for a year, and could not serve more than twice.

*bouleutērion* βουλευτήριον: council chamber, the place where the *boulē* met.

cleruchy κληρουχία (*klēroukhia*): a settlement of (usually) poorer Athenian citizens granted a piece of land (*klēros*) in conquered territory. They kept all their rights as Athenian citizens.

Cyrus: king of Persia (*c*. 550–529).

Dareios (Darius): father of Xerxes and king of Persia (c. 522–486) when the Persians sent an expedition against the Greeks which was repulsed at Marathon (490).

Delian League: an alliance of states of which Athens was the predominant member, formed after the Persian Wars to guarantee Greek security against further Persian invasion. Members paid Athens in money or ships. The treasury was moved from Dēlos to Athens in 454.

Delphic oracle: the sanctuary of Apollo (god of prophecy) at Delphi, where it was possible to consult the god. The most influential oracle in the ancient world.

deme δῆμος: local communities (cf. parishes) which formed the basis of Kleisthenes' political reforms. Membership of a deme was a requirement for citizenship. Athenians usually identified themselves by deme name and father's name.

Dēmētēr Δημήτηρ: the Greek corn goddess, who governed the fruits of the earth. She was a central figure of the Mysteries at Eleusis and of the female festival in Athens, the Thesmophoria.

*dēmokratia* δημοκρατία: democracy, lit. 'the rule of the *dēmos*', where *dēmos* = all Athenian citizens (i.e. males over 18 with Athenian mother and father).

*dēmos* δῆμος: a variety of meanings: (i) the whole adult male citizen body, (ii) the poorer (as against aristocratic) citizens, (iii) democratic constitution, (iv) democrats as against those favouring other constitutions, (v) the democratic state of Athens, (vi) the people of Athens in the *ekklēsia*, (vii) the local division, the deme (rather like our 'parish', or local district).

Demosthenes Δημοσθένης: (i) a fifth-century soldier who captured the Spartans on Sphakteria in 425 and was killed later in the Sicilian expedition: (ii) a fourth-century orator and politician who urged all Greeks to unite against the threat of King Philip of Macedon. He also wrote many private speeches for litigants on a wide range of topics.

*dikastērion* (pl. *dikastēria*) δικαστήριον (δικαστήρια): the law-courts.

*dikastēs* (pl. *dikastai*) δικαστής (δικασταί): dikast, juror. Empanelled from Athenian citizens over 30. 6,000 a year could be called up for duty in the courts. They were paid for attendance.

*dikē* δίκη: justice, law, right; penalty. Also a private lawsuit brought by an individual against another, cf. *graphē*.

Diodoros Διόδωρος fl. *c.* 40: wrote a *World History*, using sources now lost to us. Of the 40 books, 4–6 cover Greece and Europe and 7–17 from the Trojan War up to Alexander the Great.

Dionysia Διονύσια: in Athens the Lesser (or Rural) Dionysia was a smaller rustic festival than the Greater (or City) Dionysia in honour of Dionysos, at which a statue of the god was carried from Eleutherai and the major tragic and comic competitions were staged.

Dionysos Διόνυσος: god of all things living and god of transformation (hence patron god of the theatre) and of destruction. Associated with the frenzy brought on by wine. In their ecstasy his followers were said to kill and devour animals raw to get the living god inside them.

*dokimasia* δοκιμασία: an examination which state officials and *bouleutai* underwent before taking up office. It asked them about their rights to citizenship, care of family burial grounds, etc.

*dokimastēs* δοκιμαστής: the state official (in fact a slave) whose duty it was to test the purity of the coinage.

drachma δραχμή: a unit of money, within the following system:

> obol
> drachma (six obols)
> mna (100 drachmas)
> talent (60 mnas)

*eisphora* εἰσφορά: a special tax on capital, often levied when the state was at war, applicable to citizens and metics.

*ekhthroi* (*s. ekhthros*) ἐχθροί (ἐχθρός): personal enemies.

*ekklēsia* ἐκκλησία: the Assembly (lit. 'called out', 'selected'), open to all Athenian (male) citizens over the age of 18. It sat regularly 4 times a month, of which one session was the *kuria* (sovereign) *ekklēsia*, with a fixed agenda. It could be summoned at other times. It was the sovereign body of the state. It voted on all major questions and elected the most important officials. Its agenda was prepared by the *boulē*, but the *ekklēsia* could reject the *boulē*'s proposals and demand that the *boulē* do what *it* wanted.

Eleven, the οἱ ἕνδεκα (*hoi hendeka*): this board dealt with ordinary criminals, charging and punishing them. They also oversaw prisons.

Ēliaia Ἡλιαία (often given as 'Heliaia'): the body of 6,000 *dikastai* empanelled to serve on the juries for a year. (A juror can be called (*h*)*ēliastēs* as well as *dikastēs*.)

*epistates* ἐπιστάτης: chairman of the *prutaneis* and of the *ekklēsia*. Served for one day. Since there were 50 *prutaneis* serving for a period of 35–6 days, there was a good chance that any given *prutanis* would serve as *epistatēs*.

'eponymous' *arkhōn*: see *arkhōn*.

*erastēs* ἐραστής: lover. Used especially of the older, active partner in a homosexual relationship. Cf. *erōmenos*.

Erekhtheion (Erechtheum) Ἐρεχθεῖον: a temple of Erekhtheus on the Acropolis, housing the venerable statue of Athēnē Polias as well as other sacred objects.

Erekhtheus Ἐρεχθεύς: mythical king of Athens, a son of Earth and reared by Athēnē.

*erōmenos* ἐρώμενος: 'the [male who is] loved', used of the younger, passive partner in a homosexual relationship. Cf. *erastēs*.

Euripides Εὐριπίδης *c.* 485–406: Athenian tragic playwright, with a reputation for especially provocative analyses of Greek myth and of the human motivation which made the characters act as they did. Contemporary intellectual issues seem to surface in his plays more than in those of other tragedians.

*euthunai* εὔθυναι: audit, review. This was the term applied to outgoing state officials, who were subject to *euthunai* to check they had not abused their position (especially with regard to finance).

*exēgētai* ἐξηγηταί: lit. 'expounders', 'interpreters'. A body of men concerned with unwritten, sacred law and with some specific issues (especially purification and burial). They had connections with Apollo at Delphi.

genos (pl. *genē*) γένος (γένη): a small grouping of families within the *phratria*.

*graphē* γραφή: a lawsuit on a matter of public importance brought by an individual against another (there was no such thing as a public prosecutor in Athens). Cf. *dikē*.

*graphē paranomōn* γραφὴ παρανόμων: a lawsuit brought by an individual against another, alleging that the defendant had been responsible for proposing a measure which was illegal.

*hēgemōn* ἡγεμών: leader, cf. hegemony.

Hektor Ἕκτωρ: Trojan hero of the Trojan War, who killed Achilles' companion Patroklos and was killed in turn by Achilles. His maltreated body was eventually returned by Achilles to his father Priam, king of Troy.

Hellas Ἑλλάς: the Greek word for 'Greece' i.e. the Greek world (*not* a state or country).

Hellenes Ἕλληνες: men of Hellas, Greeks.

Hellēnotamiai Ἑλληνοταμίαι: state treasurers in charge of funds used for administering the Athenian empire (after 411 they absorbed also the work of the *kōlakretai*, till then in charge of domestic funds). Like *stratēgoi*, they could be re-elected every year.

Hephaistos Ἥφαιστος: god of fire, husband of Aphrodite; the craftsman's god.

Hera Ἥρα: queen of the gods, wife of Zeus. Goddess of marriage and women's life. Strong connections with Argos.

Herkeios ἑρκεῖος: 'concerned with the household', often used of Zeus in his role as protector of the house.

Hermes Ἑρμῆς: god of travel, escort of the souls of the dead, god of heralds and thieves. Hermai (s. Herm) were representations of the god consisting of a stone block, with a head on the top and phallus half-way up the block, placed outside houses in Athens.

Herodotus Ἡρόδοτος *c.* 480–420: fifth-century historian from Halikarnassos, who lived for some time in Athens. Said to have travelled widely around the Mediterranean compiling his *Histories* in 9 books of the way in which Greeks and Persians came into conflict in the Persian Wars: 'the father of history'.

Hēsiod ‘Ησίοδος (Hēsiodos): seventh-century farmer-poet, who wrote (in adapted epic style) *Works and Days* (a farmers' calendar and instruction manual) and *Theogony* (the birth of the gods).

*hiereus* ἱερεύς: priest, or 'one in charge of sacred matters'.

Hikesios ἱκέσιος: 'concerned with supplication', used of Zeus in one of his roles as protector of suppliants.

*hippeis*: see *pentakosiomedimnoi*.

Hippocrates ‘Ιπποκράτης: the famous doctor from Kōs, lived during the fifth century. Virtually all medical treatises were ascribed to him. The probable founder of scientific medicine.

Homer ″Ομηρος (Homēros): eighth-century (?) epic poet of the *Iliad* and *Odyssey* (as the Greeks believed). Came from Ionian coast. Nothing else known about him.

Hoplites ὁπλῖται (*hoplitai*): Greek warriors, fighting with shield, spear, sword and full heavy armour. The hoplite formation gained its strength from its unity, rank upon rank of closely-linked fighting men.

*hubris* ὕβρις (hybris): an act of violence or aggression, whose main purpose was to degrade or humiliate.

*hubristēs* ὑβριστής: one who commits an act of *hubris*, criminal.

*Iliad* ’Ιλίας (*Ilias*): Homer's epic version of the wrath of Achilles during the Trojan war, his withdrawal from battle but eventual return on the death of his companion Patroklos; how Achilles killed Patroklos' slayer Hektor and maltreated his body but eventually returned it to his father, King Priam.

Isaios (Isaeus) ’Ισαῖος *c.* 420–350: Athens' leading speech-writer in cases concerned with wills and inheritance.

Isokrates ’Ισοκράτης 436–448: treatise-writer and educationist, who insisted that utility in education was of more importance than abstract thought. In a number of his treatises he glorified the great days of Athens' past.

*isonomia* ἰσονομία: rule of equals, democracy, equality under the laws.

*keleustēs* κελευστής: the bo'sun of a trireme, who gave the time for the rowers to keep to.

Kerameikos Κεραμεικός: Potters' Quarter in Athens (cf. 'ceramic'); also the site of an important cemetery.

*kērux* (pl. *kērukes*) κῆρυξ (κήρυκες): herald, messenger

*khorēgos* (choregus) (pl. *khorēgoi*) (χορηγός) (χορηγοί): the wealthy (male) citizen who, as part of a *leitourgia*, met all the expenses of a tragic or comic writer's entry at a play festival.

Kimon Κίμων: aristocratic, wealthy Athenian statesman and soldier who greatly developed the Athenian empire between 476 and 460, though in some conflict with radical democratic leaders like Pericles.

Kleisthenes Κλεισθένης: Athenian statesman who in 507 reformed the Athenian constitution in a way that was to lead to the full democracy of the fifth century under Pericles.

Klutaimēstra (Clytaem(n)estra) Κλυταιμήστρα: wife of Agamemnon. She married her lover Aigisthos and killed Agamemnon on his return from Troy. She in turn was killed by their son Orestes.

*kratos* κράτος: might, rule, sway, control.

Ktesios κτήσιος: 'concerned with property', applied to Zeus in his role as protector of the home and its wealth.

*kubernētēs* κυβερνήτης: the steersman of a trireme, the most important figure in the control of the ship.

*kurios* (pl. *kurioi*) κύριος (κύριοι): valid, sovereign, empowered. Used of male heads of the household who controlled the house's people and property; also used of the 'sovereign' *ekklēsia* with a fixed agenda meeting once a month. Cf. *kurieia*: control, sovereignty.

Lakedaimonians = Spartans.

*leitourgia* (pl. *leitourgiai*) (liturgy) λειτουργία (λειτουργίαι): state duty imposed annually on the wealthiest men of Athens, who had to pay for, e.g., play productions at the festivals, the expenses of running a trireme, etc.

*logistai* λογισταί: thirty state auditors, who checked the financial dealings of all outgoing state officials as part of their *euthunai*.

Lykeion (Lyceum) Λύκειον: the grove in Athens where Aristotle established his school.

*mantis* μάντις: seer, prophet.

*medimnos* (pl. *medimnoi*) μέδιμνος: Attic grain-measure of approximately 12 gallons.

Menander Μένανδρος (Menandros) *c.* 342–290: writer of so-called New Comedy, set in contemporary Greece and dealing largely with domestic situations. Forerunner of 'drawing-room' comedy.

*metoikos* (pl. *metoikoi*) (metic) μέτοικος (μέτοικοι): resident alien (i.e. non-Athenian citizen who lived more than one month in Athens). Liable to military service and special taxes; not able to own landed property in Attica. Resident aliens were responsible for much trade.

Minoan world: i.e. Crete between 1800 and 1400 (so called after the legendary King Minos). At this time Crete was a power in the Mediterranean, before it was destroyed *c.* 1400, probably by Mycenaean Greeks.

mna (mina) μνᾶ: unit of money; *see* drachma.

*mustai* μύσται: initiates into the Mysteries of Eleusis.

Mycenaean period: 'Mycenaean' culture (so called because Mycenae seems to have been the most powerful city of the time) flourished in Greece between 1600 and 1100 B.C. After its destruction there was a 'dark age' of nearly 200 years. Homer's poetry reflects elements of Mycenaean culture.

Nikias Νικίας 470–413: Athenian politician and general, frequently elected *stratēgos*. Negotiated the peace of 421 with Sparta in the Peloponnesian War. Reluctantly led the Sicilian expedition, on which he was killed.

*nomos* νόμος: law, custom, observance, habit. Frequently contrasted with *phusis*, when *nomos* comes to take on the idea of what is conventionally right.

*nomothetai* νομοθέται: law-makers, who were called in to draft new laws (as needed) for the *boulē* and *ekklēsia* to approve.

obol; *see* drachma

*Odyssey* Ὀδύσσεια (*Odusseia*): Homer's epic tale of Odysseus' return from Troy: how, after 10 years wandering, he eventually returned home to Ithaka and killed the 108 suitors courting his wife Penelope.

*oiketēs* οἰκέτης: slave, or free house servant; also (slave) aide to state official.

*oikos* (pl. *oikoi*) οἶκος (pl. οἶκοι): household (including property and slaves).

*orkhēstra* ὀρχήστρα: circular dancing-floor in the Greek theatre where the chorus in plays danced and sang.

ostracism ὀστρακισμός (*ostrakismos*): an act of the *ekklēsia* in banishing someone from Attica for 10 years (though with no loss of property rights).

*ostrakon* ὄστρακον: the potsherd on which names for ostracism were written down.

paean παιάν: battle song, chant; song of triumph, usually to Apollo.

*palaistra* παλαίστρα: the wrestling-ground, a common feature of the gymnasia where leisured Greeks 'worked out' and relaxed.

Panathenaia Παναθήναια: an all-Athenian festival in honour of Athēnē's birthday, celebrated every year, and with special magnificence every fourth year (the Great Panathenaia). There were processions, sacrifices, and games.

Parthenon Παρθενών: the temple of Athēnē Parthenos ('the virgin'), commissioned by Pericles and built on the Acropolis in Athens.

Patrōos πατρῷος (*patrōios*): 'of the father'; used of gods in their roles as protectors of family and people.

Peiraieus (Piraeus) Πειραιεύς: the harbour of Athens.

Peisistratos (Pisistratus) Πεισίστρατος: sixth-century sole ruler (*turannos* = tyrant) of Athens, who did much to establish a sense of Athenian identity by instituting various festivals and building programmes.

peithō πειθώ: persuasion by argument, sometimes personified as a goddess.

Peloponnesian War (Second): the war fought between Athens with her allies and Sparta with hers for domination of Greece. Athens was a sea-based power, Sparta a land-based one. It lasted from 431 to 404. Athens was defeated in the end.

peltast πελταστής (*peltastēs*): Greek soldiers named from the small round shield they carried (*peltē*), who, originally skirmishers, were turned into a formidable fighting force in the fourth century.

*pentakosiomedimnoi* πεντακοσιομέδιμνοι: a property class, of people who had an estimated annual income of not less than 500 *medimnoi* of grain, or its equivalent. This was the top property class, followed by:

*hippeis* ἱππεῖς: 'knights' with annual income of 300–500 *medimnoi* or equivalent.

*sdeugitai* (*zeugitai*) ζευγῖται: 200–300 *medimnoi* annual income.

*thētes* θῆτες: less than 200 *medimnoi* annual income.

Pericles Περικλῆς *c.* 495–429: statesman and soldier, guiding spirit behind Athenian democracy and imperialism. Elected *strategos* every year from 443 till his death. Commissioned the Parthenon. Close friend of many leading intellectuals of the day.

Persephone (Proserpina) Περσεφόνη: daughter of Dēmētēr and wife of Hades, god of the dead.

Persian Wars: the wars fought between the Greeks and Persia between 490 and 480, particularly the battles at Marathon, Thermopylai, Salamis and Plataia. The Persians were driven back in 490 and were finally repelled, under Xerxes, in 480. Greeks looked back to these wars as a high point of Greek achievement. It was one of the few times when some (i.e. 31) Greek *poleis* forgot their differences to repel a common foe.

*phallos* (pl. *phalloi*) φαλλός (φαλλοί): representation of the male reproductive organ, often carried in processions, particularly those associated with fertility.

Pheidias Φειδίας: one of the finest fifth-century Athenian sculptors. Responsible for a great deal of the work on the Parthenon.

Philip II Φίλιππος reigned 359–336: king of Macedon, who unified Macedon and made it the greatest fighting force of the fourth century. His victory over the Greeks at Khaironeia (338) ended Greek independence. Father of Alexander the Great.

*philoi* (s. *philos*) φίλοι (φίλος): friends, allies; those with whom you presented a common front.

*phoros* φόρος: tribute paid by her allies to Athens for the maintenance of the empire.

*phrater* (pl. *phrateres*) φράτηρ (φράτερες): *phratria*-member.

*phratria* (pl. *phratriai*) (phratry) φρατρία (φρατρίαι): a sub-division of the *phulē*, to which only citizens could belong. It had various religious functions. New-born children were presented to it. As a body it was often called upon to witness to legitimacy and therefore rights of citizenship.

Phratrios φράτριος: 'of the *phratriai*', a title applied to Zeus and other gods in their roles as protectors of the *phratria*.

*phulē* (pl. *phulai*) φυλή (φυλαί): tribe; there were originally four of these, with various administrative and military functions. Kleisthenes, while allowing these to remain for religious functions, created ten new *phulai* in his democratic reforms, and these became the basis of state administration. There were ten *stratēgoi*, committees of the *boulē* often consisted of ten members, the *boulē* itself was made up of 50 × 10 members, and in these cases each *phulē* provided one unit.

*phusis* φύσις: nature, natural law, often contrasted in Greek thought with *nomos*, conventional law.

Pindaros (Pindar) Πίνδαρος 518–438: lyric poet from Boiotia, famous for his odes, in which he celebrates the victories of athletes at various games (e.g. Olympic).

Plato Πλάτων (Platōn) *c*. 429–347: very influential Greek philosopher who built on Socrates' teaching about how we should live our life a whole theory of metaphysics; the Theory of Forms (or Theory of Ideas) has been particularly important. A bitter rival of the sophists.

Plutarch Πλούταρχος (Ploutarkhos) *c*. A.D. 50–120: biographical historian and student of antiquities. Unreliable in use of sources, but his *Parallel Lives* of great Greeks and Romans are important.

Pnyx πνύξ: the place where the *ekklēsia* met.

*polemarkhos* (polemarch): *see arkhōn.*

*pōlētai* πωληταί: sellers. Ten (one from each *phulē*) *pōlētai* sold off the right to carry out official state business e.g. collecting taxes, mining rights, buying and putting up *stēlai*, etc.

Polias Πολιάς: an epithet for Athēnē in her role as guardian of the city, especially used of her statue in the Erekhtheion.

*polis* (pl. *poleis*) πόλις (πόλεις): the name given to the self-governing city-states of the Greek world. Each *polis* had its own laws of citizenship, coinage, customs, festivals, rites, etc. Athens, Corinth, Thebes, Sparta were all separate, autonomous *poleis*. They were quick to form alliances amongst themselves and prone to conflict over the best forms of constitution.

Poseidon Ποσειδῶν: God of the sea and earth(quakes).

*presbeis* (s. *presbeutēs*) πρέσβεις (πρεσβευτής): envoy, ambassador.

Priam Πρίαμος (Priamos): king of Troy.

*probouleuma* προβούλευμα: a decree made by the *boulē* for the *ekklēsia* to discuss and then accept, modify or reject.

*probouleusis* προβούλευσις: the act of the *boulē* in reaching a decision about what motions to lay before the *ekklēsia* for discussion.

Prometheus Προμηθεύς: Titan god who made man, gave him fire and ensured that man got all the good meat to eat at sacrifice (Zeus being left with bones and offal).

*prostatēs* προστάτης: leader of the *dēmos*; patron of a *metoikos*, who would guarantee him before the *polemarkhos* when the *metoikos* applied to live in Athens.

*proxenos* πρόξενος: the title given to someone who, as a citizen of state A and residing in state A, represented state B's views.

*prutaneis* (s. *prutanis*) πρυτάνεις (πρυτάνις): fifty members of the *boulē* who lived for 35–6 days, 24 hours a day, in the *tholos* at state expense to receive all business and determine whether the *boulē* or *ekklēsia* should be summoned to deal with it.

*psēphisma* (pl. *psēphismata*) ψήφισμα (ψηφίσματα): decrees of state passed by the *ekklēsia*.

Pythia Πυθία: the priestess through whom Apollo spoke at his oracle in Delphi.

Rhapsode ῥαψῳδός (*rhapsōidos*): a professional reciter of epic (especially Homer's) poetry at festivals.

*rhētor* (pl. *rhētores*) ῥήτωρ (ῥήτορες): lit. 'speaker', 'orator' (cf. rhetoric). Came to mean politician, i.e. someone who could speak effectively at meetings of the *ekklēsia* and persuade the people as to the rightness of his own views.

*sdeugitai* (zeugitai) ζευγῖται: *see pentakosiomedimnoi*. *sdugitai* (ζυγῖται) is used for those who rowed in the middle rank of a trireme.

Sicilian expedition: the Athenian expedition of 415–413, led by Nikias and Demosthenes during the Peloponnesian War, to try to take Sicily. It failed disastrously, the whole fleet being lost, but Athens made a miraculous recovery and continued the war till 404.

*skēnē* σκηνή: the stage building against which Greek drama was performed (cf. scene).

Socrates Σωκράτης 469–399: the philosopher most responsible for turning the trend of Greek philosophical enquiry away from questions of the nature of the physical world to questions of man's position and duties in it. He never wrote a word, versions of his thought being recorded for us by Plato and Xenophon in dialogue form. A fierce opponent of the sophists. Invented dialectic (question-and-answer technique).

Solon Σόλων: Athenian statesman and poet who, in the 590s, divided the citizen body into four classes by wealth (see *pentakosiomedimnoi*) and assigned a number of political responsibilities to them by class, opening up service in the courts to the lowest classes. Made other laws which were still observed in fifth-century Athens. A greatly revered figure.

*sophistēs* (pl. *sophistai*) (sophist) σοφιστής (σοφισταί): lit. 'wise men'; the term became applied to travelling lecturers who were prepared to impart knowledge of any number of subjects (but especially rhetoric, the ability to persuade people) for payment.

Sophocles Σοφοκλῆς *c.* 496–406: Athenian tragedian. Much-loved figure in Athens. Famous for *Oedipus Tyrannus*, which tells how Oedipus found out that he had killed his father and married his mother, and *Antigone*, which tells how Antigone went to her death for burying her brother, in defiance of an edict given by her uncle Kreon, the king.

*sōphrōn* σώφρων: modest, sensible, prudent, discreet, law-abiding. *Sōphrosunē* is a virtue constantly recommended by Athenian writers to those who want to keep their noses clean.

*stasis* στάσις: internal revolution.

*stēlē* (pl. *stēlai*) στήλη (στῆλαι): inscribed stone monuments, especially grave-markers and upright slabs on which decrees and similar public documents were inscribed.

stoa στοά: a building with a roof supported by columns, but especially a long, open colonnade. Usually it resembles a long hall with one side thrown open and supported by columns.

*stratēgos* (pl. *stratēgoi*) στρατηγός (στρατηγοί): general. Ten of them, directly elected annually by the people, and they could be re-elected. Apart from military duties, the *stratēgoi* were the most influential moulders of state policy.

*sukophantēs* (pl. *sukophantai*) (sycophant) συκοφάντης (συκοφάνται): a sycophant, one who made money by bringing charges against people in the courts and winning.

*summoria* (pl. *summoriai*) (symmory) συμμορία (συμμορίαι): a group of tax-payers who, instead of paying individually for the upkeep of a trireme (*see* trierarch; *leitourgia*), paid for it as a group. An institution of the 350s.

talent: *see* drachma.

Ten Treasurers of Athēnē: annual officials, drawn by lot from each of the *phulai*. Superintended the funds of the goddess and her statue.

Themistokles Θεμιστοκλῆς *c.* 528–462: leading Athenian general of the Persian Wars, who later ensured that Athens was defended by fortified walls against Sparta. He sponsored the fortification of the Peiraieus and the holding of a fleet.

Theophrastos Θεόφραστος *c.* 370–285: successor to Aristotle as head of the Lykeion; researcher in botany and other scientific subjects. His *Characters* is a description of 30 or so people who exhibit extremes of behaviour.

Theseus Θησεύς: legendary Athenian national hero. Supposed to have drawn all the communities of Attica into one, with Athens at their head. Slaughtered the Cretan Minotaur.

Thesmophoria Θεσμοφόρια: women's festival in honour of Dēmētēr.

*thesmothetai* θεσμοθέται: six *arkhontes*, concerned with administering justice, fixing trial dates, etc.

*thētes*: *see pentakosiomedimnoi*.

Thirty Tyrants (or oligarchs), the Thirty: leaders of the oligarchic coup in Athens of 404.

*thranitai* θρανῖται: those who rowed from the highest point of the trireme, and therefore had to pull on the longest oars at the sharpest angle: paid more than the other ranks of rowers.

Thucydides Θουκυδίδης (*Thoukudidēs*) *c.* 460–400: Athenian who wrote the history of the Peloponnesian War. Pro-Pericles, regarded as very trustworthy.

*timē* τιμή: honour, worth, status, evaluation.

trierarch τριήραρχος (*triērarkhos*): wealthy citizen chosen to pay for and captain a trireme (*see leitourgia*).

Trojan War: the ten-year siege of Troy by the Greeks, and its eventual capture (*c.* 1200, if the war occurred at all). The Greeks wanted to win back Helen, the wife of the Greek leader Menelaos (brother of the expedition's leader Agamemnon), who had been seduced back to Troy by Paris, son of the Trojan King Priam. The subject of much epic poetry, including Homer's *Iliad*.

Xenophon Ξενοφῶν 428–*c.* 354: Athenian soldier and writer of *Anabasis* (the expedition of a Greek mercenary force to and back from Mesopotamia 401–399); *Hellenika* (history of Greece 410–362); *Memorabilia* (memoirs of Socrates); *Symposium* (recollections of a party); but not of *Constitution of Athens* (the work of the so-called 'Old Oligarch', almost certainly not Xenophon), a not wholly damning critique of Athenian democracy; and perhaps *Constitution of Sparta*, in high praise.

*xenos* (pl. *xenoi*) ξένος (ξένοι): alien (i.e. in Athens, a non-Athenian resident, cf. *metoikos*). Also, a guest-friend, i.e. one with whom one has obligatory, reciprocal ties of friendship.

Xerxes: king of Persia; led the expedition against Greece in the 480s which resulted in battles at Thermopylai, Salamis and Plataia, and eventual Persian defeat.

# APPENDIX: CROSS-REFERENCES WITH THE TEXT OF *READING GREEK*

H.I. = Historical Introduction; P. = Postscript; other references are to chapters and sections.

### *Reading Greek* (Text) 1A

survival of Greek literature, 7.5
Greek alphabet, 7.2–3
ships and sailing, 1.4, 15
rhapsode and festivals, 2.45–8
grain trade, H.I.23, 40; 1.20; political importance of, 5.74–7
trade, 4.55–8; 5.69
loans on ships (and source of this story), 4.59
Peiraieus, H.I.15, 24; 1.20–4, 32
Parthenon, H.I.27; 1.18; history of, 1.25–7, 30–1, 34; art and, 7.78; temples and sanctuaries, 2.38–9

### 1B

clarity of air, 1.6
*kubernētēs*, 6.31, 34, 41, 45

### 1F

value of human life, 3.25–6
friends and enemies, 3.1–2, 13–14

### 1G

prayers 2.34; 7.11
sacrifice, 2.28

### 1H

Homer, H.I.1; 7.1; P.10–12
Socrates, 7.29–31
arguing and the power of words, 7.24
*tekhnē*, 7.64–5
*stratēgos*, 5.29–31
war, 6.1–8

### 2A

Persia and the Persian Wars, H.I.12–20 (*esp.* 18 – Salamis); P.2–6
rhetoric, 7.17

### 2B

balanced, Gorgianic style, 7.19
use of *men . . . de*, 7.9
sacrifice, 2.28ff.
supplication, 2.36
*hubris*, 3.15

### 2C

Herodotus and historical writing, 7.33–4
Aeschylus' *Persians*, 7.38, 46
religion and patriotism, 2.47; 4.82
*agōn* and competition, 3.1–2

## 2D

interventions of the gods, 2.6–8
sea-battles, 6.31ff.
Salamis, 6.37
Greek unity, 1.1, H.I.16, 29
Greek *stasis*, H.I.39, 72; 3.14
use of past to throw light on present,
    7.25

## 3A

source of this incident, 1.24
Peloponnesian War, H.I.33–56
beacon fires, 1.16

## 3B

ships and hoplites, 6.31ff.
manning triremes, 6.42–4
slaves in battle, 6.17

## 3C

Spartan history, H.I.6, 10–11; 19;
    22–4, 29
the legend of Sparta, P.7–9
Periclean policy in war, H.I.38–9
Pericles as *stratēgos*, 5.29–33
Athenian sea power and history,
    H.I.15; 5.78ff.; 6.33
trierarchs, 5.71–2; 6.41–8

## 3D

*keleustēs*, 6.31, 45
competition to get ship ready, 6.44–5
houses, 1.7, 35–7, *cf.* 4.26
deme-names, 4.16

## 3E

libations, 2.29
journeys, 2.33; 6.45

## 4A

walls of Athens, H.I.24; 1.23, 30–3
farmer's lot, 1.9, 13; 4.50–2
sea power, 6.2, 8; H.I.23

Periclean policy, H.I.36
beginnings of empire, H.I.27; 5.78ff.
plague and suffering, H.I.36; 2.7;
    Thucydides and plague, 7.34; 4.81
unpredictability of gods, 2.6–7

## 4B

death and burial, 4.77–82
*hubris*, 3.15
need to respect the gods, 2.40; 4.13, 81
human obligations, 2.25–6
pessimism about gods, 2.22–3
the gods reciprocate, 2.3; 2.24

## 4C

altar of the Twelve Gods, 1.28
supplication, 2.36–7
travelling, 1.14
the Eleven, 5.36–7
*hupēretēs*, 4.64
*kērux*, 5.39–40
sanctuary, 2.38
responsibility for suppliants, 2.25

## 4D

part-source of the story, 2.37
*presbeutēs* (pl. *presbeis*), 5.38, 41
desire for peace, 6.5

## 5A

Greek comedy, 7.35–6; 53–63
Aristophanes and Pericles, H.I.37
festivals, 2.41–8
coinage, 4.61
rich and poor, 3.18
horses, 1.13
Alkibiades and horses, 3.9
women: and marriage, 4.23–31; and
    home life, 4.32–6, 50–1;
    'dangerous' women, 3.19
town and city, 4.1–11; 1.21

**5B**

olives, 1.9, 20; 4.51, 57
slaves, 3.18; 4.62–6; slaves and war,
    4.10, *cf.* H.I.51
arguments as means to ends, 7.17
learning rhetoric, 7.18–19

**5D**

Socrates and sophists, 4.43–8; 7.20–31
intellectuals and methods of arguing,
    7.1–19 (*esp.* analogy, 7.9; the world
    as 'soup', 7.13)
importance of *logos*, 5.19, 7.17, 24
education, 4.39ff.
importance of leisure, 4.49

**5E**

physical speculation, 7.7, 22
mathematics and measurement, 7.23
Thales, 7.7

**5F**

intellectual achievement of fifth-
    century Athens, 7.14, 21
technical work, 7.22
Peloponnesian War, H.I.33ff.

**5H**

arguing from both sides of the case,
    7.26
magic, 2.18

**6A**

rhetoric and speeches, 7.16–19
lawcourt practice, 5.44–67 (*esp.* 52)
Delphi and the oracle, 2.12, 15–17

**6B**

Socrates' 'ignorance', 7.31
inspiration and creativity, 7.64–5
*mantis*, 2.19–20

**6C**

leisure and speculation, 4.49, 52

the rich, 3.18, 7.13
early arguments over the gods, 7.11; *cf.*
    2.5
questioning the gods, 2.65–6
death of Socrates, H.I.59

**6D**

words and arguments, 7.24
arguing on both sides of a case, 7.26
dissatisfaction with sophistic quibbles,
    4.47–8

**6G**

Herodotus, 7.33; P.1
*nomos–phusis*, 7.28
Greek view of women (for comparison
    with Scythians), 2.9–10; 3.18–20;
    4.22–36
*for another perspective on alien women
    see P.1*

**7A**

*for comic background, see references at
    5A*
Aristophanes: and politics, H.I.37;
    7.61ff.; and fantasy, 7.59
part-source of this scene,1.24
*agora*, 1.27–9, 33–7
*kuria ekklēsia*, 5.10ff. (*esp.* 14)

**7B**

*dikastēria*, 5.44ff.
Athenian litigiousness, 5.63
Athenians and rhetoric, 5.20–1
the 'new politicians', H.I.37
importance of aristocrats, H.I.7, 11, 37

**7C**

attitudes to Pericles, H.I.27, 5.33
benefits of empire, 5.90–1
Pericles' court case, H.I.36; 3.10;
    5.31–2
yearning for peace, 6.5
festivals, 2.41–7

pessimism, 2.21–3

**8A**

lawcourts, 1.35; 5.46–7, 3.2

**8B**

sacrifices, 1.11; 2.28–33
homosexuality, 3.21ff.

**8C**

Philēliastēs and the Ēliaia, 5.46–7

**8D**

Kleon, H.I.37, 41–2; 5.21

**8F**

pay for jury-service, 5.47, 58

**8G**

urns, 5.60
*klepsudra* (water-clock), 5.60

**8H**

coming to trial, 5.55
source of this scene, 5.59–62

**8I**

goat's milk/cheese, 1.13
witnesses and evidence, 5.53

**8J**

voting, 5.60–1

**9A**

women, 4.28–36 (*esp.* 31); 3.18–20
    (*and cf. on homosexuality*, 3.22); in
    mystery religions, 2.58; in myth,
    2.10
inconsistency of plot, 7.59
the war (as it was when *Lysistrata* was
    produced), H.I.52–3

**9B**

treasury, 1.34

economics of empire, 5.78ff., *esp.* 84–5

**9D**

purification, 2.35
male slaves caring for children, 4.64

**10A**

Solon, Kleisthenes and beginnings of
    democracy, H.I.8, 11
democracy, 5.1–22
*agora*, 1.29, 33–5; 2.40
Aristophanes and politics, 7.60–2
*kuria ekklēsia*, 5.14, 77
*skhoinion*, 5.14–15
*prutaneis*, 5.10–12, 24
countryman's love of his *dēmos*, 1.21,
    2.52
*kērux*, 5.39
'Who wishes to speak?', 5.11
*rhētor*, 5.19–21
Scythian archer, 4.64; 5.14, 37
*presbeis*, 5.41–3
Persians, H.I.12; P.2–6

**10B**

freedom and democracy, H.I.11, 53,
    55; 4.53; 7.14
debate and democracy, 5.5–7
citizen power, 5.9; H.I.38
trade and manufacture, 4.53–61

**10C**

Akharnians, 1.22
Marathōnomakhai, H.I.13
peace, 6.5
festivals, 2.52
city Dionysia, 2.46–7

**11A**

lawcourts, 5.44–67; 3.16–17; H.I.7;
    law vs. lawless, 7.17; courts and
    holidays, 2.43
on Apollodoros' history, 4.70, *and cf.*
    5.50–1; 6.40

decrees etc. in *agora*, 1.35

**11B**

meddling, 5.63
persuasion, 4.44; 7.16–19

**11C**

revenge, 3.1–4; friends and enemies, 3.13– 14
poverty, 3.18; *atimia*, 3.12; 5.64–7

**11D**

*atimia*, 3.12; 5.64–7
*psēphisma*, 5.48–51
*kurios* of a family, 4.16
*proix*, 4.21
family and women in general, 4.12–38
state and religion, 2.65–6
marriage and property, 4.4,21

**11F**

*sunoikein*, 4.24
Lysias, 1.24, H.I.57
Mysteries, 2.53
witnesses and evidence, 5.53–4
Greek alphabet and writing, 7.2–3, 15–16

**11G**

Solon, H.I.8; 5.26–7
Hippias, 4.47
sophists, 4.43–8; 7.20–1
evidence, 7.27

**11H**

wives and parties, 4.32, 37–8
metics and *xenoi*, 4.67ff.

**11I**

phratries, 2.50–1; 4.15–16
sycophants, 5.63
*polemarkhos*, 5.34–6
arbitration, 5.55

**12A**

divorce and dowry, 4.24

**12B**

women's role, 4.32ff.

**12C**

citizenship, 4.5–6
*genos*, 4.15–16
phratry, 4.15–16; 2.50–1
legitimacy, 4.17–20
oaths, 2.27; 7.16

**12E**

king *arkhōn*, 5.36; 2.53
gods in general, 2.1–5
offices of state, 5.29–34
purity of family, 4.17–20
piety and city, 2.66
marriage to Dionysos, 2.56
danger of defiance of gods, 2.65

**12F**

Areopagus, 5.26ff.

**12G**

liturgies, 5.71–2
choruses, 7.35
competitions, 3.1–4, 16

**13A**

creating citizens, 4.5–6, 70
citizen solidarity, 1.1, 4.82

**13B**

protection of women, 4.32–6; their dangerous habits, 2.10, 3.19
impiety a danger to the state, 2.65
tragedy and family chaos, 7.40

**13D**

importance of *oikos*, 4.12ff.
jealousy of citizenship, 4.4

**13E**

danger of female sexuality, 3.18–20
being *sōphrōn*, 3.17

**13F**

state pay, 5.47

**14A**

Greek tragedy, 7.35–52
burial, 4.77ff.

**14C**

women, marriage and home, 4.23ff.

**15A**

liturgies, 5.71–2
trierarchies, 5.71–2, 6.40–8
*exēgētai*, 2.4, 25
blood-guilt, 2.35
revenge, 3.1–4, 12–13

**15B**

climate, 1.5–6

**15C**

enmity, 3.13
trierarch, 6.41
*stasis*, H.I.73
ship's gear, 6.36, 6.42

**15D**

*boulē*, H.I.8; 5.15–16, 23ff.
evidence, 5.52–4
*hupēretēs*, 4.64

**15E**

self-help in law, 5.48, 62

**15F**

protection of women, 4.35 (*and source*)
self-help in law, 5.48

**15G**

climate, 1.5–6

**15H**

slaves giving evidence, 5.54
banking, 4.60, 65, 70

**16A**

houses, 1.7, 35–7; farming, 1.9–13
sheep, 1.13
slaves and slavery, 4.62–6
slaves and population, 4.10–11
slave jobs, 4.51–2
seclusion of women, 4.32ff.

**16B**

female rights in the home, 4.32–3
*kurios* of the house, 4.35

**16C**

travel, 1.14
doctors, 4.72–6; 7.10, 14, 25
*lithokopos*, 7.64–5; 4.79

**16D**

*exēgētai*, 2.35
purification, 2.35, 4.80; family and
 murder, 5.48

**16E**

friends and enemies, 3.2, 13
climate, 1.5–6

**17**

*nomos—phusis*, 7.28
sophists and civilisation, 7.25
myths, 2.9–11; 7.6
Greek speculation, 7.8

**18A**

*hubris*, 3.15
dreams, 2.13–14

**18B**

purification, 2.35, 4.80
*nomos*, P.1; 7.28
*atimia*, 3.12; 5.62–7

**18D**

public eye, 3.5–7
envy, 3.9–11
persuasion and psychology, 7.25
power of argument, 7.17

**18E**

reciprocity in human relations, 2.28–9;
  3.5, 13

**18F**

Zeus's roles, 2.8, 37, 40
*xenia*, 2.25, 36; 3.14; 4.67

injustice of the gods, 2.24–6
human responsibility, 3.25–6
Herodotus and history, 7.33

**19A**

Homer, 7.1
use of Homer, 7.4
Homer and the Greeks, P.10–12
Homer's gods, 2.59–64
dreams, 2.13–14
display and reputation, 3.1–4

**19D**

supplication, 2.36–7

**19F**

suppliants' rights, 2.25, 36

# ACKNOWLEDGEMENTS FOR PHOTOGRAPHS AND DRAWINGS

Unless otherwise stated, the photographs have been supplied by the museums and individuals listed.

Frontispiece A From E. Dodwell, *Views in Greece* (1821) pl. 15.

Frontispiece B Photo: German Archaeological Institute, Athens.

## Historical Introduction

HI:1    Photo: Alison Frantz, Princeton.

HI:2    Linear B tablet TA 641. Athens, National museum. Photo and drawing: The University of Cincinnati.

HI:3    Bronze armour. Nauplion, Museum. Photo: École Française d'Archéologie, Athens.

HI:4    Protocorinthian olpe (the 'Chigi' olpe). Rome, Museo Nazionale di Villa Giulia 22679 (H 2694). Photo: Hirmer, Munich.

HI:5    Red trachyte *stēlē* with inscribed law-code (front face). Istanbul, Archaeological Museum 1907. Drawing: from *Annual of the British School at Athens* 51 (1956) 158, fig. 1.

HI:6    Photo: Alison Frantz, Princeton.

HI:7    Relief carving from the Persian palace at Persepolis. Tehran, Archaeological Museum. Photo: Oriental Institute, Chicago.

HI:8    Photo: N.G.L. Hammond.

HI:9    Corinthian bronze figurine. West Berlin, Staatliche Museen misc. 7470.

HI:10    Photo: Professor R.V. Schoder, S.J., Loyola University of Chicago.

HI:11    Bronze column in the Hippodrome, Istanbul. Photo: German Archaeological Institute, Istanbul.

HI:12    Attic red-figure cup by the Briseis Painter. New York, Metropolitan Museum of Art 53.11.4 (Joseph Pulitzer Bequest).

HI:13    Marble relief *stēlē*. Athens, Acropolis Museum 695. Photo: German Archaeological Institute, Athens.

HI:14    Attic marble *stēlē*. Athens, National Museum EM 5384 (*IG* i$^3$ 272). Photo: from J. Kirchner, *Imagines Inscriptionum Atticarum* (1935) pl. 15.

HI:15    Photo: Alison Frantz, Princeton.
HI:16    Photo: Professor R.V. Schoder, S.J., Loyola University of Chicago.
HI:17    Photo: J. Wilson Myers, Michigan State University.
HI:18    Attic marble head. Athens, Agora Excavations S 211.
HI:19    Photo: Dr B.A. Sparkes.
HI:20    Silver tetradrachm. London, British Museum, Department of Coins and Medals.
HI:21    Gold stater. London, British Museum, Department of Coins and Medals 1871-11-7-1.
HI:22    Photo: Hirmer, Munich.
HI:23    Attic marble head. Athens, Acropolis 1331. Photo: German Archaeological Institute, Athens.
HI:24    Attic marble relief. Rome, Villa Albani H 3257. Photo: Alinari.

### Chapter 1

1:1    Photo: J.V. Noble, New York.
1:2    Photo: Athens, Agora Excavations, neg. no. LXXVI-71.
1:3    Attic black-figure amphora. Paris, Louvre AM 1008.
1:4    Attic red-figure bell-krater by the Kleophrades Painter. Basel, Herbert Cahn.
1:5    Attic black-figure skyphos. Boston, Museum of Fine Arts 99.525.
1:6    Boiotian terracotta figurine, Paris, Louvre CA 352.
1:7    Attic black-figure cup. London, British Museum, Department of Greek and Roman Antiquities B 436.
1:8    Photo: Alison Frantz, Princeton.
1:9    Drawing: J. Ellis Jones, Bangor.
1:11    Attic black-figure hydria in the manner of the Antimenes Painter. London, British Museum, Department of Greek and Roman Antiquities B 330.
1:12    Marble boundary stone. Athens, Agora Excavations I 5510.
1:13    Drawing: Athens, Agora Excavations.

### Chapter 2

2:1    Attic red-figure cup by Oltos. Tarquinia, Museo Nazionale Tarquiniense RC 6848. Photo: Alinari.
2:2    Attic red-figure cup by Douris. Paris, Louvre G 115.
2:3    Attic red-figure cup by the Brygos Painter. West Berlin, Staatliche Museen F 2293.
2:4    Attic red-figure askos. Boston, Museum of Fine Arts 13.169.
2:5    Attic red-figure calyx-krater by the Niobid painter. London,British Museum, Department of Greek and Roman Antiquities E 467.

2:6     Attic red-figure calyx-krater by the Dinos Painter. Oxford, Ashmolean Museum 1937.983.

2:7     Photo: Alison Frantz, Princeton.

2:8     Attic red-figure column-krater by the Aegisthus Painter. Boston, Museum of Fine Arts 1970.567.

2:9     Attic black-figure amphora. London, British Museum, Department of Greek and Roman Antiquities B 171.

2:10    Attic red-figure bell-krater by the Lykaon Painter. Boston, Museum of Fine Arts 00.346.

2:11    Attic black-figure amphora by the Timiades Painter. London, British Museum, Department of Greek and Roman Antiquities 97.7-27.2.

2:12    Attic red-figure cup by Makron. Toledo, Ohio, Toledo Museum of Art 72.55.

2:13    Attic red-figure cup. Florence, Museo Archeologico Etrusco 81600.

2:14    Attic red-figure column-krater by the Pan Painter. Naples, Museo Nazionale. Drawing: *Monumenti Antichi* 22 (1913) pl. 80.

2:15    Attic red-figure pelike by the Lykaon Painter. Boston, Museum of Fine Arts 34.79.

2:16    Attic red-figure lekythos by the Painter of Louvre CA 1694 (Guy). Basel, Antikenmuseum, Loan.

2:17    Relief slab from the temple of Apollo Epikourios at Phigaleia (Bassai). London, British Museum, Department of Greek and Roman Antiquities 524.

2:18    Marble altar. Athens, Agora Excavations I 3706.

2:19    Attic black-figure cup. Private. Photo: Herbert Cahn, Basel.

2:20    Attic red-figure bell-krater in the manner of the Peleus Painter. Cambridge (Mass.), Harvard University, Fogg Museum 1960.344.

2:21    Attic red-figure cup by the Triptolemos Painter. Paris, Louvre G 138.

2:22    Photo: Alison Frantz, Princeton.

2:23    Relief slab East V 31–35 from the Parthenon, the Acropolis, Athens. London, British Museum, Department of Greek and Roman Antiquities 324V. Photo: Alison Frantz, Princeton.

2:24    Attic red-figure skyphos by the Painter of the Yale Lekythos. Brussels, Musées Royaux A 10.

2:25    Attic red-figure stamnos. London, British Museum, Department of Greek and Roman Antiquities E 439.

## Chapter 3

3:1     Attic red-figure cup by the Briseis Painter. London, British Museum, Department of Greek and Roman Antiquities E 76.

3:2     Attic red-figure stamnos by the Triptolemos Painter. Basel, Antikenmuseum, Loan.

3:3     Attic black-figure hydria of the Leagros Group. Boston, Museum of Fine Arts 63.473.
3:4     Attic red-figure skyphos by the Brygos Painter. Vienna, Kunsthistorisches Museum inv. 3710.
3:5     Attic black-figure volute-krater by Kleitias. Florence, Museo Archeologico Etrusco 4209.
3:6     Attic red-figure cup by Douris. Vienna, Kunsthistorisches Museum 3695.
3:7     Attic red-figure cup by Douris. Vienna, Kunsthistorisches Museum 3695.
3:8     Attic red-figure cup by the Brygos Painter. Los Angeles, Malibu, J. Paul Getty Museum, Bareiss Collection S.82.AE.27.
3:9     Attic black-figure Panathenaic prize amphora by the Euphiletos Painter. New York, Metropolitan Museum of Art 14.130.12 (Rogers Fund 1914).
3:10    Attic red-figure cup by Douris. London, British Museum, Department of Greek and Roman Antiquities E 52.
3:11    Attic red-figure cup. Karlsruhe, Badisches Landesmuseum inv. 70/395.
3:12    Terracotta akroterion. Olympia, Museum. Photo: German Archaeological Institute, Athens.
3:13    Attic black-figure amphora by the Phrynos Painter. Würzburg, Martin von Wagner Museum 241.

## Chapter 4

4:1     Attic cover-tile. Athens, Agora Excavations P 27594.
4:2     Attic black-figure lekythos by the Amasis Painter. New York, Metropolitan Museum of Art 56.11.1 (Walter C. Baker Gift).
4:3     Attic red-figure amphora by the Nausikaa Painter. London, British Museum, Department of Greek and Roman Antiquities E 284.
4:4     Attic marble statue. Brauron, Museum. Photo: Hannibal.
4:5     Attic red-figure cup from the circle of the Brygos Painter. Cincinnati, Ohio, Art Museum 1979.1.
4:6     Drawing: J. Ellis Jones, Bangor.
4:7     Attic red-figure cup in the manner of the Sotades Painter. Brussels, Musées Royaux A 890.
4:8     Attic black-figure lekythos by the Amasis Painter. New York, Metropolitan Museum of Art 31.11.10 (Fletcher Fund 1931).
4:9     Boiotian terracotta figurine. Boston, Museum of Fine Arts 01.7788.
4:10    Attic red-figure cup by the Foundry Painter. Cambridge, Corpus Christi College, courtesy of the Master and Fellows. From *The Journal of Hellenic Studies* 41 (1921) pl. 16.
4:11    Attic red-figure cup in the manner of Douris. London, British Museum, Department of Greek and Roman Antiquities E 51.
4:12    Attic red-figure cup by Douris. West Berlin, Staatliche Museen F 2285.
4:13    Attic red-figure cup by Makron. Vienna, Kunsthistorisches Museum 3698.

4:14    Attic red-figure pointed amphora by the Kleophrades Painter. Munich, Glyptothek und Antikensammlungen 2344.

4:15    Attic black-figure cup of the Burgon Group. London, British Museum, Department of Greek and Roman Antiquities 1906.12-15.1.

4:16    Attic black-figure neck-amphora. Boston, Museum of Fine Arts 01.8035.

4:17    Attic red-figure pelike by the Syleus Painter. Geneva, Dr Jacques Chamay.

4:18    Athenian silver coins. Cambridge, Fitzwilliam Museum.

4:19    Attic red figure hydria by the Aegisthus Painter. Paris, Louvre CA 2587.

4:20    Attic red-figure aryballos by the Clinic Painter. Paris, Louvre CA 2183.

4:21    Attic marble relief. Peiraieus, Museum. Photo: German Archaeological Institute, Athens.

4:22    Attic red-figure *loutrophoros* by the Painter of Bologna 228. Athens, National Museum 1170. Photo: Hirmer, Munich.

4:23    Attic marble gravestone. Athens, National Museum 3472. Photo: Hirmer, Munich.

4:24    Attic white-ground lekythos by the Achilles Painter. Oxford, Ashmolean Museum 545.

## Chapter 5

5:1    Attic marble relief. Athens, Agora Excavations I 6524.

5:2    Photo: Alison Frantz, Princeton.

5:3    Ostraka. Athens, Kerameikos Museum. Photo: German Archaeological Institute, Athens.

5:4    Drawing: J. Travlos, Athens.

5:5    Photo: Agora Excavations, Athens.

5:7    Athenian bronze weights. Athens, Agora Excavations B 497, 492, 495.

5:8    Athenian terracotta dry measure. Athens, Agora Excavations P 3562.

5:9    Models of Athenian terracotta water-clocks. Athens, Agora Excavations P 2084.

5:10    Athenian bronze ballots. Athens, Agora Excavations B 146, 728, 1055, 1056, 1058.

5:11    Athenian bronze identity ticket. Athens, Agora Excavations B 822.

5:12    Attic red-figure cup by the Stieglitz Painter. Dijon, Musée des Beaux Arts CA 1301.

5:13    Fragment of Attic marble *stele*. Athens, Agora Excavations I 7307.

5:14    Attic marble relief. Athens, National Museum EM 2593.

5:15    Relief slab North XXXVIII 117–18 from the Parthenon. London, British Museum, Department of Greek and Roman Antiquities 325 XXXVIII.

5:16    Detail of Lykian marble sarcophagus. Istanbul, Archaeological Museum 63 (369).

## Chapter 6

6:1   Attic red-figure pelike by the Trophy Painter. Boston, Museum of Fine Arts 20.187.

6:2   Weapons from Marathon. London, British Museum, Department of Greek and Roman Antiquities.

6:3   Attic Marble gravestone. Los Angeles, Malibu, J. Paul Getty Museum, 79.AA.1.

6:4   Attic red-figure hydria. Paris, Louvre G 179.

6:5   Attic red-figure cup by the Brygos Painter. Rome, Vatican Museum. Photo: Alinari.

6:6   Attic red-figure cup by Oltos. London, British Museum, Department of Greek and Roman Antiquities E 17.

6:7   Attic red-figure neck-amphora by the Alkimachos Painter. London, British Museum, Department of Greek and Roman Antiquities E 285.

6:8   Attic red-figure cup. Cambridge (Mass.), Harvard University, Fogg Museum 1959.219.

6:9   Attic marble gravestone. Athens, National Museum 2744.

6:10  Drawing after J.K. Anderson.

6:11  Detail from the Nereid Monument, from Xanthos, Asia Minor. London, British Museum, Department of Greek and Roman Antiquities 872.

6:12  Attic black-figure cup. Paris, Louvre F 123.

6:13  Drawing after J.K. Anderson.

6:14  Photo: Professor R.V. Schoder, S.J., Loyola University of Chicago.

6:15  Attic red-figure lekythos by the Brygos Painter. New York, Metropolitan Museum of Art 25.189.1 (Funds from various donors).

## Chapter 7

7:1   Fragmentary papyrus. Oxford, Bodleian Library MS Gr. class c. 76/1(P).

7:2   Attic marble relief. Athens, National Museum 4465.

7:3   Attic red-figure bell-krater by the Hephaistos Painter. Frankfurt am Main, Museum für Vor- und Frühgeschichte VF β 413.

7:4   Attic red-figure cup by Onesimos. Oxford, Ashmolean Museum G 138, 3, 5 & 11.

7:5   Attic red-figure neck-amphora by the Kleophrades Painter. London, British Museum, Department of Greek and Roman Antiquities E 270.

7:6   Attic red-figure pelike by the Pan Painter. Athens, National Museum 9683.

7:7   Attic head vase. Boston, Museum of Fine Arts 00.332.

7:8   Attic red-figure hydria by the Leningrad Painter. Boston, Museum of Fine Arts 03.788.

7:9   Attic red-figure column-krater. Basel, Antikenmuseum BS 415.

7:10  Attic red-figure bell-krater. Ferrara, Museo Nazionale di Spina T 173C VP (inv. 20299).

7:11     Attic red-figure calyx-krater by the Dokimasia Painter. Boston,Museum of Fine Arts 63.1246.

7:12     Attic red-figure calyx-krater by the Dokimasia Painter. Boston, Museum of Fine Arts 63.1246.

7:13     Attic red-figure hydria. West Berlin, Staatliche Museen 1966.18.

7:14     Attic red-figure pelike. West Berlin, Staatliche Museen inv. 3223.

7:15     Photo: The Tourist Office, Athens.

7:16     Drawing after Oliver Taplin.

7:17     Attic black-figure amphora by the Painter of Berlin 1686. East Berlin, Staatliche Museen F 1697.

7:18     Attic terracotta figurines. New York, Metropolitan Museum of Art 13.225.13–28 (Rogers Fund).

7:19     Grave-vase from Athens. Athens, National Museum 804. Photo: Alison Frantz, Princeton.

7:20     Bronze statuette from Samos, now lost. Photo: German Archaeological Institute, Athens.

7:21     Ivory figure from the Dipylon Cemetery, Athens. Athens, National Museum 776.

7:22     Protoattic grave-vase from Eleusis. Eleusis Museum. Photo: German Archaeological Institute, Athens.

7:23     Marble statue from Sounion. Athens, National Museum 2720.

7:24     Drawing from H. Payne and others, *Perachora* I (Oxford 1940) pl. 9b.

7:25     Limestone gorgon from pediment of Temple of Artemis, Corfu. Corfu Museum.

7:26     Attic black-figure bowl and stand signed by the painter Sophilos. London, British Museum, Department of Greek and Roman Antiquities 1971.11-1.1.

7:27     Attic black-figure amphora by Exekias. London, British Museum, Department of Greek and Roman Antiquities B210.

7:28     Attic red-figure calyx-krater signed by potter Euxitheos and painter Euphronios. New York, Metropolitan Museum of Art, Bequest of Joseph H. Durkee, Gift of Darius Ogden Mills, and Gift of C. Ruxton Love, by Exchange, 1972. (1972.11.10)

7:29     Marble statue from the Acropolis, Athens. Athens, Acropolis Museum 679. Photo: Alison Frantz, Princeton.

7:30     Marble pediment figure from Acropolis, Athens. Athens, Acropolis Museum 631C. Photo: German Archaeological Institute, Athens.

7:31     Marble pediment figure from the Temple of Aphaia, Aiginē. Munich, Antiken Sammlungen.

7:32     Marble statue from Acropolis, Athens. Athens, Acropolis Museum 698. Photo: Alison Frantz, Princeton.

7:33     Marble group from west pediment of Temple of Zeus at Olympia. Olympia Museum. Photo: Alison Frantz, Princeton.

7:34    Parthenon from north-west. Athens, Acropolis. Photo: Alison Frantz, Princeton.

7:35    Marble figure from west pediment of Parthenon. London, British Museum, Department of Greek and Roman Antiquities 304A.

7:36    Marble figure from west pediment of Parthenon. London, British Museum, Department of Greek and Roman Antiquities 303J.

7:37    Part of marble slab from north frieze of Parthenon. London, British Museum, Department of Greek and Roman Antiquities 325 XLII.

7:38    Bronze statue from Riace, Calabria. Photo: Alinari.

7:39    Attic red-figure cup from Vulci, signed by potter Brygos. Paris, Louvre G152. Photo: Giraudon.

7:40    Attic white funeral lekythos from Eretria. Athens, National Museum 1816. Photo: Alison Frantz, Princeton.

7:41    Attic red-figure calyx-krater from Orvieto. Paris, Louvre G 341. Photo: Giraudon.

7:42    Attic red-figure hydria signed by the potter Meidias. London, British Museum, Department of Greek and Roman Antiquities E224.

7:43    Marble Karyatid porch of Erekhtheion. Athens, Acropolis. Photo: Alison Frantz, Princeton.

7:44    Marble relief slab from parapet of temple of Athene Nike. Athens, Acropolis Museum. Photo: Alison Frantz, Princeton.

7:45    Marble grave-relief from Athens. Athens, Kerameikos Museum. Photo: Alison Frantz, Princeton.

7:46    Marble grave-relief found near the Ilisos. Athens, National Museum 869.

7:47    Bronze statue from sea off Marathon. Athens, National Museum 15118. Photo: Alison Frantz, Princeton.

7:48    Marble statue. Vatican. Photo: German Archaeological Institute, Athens.

7:49    Wall painting from Vergina. Photo: M. Andronikos.

7:50    Mosaic floor from Pella. Pella Museum.

7:51    Mosaic floor from the House of the Faun. Naples, Museum 10020.

7:52    Detail of above.

# INDEX

References in bold type are to the maps on pp. xiiiff. The map number is followed by a grid-reference. Places appearing on the plans on p. 79 are so referred.

## 1. GENERAL INDEX

Academy, 1.36, 2.46, 4.42, 4.47, p. 79
accountability in democracy: of officials, 5.32; of private citizens, 5.50
Achilles, 2.7, 3.4, 3.5, 3.6, 7.1, 7.23, 7.72. P.11
Acropolis, H.I.26, H.I.27, H.I.84, 1.6, 1.25, 1.26, 1.27, 1.29, 1.30, 1.31, 1.34, 2.45, 5.87, 7.73, 7.74; Erekhtheion, 1.34, 2.39, 4.65, 7.78; Parthenon, H.I.27, 1.18, 1.31, 1.34, 2.39, 2.44, 7.22, 7.75–6, 7.78; Propylaia, 1.34, 7.78; temple of Athēnē Nikē, 7.78; treasury, 1.34, 5.82, p. 79
actors, 7.35, 7.37, 7.45, 7.46, 7.47, 7.50–1, 7.53, 7.56, 7.59
Adeimantos, 1.24
adoption, 4.21, 4.22
adultery, 4.25
Aeschylus, H.I.13, 5.5, 5.15, 5.28, 6.17, 7.36, 7.37, 7.38, 7.39, 7.46, 7.48, 7.49, 7.59, P.10
Africa, H.I.4, 1.20, **1Ab**
afterlife, 2.1, 2.4, 2.53, 4.82
Agamemnon, 2.13, 3.5, 3.7, 3.19, 7.36, 7.39, 7.40
Agaue, 7.43
Agēsilaos, H.I.61–2, H.I.66, H.I.67, H.I.70
Agiadai, H.I.6
Agis, fifth-century king of Sparta, H.I.46, 6.9, 6.12
Agis, fourth-century king of Sparta, H.I.84
agkhisteia, 4.15
agōgē, H.I.6
agōn, 3.2, 5.52, 7.52, 7.58
agora, 1.27, 1.28, 1.29, 1.33, 1.35, 2.40,

4.58, 5.13, 5.14, 5.17, 5.56, 5.60, 5.66, 5.67, 7.15, 7.78
agoranomoi, 5.38, 5.76
Agrai, 2.54, p. 79
agriculture, 1.10–13, 7.25
Agyrrhios, 5.69
aidōs, 3.6, 7.25
Aigaleos, 1.17, 1.25, **3Aa–b**
Aigeus, 5.28
Aigilia, 2.13, **3Bb**
Aiginē, H.I.18, H.I.30, H.I.32, H.I.34, 1.18, 6.9, 7.73, **3Ab**, **4Bb**
Aigisthos, 7.40
Aigospotamoi, H.I.54, H.I.56, **4Ca**
aikeia, 3.15
Aineias the Tactician, 6.30
Aiskhines, H.I.78, H.I.80, H.I.84
Aitolia, H.I.39, 6.22, **2Aa**
Akharnai, 1.22, **3Aa**
Akheloion, 5.95
alastores, 2.32
Alexander, H.I.82–4, 6.23, 6.49, 7.79, 7.81, 7.82
Alexandria, H.I.82, 7.5, 7.32, **1Cb**
Alkibiades: and Aristophanes, 7.61; career, H.I.46, H.I.48, H.I.50, H.I.52, H.I.54, 3.9, 6.25, 6.34; character, H.I.46, H.I.52; friendship with Socrates, 3.24, 4.47; mutilation of Hermai, H.I.49; private life, 4.37; profanation of Mysteries, H.I.49, 2.55
Alkmaion, 7.9, 7.10
Alkmaionids, H.I.10–11, H.I.27
Alkman, 7.1
Alkmene, 2.9

## 2. INDEX OF PASSAGES QUOTED

## INSCRIPTIONS